PRICE

THEORY

SIDNEY WEINTRAUB
Professor of Economics, St. John's University

GREENWOOD PRESS, PUBLISHERS
NEW YORK   1968

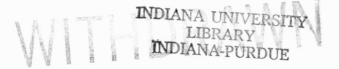

TO

Sheila E. Weintraub

Preface

IN THIS BOOK I HAVE TRIED TO
present a systematic and reasonably complete statement of modern
price theory for students who already have some acquaintance with
the subject. It is my thought that it will also prove useful to specialists in economics who have read the major works and require some
integration of the literature before proceeding with confidence at the
professional level. Likewise, the book is aimed at the numerous non-
specialists who take courses in advanced economics but have neither
the time nor the inclination to read extensively, yet are willing to exert
the effort necessary to master one book containing the requisite materials. I have myself used parts of it with good success in teaching
students who come from an elementary course and who lack any
special mathematical equipment.

Many major topics of economic theory have been omitted. I have
not dealt with either the theory of aggregate income, the theory of
income division, or with the growing body of welfare theory. Fortunately, there are now several good works on aggregate-income analysis.
The theory of income division, on the other hand, is in a more chaotic
state; a laborious job of reconstruction, in my opinion, is necessary.
My reasons for failing to develop to any important degree the welfare
implications of price theory are indicated in an Appendix. I hope,
however, to develop these topics in a future work.

At this date I take it that there is no need to defend the thought-
clearing that economic theory provides in approaching concrete economic problems. With this viewpoint in mind I have abandoned a
lengthy introductory discussion on the nature and content of economic
analysis. I doubt that remarks on the scientific character of analytic
thinking convince anybody not already impressed with the legitimacy
and importance of theoretical study. It happens, too, that economists
are more at home in doing their work than in preparing significant
generalizations on their methods and techniques.

Professional readers will recognize my indebtedness to the main
stream of the literature. The writings that I have found most useful

are indicated in the bibliographical notes appended to each chapter, which also contain suggestions to the student for further reading.

It is a pleasure to record my obligations to those who were helpful and patient with me during the long period, interrupted by wartime military service, over which this was written. Professor H. B. Dorau of New York University and Dr. T. F. P. McManus gave direction to my learning as a student. The late Dr. Horace White, Jr., offered some constructive comments on a much earlier version of the manuscript before his untimely death in 1943. Dean William J. Weary of St. John's University has been keenly sympathetic to the project since its inception. His planning of my teaching program and his encouragement to use parts of the manuscript in class facilitated its completion. Mr. Mulford Martin, Librarian, New York University School of Commerce, generously placed his fine collection of books and periodicals at my disposal. My own graduate study at the London School of Economics also helped make this a better book than it otherwise would have been.

I have also benefited from the invaluable counsel and friendship of Professor Joseph Dorfman of Columbia University. Many improvements in the final manuscript are due to discussions with him. My wife, Sheila Ellen Weintraub, endured, assisted, and encouraged beyond all measure. Without her labors the work could not have been completed.

SIDNEY WEINTRAUB

Contents

PART III. MULTIPLE-PRODUCT FIRMS

PART IV. DYNAMIC ANALYSES

CONTENTS

PRICE THEORY

Abbreviations and Symbols

AC	Average cost
AP_x	Average product of factor X
AR	Average revenue
D	Demand
E_c	Elasticity of total costs
E_d	Elasticity of demand
E_p	Elasticity of productivity
E_s	Elasticity of supply
E_{ss}	Elasticity of substitution
$_IE_x$	Income elasticity of demand for X
$_{px}E_y$	Cross elasticity of demand
$I\text{-}C$	Income-consumption curve
MC	Marginal cost
M_L	Index of monopoly power
MP_x	Marginal product of factor X
MR	Marginal revenue
MRS	Marginal rate of substitution
$P\text{-}C$	Price-consumption curve
P_m	Monopoly price
P_x, P_y, P_z	Price of commodity X, Y, Z
S	Supply
TC	Total cost
TP_x	Total production, with factor X variable and other factors constant
TR	Total revenue
ΔX	Increase in X (say from 19 to 20)

Part I

DEMAND AND COST

ANALYSIS

Introduction

Economic activity in free econ-
omies is organized through the price system. It is not uncommon in
economic analysis nowadays to depreciate the study of price making
and to stress, instead, the forces determining the volume of income,
output, and employment. Despite the intrinsic importance of these
topics, their study lacks cohesion and relevance unless the forces
responsible for the particular price and output magnitudes, which
comprise the national income aggregate, are understood. Major
questions concerning the kinds of goods produced, their individual
quantities, and the productive factors engaged in their production can
be answered only by a study of price formation. This book deals with
this array of subjects, the older sphere of value theory.

Part I is devoted to a consideration of some of the preliminary
materials essential to the study of price theory. Chapter 1 discusses

3

the market behavior of the individual consumer faced with prices which limit his ability to make purchases. Herein lies the typical problem of the consumer market. And yet it is from the individual actions that market-demand phenomena arise. Aspects of market-demand analysis are developed in Chapter 2.

Temporarily, this ends our preoccupation with the theory of demand; the treatment will be sufficient to prepare us for the studies in price determination in Part II. Chapter 3 outlines certain problems in the theory of production, especially those associated with the selection of productive factors at each level of output when firms are guided by the principle of minimizing total production costs. The elucidation of this condition of cost minimization will facilitate the analysis of a broad range of problems. The significance of the insight imparted by this principle becomes apparent when we introduce the additional assumption that price making is directed, ordinarily, to profit making. But it also has even deeper implications: unless the principle of minimum-cost output is grasped, the concept of economical production and resource management escapes us. In the welfare propositions drawn from modern economic analysis this relationship has a profound and persuasive bearing.

Chapter 4 is a further extension of the study of production. The major cost concepts are sketched and the laws of returns are elaborated; these concepts and laws constitute the contemporary version of the older principle of diminishing returns. A careful attempt is made to weld the ideas on physical returns with the movements in production costs. After having reached this stage we are ready for market analyses, to investigate the determination of prices and output quantities in various concrete circumstances.

The word *theory* has been stressed in these initial remarks. We shall use the word synonymously and interchangeably with analysis. Only the obstinate would contend that theory and analysis have a meaning which is the antithesis of fact. All that is meant to be conveyed by either term is that we are in studious pursuit of *relationships*. Facts are independent entities, individual events limitless in number. To bring some order among them, to detect their causal sequence or mere interdependence so that we may interpret real world occurrences, is the task of analytic study and the aim of serious study in all fields. But, it is to be observed, we seek to ascertain *important* relationships, those that are revealed in a wide range of phenomena. It is the latter uniformities which aspire to the status of a law or scientific principle.

Inherently, it is frivolous and academic to dispute or attempt to arbitrate the issue of whether economics "really" is a science. Whether physics is or is not a science is unimportant. The vital point is that the study of physics casts light upon a range of matters that are inscrutable without its devices. Similarly, the illumination that economic analysis can throw, however dim and obscure it is in certain sectors, is such that no one who has acquired a working knowledge of its perceptions will readily sacrifice it. Its deficiencies invite repair.

We shall find that most of the significant relationships extracted by economic theory can be described verbally. Many parts of economic theory—maybe all of it—admit of treatment by mathematical methods. But there is little reason to believe that this method must be employed or that it is superior in all contexts; the account that follows is innocent of any high mathematical pretensions. Geometrical devices are introduced where these are suitable and enlightening. Abbreviations, which border on mathematical symbolism, have been incorporated to avoid tedious repetition of familiar concepts. The book's one main debt to mathematics consists in extensive usage of the incremental idea, or symbol *delta*, written Δ. Curiously, we recognize it for what it is—a bit of harmless symbolism—when it appears on the doorplate of a fraternity house, and we impute to it a simple and comprehensible meaning. Yet when we meet it in mathematics we are prone to become alarmed and ascribe to it all sorts of dreadful connotations. Once this initial fright vanishes we shall discover it to be an expedient means of communication, for it is intended merely to signify a difference, usually a small difference. Thus

$$X_2 - X_1 = \Delta X.$$

Hence if the value of X_2 is 20, and X_1 is 19, then ΔX is of course 1. Or when we regard $X_1 + \Delta X = X_2$, then ΔX is described as an *increment*. With a minus sign before it, it would denote a decrement, as it would if in the preceding equation $X_1 > X_2$.

CHAPTER 1

Consumer Behavior

THIS CHAPTER IS DEVOTED TO A study of certain aspects of the theory of consumer behavior. This analysis provides a logical beginning, for it is in response to demand forces that economic activity is undertaken. The critical problem is to demonstrate the properties of the equilibrium position on the assumption that a consumer of definite tastes and income, faced with externally determined prices, makes his purchase selection on the principle of maximizing his satisfaction. This is the maximizing problem of the household, the first of several maximizing problems that we shall meet. Solving it, our analytical progress will be greatly accelerated, for the techniques and the details of the solution appear in countless other situations. We turn first to a consideration of the intricacies involved in defining consumer tastes precisely.

THE COMPLEX OF PREFERENCES

Ordinarily an individual will be aware of the goods he prefers if he is placed in a position to choose among them. Actually his choice in the market place will be colored not only by his tastes but also by his income and by the market prices confronting him. These relations can be clarified by means of an indifference map.

The Individual's Indifference System

Imagine an individual, possessing definite quantities of several goods denoted as $A, B, C \cdots$, to be confronted with two other goods, X and Y. They may be specific commodities or broad classes of goods, as food and clothing. If he selects at random any one combination of the goods, there will be other combinations of the goods that will be regarded as neither better nor worse; they will be combinations of indifference or composites of equal preference. Indifference curves illustrating these ideas are drawn in Figure 1A. Attention being focused on the curves 1, 2, 3 · · · , combinations of equal preference are found along each separate curve; thus the individual will feel equally content with any of the quantities of X and Y depicted along the curve with index 1. Likewise, curve 2 represents other indifference combinations. On curve 2, each combination is preferred to any combination on curve 1; at P as compared to Q, for example, there is at least the same amount of Y plus more of X. And so it goes. Moving from curves of lower index to curves of higher index, we ascend to

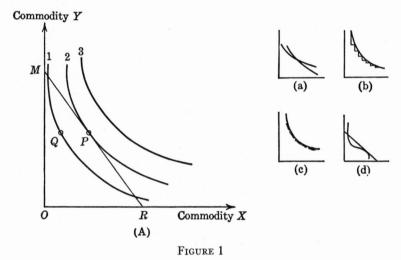

FIGURE 1

more highly preferred positions, because there is at least one commodity that is increased in amount while the other commodity is unchanged; or the increase in one commodity more than offsets a decrease in the other.

Tastes are thus defined independently of either income or prices. If income were large enough, the individual would select a combination of maximum gratification; more goods would then diminish well-being.* More important, it should be observed that the separate indifference curves may not intersect; if they did, as in Figure 1a, it would imply that certain combinations of the goods are equal simul-

* This is at the summit of Pareto's "colline de plaisir," *Manuel d'Économie Politique,* 2nd edition, A. Bonnet, trans., p. 171. If utility were measurable we could employ a three-dimensional figure with heights above each indifference curve representing an actual quantity of satisfaction, rising according to some definite rate as we mounted the preference hill. If we are unable to measure utility, but can describe combinations of goods as embodying greater or lesser satisfaction, the three-dimensional representation fails. In the first view, utility is a cardinal quantity; in the second, it is an ordinal amount.

taneously to combinations of both higher and lower preference: this is either nonsense or evidence of consumer irrationality. Manifestly, the indifference system will have to be redrawn whenever tastes change. Likewise, the indifference curves pertain to two goods; they therefore presume the individual's stock of other goods constant. Changes in the quantities of consumer commodity holdings will entail a redrawing of the curve system.

The Major Characteristic of the Indifference System

A scientific advantage of the indifference system is that the sole allusion to utility and satisfaction is in a relative sense; all that it is necessary to suppose is that an individual has preferences. The curve system crystallizes the onerousness of living on a human plane—the continual necessity of choosing, of selecting, of making decisions.* Rather than being two-dimensional, choice in the real world is n-dimensional, immune to any simple graphic representation. Normally, an individual will not know his preferences at consumption levels differing markedly from those to which he is accustomed. This unawareness would preclude the drawing of the full indifference map beyond the range of small changes, perhaps the usual changes in income; thereafter the system of indifference curves will either be discontinuous or blank.†

THE MARGINAL RATE OF SUBSTITUTION

Let us see how the concept of marginal utility and the principle of diminishing (marginal) utility fit into the modern analysis which eschews the older version of utility as an absolute quantity. Marginal utility referred to the increment in total utility made by the $(n + 1)$th unit to a stock of n units of a good. That is, if 10 units of a good afforded 250 units of satisfaction, and 11 units of the good afforded 260 units of satisfaction, the marginal utility of an 11th unit was 10 units of satisfaction. All units were deemed perfectly substitutable for one another so that the loss of any one unit would lead to the same diminution in total utility.

The Relativity of Subjective Valuation

The objection to the notion of marginal utility is its suggestion of the measurability of utility. Confessing that we have no idea of the size or

* F. H. Knight, *The Ethics of Competition*, p. 88.

† Pareto mentions the absurdity of questioning a peasant on her preferences for diamonds if she becomes a millionaire. *Manuel d'Économie Politique*, p. 260.

dimensions of a unit of utility and accepting preferences as the fundamental fact, it is best to drop utility terminology, for unless extreme care is taken absolutistic ideas and inferences on the measurability of utility would seep in.* As the propositions of analytical economics seldom if ever depend on the measurability of utility, it is wise to dispense with terminology that seems to imply it.† Only the relativity of subjective valuation needs to be stressed.

Marginal utility, in the older theory, was but a first step in the formulation of the principle of diminishing utility, according to which continuing increments to an individual's stock of goods yielded decreasing additional amounts of satisfaction. Obviously, this "law" has no content if absolutistic ideas on utility are abandoned. The loss appears less disastrous when we recall that exceptions to it were always recognized: it was always qualified to exclude the "initial units" consumed over which rising marginal utility might be experienced. More significant is the fact that the principle itself was quite irrelevant, if not wrong, as a description of typical market phenomena. Individuals seldom cease their purchases of a "piece of pie," or of a radio, of a suit of clothes, because of some patently diminished marginal satisfaction; instead it is the reduced income available for other expenditures as a result of any particular purchase which constitutes the decisive factor. Most people would, for most commodities, hardly get beyond the rising portion of a marginal-utility curve; illustrations of consumers eating apples until they are sick are crude explanations of the facts of market behavior. A person's income might have to be spent many times for such a surfeit to occur in his commodity purchases.

The *MRS* and Relative Marginal Utility

Rather than the consumption of a commodity until satiety, it is the pull of competing demands that limits the purchase of any particular good. However, for the analytical purposes which it served in explaining the equilibrium position, the principle of diminishing utility must be replaced by that of a diminishing marginal rate of substitution among commodities.‡ The marginal rate of substitution (*MRS*) is defined as *the decrement in Y which will just compensate for an increment in X, leaving the individual in neither a better nor worse position.* Thus it refers to

* See J. R. Hicks and R. G. D. Allen, "A Reconsideration of the Theory of Value," *Economica* (1934), p. 56.
† See a path-breaking article by W. E. Johnson, "The Pure Theory of Utility Curves," *Economic Journal* (1913), p. 490.
‡ See J. R. Hicks, *Value and Capital*, (1st edition), p. 20.

a movement along an indifference curve.   The decreasing rate reflects the fact that as X continues to be substituted for Y the MRS ratio will be lowered: the unit increment in X will command an ever smaller decrement in Y if the level of well-being is held constant.   Table 1 illustrates these relations.   In column 1 combinations of equal preference are listed; each of the combinations of X and Y are located on an indifference curve similar to curve 1 in Figure 1.   Commodity Y, say, represents neckties, and commodity X, shirts.   Column 2 shows the individual's evaluations of the ability of a further quantity of X to replace an amount of Y without any diminution in well-being.   Thus when $27Y$ and $6X$ are at hand the individual would be willing to release $5Y$ for $1X$.   When $10Y$ and $16X$ are held, he would want $4X$ before surrendering only $1Y$.   In column 3 we have the marginal rate of substitution; this is the ratio derived by placing in the numerator the quantity of Y that would be sacrificed for a further increment of X, which becomes the denominator.   The MRS can thus be computed at each point along the indifference curve; as we move down the curve to the right, with the stock of Y becoming relatively depleted and X augmented, the MRS must fall.   Drawing an indifference curve convex to the origin, as we have done, implies this very fact, namely a decreasing capacity of X to replace Y.

TABLE 1.   Indifference Combinations and the Marginal Rate of Substitution

Indifference combinations	Subjective valuation of ΔX and ΔY	Marginal rate of substitution of X for Y ($\Delta Y/\Delta X$)
$27Y, 6X$	$5Y = 1X$	5/1
$22Y, 7X$	$4Y = 1X$	4/1
$18Y, 8X$	$3Y = 1X$	3/1
$15Y, 9X$	$2Y = 1X$	2/1
$13Y, 10X$	$1Y = 1X$	1/1
$12Y, 11X$	$1Y = 2X$	1/2
$11Y, 13X$	$1Y = 3X$	1/3
$10Y, 16X$	$1Y = 4X$	1/4

Writing $-\Delta Y$ to represent the amount of Y that will be released for a further unit of X, symbolically ΔX, the MRS can be denoted by the ratio

$$-\Delta Y/\Delta X.$$

In our table this ratio fell from 5/1 to 4/1, and ultimately, to 1/4. In the form $-\Delta Y/\Delta X$ the MRS can be discerned for what it is, namely a rate of change along an indifference curve, measuring the descent downwards on OY for an outward movement of one unit on OX. A "staircase" to exhibit this change, as in Figure 1b, can be drawn. Mathematically, the movement in the MRS can be traced by drawing a tangent to each point on the indifference curve, for the value of the tangent is the measure of the slope or rate of change of the curve, and is equal exactly to $-\Delta Y/\Delta X$. The slope of the tangents, as in Figure 1c, will vary from point to point on the indifference curve or, more concretely, with changes in the relative quantities of X and Y on hand. The tangents will flatten out and lose their steepness as the stock of X increases and that of Y diminishes, signifying a lower $-\Delta Y/\Delta X$ ratio and thus a decreasing MRS.

Basically, the notion of a decreasing MRS has its roots in the idea of diminishing marginal utility; the latter also fell as the quantities consumed increased, or rose as the quantities decreased. Thus, suppose that when $27Y$ and $6X$ were possessed, the marginal utility of $1X$ (MU_x) amounted to 50 and of $1Y$ (MU_y) to 10 units of satisfaction. The ratio of marginal utilities would be

$$MU_x/MU_y = 50/10,$$

so that our individual would be willing to surrender $5Y$ for $1X$. But this is simply an alternate statement of the MRS of X for Y: hence we can write

$$MU_x/MU_y = MRS = -\Delta Y/\Delta X.$$

If the $5Y$ were actually traded for the $1X$, leaving $22Y$ and $7X$, the MU_x would fall, say to 44, in the light of the increase in X, and the MU_y would rise because of the decrease in Y, say to 11; the new ratio of marginal utilities would be $44/11$. This is tantamount to an MRS of $4/1$; the decline in the ratio of relative marginal utilities is thus equivalent to a decreasing MRS. If we always remembered to speak of *relative* marginal utility and always compared the utility of one good to another while maintaining our level of well-being constant, the central thought of the decreasing MRS could be conveyed just as pointedly and precisely.

THE PRICE LINE AND THE EQUILIBRIUM PURCHASE COMBINATION

Let us suppose that an individual having a definite amount of money income (I) comes to the market to purchase commodities X and Y at the market prices P_x and P_y. The problem is to determine the quantities of each commodity that he will purchase on the principle that the consumer so allocates his income expenditure as to maximize his well-being.

The Price Line

We have already learned how to depict the tastes of the individual; these tastes are subjective facts.   Purchases, however, will depend not only on his tastes, as reflected in the indifference curves, but also on his income and on the ruling prices.   Let us represent schematically the objective facts of prices and income.   Thereafter we ought to be able to combine the subjective and objective phenomena and describe the forces determining the equilibrium-purchase intake of our individual.

Suppose our consumer spent his full income I, equal say to $100, on commodity Y selling say at a price of $1.   To compute the maximum quantity of commodity Y that could be bought, we divide I/P_y = ($100/$1) = 100.   On the indifference map of Figure 1 this Y quantity is represented by the distance OM.   Similarly when the consumer is directing all of his income to the purchase of X, the maximum purchase intake would be I/P_x, or amount OR equal to 50 units if $P_x = $2.   Since $P_x = 2P_y$, if the same distance represents a unit of a commodity along both OY and OX, then $OM/OR = 2$.   In view of the price relations, by foregoing the purchase of $2Y$ our individual can, in real terms, always acquire $1X$, signifying a value relationship or market rate of exchange of $2Y = 1X$.   Thus $P_x/P_y = -\Delta Y/\Delta X$, where the latter ratio signifies the market rate of exchange between the two goods.   In our problem,

$$P_x/P_y = \$2/\$1,$$

so that

$$-\Delta Y/\Delta X = 2/1.$$

Concretely, by withdrawing $2 from expenditure on Y our consumer sacrifices $2Y$ (thus, $-\Delta Y$) and accumulates a sum of money with which to purchase $1X$ (thus ΔX).   As this market exchange rate $P_x/P_y = -\Delta Y/\Delta X$ is constant and equal to 2, a straight line such as MR in Figure 1 contains all the maximum purchase combinations of X and Y open to the consumer.*   The line MR is termed a *price* line.†

* As with the MRS, the slope of the line MR can be measured at each point by the ratio of the vertical descent ΔY with the unit outward movement in X, ΔX.   As this ratio $-\Delta Y/\Delta X$ is constant in our illustration at 2/1, the slope of the price line is invariant and MR is a straight line.

† The price line is also called a *budget* or *opportunity* line.   The budget equation may be written $P_x X + P_y Y = I$.   With income and prices constant, if less is spent on Y, in

In contrast to the indifference curve which mirrors the subjective taste phenomena, the price line portrays the external objective facts of prices and income and thus the alternative purchase possibilities. All combinations on and below the price line can be bought in the given income and price circumstances. The price line will be linear only when the ratio of market prices (or, identically, the rate of exchange between the goods) is constant.

The Equilibrium Position

After displaying the quantities of X and Y that *can* be purchased, the next step is to elicit the equilibrium position, consisting of the quantities that *will* be purchased. Generally there will be one combination of the goods X and Y that can be bought which will be preferred to all other combinations. In Figure 1, at the income level OM in terms of Y (or OR in terms of X), although the individual can buy any of the quantities located along the price line, the position of maximum well-being is at point P where the price line MR is tangent to the indifference curve 2. At the point of tangency the slope of the indifference curve, measured by $-\Delta Y/\Delta X$ and equal to a definite marginal rate of substitution, equals the slope of the price line, also measured by $-\Delta Y/\Delta X$ and equal to P_x/P_y.* Hence at the tangency position and for the full-income expenditure, $MRS = P_x/P_y$. In words, the rate at which individuals are willing to substitute goods in their purchase scheme in view of their tastes is brought into harmony with the market-price ratios or rates of exchange. This equilibrium property thus evolves out of a balancing by the individual of the subjective and objective facts of tastes, income and prices.

To prove that the point of tangency between the price line and the indifference curve represents the most preferred purchase opportunity, we can imagine the consumer contemplating the expenditure of all his income on commodity Y. Thereafter we visualize him as pondering whether it is desirable, in view of the prices, to forego $2Y$ for the purchase of $1X$. Whenever the price line intersects the indifference

---

amount $P_y\Delta Y$, more can be expended on X, in sum $P_x\Delta X$. Thus: $P_x\Delta X = -P_y\Delta Y$, and $P_x/P_y = -\Delta Y/\Delta X$; the latter ratio is the rate of exchange of the two goods and denotes the slope of the price line which, in view of the constant prices, is constant.

* The slope of the indifference curve and of the price line are both measured by $-\Delta Y/\Delta X$. But we must not make the mistake of assuming that their values are always the same; $\Delta Y/\Delta X$ is a mathematical measure used to evaluate all slopes. Referred to the price line $\Delta Y/\Delta X = P_x/P_y$; referred to the indifference curve it equals MRS. MRS equals P_x/P_y only when $\Delta Y/\Delta X$ is the same for each as at the point of tangency between an indifference curve and the price line.

curves, as it will at other than the tangency point, this implies that the slope of the price line, measured by $-\Delta Y/\Delta X$ (equal to P_x/P_y), differs from the slope of the indifference curve, measured by $-\Delta Y/\Delta X$ (equal to MRS). Thus at any maximum purchase combination other than the tangency position $P_x/P_y \gtrless MRS$, signifying that the market exchange rate differs from the preference ratio. When the slope of the indifference curve exceeds that of the price line, or $MRS > P_x/P_y$, the actual or tacit surrender of some Y (by a failure to buy it) will lift the individual onto a higher indifference level. If the MRS is $4/1$, meaning that the individual regards $1X$ as the equivalent of $4Y$, and if the exchange ratio is but $2/1$, the sacrifice of but $2Y$ will enable $1X$ to be bought, thus enabling well-being to be augmented by the mental equivalent of $2Y$; the individual will therefore hasten to purchase $1X$ and, implicitly, divest himself of $2Y$.

Similarly, when $MRS < P_x/P_y$, as $1/1 < \$2/\$1$, the individual will observe that by mentally foregoing the purchase of $1X$ he can be equally satisfied by acquiring $1Y$. But the market facts enable him to purchase $2Y$ when he cuts his X intake by one unit. Obviously there is an incentive to buy more Y and elevate his level of well-being. To conclude: when $MRS > P_x/P_y$, more X will be bought and less Y; when $MRS < P_x/P_y$, more Y will be acquired and less X. When for the full income disposal $MRS = P_x/P_y$, diagrammatically, where the slope of the price line is tangent to an indifference curve, the incentive to alter the purchase combination vanishes: here the subjective attitudes are consistent with the external price and income data. This is the equilibrium position; it represents the purchase combination of maximum satisfaction in the particular taste, price and income circumstances. Until this position is realized there will be a reshuffle in the expenditure plan.

INCOME AND PRICE VARIATIONS

After this exposition of the character of the equilibrium position we can relax some of our previous hypotheses. Continuing the assumption of constant tastes, and thus the assumption of a rigid indifference map, let us suppose that income moves from I_1, to I_2, to $I_3 \cdots I_n$, where $I_1 < I_2 < I_3 \cdots < I_n$. Prices are assumed to be constant while income varies.

The Income-Consumption Line

To represent constant tastes and prices with rising income, we need only to elevate the price line parallel upward, as from MR to $M'R'$ in

Figure 2. Another point of tangency ensues between the new price line and a higher indifference curve, as at L; for a further rise in income, point T would be the equilibrium point. Connecting the equilibrium points at each income level, as QLT in Figure 2, we describe an *income-consumption (I-C)* line. As the market prices are constant, and as in equilibrium at each income level the price ratio $P_x/P_y = MRS$, the income-consumption line relates points of identical MRS. Normally, the income-consumption line will reveal that as I rises with prices unchanged, the consumption of both (all) commodities will increase. The effect of the income change, from

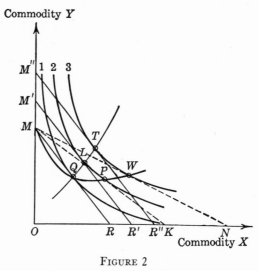

FIGURE 2

I to $(I + \Delta I)$ on the purchases of X and Y at the given prices, is termed the *income effect*.

The Price-Consumption Line

As another sample of the insight afforded by the indifference map in probing and elucidating certain problems in the theory of demand, assume that there is a change in P_x while I and P_y remain constant. This can be represented by a nonparallel shift in MR to MK, indicating a fall in P_x, since at the constant level of I more units of X and the same amount of Y can be purchased; the tapered slope of the price line indicates also that fewer Y need be offered in exchange for a unit of X, which is an aspect of a lower P_x. Just as with income, the full plane can be covered with price lines emanating from M, showing the new price relations consequent upon the variation in P_x, with I and P_y constant. Connecting the points of tangency of each price line with the indifference map, a *price-consumption (P-C)* curve can be constructed, as $MQPW$ in Figure 2.

Income and Substitution Effects

There is this to notice with respect to the price-consumption curve: a movement in P_x generates two effects, namely (1) an *income* (I)

effect corresponding to the change in the level of real income, and (2) a *substitution* (S) *effect* through which the relatively high-priced commodity, Y in this case, is replaced at the initial (or any) income level by the commodity that has fallen in price—commodity X in our illustration. Starting from a particular price line, as MR in Figure 2, the price-consumption line based on hypothetical decreases in P_x with P_y constant will, because of the S effect, lie below and to the right of an income-consumption line which presumes that the initial prices are constant and that only I varies.

Figure 3 demonstrates these relations.

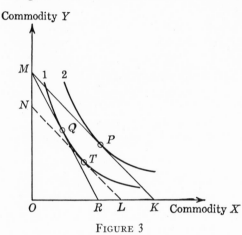

Commodity Y

FIGURE 3

A fall in P_x is indicated by the movement in the price line MR to MK. The new equilibrium adjustment is at P, compared to the old position at Q. The movement from Q to P can be thought of as occurring in two stages: *first*, an S movement from Q to point T, which assumes that the new price relations OM/OK (equal to ON/OL) have been established but that the original real-income level is maintained, and *second*, an I effect, a movement from T on curve 1 to P on indifference curve 2, as a consequence of the rise in real income; the magnitude of the I effect is equivalent to an increase in money income, in amount $P_y \cdot MN$, or to the new $P_x \cdot LK$.*

At first sight, the purpose of separating the effects of a price fall in this way is perplexing and obscure. But we shall see that the two effects need not work in the same direction, and hence that their analytic separation is imperative. This will be elaborated at page 17.

Price-Income-Consumption Lines

A third consumption line may be derived. Later, the emphasis will be upon the simultaneity of price movements, suggesting a syn-

---

* Hicks usually measures the substitution effect along the new rather than the old indifference level. (*Value and Capital*, p. 31.) The sum of the effects, under either method of measuring them, must be the same: the new equilibrium position must culminate at P. But the income component and the substitutionary component will have slightly different values under each procedure. See J. Mosak, "On The Interpretation of the Fundamental

chronized fall in both P_x and P_y. Hence even at this stage it is unrealistic to overwork the fiction of P_y remaining constant while P_x falls, or vice versa. The relative price movements, however, may well be disproportionate.

First, it should be clear that a proportionate price fall in P_x and P_y is tantamount to a proportionate increase in money income. A proportionate fall in P_x and P_y, therefore, will drive the price lines parallel upward and generate an income-consumption line. If the relative fall in P_x were always disproportionate to the fall in P_y, another consumption line could be traced. The new curve might be termed, in recognition of the mixed phenomena, a *price-income-consumption* (*P-I-C*) line, for the effects on consumption will be due to the shifts both in the income level and in relative prices. Unless we specify some particular price path, the location of the curve relative to the *I-C* and *P-C* curves is indeterminate. Starting at some definite P_x-P_y relationship, if P_y invariably rises as P_x falls, the *P-I-C* line may become fairly horizontal.

NEGATIVE INCOME EFFECTS

Usually an increase in income with prices and tastes unchanged will increase the quantities purchased of both X and Y. To list all the possibilities: (1) the quantities purchased of both X and Y may increase; (2) the quantity of X (or Y) may increase with Y (or X) unchanged; (3) purchase of X may increase while the quantity demanded of Y decreases, or vice versa.

Inferior Goods

The third case admits the possibility that Y (or X) may be an *inferior* good, so that the I effect will be negative. An inferior good is one consumed at lower income levels which drops out of the purchase plan as income rises and a shift to *superior* goods sets in. Bread, oleomargarine, cheap clothing, etc., can be cited as illustrations of inferior goods. The possibility of a negative I effect is important from a theoretical standpoint because it explains an interesting and abnormal demand situation in which the sales quantity falls despite a lower price for a good.

The various I effects can be shown graphically by following the course of diverse income-consumption curves. On a backward-bending income-consumption curve that curls up to the Y axis, X is the inferior good, less of it being bought as income rises.* On a downward-sloping I-C curve, Y is the inferior good. On a fairly horizontal (vertical) curve the demand for X alone (or Y alone) is increased with a rise in income; purchases of the other commodity are unaffected. With a normal I effect the demand for both X and Y will be increased simultaneously.†

The interpretation of a negative I effect can be facilitated by considering it in relation to the MRS. Given the ruling prices, say $P_x/P_y = \$3/\$1$, for equilibrium the MRS must be equated to P_x/P_y at each income level. Normally, after a rise in I (equal to ΔI), the preservation of the equality will involve the purchase of more of both X and Y. But if X is the inferior good, less X will be bought despite ΔI. Implicitly, this suggests that if there were a vertical upward movement on the indifference map, with more Y and an unchanged amount of X bought, or a horizontal rightward displacement with more X and the same Y purchased, the MRS at either of these positions would be less than $3/1$—for it is only $3/1$ with fewer units of X bought, and the law of decreasing MRS must hold at the new indifference level. As the consumption of X is decreased when it is an inferior good, the implications in utility terms are that the marginal utilities are interdependent to the extent that an increment in Y so reduces MU_x that the former stock of X must be *reduced* to equate the MU_x/MU_y ratio to the price ratio after the income improvement.‡

Negative Income Effects and a Price Fall

To appraise the importance of the income effect released by a price fall, let us develop the possibilities of a fall in P_x, with P_y unchanged, on the quantities wanted of X. Since a fall in P_x occasions an S effect, rotating a price line from M in Figure 3 will invariably increase the quantity

---

* The appropriate indifference field can be superimposed by remembering that each point on the income-consumption line represents a point of tangency between an indifference curve and a price line for higher income at unchanged prices.

† The income elasticity of demand for X, measuring the proportionate increase in the purchase of X with a relative rise in income, can be written as

$$_IE_x = (\Delta X/X)/(\Delta I/I) = I\Delta X/X\Delta I \gtreqless 0,$$

being < 0 if X is an inferior good. A similar measure can be formulated for Y.

‡ The marginal utilities cannot be *independent;* if they were, the restoration of the equilibrium-utility ratio would involve more of X and Y. But this would preclude the possibility of an inferior good. Thus the law of a decreasing MRS involves more than merely the retention of the law of diminishing utility.

wanted of X at the original indifference level. This much is certain: the increase in quantity is a consequence of drawing indifference curves convex to the origin.* But the I effect is not so definite; normally, it will be positive and will also work to expand the sales of X. If the income effect is abnormal and negative, with X an inferior good, there are the three possibilities—namely that the effects of S are less than, equal to, or greater than the effects of I $\left(\text{written } S \overset{<}{\underset{>}{=}} I\right)$. The quantity purchased, in the last instance, would still increase as P_x fell. In the second case, purchases of X would be unchanged despite the fall in P_x; finally, when the I effect overshadows the S effect, the X purchases will fall off.

As a practical matter, a negative I effect is unlikely to exceed the S effect except when the individual is spending a large part of his income on the commodity.† Then the savings on the price fall are so substantial and the prospect of consuming other superior substitutes is so bright that the individual's purchases of the particular good may decrease. But almost invariably we can expect that the quantities wanted will steadily increase as prices fall. For the complete market this is the more likely, because even if there are decreased purchases by some consumers their diminished intake will be counterbalanced by the increased quantities wanted by lower-income groups who are better able to include the good in their consumption plan as its price moves down. Though we have an explanation of a curious demand phenomenon, this phenomenon must not be interpreted as the typical situation.

SUBSTITUTES AND COMPLEMENTS

At a constant level of real income in a two-commodity world, goods can only be substitutes for one another; an increase in the consumption of one commodity, with the indifference level unchanged, requires a decrease in the intake of the other. But when we introduce three or more commodities it is possible for two of the goods to be *complementary* at the assumed income level and for their consumption to increase at the expense of other commodities.

Substitutes and Complements

Rather than symbolize the third commodity Z, whose presence permits complementarity relationships, as merely a simple commodity, we

* See the odd curves drawn in the fresh and lucid work by Ruby Turner Norris, *The Theory of Consumer's Demand*, Chapter II especially.
† As in Marshall's famous "Giffen case." *Principles of Economics*, 8th edition, p. 132.

might regard it as a sum of money. Since money represents purchasing power over all goods, commodity Z is in effect a composite of all commodities; they may be lumped together in this one composite so long as the relative prices of the commodities subsumed—those that can be purchased for the money sum—are constant.* Viewing Z in this way, we can define Y as a substitute for X if the *MRS* of Z for a unit of Y decreases when X is increased by a unit and Z is decreased by an amount necessary to keep the level of well-being unchanged. Y can be declared complementary with X if the *MRS* of Z for a unit of Y increases as a unit of X is substituted for Z at the constant indifference level.† Y, a substitute for X, may itself have other substitutes or complements. Commodities will thus be interrelated to one another, either faintly or firmly, as substitutes or complements, or competing or completing goods in the full-preference system.

To elaborate these relations, assume that X is substituted for Z at a constant indifference level when, say, $100X$, $100Y$, and $100Z$ are possessed and the *MRS* ratios, neglecting the negative signs, are: $\Delta Z/\Delta X = 6/1$ and $\Delta Z/\Delta Y = 4/1$. As X rises to $101\,$., and Z falls to $94Z$, a fall in the *MRS* of Z to X from $6/1$ to say $5/1$ must occur. If the *MRS* of $\Delta Z/\Delta Y$ also diminishes as compared to former ratios, from $4/1$ to $3/1$ despite the constancy in Y holdings, then X and Y are substitutes. Additional Y, because of the additional X, has become less important in the individual's desire schema. In the contrary instance when X is increased and the individual is prepared to sacrifice more Z than formerly to acquire a unit of Y—for example, to sacrifice Z for Y at the rate of $5/1$ rather than $4/1$—then X and Y are complements. Literally, Y is more essential after the expansion in X. As Z has been exchanged for X at the particular income level, these commodities must be substitutes. In short, to discover the nature of the interrelations between X and Y we are compelled to examine the changed relative importance of Y, whose stock is constant, with commodities such as Z, whose stock has been decreased when X expands.

The definitions of commodity interrelations presumed a given indifference level. Undoubtedly the degree of substitution and complementarity is likely to alter with the income level. As an example, at low levels of income bread and cake are likely to be substitutes against, say, savings. As income rises they are more likely to be viewed by the valuing subject as complementary items.

---

* This device for handling commodity interrelations has been termed the "law of composition of goods." See O. Lange, *Price Flexibility and Employment*, p. 106.

† Hicks, p. 44.

Implicit Relations

Analytically, if the MRS between Z and X and between Z and Y are given, there is also an implicit MRS between X and Y. If $6Z = 1X$ and $4Z = 1Y$, then $1.5Y = 1X$. Conceivably, if X and Y are substitutes, as Z is reduced and X increased, then the individual may be ready to part with *more* Y to acquire $1X$; in our illustration, say $1.6Y$ for $1X$. For complements the reverse would hold; less Y would be offered for $1X$. It is possible to construct illustrations where on the indirect evidence provided by the MRS ratios between $\Delta Z/\Delta X$ and $\Delta Z/\Delta Y$ the commodities will be defined as substitutes, even though a direct comparison of MRS ratios may not disclose this fact. If $20Z = 1X$ and $10Z = 1Y$ before the decrease in Z and the increase in X, and if $10Z = 1X$ and $5Z = 1Y$ after the variation, then the direct comparison yields an MRS of $2Y = 1X$ before and after the quantity variations, even though on the indirect relationship X and Y are deemed to be substitutes.*

PRICE INTERRELATIONS

Commodity interrelations are essential as a preliminary to explaining the interdependence of market prices. Suppose that P_x should fall slightly; the quantity demanded of X will normally increase as the MRS is equated to the new and lower P_x/P_z. Thus if the former price ratio was \$5/\$1 and the new ratio is \$4/\$1, then the purchase of X must increase before the MRS of X with Z is reduced to $4/1$. If X and Y were interrelated at the former income level, and Z is the composite money commodity, the MRS ratio between Z and Y and P_y/P_z will be unbalanced: if X and Y are substitutes, the individual will be reluctant to part with the same Z quantity as formerly for an increment of Y; hence there ought to be a diminution in the intake of Y at the prevailing P_y as the MRS of Y for Z decreases, following the augmentation of X purchases and the depletion of the Z intake. On this score, P_y should tend to fall unless the normal I effect exceeds the S force and sustains the demand price for Y. On the other hand, if X and Y were complements originally, the fall in P_x would augment the demand for Y, because both the normal income and complementarity forces would operate in concert: Y would rise in importance relative to Z, foreshadowing a rise in the individual's demand price for the same quantity of Y as was formerly purchased. Thus with positive and small income

* It would seem that the implicit relationship is simpler to grasp; however I have followed Hicks' definitions, for they overtly fasten attention on the variation in other commodities which, on the implicit relationship, might be ignored.

effects for Y, the prices of substitutes ought to move synchronously, in the same direction, while the prices of complements take opposite paths. With negative income effects for Y, these price interrelations are even more certain for substitutes; their demand will fall off on both counts although for complements a negative income effect may upset the usual rule. It is not to be overlooked that as P_x continues to fall, raising the level of real income, the I effect may greatly outweigh the S effect. Interrelations which follow for small movements in P_x may not survive a sharp change in P_x. Ostensibly, as the degree of substitute and complementarity relations oscillates with the income level from which we start, it becomes difficult in practice to denote commodities as typical substitutes or complements.

Causes of Movements in P_x

Assuming that substitutionary and complementarity relationships are rigid, we may wonder about the source of the initial movements in P_x that kindle the price repercussions among the markets. It may be that a new group of consumers appear in the market for X. Or, some of the previous consumers of X buy more of it without reducing their purchases of any other commodity; their diversion of purchasing power to X may be at the expense of saving. Or for a few consumers there may be a shift to X from but one good Z. Finally, altered cost conditions may lead to a change in P_x. Categorizing goods as substitutes and complements, and invoking these relations to explain price movements, is thus contingent upon a high degree of stability in the indifference relations among X and Y for an important group of consumers. If widespread changes in tastes are common, involving a revision of the preference systems of many consumers, the change in tastes rather than the commodity interrelationships would explain the price movements.

As evidence of the importance of the exact nature of the changes in external phenomena, suppose that for complementary goods, where P_y ought to fall with a higher P_x, new consumers with tastes similar to those of present buyers enter the market. Here P_y is unlikely to fall because of a higher P_x; instead it will probably rise in view of the greater demand for the complementary pair even though some of the original purchasers whose tastes are unaltered may shift from the complementary pair to substitute goods and dampen the price rise. The term *sympathetic goods* has been reserved for those goods for which the demand changes in the same direction, with more of both X and Y wanted at the same prices as formerly. Thus, such technical complements as the automobile and gasoline, bread and butter, tea and lemon, etc., are in *sympathetic demand.* Goods are in *antagonistic relationship* if the shift in demand in favor of one is usually adverse to the other; otherwise, they are in *neutral demand.* These relationships revolve upon certain empirical rules of the typical variation, whereas the previous definitions of substitutes and complements were properties of a *given* structure of tastes.*

The Instability of the System

The availability of a substitute good tends to restrain a price rise, originating (say) in P_x, by causing a diversion in demand to substitutes and diffusing the rising-price forces in P_x over a wider area. The effect of numerous substitutes, therefore, is to render a particular market more stable than otherwise. But for the economic system as a whole a preponderance of substitute relations contains an omen of instability, since a price movement in one market will have ramifications, identical in direction, in all the other markets comprising the price chain. Their calm will be destroyed and the entire system disrupted, however small the initial force.

SUMMARY

The indifference-curve approach has illuminated certain dark corners in the theory of consumer demand. In concluding this survey we might assess certain key assumptions and ponder some of the stumbling-blocks that halt any theory of rational demand.

The indifference-curve technique assumes that the individual knows his preferences and that they are consistent, in the sense that if A is preferred to B, and B to C, then A is more highly valued than C. Ruled out, therefore, are cases of impulsive behavior that do not involve an estimate of preferences, and irrational (inconsistent) behavior. It would be vain to deny their occurrence, but little can be said of them on a general plane. Either we must grant that they are the less important manifestations or else forego the prospect of developing a theory of economic behavior to describe the market facts.

In terms of fully measurable quantities, if X represents one batch of goods and Y another, and P_1 and P_2 are distinguishable average prices per unit of goods in each batch, then if $P_1 X \geq P_1 Y$ and basket X is

---

* See the note of O. Lange, "Complementarity and Interrelations of Shifts in Demand," *Review of Economic Studies* (October 1940), pp. 58–63, and the reply by Hicks, pp. 64–65; also the notes by D. H. Robertson, J. R. Hicks, and O. Lange in the same journal (1944–1945 issue).

selected for consumption, after a price change such that $P_2X \geqq P_2Y$, consistent behavior would require that the X batch again be chosen.*

The stipulation of a decreasing MRS to accompany the theory of calculated choice must be invoked for the same reason, otherwise an increasing MRS would imply that the consumer was willing to offer ever greater amounts of Y for X as his stock of the former decreased and the stock of the latter increased, with well-being unchanged; ultimately consumers would be pictured as allocating their full outlay to but one commodity. This would constitute an evasion of the market facts although it might have some bearing in the actions of the drunkard. But we do class (and dismiss) such action as irrational. Likewise, if the indifference curves contained a concave kink, as in Figure 1d, it could be shown that the tangency of the concave portion of the curve to the price line denoted a minimum rather than a maximum position of well-being. So long as we are prepared to grant, on introspection or empirical investigation, that when consumers buy commodities selling for $2 and $1 they expect to derive twice the satisfaction from the former as from the latter, then our concepts and the equilibrium solution hold firm.

More vulnerable to the structure is the postulate that tastes are unchanged. The entire indifference map is drawn on this basis and remains valid only if the preference relations are rigid. The definitions of substitutes and complements were themselves expressed as properties of a given taste structure. If tastes are ephemeral and volatile, subject to chronic and unpredictable flux, then the entire superstructure of the indifference analysis rests on shaky foundations. Systematic methods for dealing with the interrelations among tastes (and thus among markets) would have to be abandoned. Considering that the impact of knowledge and education in our world is very gradual, and acknowledging the weight of habit, perhaps the hypothesis of a given taste structure is close enough to the facts. Its static nature is generally a simplifying advantage, but a distortion under more dynamic taste circumstances.

A technical disadvantage of the indifference curve lies in its inability to deal diagrammatically with more than two, or at most more than three goods. Throughout the discourse the stock of other goods must be held constant, otherwise the preference ratios for the two goods under consideration will be upset. In effect, it must be assumed that there are but two goods available for purchase or that expenditure equilibrium has been established in other markets, between all pairs of goods and

---

* See P. A. Samuelson, *Foundations of Economic Analysis*, p. 110.

between goods and savings, and that the individual has ready for expenditure on the remaining two commodities an income sum that will, after allocation among the two commodities, assure him of maximum satisfaction. The importance of the stocks of goods on hand cannot be exaggerated in evaluating market behavior with respect to durable goods. For perishables its significance diminishes.

In the same vein, preference ratios will also be contingent upon stocks held by other consumers. There are the two cases of taste interdependence: some goods are more highly desired when there is a widespread consumption of them. The "keeping up with the Joneses" phenomenon of goods in "emulation demand" would to some extent comprise one category. A less invidious instance are those goods bought in conjunction with purchases by friends: the purchase of golf clubs becomes more important when friends take up the game. The second case consists of goods that appeal to the snob as a vehicle for "conspicuous consumption," as Veblen called it, only when the price goes sufficiently high to prevent these items from being widely bought. In either event, indifference systems change with the possession of the goods by others; in the one case presumably because price has fallen and purchases have become more universal, and in the other case because prices have risen. Both situations are inimical to ordinary analysis; rather than taste phenomena being, along with cost phenomena, the ultimate explanation of price phenomena, it is the price phenomena that are causal in the formation of tastes. Our methods are unsatisfactory here. But their shortcomings are not a serious drawback if these situations do not comprise the major cases of the consumer market.*

A NOTE ON COMPENSATING
AND EQUIVALENT INCOME VARIATIONS

The indifference-curve approach does place the demand curve on a firmer footing besides underscoring the interrelations among tastes and thus among markets. To appreciate its effectiveness in many other questions, consider a fall in the price of one commodity, other prices remaining unchanged. We might ask, by how much does this price fall improve consumer well-being? This was the sort of problem incorporated in the older literature under the guise of "consumer's surplus." Analogously, we might want to discover the income rise at unchanged

---

* Once the stocks held by others are stabilized, the indifference maps can be drawn and the technique brought into play. But if the external holdings are in continuous flux the individual maps will themselves reflect this fact and become subject to constant revision.

prices that would be as satisfactory to a consumer as a fall in P_x. Both answers, we shall see, are not quite the same.   Indifference-curve analysis can illuminate this puzzle and enable us to extract more precise results than with the older methods.

Compensating Income Variations

The analysis can be simplified by measuring amounts of money (instead of a commodity) vertically and amounts of commodity X horizontally.   This procedure is valid if we suppose that the prices of

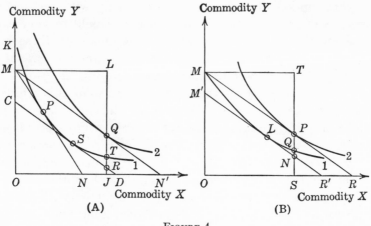

(A)   (B)

FIGURE 4

all other commodities are constant so that each amount of money corresponds to a definite amount of other goods.   Hence the indifference curves now touch the vertical axis; for each quantity of money ("other things") connotes a definite level of well-being.   Heretofore, as both X and Y were essential to life, the indifference curves did not touch the axes but instead became asymptotic to them.*

In Figure 4A the original income and price relations are indicated by the opportunity line MN; the equilibrium adaptation is at P.   The price line MN' informs us that P_x has fallen while other prices are unchanged; the new equilibrium is at Q.   At Q the individual purchases OJ of X, and JQ of Y (other things), having parted with LQ of money for the OJ amount of X.   If we measure the actual money value of the improvement in well-being conferred by the fall in P_x, one answer would be that the consumer benefits in amount equal to TQ, for this sum might be exacted from him, perhaps in direct taxation, without any

* A. G. Hart, "Peculiarities of Indifference Maps Involving Money," *Review of Economic Studies* (1941).

diminution in well-being as compared to his original indifference status. The money sum TQ might, with propriety, be described as a compensating income variation. Since it presumes the OJ purchases will continue, TQ can be further distinguished as a *quantity*-compensating variation.

In fact, if TQ alone were expropriated, the consumer would be better off than he was originally, despite the tax payment. For after the loss in TQ of money income, a price line parallel to MN' would run through T and would be tangent to a higher indifference curve than that carrying the index 1. If the consumer was to be restored to indifference level 1, a sum equal to QR ($= MC$) would have to be extracted from him after the price fall. For when a money sum QR ($> TQ$) is recovered from the individual, the new price line CD is tangent to indifference curve 1 at point S, ensuring the return to the original indifference level 1; a price line passing through T and parallel to CD would raise the income status. The sum QR, therefore, measures the change in income that exactly describes the gain in well-being occasioned by the price fall. This can be termed the *price-compensating variation in income;* it is the full measure of the income enhancement consequent upon a price fall.

Conceivably, if CD were tangent to curve 1 vertically below Q, the point of tangency of MN' with curve 2, then $QR = QT$. This would mean that the MRS was equal in both instances despite the $\pm \Delta Y$ at the amount OJ of X—for prices are the same—and that a rise in income, if accompanied by more X, would reduce the MRS. The change in the demand for X, with respect to income changes, would then be zero.* In utility terms the marginal utility of Y could be described as constant, for even as the Y holdings alter (as we move vertically up or down on the indifference map) the ratio MU_x/MU_y ($= MRS$) would be unchanged.† Barring this exception, the price-compensating variation QR will exceed the quantity variation TQ.

Equivalent Income Variations

Modifying the query, we may inquire what gain in income at the original prices would be equivalent to the fall in price represented by the rotation of the price lines from MN to MN'. The price change is presumed to be suspended and the initial prices embodied in MN are to rule; the consumer is to be lifted onto indifference curve 2 by a grant of

---

* The income elasticity of demand would be zero; see note above.

† In indifference terms this is the meaning frequently attached to Marshall's premise of a constant marginal utility of money in drawing the demand curve.

money income in lieu of a price fall.   This type of variation is termed an *equivalent income variation.*

There are at least two ways in which the income level can be elevated. First, we can suppose that the quantity of X to be purchased after the income rise is indicated at P (or, on the indifference map, the commodity intake can be found vertically upward on curve 2).   This change of income can be called a *quantity-equivalent variation.*   Unless the MRS is constant for the fixed X regardless of the change in Y, the new price line would intersect curve 2 and well-being would exceed the level defined by curve 2.   Second, in contrast, the price line MN could be edged upward, always parallel to MN, until it became tangent to curve 2. The money sum necessary for this movement can be denoted as a *price-equivalent variation.*   It may, in the one case of constant MRS ratios of X for Y, despite altered Y holdings, be equal to the quantity variation, but otherwise it will be smaller.

Although it can be proved rigorously that the equivalent variations exceed the compensating variations, the following simple fact can be adduced to corroborate this view.   Since P_x is higher under the hypothesis of an equivalent variation than with the compensating variation, to lift an individual from indifference level 1 to indifference level 2 requires a greater sum than would be necessary at a lower P_x.   If the lower price prevailed, remembering P_y is constant throughout, and if an individual was already on curve 2, a given money sum taken from him which forced him down to curve 1 would be insufficient if handed to him to restore him to curve 2 when he was already on curve 1 and faced with higher prices.   Thus, in descending order of magnitude, the quantity equivalent variation, for a price fall, exceeds the price equivalent variation, both of which exceed the compensating variations; of the latter, the price variation is the greater magnitude.   Although we have looked at these measures from the standpoint of a price fall, if P_x rises then what were hitherto compensating variations become equivalent variations.

Further Applications

So far the analysis has been intricate largely because of the variety of measures turned to light; it is not possible, however, to declare which measure is best, for each has its use depending on the question to be solved.   Some further applications of these ideas may be examined.

MR and $M'R'$ in Figure 4B represent price lines at varying income levels but with constant prices for X and for the other commodities subsumed in Y.   Let us measure the gain in money secured by the presence of a commodity compared to the pecuniary loss in well-being suffered by its complete withdrawal from the market. When X is withdrawn, according to Figure 4B, the maximum position of well-being is at M, on the vertical axis, of indifference curve 1. When X is available at the market price, well-being rises to the level indicated by indifference curve 2. By having commodity X in the market at the given price, an individual enjoys an enhancement of real income measured by PN ($= MM'$). On the removal of commodity X, without a new substitute to replace it and with other prices constant, he would retain PT to spend on other things (the Y commodities), but his pocket would literally be picked in sum PN; the individual would be driven to the level of well-being represented by point M on curve 1. The sum PN is thus a measure of the economic importance of the commodity to him.

As an alternative problem, let us ascertain the maximum sum an individual would offer in order to purchase a particular quantity of a commodity as compared to the sum that he does pay in view of market prices; this problem is interesting in connection with all-or-nothing types of bargains. Possessed of money income OM at the prevailing MR price structure in Figure 4B, the consumer will purchase OS of commodity X, spending SP on all other commodities and PT on X. Confronting the individual with the alternative of paying a higher sum for the quantity OS of X or not being permitted to buy any of it at all, at a maximum he would tender the sum TQ for OS of X, or an amount PQ above his expenditure when he is free to purchase at the market price. The sum PQ thus represents his *consumer's surplus* on being able to purchase at the market price rather than being compelled to submit a maximum offer for this quantity.

BIBLIOGRAPHICAL NOTE

On the materials of this chapter, see J. R. Hicks, *Value and Capital*, Chapters I–III. Most of this chapter follows Professor Hicks' development. Other important studies are H. Schultz, *The Theory and Measurement of Demand*, Chapters I, XVIII, and XIX, and Paul A. Samuelson, *Foundations of Economic Analysis*, Chapters V and VII. Two earlier articles of J. R. Hicks and R. G. D. Allen, "A Reconsideration of the Theory of Value," *Economica* (1934), ought also to be included. A summary of these developments is provided by B. F. Haley's "Value and Distribution," in *A Survey of Contemporary Economics*, H. S. Ellis, ed.

On the measurability of utility, see the discussion on "The Determinateness of the Utility Function," *Review of Economic Studies* (1934–1935), to which Allen, Brown, Bernardelli, Lerner, and Lange contributed. Certain aspects of this old discussion were recently revived and in general a critical tone towards indifference analysis was adopted by Professor F. H. Knight in his "Realism and Relevance in the Theory of Demand," *Journal of Political Economy* (1944). See also the reply by R. L. Bishop, and the comments of Professor Knight and Professor J. M. Clark, in the April and August 1946 issues of the same journal.

On the modern theory of consumer's surplus, see Hicks, *Value and Capital*, p. 41, and his several articles in *The Review of Economic Studies:* "The Generalised Theory of Consumer's Surplus" (1945–1946); "The Four Consumers' Surpluses" (1943); "The Rehabilitation of Consumer's Surplus" (1941), and "Consumer's Surplus and Index Numbers" (1942). An excellent short note by A. Henderson, "Consumer's Surplus and the Compensating Variation," appears in the latter issue. Also, K. Boulding, "The Concept of Economic Surplus," *American Economic Review* (1945), and an important initial study on the subject by M. F. W. Joseph, "The Excess Burden of Indirect Taxation," *The Review of Economic Studies* (1939). Further, H. W. Robinson, "Consumer's Surplus and Taxation: Ex Ante or Ex Post?" *South African Journal of Economics* (1939), and the discussion of Knight and Bishop, "Realism and Relevance in the Theory of Demand," especially Bishop's reply. For a summary survey and additional references, see J. N. Morgan, "Measurement of Gains and Losses," *Quarterly Journal of Economics* (1948).

The classic exposition of the theory of rational choice is that of P. H. Wicksteed, *The Commonsense of Political Economy*. An endeavor to subject the Veblen case of "conspicuous consumption" to an indifference-curve analysis has been made by A. Kozlik, *American Economic Review* (1943).

CHAPTER 2

Market Demand

THE ANALYSIS IN THE PRECEDING chapter has carried us a good distance into the theory of demand. The present chapter proposes to review some familiar demand ideas such as the demand curve, the elasticity of demand, and total, average, and marginal revenue. Much use will be made later of these familiar tools of the economist's workbench. To conclude this chapter we consider the meaning of a commodity. Linking up these materials with the previous development we first demonstrate the connection between the demand curve and the price-consumption curve of the indifference map.

THE DEMAND CURVE

Technically, the individual demand curve is a geometrical expression of the functional relationship between market prices and the quantities wanted of a commodity by an individual at each possible price. If we measure prices vertically and quantities wanted horizontally, the curve embodying the relationship between the two is termed the demand curve. An illustration is provided in Figure 1A where D_1D_1' is a demand curve. Rather than refer to the demand curve, we may on occasion wish to specify the demand schedule, which is but a tabular statement of the actual numerical relationships between prices and quantities wanted. Table 2 contains part of a demand schedule for neckties. At a price of $5, it can be seen that 3 ties will be bought. At

TABLE 2.   Demand Schedule for Neckties

Price	Quantity Wanted
$5.00	3
4.00	5
3.00	7
2.00	12
1.00	20
0.50	35

31

a price of \$4, 5 ties, at \$3, 7 ties, etc.   For simplicity, the intermediate price and demand quantities have been omitted.

If the points of this demand schedule are plotted in the usual coordinate field and then connected, the familiar demand curve emerges. Since our demand schedule pertains to but one individual, the demand curve is likewise an individual phenomenon.   By constructing demand schedules for each prospective purchaser and then adding the quantities wanted by the full market group at each price, we can derive the

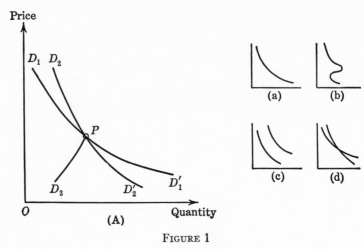

FIGURE 1

market-demand schedule.   Plotting this on our chart field gives a market-demand curve.   There is this fact to note about the demand curve or schedule: each point on it represents an *alternate* market possibility for the period of time in which we are interested.   Since prices are taken as external to each consumer, each point on the curve reveals the quantities that will be bought if the corresponding price is announced in the market.   The curve (or schedule) is not to be interpreted to mean that, if a price of \$4 is named, 5 ties will be bought by our individual, or that, if immediately thereafter the price falls to \$3, he will buy 7 additional units.   Each point on the curve is to be understood as signifying the quantities that will be bought if a price (externally determined) is named to prevail for the period of time that we are investigating. Strictly, the time length of each point on the curve pertains only to this one period; and in this time length only one price is supposed to rule.

Proceeding to the analytical derivation of the curve, the individual demand curves can be elicited from the price-consumption curve of the indifference system.   It will be recalled that this represented the path of purchases of maximum satisfaction on the assumption of constant tastes, income, price of commodity Y (other prices), and a varying price of commodity X. Going back to Figure 2, Chapter 1, and concentrating on the demand for X to the complete exclusion of commodity Y, we find that the quantities wanted of X at each successive P_x can be read off the price-consumption curve. Invariably, excepting only those inferior goods in which the I effect exceeds the S effect, the quantity demanded of X will increase as its price falls; the normal demand curve thus falls downward to the right, as in Figure 1a. If this holds for each individual it will also hold for the full market. For those inferior goods (probably rare) in which $I > S$ and I is negative, the demand curve will be backward-falling, at least over some range, as in Figure 1b. So long as this reaction is typical of but a small portion of the aggregate of individual responses to price decreases, while for the greater part of the market the demand curve is of normal form, then the market-demand curve will slope continuously downward to the right.

When we speak of demand we shall have in mind the full course of the demand curve or schedule, either individual or market. The quantity wanted at a particular price will be described as the demand quantity; this quantity will, in the normal case, increase as price falls. The price that will be paid per unit for a particular demand quantity will be referred to as the demand price. This price will normally fall as the demand quantity rises. Although the former statement is often heralded as the "law of demand," it may fail to apply to inferior goods.

Premises of the Demand Curve

If other prices vary concomitantly with P_x we can determine the quantities demanded of X by following the course of the price-income-consumption curve referred to in Chapter 1. Thus in eliciting the demand curve we are not restricted to the hypothesis of constancy in P_y (P_y being representative of other prices); instead, so long as the variation in P_y with each P_x is postulated, the demand curve for X can be traced quite readily. A fixed P_y, while P_x varies, is only a special rather than a general condition.

The demand curve must rest on at least the following premises: (a) given tastes, so that the indifference map is determinate; (b) given money income, so that, whatever the price ratios, the price lines may be drawn; (c) given other prices, or their mode of variation with each P_x, so that the slope of the price line for the fixed income is settled. A change in the data, which also involves implicitly the number of con-

sumers in the market and the relative distribution of income, will shift
the entire course of the demand curve. Consequently when we say
demand increases we have in mind a complete rightward shift in the
demand curve, as in Figure 1c, so that, at the same prices as formerly,
individuals will buy greater amounts, or they will be willing to pay
higher prices for the same amounts as they formerly purchased. A
decrease in demand signifies a leftward shift in the entire schedule.
Thus, while the demand quantity has reference to a point on a particular curve, a change in demand connotes a movement from one curve to
another. Sometimes the shift in demand will be erratic, as in Figure
1d, so that there is an increase in demand above the intersection of the
old and new curves, and a decrease below the intersection. Consequently, changes in the rate at which consumers desire to make purchases in the market, when market price is constant, will be ascribable
to a change either in tastes, income, or in movements in other prices.

Variations in Other Prices

Suppose that P_y (where Y is a widely recognized substitute good for
X) is constant while P_x rises, say from the level denoted at point P in
Figure 1A. The portion of the market-demand curve that ensues for
commodity X will follow the course, we can suppose, of D_1P, with sales of
X falling off rapidly as P_x mounts because of the shift of consumers away
from X to Y at the constant P_y. Conversely, if P_y holds firm as P_x falls,
the diversion of purchases will be from Y to X; the PD_1' portion of the
curve represents this situation.

As a similar experiment we can envisage that as P_x rises the diversion
of demand to Y causes a rise in P_y. If the rise in P_y is always synchronized with that in P_x, then the demand curve for X will follow the
course D_2P in the upper regions; for, as P_y is higher, the quantities
wanted of X will be greater at the same P_x prices as before. Hence the
curve segment D_2P will lie to the right of D_1P. Similarly, P_y may follow P_x downward, below point P, perhaps because of the fall-off in the
sales of Y as P_x is lowered. The new curve section for commodity X
is thus PD_2', compared to PD_1'. In brief, D_1D_1' is a demand curve for
X drawn on the hypothesis of other prices constant (P_y being representative), while D_2D_2' assumes variations in other prices as P_x alters.
Undoubtedly the slope of the curve drawn on the constancy hypothesis
is gentler than that of the curve drawn on the assumption of concomitant variations in other prices moving in the same direction as P_x.
The explanation is of course that if P_y rises with P_x, the sales of X hold

up better; while if P_y falls with P_x the sales of X do not expand quite as rapidly.

Finally, if as P_x falls from the height indicated at P, and if other firms take active measures to counter the price fall, lowering their price say by 10% for each 1% fall in P_x, then the quantities wanted of X may slump precipitately despite the reduction in P_x. The lower bend of the demand curve for X may thus turn backward, as does PD_3. If the rival firms accede to a price rise in X by raising their own prices, while replying sharply to a price fall, then the demand curve for X will take the form D_2PD_3, with the sharp corner at P. If the rival's prices are constant, for a rise in P_x, but decline disproportionately to a fall in P_x, the demand curve for X will be similar to D_1PD_3. Many applications of these demand-curve ideas will be observed later.

Sometimes a distinction is drawn between *short-* and *long-run* demand curves. Whatever the assumption regarding other prices, if price P has been ruling for some time a demand curve such as D_2D_2' can be interpreted as listing the immediate demand quantities of X if P_x suddenly changes to any of the possible levels to which it might go. Whatever the new P_x that appears in the market, as time passes and consumers become more aware of alternate purchase opportunities, the sales of X will recede, as compared to the immediate response, if the new P_x exceeds P. If the ruling P_x lies below P, it is argued that other consumers acquire this knowledge only slowly, fitting X into their purchase scheme so that sales are gradually enlarged at the lower P_x levels. The demand curve for the "short-run" is thus D_2D_2', but for the "long-run," if each P_x held firm for a longer time duration, the demand curve would be D_1D_1'. The pivot at P indicates that this is the contemporaneous price.

Demand Curve = Sales Curve = Average-Revenue Curve

There are other names current for the demand curve which might, in passing, be brought forward. The curve showing the relations between quantities wanted and prices, or quantities that will be purchased and prices, or quantities bought and prices—all interpretations will come to the same thing in practically all circumstances—has been termed the demand curve. Looked at from the point of view of the seller, this curve can be described as a *sales curve*, for each point on it denotes the sales that can be made at each price. Some writers are fond of terming it an *average-revenue curve*, since each ordinate price point represents the average revenue received by the seller for the corresponding quantity of market sales. Some writers draw a distinction between the demand curve of an industry and that for a firm, reserving the older term, demand curve, for the former relationship and christening the diagram a sales curve when it is interpreted as a phenomenon of the sales market of the firm. We shall, however, use the three names synonymously and interchangeably. There seems little to be gained by terming inherently like phenomena differently.

A more fundamental issue is whether the demand curve is a subjective fact—a mental image in the mind of the entrepreneur—or whether it is a market fact, an objective phenomenon which, with painstaking empirical investigation, can be revealed; or whether the dual phenomena exist. Later we shall disentangle these ideas and explain the possible coexistence and divergence of subjective and objective sales curves. For the moment, however, we can postulate the coincidence of the two so that these ultimate questions are temporarily shelved.

REVENUE CONCEPTS

The demand curve has already been denoted as an average-revenue curve. The concepts of total revenue (TR), average revenue (AR), and marginal revenue (MR) ought to be developed more systematically and the corresponding curves drawn. Although the revenue sums do refer to demand phenomena, they are looked at from the standpoint of the seller or business firm, the recipient of the consumer outlays.

In brief, writing P to symbolize price and X to symbolize sales quantities, with the subscript n indicating that the sums change with changes in the sales volume, the revenue concepts can be defined algebraically as

$$TR_n = P_n X_n,$$
$$AR_n = \frac{TR_n}{X_n} = \frac{P_n X_n}{X_n} = P_n,$$
$$MR_n = \frac{\Delta TR_n}{\Delta X_n} = TR_n - TR_{n-1}.$$

In words, the total revenue refers to the total expenditure of consumers, or price multiplied by the demand quantity. The TR curve indicates the total amount spent by consumers in buying successively larger quantities of a commodity. Measuring total revenue on the vertical axis, each ordinate value depends on the number of units bought multiplied by the purchase price. In Figure 2A the abscissae points represent the quantities bought for each TR, and thus implicitly at each P.* Normally, the curve is bell-shaped—for, at a very high price sales are zero—so that the curve originates at O, rises and reaches a maximum, and ultimately (because price approaches zero when very large quantities are sold) turns back again to the horizontal axis.

Average revenue or the demand price is equal to the total consumer outlay on a given number of units, divided by the selfsame quantity. Thus the average revenue per unit of sales is ordinarily the market price; the AR curve and the demand curve are one and the same. Marginal revenue refers to the change in total revenue resulting from a

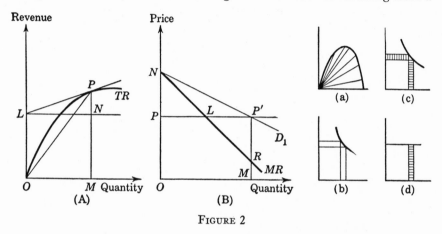

FIGURE 2

further increment in sales volume; the MR curve thus depicts the changed TR resulting from further sales.

The typical relations between the three curves are shown in Figure 2. Although all three curves can be drawn on the same chart field (since money sums are measured in all cases on the vertical axis), to avoid encumbering the diagram the TR curve is placed in Figure 2A and the AR and MR curves in Figure 2B. In Figure 2A we measure total sales revenue, or consumer expenditure, vertically, while horizontally we mark off the quantities purchased at each total expenditure. If the firm sells in a purely competitive market in which the price remains constant whatever quantity it sells, the TR curve becomes a straight line starting at the O origin (for perfectly divisible goods) and rising at a constant rate equal to the price for each further unit of sales. AR and MR, for this case, are equal to one another and thus both are equal to the price.

In the typical monopoly situation the seller can dispose of further

* With price discrimination, AR or price is not unique per unit of sales.

units of output only at a lower price per unit.   The total-revenue curve would then resemble the TR of Figure 2A.   To derive the unit price or average revenue geometrically from the TR curve, we can extend a vector from O to the point on TR for the sales quantity in which we are interested and note its slope; for example, the demand price for the quantity OM would be indicated by the ratio PM/OM, which is also the slope of the vector from O.   It should be observed that ordinarily a vector from O cuts TR in only *one* point, otherwise a multiple sales volume would be indicated at the same sales price.   Moreover, as we move rightward, out to greater sales quantities, the slope of the vectors continually fall, as in Figure 2a, denoting a lower price for greater sales volumes.

MR can be deduced from the TR curve by drawing a tangent to the TR curve and extending it to the ordinate axis; the slope of the tangent would indicate the additions to total revenue made by a further increment in sales.   Its value is given by the ratio PN/LN in the figure. When TR reaches a maximum, $MR = 0$; a tangent to the TR curve would thus become horizontal, indicating no change in TR as sales increase.   Almost invariably (aside from the case of pure competition in which the market price is constant and $MR = AR$) MR will be less than AR.   Let us investigate this last relationship more thoroughly.

Price and Marginal Revenue

The normal downward-sloping demand curve reveals that to sell an additional unit of output, price must fall.   Marginal revenue, the change in total revenue consequent upon a further unit of sales, is thus a resultant of the two forces: (1) the income derived from the additional unit sold, which is equal to the new price, and (2) the loss in income due to the fact that all those units salable at a higher price must be marked down to the new price because, aside from discriminatory pricing, only one price can rule in the market for the full sales quantity. TR will increase only if the magnitude of the first sum exceeds that of the latter sum.   When TR increases, MR will be positive.

Algebraically, the relations can be shown as follows.   Write:

MR = marginal revenue,
P_1 = the initial price,
P_2 = the new (lower) price,
X_1 = the (smaller) sales quantity at price P_1,
X_2 = the (larger) sales quantity at P_2,

$\Delta X = X_2 - X_1 =$ the unit increase in sales as price falls
from P_1 to P_2,

$\Delta P = P_1 - P_2 =$ the fall in price necessary to increase sales
by ΔX.

Then

$$MR = P_2 X_2 - P_1 X_1.$$

Substituting,

$$MR = P_2(X_1 + \Delta X) - X_1(P_2 + \Delta P)$$
$$= P_2 \Delta X - X_1 \Delta P.$$

Or (to generalize), where P_1 and P_2 as well as X_1 and X_2 are very close
to one another,

$$MR = P \Delta X - X \Delta P.$$

As ΔP is conceived to be just large enough to extend sales by one unit,
$\Delta X = 1$. Thus the formula is simplified to:

$$MR = P - X \Delta P.*$$

This relationship is the meaning attached to MR and a full statement of
its components.

If, as under competitive market conditions, the firm can dispose of
additional units at the market price, ΔP reduces to zero and $MR = P$;
price and marginal revenue become one and the same. Otherwise, so
long as price falls as sales expand, $X \Delta P$ is of definite magnitude and
hence $P > MR$. Each point on the normal demand curve will thus
lie above the point corresponding to the same sales volume on the MR
curve. The greater the size of X, and the sharper the price fall ΔP,
the larger the spread $(P - MR)$. Clearly, MR may be positive or
negative; it will be negative when $X \Delta P > P$, implying that the price
sacrifice on the previous volume of sales overshadows the additional
price from extending sales.

MR, which represents the movement in total revenue, can be related
to the area under the demand curve. If from any point on the demand
curve we extend perpendiculars to both the X and Y axes, so as to
enclose a rectangle, as in Figure 2b, and do the same at the neighboring
demand point, then if the area of the new rectangle exceeds that of the
old, MR is positive. This requires that the area added to the portion
of the rectangle common to both prices exceeds the area lost. Thus in

---

* Writing the equation for the demand curve as $P = f(X)$, then $TR = Pf(X)$ and
$MR = dPX/dX = P + X(dP/dX)$, where dP/dX is negative.

Figure 2c the cross-checked horizontal segment indicates the revenue lost as price falls and sales expand by one unit (the $X\Delta P$ magnitude of the formula), while the cross-checked vertical segment is the equivalent of the new price P. When the latter exceeds the former, MR is positive; when the two are equal, $MR = 0$. In the limiting case of a horizontal demand curve, as in Figure 2d, (which we will shortly describe as a perfectly elastic demand curve) $P = MR$. Otherwise, invariably, $P > MR$.*

Average- and Marginal-Revenue Curves

Let us examine the geometrical relations of the demand and marginal-revenue curves. In Figure 2B a linear AR curve, D_1, is drawn, together with the corresponding MR curve, lettered MR; the latter curve denotes the additions to total revenue made by each further unit of sales. Let us see how the marginal-revenue curve may be deduced from the demand or AR curve.

One way to derive the points on MR accompanying each demand point would be to drop perpendiculars from two successive points on the demand curve, to both the OX and OY axes; the difference in the areas of the rectangles so formed would be the marginal revenue for the additional unit of sales. MR may be either positive or negative, depending on the movement in total revenue or the change in the area of the demand-curve rectangles.

There is a simple geometrical relation between AR and MR curves for linear demand curves, as D_1; it can be proved that the descent of the marginal curve is twice that of the average-revenue curve. Thus MR will cut the horizontal axis—or any line parallel to OX—only one-half as far along as does the D_1 curve. Merely by drawing tangents from the OY axis to any point on any demand curve whatever, we can ascertain the marginal revenue for the sales volume indicated at the tangency point; this can be done by directing another straight line from the OY intercept of the tangent to the demand curve and running this new line to only one-half the OX abscissae intercepted by the tangent itself. The MR can be read off the new correspondent line at the ordinate height (above the sales volume) of original tangency. Thus, in Figure 2B, at price P the total revenue is equal to $OM \cdot PM$, which is also equal to the full area under the MR curve, $ONLRM$. By similar triangles,

---

* This typical relationship will be reversed when the demand curve is abnormal and upward rising to the right. Then $MR = P + X\Delta P$, with the minus sign which normally separates P and $X\Delta P$ yielding to a positive magnitude.

because the area of the $P \cdot X$ rectangles, denoting total expenditure, are constant on a rectangular hyperbola. If expenditure increases, it can be shown that $E_d > 1$ and demand is declared to be elastic. If $E_d < 1$, or a smaller sum than formerly is spent on the good after the slight price fall, the demand point is denoted as inelastic.

To prove these relations between the elasticity of demand and total expenditure, we note that if $E_d > 1$ the numerator of the elasticity formula exceeds the denominator, thus: $P\Delta X > X\Delta P$. But $P\Delta X$, the numerator, corresponds exactly to the first part of the marginal-revenue formula, while the denominator, $X\Delta P$, is the remainder of the MR expression. Total revenue or total consumer outlay, we know, increases when MR is positive and thus when $P\Delta X > X\Delta P$, or when $E_d > 1$.* When demand is inelastic, then $P\Delta X < X\Delta P$; but then MR would be negative and the TR curve would turn down, implying that total consumer outlay would decrease as price falls. Sometimes it is useful to know that if the demand curve is a rectangular hyperbola, as $PX = k$, then its elasticity is unity throughout and marginal revenue is always zero.

Elasticity and Marginal Revenue

Algebraically, the demand elasticity can also be computed by the following formulas which relate P, MR and E_d. Knowing any two of these we can immediately deduce the third.†

Since

$$E_d = \frac{P\Delta X}{X\Delta P} \quad \text{and} \quad MR = P\Delta X - X\Delta P,$$

Then

$$E_d = \frac{P\Delta X}{P\Delta X - MR} = \frac{P}{P - MR}; \tag{a}$$

$$MR = P\left(1 - \frac{1}{E_d}\right) = P\left(\frac{E_d - 1}{E_d}\right); \tag{b}$$

$$P = MR\left(\frac{E_d}{E_d - 1}\right). \tag{c}$$

Also, from (c),

$$\frac{P}{MR} = \frac{E_d}{E_d - 1}. \tag{d}$$

* A minor discrepancy, however, is that in the MR formula P is the "new" (lower) price while X is the "old" sales quantity. The proof can then be approached in this way: $MR = (P - \Delta P)(X + \Delta X) - PX$. Multiplying, canceling, and dropping $\Delta P\Delta X$ as being of an extremely small order, $MR = P\Delta X - X\Delta P$. Thus MR depends, as before, on whether $\dfrac{P\Delta X}{X\Delta P} \begin{array}{c}>\\=\\<\end{array} 1$. But this last relationship is, of course, E_d.

† Mrs. Robinson, p. 36.

In all of these formulas, for the normal demand curve E_d is construed as positive. According to (a) above, $P - MR = P/E_d$. Hence, diagrammatically, the distance $P'R$ in Figure 2B is equal to P/E_d.

Geometrical Measures of Elasticity

Occasionally, we might find Marshall's geometrical measure of demand elasticity useful. Drawing the tangent to a demand curve at a point P, and extending it to cut OY at t and OX at T, the ratio of the lengths PT/Pt would yield E_d. When both lengths are equal, demand is of unity elasticity; when PT exceeds Pt, demand is elastic or of greater than unity elasticity.*

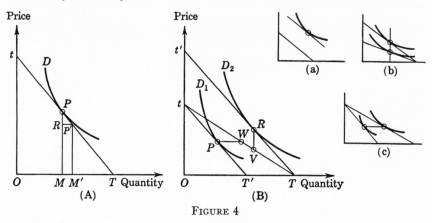

FIGURE 4

To prove that $E_d = PT/Pt$, consider the diagram in Figure 4A. According to the rules for similar triangles, and neglecting the negative sign,

$$E_d = \frac{P'R}{OM} \div \frac{PR}{PM} = \frac{P'R}{PR} \cdot \frac{PM}{OM} = \frac{TM}{PM} \cdot \frac{PM}{OM} = \frac{TM}{OM} = \frac{PT}{Pt}.$$

Consequently, when the segment $P - P'$ approaches zero, PP' becomes a point of tangency to a demand curve and either PT/Pt or TM/OM is a suitable measure of the elasticity.

Sometimes it may be difficult to estimate visually whether the length $PT \gtrless Pt$ and thus whether demand is elastic. As an alternate mode of visualizing the elasticity, which also possesses merit in underscoring the fact that elasticity and slope of the demand curve are not the same thing, we can write

$$E_d = P\Delta X/X\Delta P = (P/X)/(\Delta P/\Delta X).$$

* Alfred Marshall, *Principles of Economics*, 8th edition, pp. 102, 103, and 839.

The denominator $\Delta P/\Delta X$ is of course the tangent to the demand curve, or the *slope* of the demand curve at the point in question. Likewise, if from OY, at an ordinate equal to the price height P, a diagonal is drawn to the demand-quantity abscissae of X on OX, the resulting diagonal bears the same relation to P/X as the tangent to the curve does to $\Delta P/\Delta X$. Comparing these *two* slopes, if the P/X diagonal is parallel to the tangent, as in Figure 4a, then $E_d = 1$. If the PX diagonal (which bisects the total revenue rectangle) has a gentler slope than the tangent, the two would meet on or below the horizontal axis if they were both extended; demand is then inelastic. Converging at or to the left of the vertical axis, demand is elastic.* Elasticity of demand is thus a relation between two slopes. Manifestly, if the demand curve (and thus the tangent) is fairly flat, demand will be elastic.

Geometrical Comparisons of Demand Elasticity

Although these devices are serviceable for estimating the elasticity at different points along a demand curve, they are less valuable for comparing the respective elasticities of points on different demand curves. For this purpose a modified version of the Marshallian measure has been proposed.†

To compare the elasticity at points P and R on demand curves D_1 and D_2 respectively, draw the usual Marshallian tangents to each point, extending them to cut the axes in Figure 4B. Connecting the alternate extremities, t and T, the line Tt is formed. Then draw PW horizontally and RV vertically, to cut Tt at W and V.

The elasticity at R is

$$RT/Rt' = VT/Vt.$$

This last result follows from the laws for similar triangles. Similarly, the elasticity at P is

$$PT'/Pt = WT/Wt.$$

Hence the relative elasticities can be elaborated with reference to the division of the one line, Tt. If $W = V$, then the elasticities are the same: R would lie directly above W. If WT exceeds VT, as in the figure then the denominator $Wt < Vt$ and thus the elasticity at P is necessarily greater than the elasticity at R.

---

* C. Holt and P. A. Samuelson, "The Graphic Depiction of Elasticity of Demand," *Journal of Political Economy* (1946), pp. 354–357.

† A. P. Lerner, "Geometrical Comparison of Elasticities," *American Economic Review* (March 1947), p. 191. For an approach in terms of angles, see John S. Henderson, "Geometrical Note on Elasticity of Demand," same journal (September 1946), pp. 662–663.

By geometrical considerations it would then be possible to prove the following propositions. First, for parallel linear demand curves, a vector projected from the 0 origin will intersect both curves at points of equal elasticity; if the tangents to nonlinear demand curves are parallel at different prices, and a vector can be drawn from the origin through these points, then E_d will be the same at each point; in Figure 4B, R would lie directly above W. Also, for parallel linear demand curves or for curves having similar tangents, a line perpendicular to the OX axis will intersect the upper curve at a point of greater E_d than the lower; but a perpendicular to OY would intercept a greater E_d on the lower than on the higher curve. Analogously, if E_d is the same at a given *output* along two demand curves, the separate tangents will have a common node on OX. If E_d is equivalent at a certain price, then the tangents will have a common meeting place on OY. (See Figures 4b and 4c.) If the tangent to a higher curve, as D_2 in Figure 4B, intercepts a lower OY point than the tangent to an inner demand curve, as D_1, the E_d of the higher curve will be the greater.

ARC ELASTICITY OF DEMAND

In the real world, changes in price are generally finite. The concept of demand elasticity, properly interpreted, refers to incremental movements from point to point along the demand curve and, when fully described, is termed the point elasticity. Often the best we can do in practice is to learn whether total expenditure increases or decreases, and then state in broad terms whether demand is or is not elastic over the range of variation. If we desire to measure the change more precisely there are a number of formulae that we might use to measure the *arc* elasticity; none of them provide the same answer as the true point elasticity. The smaller the price difference $P_1 - P_2$, where $P_1 > P_2$, the better will be the approximation. If P_1, X_1 is the original set of price and quantity coordinates, and P_2, X_2 is the new set after the finite price change, the ratio $(X_2 - X_1)/(P_2 - P_1)$ must figure as part of any measure of arc elasticity, for this is the $\Delta X/\Delta P$ component of the point E_d. To make this ratio independent of units, or to measure the proportional changes as in the point elasticity, we need multiply the numerator by a P and the denominator by an X.

But this is precisely the area of arbitrariness. If we are contemplating the demand elasticity for a price fall we could multiply by P_1/X_1 and endow our measure with an air of consistency with the point elasticity. Or, for a price rise, we could multiply by P_2/X_2. But both measures would be defective in that they involve asymmetry (a different value for the downward movement as compared to the upward price movement), and, what is worse, neither of the measures would equal unity, as would the point elasticity when total expenditure in the two price situations is the same. Slight arithmetical tests would prove this contention. For example, take $P_1 = \$2$, $X_1 = 300$, $P_2 = \$1$, $X_2 = 600$; then

$$\frac{P_1(X_2 - X_1)}{X_1(P_1 - P_2)} = \frac{\$2(300)}{300(\$1)} = \frac{\$600}{\$300} = 2,$$

or

$$\frac{\$1(300)}{600(\$1)} = \frac{\$300}{\$600} = \frac{1}{2}.$$

It would be desirable for a measure of arc elasticity to equal unity when total consumer outlay is constant, as in the illustration. If we used P_1/X_2 or P_2/X_1 as our multiplier, this condition of unity elasticity for a fixed outlay would be satisfied. But each of these measures would still exhibit some asymmetry, furnishing a different value as we move up the arc for a price rise from P_2 to P_1 as compared to a price fall from P_1 to P_2.* Logically, the elasticity should be the same in either direction.

The Measure Recommended

To eliminate this shortcoming, as well as to retain the virtue of a unity value whenever total expenditure remained constant, it has been suggested that an average of P_1 and P_2, and X_1 and X_2 be used as a multiplier. The most suitable arc elasticity, on these considerations, thus becomes

$$\text{arc elasticity} = \frac{\dfrac{(P_1 + P_2)(X_2 - X_1)}{2}}{\dfrac{(X_2 + X_1)(P_1 - P_2)}{2}}$$

$$= \frac{(P_1 + P_2)(X_2 - X_1)}{(X_2 + X_1)(P_1 - P_2)}.$$

In our simple illustration,

$$\frac{(\$1 + \$2)(300)}{(300 + 600)\$1} = \frac{900}{900} = 1.$$

Though this measure is slightly more cumbersome than the arc measures

* In all but the unity case.

containing the simpler multipliers, its advantages outweigh the further complexities.   All the various measures, however, yield more uniform results as the arc in question grows smaller.

With the measure suggested, geometrically the elasticity would still be the Marshallian ratio PT/Pt; but P this time is located midway between P_1 and P_2, bisecting the chord connecting the two points, for we have taken the average $(P_1 + P_2)/2$ and $(X_2 + X_1)/2$ as the multiplier.   The demand curve, therefore, is implicitly assumed to be linear between the two points P_1 and P_2.

THE CROSS ELASTICITY OF DEMAND AND PRICES

Another demand-curve idea is the concept of the cross elasticity of demand.   As a matter of fact, we have already made extensive use of its central thought though refraining from the use of the term.

The cross elasticity of demand is the ratio of the relative movement in the quantity demanded of Y, given a relative change in P_x, with P_y constant.   Thus the cross elasticity is

$$_{px}E_y = (\Delta Y/Y)/(\Delta P_x/P_x) = P_x \Delta Y/Y \Delta P_x.$$

This offers an immediate contrast to the normal direct point elasticity of

$$_{px}E_x = P_x \Delta X/X \Delta P_x.$$

The cross elasticity can assume positive, negative, or zero values, in contrast to the direct elasticity which, when uncorrected for sign, will invariably be negative for a price fall, excepting only the backward-bending demand curves.   On the indifference field, the value and sign of the cross elasticity of demand will depend on whether the Y demand quantity increases or decreases as P_x falls.   For two goods, if total expenditure is constant and the demand for X is elastic, the cross elasticity will have to be positive.   It would be negative if the demand curve for Y shifted to the right after the decrement ΔP_x; the direct elasticity $_{px}E_x$ would then be inelastic.   Nothing very definite can be said on the magnitude of $_{px}E_y$, for this also depends on the level of P_y and Y.   If the cross elasticity is small the markets for X and Y can be considered as effectively independent.

Cross Elasticity and Commodity Interrelations

Graphically, the cross elasticity measures the lateral shift, at the ruling P_y price, in the quantity demanded of Y as P_x varies; this thought was at the bottom of our examination of demand interrelations. Normally, if X and Y are substitutes, $_{px}E_y$ will be positive whether P_x rises or falls. Conversely, if the goods are complements the cross elasticity of demand ought to be negative as P_x varies. Independent goods, according to this empirical measure containing only fully objective quantities, are those goods whose demand is unaffected by (a range of) movements in other prices, such as P_x. Barring inferior goods, the negative or positive price interdependence revealed by $_{px}E_y$ conforms to the earlier ideas on substitute and complementary relationships.

Just as with direct arc elasticities of demand, measures of arc cross elasticities of demand can be formulated. Measures similar to those described in the previous section can be devised, but this time the P's would refer to the P_x prices while the X's would instead be replaced by Y quantities.

The Coefficient of Price Interdependence

Instead of linking relative changes in the sales of commodity Y to proportionate price movements in X, we sometimes want to measure the degree of price interdependence, for in some monopoly problems the markets are interrelated, and a change in one price, as ΔP_x, will engender a movement in another price. Thus we can relate the relative movements as follows, assuming the initial change ΔP_x:

$$_{px}E_{py} = \frac{\dfrac{\Delta P_y}{P_y}}{\dfrac{\Delta P_x}{P_x}} = \frac{P_x \Delta P_y}{P_y \Delta P_x}.$$

Normally, the value of this coefficient of price interdependence ought to range between positive and negative values of unity. For substitutes, a price rise of commodity X in the order of 1 per cent ought at most to elevate P_y by the same proportion. For complements the price interdependence will appear to be negative.

COMMODITY DIMENSIONS

As a final topic for this chapter, we might consider the definition of a commodity, a term we have been using frequently. Its casual meaning is clear: items which in all external manifestations exhibit the same bundle of physical characteristics are identical commodities. Immediately we are thrown against the venerable query of whether technical substitutes located in different places are, after all, perfect substitutes.

Most of us would agree that they are not; that wheat in Chicago is not the equivalent of identical wheat in New York; an appeal to the market would dispel any doubts on this score. As consumers in the one place usually pay a price differing from that in the other market, apparently the items purchased are not identical. As each purchase consists of a bundle of form and time-and-place utility, it has been customary to assert that goods must, at a minimum, be defined with respect to these indices. Actually, what is ordinarily bought as a single product is a complex joint product, composed not only of elemental stuff available at a certain time and place, but also packaged in a definite way, associated with a particular type and volume of advertising, sold on specific credit terms in a certain "toned" shop, and with some proviso as to delivery. Normally, a commodity contains at least these many facets.

If items of a commodity class had to be identical in all these dimensions, by definition we would probably preclude any prospect of perfect competition. Each seller would be offering a different product and each would be a "monopolist."* However intense the competition in any more fundamental sense, the world would be described as one of ubiquitous monopoly. This definition is thus too stringent; red tennis balls would be different commodities than white tennis balls even though consumers might be completely indifferent between the two.

This last remark furnishes a clue to a sounder basis of classification than an appeal to technical and institutional dissimilarities. Ultimately, consumers judge whether commodities are identical or not. Fully substitutable in all uses, from the standpoint of consumers, the goods are the same. After all, this is the reason why goods with the same technical attributes are commonly regarded as identical and why, when separated in space, they are viewed as different goods. Perfect substitutability is thus the criterion. In terms of MRS ratios, these would always be constant and, generally, equal to unity. The indifference curves would degenerate into straight lines, normally running say from $1X$ to $1Y$, $2X$ to $2Y$, etc. Price discrepancies between the goods would not be tolerated; as the elasticity of demand for any one seller, at the price charged by his competitors, would be infinite, a higher-priced seller would have to meet the lower price of the competitor turning out the same good, or watch his sales fall to zero.†

---

* As Mrs. Robinson has described it.

† This holds true unless sales quantities are rationed by the lower-priced seller. The case of linear indifference curves running say from $2Y$ to $1X$, $4Y$ to $2X$, etc., would also yield

Consumer Determination

Consumers, on this view, adjudge the degree of identity of goods and the interdependence of markets. Practically everything that is of interest to the economist in distinguishing among commodities resides in their valuations. When consumer valuations indicate less than full substitutability, we are dealing with different commodities. A major complication of this approach is that all consumers will seldom evaluate commodities identically; their indifference maps will rarely be exact replicas of one another. But if *MRS* ratios between two (or several) goods are constant, and roughly the same for a goodly number of purchasers, there will be a high degree of demand elasticity among the separate commodities; when price ratios departed from the substitutionary ratios, a precipitate replacement of one good by the other would set in. In practice, a high degree of price sensitivity of a substantial body of users will denote the presence of an alternate, almost identical product.

BIBLIOGRAPHICAL NOTE

On the demand curve and demand elasticity the treatment in Marshall's *Principles* is still fresh. Mrs. Joan Robinson's *Economics of Imperfect Competition*, Chapter II, contains an original and thorough explanation of the relations between average and marginal revenue and the geometry of the ideas. Although the drawing of the demand curve on the hypothesis of other prices varying is now commonplace, an important later contribution to the subject was the short note of Paul M. Sweezy, "Demand Under Conditions of Oligopoly," *Journal of Political Economy* (1939). A stimulating, if critical, reappraisal of the entire demand concept is Oscar Morgenstern's "Demand Theory Reconsidered," *Quarterly Journal of Economics* (1948).

On the arc elasticity of demand, see R. G. D. Allen, "The Concept of Arc Elasticity of Demand," *Review of Economic Studies* (1934), and the remarks of A. P. Lerner in the same issue. The concept of the cross elasticity furnishes the key to Robert Triffin's classification of market structures in his *Monopolistic Competition and General Equilibrium Theory*, p. 104. A discussion of the definition of a commodity is also offered by Triffin, pp. 90–95, as well as in an article of Lionel Robbins, "Production," *Encyclopedia of the Social Sciences*, Vol. 12, p. 463.

---

perfectly elastic demand curves and would imply identical commodities; as an illustration, different-sized coals might provide heat in the constant ratio, say, 2/1. If the indifference curves indicate perfect substitutability in their central regions, but become perpendicular near the axes, the derivative-demand curves would be elastic over a good part of their range.

CHAPTER 3

Production and Costs

A̲FTER THE FOREGOING SURVEY OF demand theory our attention turns to the theory of production. Two aspects of this study are developed in this chapter: there is the purely technical side consisting of the input-output relations, for generally a product can be produced in manifold ways—the technological forces are seldom such as to impose a unique factor combination. The relation between the various factor combinations and the output of the particular commodity is expressed in a production function such as $X = f(A, B, C \cdots)$, where X refers to the quantity of output and $A, B, C \cdots$ are the factors used in its production. The production function pertains to a given state of knowledge, for with new achievements in the technological arts the possible input combinations to obtain a definite output are multiplied.

Because there are manifold technical possibilities, factor costs will prove to be the decisive element in determining the precise combination of resources selected for production. An entrepreneur bent on maximizing income will choose the least-cost combination for each quantity of output; this introduces an economic aspect to production. As a parallel to the theory of consumer behavior where the consumer was engaged in maximizing satisfaction, the firm is presumed, in general, to be striving to minimize the cost of producing any given level of output. As a continuance of the competitive hypothesis, factor prices are postulated as beyond the control of the firm, for otherwise we are face to face with a monopsony (buyer's monopoly) type of problem. Before we begin the particular studies of this chapter certain terms must be defined.

FACTORS OF PRODUCTION

Using as synonyms the terms resources, factors and agents, all human and nonhuman *tangible* sources whose presence (or absence) makes a difference to output are defined as *potential* agents of production. It is the productive factors that provide the inputs responsible for the output. It is of the essence that the use of these factors be subject to human control, or that their results be subject to human appropriation and prediction, for then rational valuation and utilization become possible. Still, factors so defined are only potential agents of production; whether they will actually be employed will depend upon the market demands for their services and upon the income-leisure valuations of factor owners. Our definition, it should be observed, places its stress upon the output effect of a tangible factor. Yet firms will pay for the services rendered by intangible sources, such as advertising, patents, insurance, "good will," and, occasionally, will pay to influence legislation and social attitudes. Although these outlays are not directed toward the use of productive factors they are, nonetheless, outlays that are productive of income. Hence it is feasible to distinguish between *output* factors and *income* factors; the former contribute to output and income while the latter are significant solely because they augment income, even though a definite physical quantum of output cannot be ascribed to their presence.*

Literally, there are myriads of potential productive agents. The classical trinity of land, labor, and capital (goods) is defective from a realistic standpoint except as a shorthand classification that magnifies similarities and minimizes differences. A more precise diagnosis would suggest that insofar as agents are imperfect technical substitutes one for the other, they belong to separate factor classes. Complete substitutability of one agent for another in each of the diverse uses would thus be characteristic of all resources comprising a factor class.† Being perfectly substitutable, the members of a factor class can also be described as *homogeneous* factors; in terms of the indifference curves, the MRS among them would always be unity.‡

On the basis of these views we are compelled to abandon the tradi-

---

* Judicious legislation may likewise facilitate production and thereby be subject to some social valuation, as compared to unwise legislation. But to the valuing subjects legal institutions are data around which production is organized; they affect the content of economic life though they generally leave the formal nature of the underlying relationships unaffected. They may well be excluded at the present stage, although they can be regarded as intangible *institutional* factors of production that contribute to the social output and income.

† Factor classes are thus regarded from the standpoint of the entrepreneur. To make sure that owners of the homogeneous factors will view all employment in the same way, and thus will accept identical incomes for each output of which they are capable, we must posit that they are identically natured.

‡ Or constant although not necessarily unity. See the definition of a commodity, p. 50.

tional classification of productive factors, though occasionally, in view of their concrete content, we can, for some uses, retain the ancient categories.   Actually the main classification we require in the theory of production and price is between *fixed* and *variable* factors, while in the theory of income determination we need the separation of versatile and specific factors.   In general, we shall perceive that whatever vitality the older classification possesses is due to its fairly high correlation with the mental constructions necessary in price and income theory, with land being generally a fixed factor, labor a variable one, and equipment sometimes one and sometimes the other.

In a nonintegrated output structure, firms will generally purchase unfinished materials from other firms.   Certain products are thus *intermediate* factors that, to the using firm, are factors of production indistinguishable in principle from other productive factors.   Intermediate factors vanish, however, being embodied in other products, when we view output as a whole or visualize a fully integrated output structure in which a firm completes all the materials and processes incident to final production.

Versatile and Specific Factors

Among the categories of imperfectly substitutable factors, *versatile* factors can be separated from *specific* factors.*   Versatile factors can be consigned to more than one output use; specific agents are adapted solely to a unique output.   Although versatility and specificity are in practice a matter of degree, the sharp classificatory demarcation is useful and significant; for a purely specific good, the economic problem of its use is the simple one of deciding whether the one product that it can produce does have a positive value.   Versatile factors pose a more complex problem; the significant economic issue involves an appraisal of the most valuable of their diverse uses.

Although we speak of a firm hiring or purchasing productive factors, it is only the services provided by the factor that are sought.   The factor's services, and not the factor, are wanted, valued and paid for by the entrepreneur: it is the services that comprise the productive inputs. A firm, for example, pays wages not to the laborer as an individual but for his productive services, values not the land as such but the services it renders, etc.   Even in a slave economy the outlay for the slave is intended to acquire control of his services.

* These terms should be a useful complement of static analysis.   See F. von Hayek, *The Pure Theory of Capital*, p. 251.   The term *specific goods* is attributed to F. von Wieser, *Social Economics*, pp. 81–85, A. F. Hinrichs, trans.

FIXED AND VARIABLE FACTORS

The division between fixed and variable factors, which is the fundamental classificatory segregation for the theory of production, deserves further elaboration.

Fixed Factors

Fixed factors are those factors whose total cost is constant over some range of output. For example, assuming zero depreciation through use, the total cost of using machinery (consisting of interest charges on the sum invested and depreciation charges as a result of the passage of time) remains constant whether output is at zero or rises to 10,000 units; greater output, however, might entail the introduction of, and expenditure upon, additional equipment. The services of some factors will be fixed for greater ranges of output than for others. The machinery in the foregoing illustration may be contrasted with an inspection foreman who can serve, say, for 1 to 500 units of output.

Variable Factors

Variable factors are those whose quantity and cost alter with movements in output. The precise line for distinguishing them from fixed factors is in the increased total cost of using them with continuously increased output. Sometimes a factor is technically fixed although the payment for its services is variable, for example, machinery installed as a unit but paid for according to use. Or it may be the other way around, as in the case of flat monthly charges for telephones in homes regardless of the number of calls made. From the standpoint of the entrepreneur, the essential feature is not the technical nature of the factor, whether fixed or variable, but the terms of hire. Analytically, however, the technical nature is of the utmost importance in devising the most economic method of hire.

Divisible and Indivisible Factors

As a further distinction among fixed factors, some are divisible while others are not. Divisible fixed factors are those whose total cost is constant, although technically the factor consists of separable units which may be independently utilized. Fundamentally they are variable factors, though the exigencies of construction or the mode of hire may compel that they be purchased as a unit. For example, if 1,000 acres of land are rented, the full acreage need not be cultivated when only one man is used to farm it; it may be more sensible for him to till part of it more intensively. Or plant may be purchased as a unit although it may contain a dozen identical wings or units of independent, identical machines. Indivisible factors, on the other hand, are constructed as a single mass: the irreducible unit must serve over a wide range of outputs. Divisibility or indivisibility thus refers to the mode of use, and not to the terms of payment for fixed factors. We shall find that the degree of technical divisibility of the factor is of crucial importance in shaping the course of the marginal-cost curve.

CONSTANT-PRODUCT CURVES

Fortified with this definitional array for handling our materials, we can now make more rapid progress in our study of the theory of production. Recalling the indifference map of Figure 1, Chapter 1, let us suppose that quantities of productive factors instead of quantities of goods are measured along OX and OY. Furthermore, whereas an indifference curve associates product combinations affording equal satisfaction, let each curve now connect factor combinations capable of producing the same output, while positing that the ascent up the curve system now is toward higher output levels rather than toward greater satisfaction. What were called the indifference curves in the theory of consumption are, in the theory of production, *isoquants* or *constant-product curves*. Once more the major restriction on the field is that the isoquants may not intersect one another. Analogous to the indifference map, the isoquant field reveals that factors X and Y are substitutable at each output level. Normally there will also be some other factors employed, resources other than quantities of X and Y; in drawing our chart these must be assumed as constant, for otherwise a particular combination of X and Y will not always culminate in the same output. A similar proviso was invoked for the indifference field.

Exploring some further aspects of the constant-product curves, we are able, as with the indifference curves, to compute the MRS between the factors. For two factors this is the ratio of the decrement in Y required to compensate for a unit increment in X while leaving output unchanged. Thus

$$MRS = -\Delta Y/\Delta X.$$

Alternately, if we define the marginal product of a factor as the addition to total output made by a further unit of that factor, the MRS

can also be referred to as the ratio of the marginal products of X and Y; thus if the MRS is $2Y$ for $1X$, the marginal product of X (or MP_x) must be twice that of Y (or MP_y). If a unit of X adds 10 units to total output, a unit of factor Y adds only 5 units to total output. Thus

$$MP_x/MP_y = MRS = -\Delta Y/\Delta X.$$

More realistically than in the theory of consumption, where the MRS can be detected only by introspection or by a rigorous and intricate questionnaire, in production the MRS is open to observation and entrepreneurial verification.

Ridge Lines and Isoclines

In the theory of consumption the MRS, or $\Delta Y/\Delta X$, was always negative; on any other representation the individual would be depicted as being only as well off as before, despite an increase in the quantity of both X and Y. In production this anomalous situation does appear; it is only the good sense of the entrepreneur that rules out the excess quantities of factors implicit in a positive substitution ratio; manifestly it would be unprofitable for an entrepreneur to employ more factors than the minimum quantity necessary for the output volume.* Ridge lines OA and OB are consequently drawn in Figure 1A to rope off the area of rational factor use, containing within their bounds the curve sections in which the MRS is negative and whose slopes are convex to the origin; factor combinations outside these confines are uneconomic. At each point on the ridge line, beyond which factor combinations are excluded, tangents to each particular constant product curve are parallel to either the OX or the OY axis. This denotes an infinite or zero MRS and implies that the marginal product of one of the factors is zero at the particular output level. When the tangent to a constant-product curve is vertical, the MRS is infinite (written ∞); when it is horizontal, the MRS is zero. Thus, on the ridge line, if

$$-\Delta Y/\Delta X = MP_x/MP_y = \infty,$$

then

$$MP_y = 0;$$

or if

$$-\Delta Y/\Delta X = MP_x/MP_y = 0,$$

* The possibility, in practice, is not to be ruled out entirely. A large firm located in a small community might "over-employ" factors merely to retain local good will. Analogously, labor unions often insist upon antiquated hiring practices; two electricians might be ordered for work when one man's services might suffice, with one electrician standing idly by, watching the other labor.

then

$$MP_x = 0.$$

If we draw the segments of the isoquant curve that lie outside OA and OB, they assume an elliptical shape, as the dashed lines in Figure 2a, evidencing that the same output can be produced with multiple quantities of X (or Y) and a constant quantity of Y (or X). But in these areas outside the ridge lines the MRS is positive, implying that if X, say, is increased, Y must also be increased if output is merely to be held constant. If X has a positive marginal product, that of Y must be negative, and vice versa. The ridge lines exclude, therefore, the

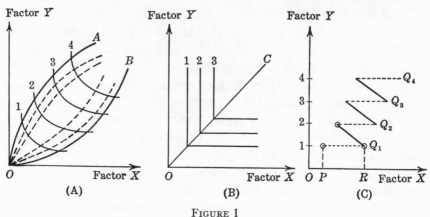

FIGURE 1

areas of excess quantities of factors or negative marginal products of one or the other factor. Within the ridge lines, the condition of a decreasing MRS prevails along each constant-product curve, so that in this area each isoquant is convex to the origin.

Ridge lines OA and OB connect points of equal (infinite or zero) marginal rates of substitution or ratios of marginal products. Within the ridge lines, points of equal MRS, or relative marginal products, can also be isolated and then connected. Doing so, we derive the faint lines in Figure 1A which correspond in shape, nature and direction to the ridge lines; these are termed *isoclines*. Along each isocline the MRS (or the ratio MP_x/MP_y) from isoquant to isoquant is constant. Ridge lines are thus a special type of isocline, at which one MP is zero and the other relatively infinite. Writing K to symbolize some constant along each isocline, including the ridge lines, we obtain as the defining characteristic of an isocline

$$MRS = -\Delta Y/\Delta X = K.$$

Unique Factor Combinations

Products that can be expanded only by a unique simultaneous increase in both factors imply an isoquant field such as that of Figure 1B. Increases in one factor unaccompanied by increments in the other would be futile. The usually divergent ridge lines OA and OB coincide in this case and the result is the straight line OC in the figure. In contrast, when factor X is perfectly substitutable for Y the isoquants would be straight lines running say from $1X$ to $1Y$, $2X$ to $2Y$, etc. Axes OX and OY would then constitute the ridge lines and the isoclines would be straight lines emanating from the O origin.

THE MINIMUM-COST CONDITION

The isoquant study has disclosed the various input-output relations. As there are many ways of producing the same output, the factor combination actually selected will depend on factor prices; rationally, the entrepreneur will choose the least-cost combination for each output. Diagrammatically (just as with the indifference system), a price line, now termed a *factor-cost line* (or an *isocost curve*), can be drawn from the vertical to the horizontal axis on the assumption of a given total cost outlay and a given set of factor prices. The factor-cost curve thus indicates the maximum factor combinations that can be hired under these hypotheses.

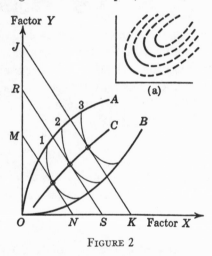

FIGURE 2

Since the market rate at which the X factor can be hired to replace the Y factor at the given total cost outlay depends upon the ratio of factor prices (P_x/P_y), the slope of the factor cost line $(\Delta Y/\Delta X)$ is equal to this ratio. Just as in the consumer analysis, an entrepreneur will substitute one factor for another at each total-outlay level until the MRS is equal to the ratio of factor prices; again, this involves the tangency between isocost and isoquant, as shown in Figure 2. Unless these factor quantities are chosen the entrepreneur is not maximizing output for his cost outlays on factors. Alternately, the total cost outlay for the particular output is not being minimized. In the older formulation the equilibrium condition of minimum cost at each level of output stressed the equality between the ratios of marginal products and factor prices. All these formulations are equivalent.

To elaborate: at the tangency position the slope of the isoquant, which is the MRS and is measured by $\Delta Y/\Delta X$, equals the slope of the isocost, which is also measured by $\Delta Y/\Delta X$ and is equal to the ratio of factor prices. Thus

$$MRS = P_x/P_y.$$

Alternately,

$$MP_x/MP_y = P_x/P_y,$$

or,

$$MP_x/P_x = MP_y/P_y.$$

If several factors are hired,

$$MP_x/P_x = MP_y/P_y = MP_z/P_z = J,$$

where J is some constant typical of all these ratios.

A numerical illustration can be considered as a tentative proof of this proposition. To the left of the tangency position the slope of the factor cost line is less than that of the isoquant it intersects, implying that the $MRS > P_x/P_y$. Suppose that

$$MRS = 4Y/1X,$$

or

$$MP_x/MP_y = 4/1,$$

while the factor price ratios are

$$P_x/P_y = \$2/\$1.$$

Refraining from the hire of $2Y$ the firm can acquire $1X$; in productivity, however, $1X = 4Y$. Consequently, output can be augmented by the switch in factor hire or, alternately, the given output can be produced at lower cost, for $4Y$ can be released on the addition of $1X$, involving a total cost saving of \$2. If the $MRS < P_x/P_y$, the results would be similar except that now the hire of factor X would be reduced, while that of Y would be increased. The incentive to alter factor use disappears only when $MRS = P_x/P_y$. When this condition prevails the factors hired represent the equilibrium combination—that is, the minimum-cost combination for the particular output—or the factor combination of maximum output for the given total cost, given the factor price and factor productivity circumstances.

THE EXPANSION PATH

Superimposing a number of isocosts on our figure, as MN, RS, JK, each parallel to one another to indicate the constancy of factor prices, and noting their points of tangency to the isoquants, we can extract the factor combinations that will be selected as output expands and factor outlays are increased while factor prices are constant. Linking up the various equilibrium combinations traces the *expansion path* of the firm. This path is the locus OC in Figure 2, representing the minimum-cost factor combinations for the successive levels of output.

When factor prices are constant, the expansion path follows the course of an isocline, since the latter is defined as connecting points of constant MRS, while the expansion path connects points at which $P_x/P_y = MRS$. Hence when the ratio P_x/P_y is constant, the MRS along the expansion path is always the same and thus isocline and expansion path coincide. Under these hypotheses the expansion path has its counterpart in the income-consumption curve analyzed in Chapter 1, but rather than alluding to an income effect in the demand for factors as production expands, we refer instead to an output effect. The expansion path departs from a given isocline only when factor prices vary with changes in the output level.* If the relative factor prices confronting the firm changed independently of its own output and factor demand, a new series of isocosts would have to be drawn and a new expansion path would emerge, coinciding with another isocline. As would be expected, if P_x fell relatively to P_y, more of X would be utilized, with X substituted for Y at each output level. There are no paths strictly analogous to the price-consumption curves of Chapter 1 which resulted from varied prices with fixed consumer income, for, in the theory of production, expenditures on factors are not limited as is consumer's income; producers are envisaged as able, through borrowing (or lending excess sums), to command the outlays necessary for expansion to any output point that they choose along the appropriate path.

Expansion Path and Factor Productivity

Moving upward along the expansion path, as the factor combinations are being successively enlarged, on the assumption that factor prices are constant, the relationship that will be satisfied is

$$MP_x/MP_y = P_x/P_y = K.$$

* See below, pp. 257–258.

If the expansion path is a straight line, with a slope of $\Delta Y/\Delta X = C$, then, in order to hold the ratio of marginal products unchanged, the increase in the hire of factor Y relative to that of X is never altered; the marginal products of X and Y can be described as falling (or rising) in a constant proportion as output advances along the path of minimum cost.   If the expansion path is linear and passes through the O origin, the ratio of factor use is never altered; the expansion path may, instead, wind around toward the OY axis, implying an ever-rising slope and enabling us to infer that as output advances the marginal product of the X factor falls faster than that of Y, with the latter better suited to the higher levels of output.   Conversely, if the expansion path flattens out, becoming almost parallel with the horizontal axis, it will be the X factor that is most effective at the higher output levels.   If the expansion path is linear, but with a slope greater than unity, the marginal product of X falls faster (or fails to increase as fast) than that of Y as output grows.   Strictly, although these remarks apply to the expansion path when factor prices are constant, they are always relevant in describing the shape of the isoclines that are of course independent of factor prices.

NONMINIMUM COSTS

Certain aspects of the treatment of the principle of minimum-cost output ought to be thrown into bolder relief.   The theory of the expansion path, for one thing, presumed that the firm always had or was able to borrow the necessary sums to hire the factors indicated at each point along the expansion path.   Some consequences of the denial of this hypothesis are best considered later when we analyze the forces determining the output level of the firm.   Even now, however, we are prepared to realize that if the firm's output volume is limited by its financial capacity, a fall in the price of a factor will generate both a substitution effect and an output effect, on a parity with the substitution and income effects of price theory.

But there is an even more important matter.   In outlining the condition of minimum cost there is the tacit suggestion (1) that firms consciously strive to produce at minimum cost and (2) that they are competent to secure this objective.   If ignorance in calculation prevents them from producing as economically as possible, then the subject can be disposed of abruptly; resources valued at say $100 by the community will be devoted to producing 70 units of output when the same output can be turned out at perhaps $40.   This will imply economic waste and inefficiency, pure and simple.   Invariably, excess factor

use will be due to an inadequate conception of the production function—
that is, of all the points on the isoquant curves in the two-factor model.

The more interesting case, however, is that in which the firm does
apprehend the condition of minimum cost yet *prefers* to lavish a greater
outlay sum on an output rather than to undertake the entrepreneurial
efforts associated with cost reduction.   All along we have been writing
as if minimum cost equilibria automatically emerged, without entrepreneurial evaluations and judgments of factor productivity, without

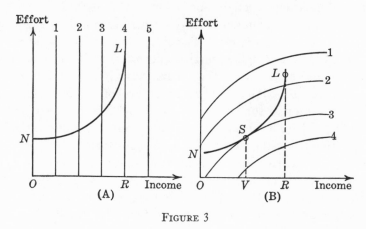

FIGURE 3

efforts in the way of hiring some factors while releasing others.   Realistically, these elements must be introduced.

In Figure 3A, amounts of entrepreneurial effort are measured along
the vertical axis, with each unit of effort conceived of as perhaps an
hour of work of a given intensity.   Amounts of income or sums of
money that can be saved by observing the minimum-cost condition
are measured horizontally.   The curve *NL* denotes the way in which
income can be raised (or total cost reduced) by reducing to a minimum
the total cost of producing a particular output, with each increase in
income (or each total cost reduction) presumed to be linked with greater
entrepreneurial effort.   At a maximum, therefore, whatever the output
level may be, the sum *OR* can be eliminated from total costs.   *NL* can
be termed an *income-effort opportunity line.**

In Figure 3A, assume that the entrepreneur is completely inured to
work, willing to exert an interminable amount of effort in order to
secure a particular level of income.   The indifference curves between
income and effort are thus perfectly vertical lines, with higher indifference levels indicated by the curves further to the right.   In this event

* *NL* may turn back to *OY*.   Compare Figure 5, p. 153, where the axes are reversed.

the individual will minimize the total cost of production for the given output, saving the full sum open, *OR*, by putting out the amount of effort prescribed by the ordinate height *LR*.   It is not inaccurate to describe this as the typical hypothesis of entrepreneurial behavior underlying the description of the minimum-cost factor selection.

In Figure 3B, the *NL* income-effort opportunity line is repeated. However, it is presumed that cost cutting involves effort on the part of the entrepreneur and that the entrepreneur is willing to forego income if it must be earned through more effort.   Curves 1, 2, 3, 4 · · · are thus income-effort indifference curves, with curve 2 denoting a higher indifference level than 1, etc.   The flattening out of the indifference curves conveys the fact that further entrepreneurial effort becomes so irksome that even a substantial income sum is barely able to entice more entrepreneurial labor.   The highest level of well-being obtainable, in view of the opportunity line *NL* and the income-effort curves, is located at *S*, where income is *OV* and entrepreneurial labor is the height *VS*.   At this point the marginal rate of substitution between income and effort—the entrepreneur's evaluation of the two—is equal to the marginal availability of these alternatives.   The entrepreneur fails to minimize costs at the particular output level by the amount *VR*.

Considerations of this sort throw a cloud over the concept of cost minimization and shake our confidence in the fidelity of concrete instances to our sharp mental images.   The degree of error occasioned by the stronger presentation of the theory will be less serious whenever businessmen are largely driven by income incentives, while appraising the ardors of their own efforts only lightly.

FACTOR SUBSTITUTES AND COMPLEMENTS

At a fixed indifference level in the two-commodity world the commodities were substitutes for one another.   In production, beyond the ridge lines and at the constant-output level, an expansion in one factor requires a simultaneous expansion in the other factor merely to maintain output; algebraically, the *MRS* would be positive in this area rather than negative, implying that one factor has a negative marginal product.   Outside the ridge line *OA* in Figure 1A, factor *Y* is a *redundant* or excess factor, whereas outside the ridge line *OB*, *X* becomes a redundant or excess factor with a negative marginal product.   Redundancy is, therefore, an independent relationship distinct from substitution even in the two-factor model.

Superficially, the redundancy relationship has a semblance to complementarity in that it portends a joint increase in the factors at the constant-output level. But we can see that this is a spurious view of complementarity: one factor is so negatively productive, tending by itself to decrease output, that the other factor has to be augmented in order to recover the output level. Complementary relations, instead, belong to a world of three or more factors. Factors X and Y are substitutes if the unit increase in factor X, and the consequent decrement in Z, to keep output unchanged, decreases the MRS of Y for Z. Another way of looking at it is to describe the MP_y as falling at the given output level as X is increased and Z decreased. Y is complementary to X if the MP_y rises as X is increased and Z decreased; or, identically, if the MRS of Y for Z rises as X is increased and Z diminished at the constant-output level.*

Although, at a given output level, factors are thus generally likely to be substitutes, as output expands the output effect is likely to lead to an increased use of all factors, especially if the ridge lines form a fairly narrow band. In a very real sense, therefore, factors may be regarded as "complementary" as output advances.

Limitational Factors

A further type of factor relationship may be unearthed. Conceivably, a given volume of output will not be possible without a very definite and irreducible quantity of factor X, while further increases of X for the same amount of output may be unavailing so far as replacing other factors is concerned. Perhaps for every *additional* unit of output, factor X will have to be increased by one unit, otherwise output will be frozen; X can then be termed a *limitational* factor. In food processing, for example, more of a particular ingredient may be an indispensible prerequisite for a further unit of output, although labor and equipment may be substitutable in combining the ingredient and producing the final product.

Substitution then is not possible for the limitational factor at each output level while, with varying output, the marginal product of all other factors will be zero unless the appropriate elemental quantity of the limitational factor is also added. Thus, at each level of output a limitational factor is rigidly independent of all other factors; the constant-product curves composed out of the limitational factor and

---

* Professor Hicks defines factor relations at varying output levels in his *Value and Capital*, pp. 93–98. The regressive relationship of a factor and product which he adduces has a certain counterpart in the redundant factor.

every other factor will thus be rectangular projections of the axes (See Figure 1B).

Indivisible Factors

Besides the limitational factors for which substitution is impossible at any output level, there may be indivisible factors that permit only very limited substitution. Machinery, for example, is often erected only in discrete standardized "lumps." Technological considerations, let us say, require output to be produced only with this equipment, although within limits labor is substitutable. Factor Y in Figure 1C, where the OY scale contains only the real integers, and is blank at other than constant additive amounts of Y, is the indivisible factor; only the discontinuous 1, 2, 3, · · · units of Y can be engaged while factor X is regarded as perfectly continuous. Using $1Y$, output can be expanded by using more of X; OP of X is perhaps essential at a minimum. When output goes to Q_1, however, it may be produced either with $2Y$ and just over OP of X, or $1Y$ and OR of X. Some substitution thus remains; a type of constant-product curve can be derived by connecting these two points. Similar isoquants can be traced, connecting other points of constant output with diverse factor combinations. It can be seen by drawing in the isocosts that as the total outlay increases the tendency will be for more equipment to be ordered.

Fixed Factors and Heterogeneous Factors

As we look back over this chapter, we must stress the fact that if the volume of fixed factors changes, in all likelihood the entire isoquant field (and hence the expansion path), will have to be redrawn. For relevance, therefore, the analysis must postulate either that fixed factors are missing from the production process or that, whatever their quantity, their total is constant over the range of output likely to be chosen by the firm.

The factors that comprise the isoquant field, among which the firm can choose, are variable factors. These factors are individually part of a homogeneous group, or factor class. If all factors were heterogeneous, completely dissimilar in respect of productivity, it would not be possible to depict the minimum cost combination schematically, as in a diagrammatic field, even though the factors were variable. To maximize output for any given outlay the firm would have to be envisaged as selecting first those factors whose marginal physical product, relative to their price, was a maximum. Any other mode of expansion would fail to minimize output costs. Sometimes as more heterogeneous factors are added and the total factor combination enlarged, the marginal physical product of factors already hired may decline. If so, and if the ratio of its marginal product to its price is below that of another factor, opportunities for profitable replacement are at hand.

A NOTE ON THE ELASTICITY OF SUBSTITUTION

The crucial importance of the MRS among factors, or among commodities for consumers, in determining the hire or purchase combination has been underscored. So far we have not provided any measure of the *degree* of substitution between X and Y; the type of measure wanted is one that relates movements in MRS to changes in the combination of either factors or commodities; the elasticity of substitution (E_{ss}) has been designed to fill the void. Since it is formulated in terms of proportional movements, the measure is independent of units; E_{ss} will be uninfluenced whether one commodity is stated in terms of tons and the other in ounces, or whether one factor is stated in acres and the other in numbers of men.

If we write X and Y to represent the initial quantities of commodities or factors on hand, and $\Delta(X/Y)$ for the ratio of the changes in their amounts, with ΔMRS reflecting the change in the marginal rate of substitution as the quantities possessed varies, E_{ss} is formulated as follows:

$$E_{ss} = \frac{\Delta(X/Y)/(X/Y)}{\dfrac{\Delta MRS}{MRS}}.$$

Translating the symbols into words, E_{ss} is equal to the relative change in the ratio of factors (or commodities) used, divided by the relative change in the marginal rate of substitution. The changes are measured at a constant level of well-being (and thus, along an indifference curve for commodities), and along an isoquant (or for a definite level of output for factors). Let us examine the meaning of E_{ss} diagrammatically.

Graphic Representation of E_{ss}

In Figure 4A we measure the MRS vertically; the MRS starts at zero and rises to infinite values. Along the OX axis, the ratio (X/Y) of factor (or commodity) X to factor Y can be plotted. This ratio also will begin at zero for at the origin zero X will be associated with a large amount of Y. Choosing either an indifference curve or an iso-quant as the source of our data, we can locate points in the chart field of Figure 4 by associating the MRS ratios to the respective X/Y ratios. In this way a marginal rate of substitution curve, such as SPR, can be traced. The MRS curve will be extremely steep when a small variation in the ratio of the factors used causes a severe change in the MRS; it will be flat when the MRS scarcely changes despite a substantial dislodgment of the relative quantities of X and Y. In the former case the indifference curve will tend to be parallel to either axis, whereas when

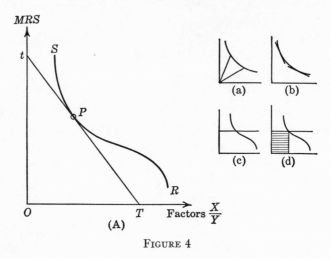

FIGURE 4

SPR is horizontal the indifference curve will approximate the straight line typical of perfect substitutes.

The slope of a tangent drawn to any point on SPR is equal to:

$$\Delta MRS/\Delta(X/Y)$$

Relating this change to the former values of MRS and X/Y at the point of tangency, we have the E_{ss}. Thus the elasticity of SPR discloses the movements in E_{ss}. Recalling the geometrical measure of the elasticity of demand (p. 44), if we draw a tangent to any point of SPR, as at P, and extend it to cut OX at T and OY at t, then $E_{ss} = PT/Pt$.

When SPR is flat this measure tends toward infinite values so that X and Y are perfect substitutes. Conversely, when SPR becomes vertical, with PT finite and Pt endlessly large, E_{ss} is zero, denoting an utter lack of substitutability. These are the limits that E_{ss} can take. If we examine the algebraic formulation, when ΔMRS is zero (as with perfect substitutes) we find that E_{ss} becomes very large; when ΔMRS is extremely large as the X/Y ratio varies, then E_{ss} approaches zero.

An Indifference-Curve Interpretation

To align the E_{ss} even more closely to the isoquant and indifference field, let us draw gradients from the O origin to a point on a particular indifference curve, and compare the relative decrease in the slope of these gradients as the use of X is expanded and Y curtailed, as in Figure 4a. Then if we compare this relative change to the relative decrease in the MRS, as shown by the slope of the tangents in 4b, we have a visual indifference-field interpretation of E_{ss}. The change in the gradients radiated from the origin indicates the movements in the E_{ss} numerator, in the ratio of the absolute amounts of factors used; changes in the tangents disclose the relative change in the MRS ratios.

Derived as it is from the indifference curves, the E_{ss} presumes that the quantities of other commodities are constant while X and Y vary; if these vary in any way it will generally be reflected in an altered E_{ss} even if the ratio X/Y is unchanged. In discussing productive factors we can substitute marginal products and their changes for the MRS and ΔMRS components of the formula.

The MRS Curve and Relative Prices

The SPR or MRS curve can be linked with the equilibrium hire of factors or purchases at a given level of well-being or output. To do so, we must now measure the price ratio P_x/P_y on the vertical axis, beginning at a zero P_x and rising to substantial P_x sums. Since market prices to the firm or consumer under competitive conditions are constant regardless of the quantities purchased, a horizontal line can be directed from the price ratio on OY corresponding to the market prices. Because in equilibrium $MRS = P_x/P_y$, the equilibrium position lies at that point at which the horizontal price ratio line intersects the MRS curve, as in Figure 4c. At the equilibrium point of intersection the rectangular areas under the MRS curve and under the market-price ratio line are equal; in the miniature diagram of 4d, these coincident areas are cross-hatched. Algebraically, the equality is

$$(MRS) \cdot (X/Y) = (P_x/P_y) \cdot (X/Y).$$

Thus if a fall occurs in P_x, the expansion in the use of X will proceed until

$$MRS' \cdot (X'/Y') = P_x'X'/P_y'Y',$$

where X'/Y' are the amounts of factors at the new intersection and P_x'/P_y' are the new prices. If the numerator $P_x'X'$, or the new expenditure on X increases after P_x falls, so that the area under the MRS curve grows, then the E_{ss} between X and Y would exceed unity. If the relative expenditure on X and Y is the same as before, and thus P_xX/P_yY is unchanged before and after the price fall, then $E_{ss} = 1$. Thus with a small fall in P_x relative to P_y, signifying a horizontal lowering of the market price line on the MRS curve field, the increase in the demand for X at the expense of Y (with real income or output unchanged) will hinge upon the elasticity of substitution. For the full effect of a fall in P_x on the demand quantity of X we would also have to include the income or output effect.

Demand Elasticity and the Elasticity of Substitution

It is possible to associate E_d with both E_{ss} and the income and substitution effects elaborated earlier. If we write E_x for the elasticity of demand for X with respect to a change in income, and E_{ss} for the elasticity of substitution, with K_x the proportion of income spent on X, and K_y the proportion of income spent on Y, for two commodities the elasticity of demand for X is:

$$E_d = K_xE_x + K_yE_{ss}.*$$

In terms of Figure 4 we measure the movement down one MRS curve and then allow for the rise in income.

Thus where E_{ss} is zero, E_d will be greater depending on the proportion of income spent on X and the magnitude of the income elasticity E_x. When E_{ss} is large, infinite as for perfect substitutes, even if K_xE_x is zero E_d will still be substantial. If $K_x = K_y$ (approximately), then E_d will depend on the relative magnitudes E_x and E_{ss}: if the latter is fairly large E_d will be large. Although in practice these separable components of E_d are hopelessly confused in the final purchase decision, so that an attempt to measure these categories would appear to be a rather elusive pastime, the measure does elucidate the underlying taste and income components that shape E_d.

BIBLIOGRAPHICAL NOTE

On the material of this chapter see Sune Carlson, *A Study on the Pure Theory of Production.* Many of the ideas of this chapter were suggested by

* For three or more commodities the formula is more complex: we can still employ, however, the dodge of lumping all other commodities together as one good. See the bibliographical references at the end of this chapter.

this stimulating work. There is also an excellent treatment of cost ideas running through R. G. D. Allen's *Mathematical Analysis for Economists*. Also K. Boulding, *Economic Analysis*, 1st ed., Chapter 23, and P. Samuelson, *Foundations of Economic Analysis*, Chapter IV. Various empirical studies of Joel Dean, such as "Statistical Cost Functions of a Hosiery Mill," *The Journal of Business* (1941), are also of interest.

An able discussion of the definition of a productive factor appears in L. M. Fraser, *Economic Thought and Language*. For the effects of indivisibility on costs, see G. Stigler, "Production and Distribution in the Short Run," *Journal of Political Economy* (1939). On limitational factors N. Georgescu-Roegen, "Fixed Coefficients of Production and Marginal Productivity Theory," and N. Kaldor, "Limitational Factors and the Elasticity of Substitution," both in *The Review of Economic Studies* (1935–1936), as well as in Allen, *Mathematical Analysis*, pp. 381–382. An elaborate discussion of fixed costs is contained in W. Arthur Lewis, "Fixed Costs," *Economica* (1946).

Nonminimum cost motivation is discussed in T. de Scitovsky, "A Note on Profit Maximization," *Review of Economic Studies* (1943), and M. W. Reder, "A Reconsideration of the Marginal Productivity Theory," *Journal of Political Economy* (1947). Most of their remarks pertain to nonmaximum profit behavior, of which the failure to minimize output costs is but one element.

For the original literature on the elasticity of substitution, see J. R. Hicks, *The Theory of Wages*, Chapter VI and Appendix, and Mrs. Joan Robinson, *The Economics of Imperfect Competition*, pp. 256, 330. For the later development and other bibliographical references see Allen, *Mathematical Analysis*, pp. 340–345; Hicks, "Distribution and Economic Progress," *Review of Economic Studies* (1936–1937); A. P. Lerner, *The Economics of Control*, Chapter XIII. An extremely lucid article is that by Fritz Machlup, "The Commonsense of the Elasticity of Substitution," *Review of Economic Statistics* (1935). Everett E. Hagen, "Capital Theory in a System with No Agents Fixed in Quantity," *Journal of Political Economy* (1942) also makes an illuminating and original contribution. Formulas for the elasticity of demand containing the E_{ss} concept are developed by Hicks and Allen, "A Reconsideration of the Theory of Value," *Economica* (1934), p. 202, and Henry Schultz, *Theory and Measurement of Demand*, p. 41, as well as J. R. Hicks, *Théorie Mathematique de la Valeur*, p. 18. An empirical study is that by J. Tinbergen, "Some Measurements of Elasticities of Substitution," *Review of Economic Studies* (1946). The more recondite concept of the elasticity of complementarity is referred to in the Hicks and Allen article.

CHAPTER 4

Costs and Factor Productivity

THE COST CURVES, WHICH ARE SO prominent in economic thinking, have not as yet been described. Although they were not required in the analysis of the firm that is bent upon minimizing the total cost of a particular output level, they will appear later in the studies of price behavior. Following a discussion of the cost-curve concept, the law of diminishing returns (redefined as a law of variable factor proportions) will be derived from further analysis of the production function. Superficially, the first two sections of this chapter stand as independent entities but they will be locked together by a demonstration of the relationship between factor productivity and costs. This aspect of the "law of diminishing returns" is seldom clarified, and yet the vitality of the study of the laws of return in a price economy is ascribable almost entirely to its implications for costs. To round out the treatment of cost curves, planning curves will also be discussed, as well as the measures of cost and supply elasticity which enjoy many applications in the analysis of cost phenomena.

TOTAL, AVERAGE, AND MARGINAL COST

The cost curves of economics relate factor cost outlays and output; curves of total, average, and marginal costs have their uses and need be explained. They have their analogy with the revenue curves elucidated earlier. We might build our cost concept with certain definitions, as follows:

$$TC = \text{total costs,}$$
$$TVC = \text{total variable costs,}$$
$$TFC = \text{total fixed costs,}$$
$$MC = \text{marginal costs,}$$
$$AC = \text{average total costs,}$$

72

AFC = average fixed costs,

AVC = average variable costs.

Recognizing that the various cost values fluctuate with output, we must attach a subscript n to each symbol to denote the output quantity, as TC_n, AVC_n, MC_n. The definitions follow:

$$TC_n = TVC_n + TFC,$$
$$AC_n = TC_n/n,$$
$$AVC_n = TVC_n/n$$
$$AFC_n = TFC/n,$$
$$MC_n = TC_n - TC_{n-1}.$$

Viewing this array of cost ideas we cannot hereafter conscionably speak of costs without specifying what cost concept and what output level we are considering. Further, as a greater quantity of output always involves some additional costs—some more labor or materials, for example—we can posit, as the "law of costs," that total costs

TABLE 3. Costs and Output

Output (n)	Total costs (TC)	Total fixed costs (TFC)	Total variable costs (TVC)	Average costs (AC)	Average variable costs (AVC)	Average fixed costs (AFC)	Marginal costs (MC)
							30
1	$130	$100	30	$130.0	30.0	100.0	
							24
2	154	100	54	77.0	27.0	50.0	
							15
3	169	100	69	56.3	23.0	33.3	
							11
4	180	100	80	45.0	20.0	25.0	
							20
5	200	100	100	40.0	20.0	20.0	
							26
6	226	100	126	37.6	21.0	16.6	
							28
7	254	100	154	36.3	22.0	14.3	
							31
8	285	100	185	35.6	23.1	12.5	
							32
9	317	100	217	35.2	24.1	11.1	
							34
10	351	100	251	35.1	25.1	10.0	
							35
11	386	100	286	35.0	26.0	9.1	
							36
12	422	100	322	35.1	26.8	8.3	

increase with a rise in output.   Average costs or marginal costs may fall but total costs must rise.   Relating this discussion with the isoquant and expansion-path analysis of the preceding chapter, we see that the minimum total cost for each quantity of production (or the maximum output associated with each level of total cost) can be read off the expansion path, from the total factor cost responsible for the output indicated by the isocost that is tangent to the particular isoquant along the expansion path.   Each point on the *TC* curve thus represents the *minimum* cost of producing the particular amount of output.

A hypothetical illustration of the relations between the various cost categories and output is provided in Table 3.   Total costs, it will be

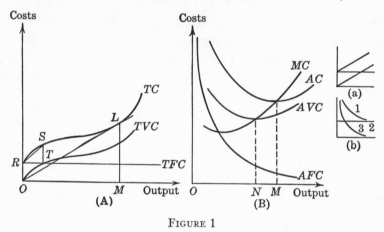

FIGURE 1

observed, always rise as output increases.   The same is true of total variable costs.   Total fixed costs, however, are rigid despite the movements in output.   Average fixed costs invariably fall with greater production.   Marginal costs may be derived as the difference between the total costs of two successive output levels or the spread between successive total variable costs.   Generally, average total and average variable costs first fall and then rise; at their minimum values they are equal to marginal costs.   The *AVC* minimum is reached before the *AC* minimum.

In Figure 1A, costs are measured along the vertical axis and output along the horizontal axis.   If total fixed costs are equal to *OR*, total costs will start at *R* and run the gamut *TC*: the *TC* curve of Figure 1A is regarded as a typical total-cost curve.   Each point on *TC*, tied as it is to the expansion path, discloses the minimum total cost of producing the particular quantity of output.   The *TVC* curve originates at *O* and runs parallel to TC, but always at a distance OR below it; for, as the definitions disclose, this sum (OR) always separates the curves. The TFC curve is always horizontal, at a height equal to the total sum of fixed costs.

The AC of any output can be discovered diagrammatically by drawing a vector, such as OL in Figure 1A, from O to any point on TC; the slope of this line, which is measured by LM/OM, yields AC. If the slope of the vector falls as output increases, this condition would reflect a falling AC. Likewise, starting from OR (the height of TFC), the slope indicated by ST/RT always indicates the AVC. A vector from O to TFC, whose slope must fall as output increases, would denote the movement in AFC; since the vertical component is always constant while the horizontal segment always increases, AFC must fall with advancing output.

Marginal Costs

Marginal costs (MC) are the additions to total cost accompanying an increment in output. In Table 3 they were obtained by deducting the total cost of producing $n - 1$ units from the total cost of n units. Thus, algebraically,

$$MC_n = TC_n - TC_{n-1}.$$

Diagrammatically, the marginal costs can be ascertained by drawing a tangent to TC at each output, because the tangent would measure $\Delta Y/\Delta X$, or the increase in total costs as output expanded. In following the movements of the tangent to TC we would observe that generally it tends to fall as output moves on from low levels, diminishing in slope until it reaches a minimum gradient, and then gradually increasing. Hence MC falls, reaches a minimum, perhaps remaining constant over a slight range of output, and then rises. The paths of the AC, AVC, AFC and MC curves accompanying the total curves of Figure 1A are sketched in Figure 1B; they could all be superimposed, of course, on the chart field of Figure 1A, although we have drawn them separately to avoid encumbering the figure.*

---

* It might be asked why there is but one marginal-cost curve whereas there are three average-cost curves. Literally, our MC is one of marginal *total* costs. If we chose instead to speak of marginal variable costs, using TVC_n and TVC_{n-1} in our formula, the results will of course always be the same as when the TC values are used, for the TFC, which separates TC and TVC, will not affect the difference in the totals that comprise marginal costs. Marginal fixed costs, on the other hand, are always zero, for there is no change in TFC as output advances. Hence there is but one marginal-cost concept and it reflects the changes in total variable costs.

There will be one output at which $MC = AVC$ and another at which $MC = AC$. At the latter output the tangent to TC would, if extended, coincide with the AC vector from O; at this output $MC = AC$. At this output the slope of the vector from O to TC would be at a minimum: this implies that $MC = AC$ at the lowest level of AC. Also, the coincidence of a tangent to TC and a vector from R to TC, would reveal that $MC = AVC$ at a lesser output than that at which $MC = AC$: the fall in average fixed costs as output increases allows AC to fall even after AVC turns up. The AC, AVC and MC curves of Figure 1B can be deduced, in the manner indicated, from the movements in the total curves of Figure 1A. AVC and MC start at the same cost height on OY. Marginal costs decline, reach a minimum, and then rise. AVC falls and rises more gradually than MC, since it will fall when $MC < AVC$, and rise when $MC > AVC$; for whenever a value below the average is added onto a total, then the new average will be lower, and vice versa. Finally, $MC = AVC$ at the minimum point on the AVC curve.* $MC = AC$ also at the latter's lowest point for the same reason; as AFC is now added to AVC this intersection is to the right of the previous one: even though $MC > AVC$ (thus tending to push AC upward) the continued fall in AFC delays the rise in AC a while longer. AVC approaches AC asymptotically, for AFC plays an ever smaller part in determining AC as output grows.

Although the TC and TVC curves of Figure 1A are regarded as typical total cost curves—for they generate the U-shaped AC and AVC curves of 1B—some other important curve sets ought to be considered. Suppose MC was always constant so that the MC curve was a horizontal line. Inasmuch as the addition to total costs would then always be the same, AVC would also be constant and the AVC curve would coincide fully with MC. The AC curve, however, would fall and approach

---

* To prove this analytically, write T for TVC and X for output. Then, at the minimum AVC value,

$$\frac{d(T/X)}{dX} = 0.$$

Thus

$$\frac{X(dT/dX) - T}{X^2} = 0.$$

Therefore

$$\frac{dT}{dX} = \frac{T}{X}.$$

Hence marginal costs equal average variable costs. To prove that this is at a minimum rather than a maximum AVC would require that we show the second derivative to be positive. A similar proof holds for the derivation of $MC = AC$ at the latter's minimum point.

AVC asymptotically. *TC* and *TVC* would in this event be linear and
rising; *TFC* is, of course, always horizontal. As AFC_n (the *Y* value)
multiplied by the number of units (the *X* value) is always constant and
equal to *TFC*, the *AFC* curve is always a rectangular hyperbola, thus:

$$n \cdot AFC_n = TFC,$$

or,

$$X \cdot Y = k.$$

AFC is always independent of the shape of the variable cost curves, *TVC*,
AVC, or *MC*. The relevant total curves are drawn in Figure 1a and
the average curves in Figure 1b. In 1b, the curve lettered 1 is *AC*,
curve 2 represents *MC* (= *AVC*), and curve 3 represents *AFC*.

Since the cost curves are derived implicitly from the expansion path,
which discloses the minimum cost factor combinations, at each point on
the total (average or marginal) curves the variable factors are presumed to be hired in such proportions that the ratios of marginal physical products to factor prices, for all factors used at each output level, will
be equal: this ratio will not, of course, be constant as output advances.
If the firm does not endeavor to minimize total costs for each output
level the *TC* curve will be given a lift: the *TC* points would then not
represent the minimum total cost of producing the corresponding
output.

LAW OF VARIABLE PROPORTIONS

Abandoning temporarily the further study of the cost curves and
returning to the isoquant field, we observe that there is another aspect
of the production function that will repay study. Assuming that there
are but two factors of production, let us probe the output consequences
of holding one factor constant while altering the amount of the other.
This is the method of the traditional theory of the law of diminishing
returns which is, more accurately, a law of *variable proportions* in factor
use, for one factor is constant while the other is increased relative to it.
In our isoquant field we can visualize that at some height on *OY*, representing a fixed amount of factor *Y*, we draw a horizontal line parallel to
OX which would cut across the field, beginning at factor combinations
outside the pale of economic rationality—to the left of the ridge line *OA*.
As it moved to the right, denoting an expanding *X* and still constant *Y*,
it would intersect curves of ever higher output, reaching a maximum at
the ridge line *OB*; beyond *OB* total output would decline.*

* Another concept of "diminishing returns" assumes that factor *Y* decreases as *X*
increases, or vice versa. Essentially it amounts to taking a cross-cut of the production
function along a path such as that normally traced by the factor cost lines.

Total-Product Curves

Let us develop these ideas more schematically. Suppose we inserted some pins into a horizontal line, such as that drawn in Figure 2a, while traversing the isoquant field at a height equal to the fixed amount of factor Y; in length the pins ought to be proportionate to output so that we would have a model, drawn to correct scale, of the relative size of output as more X was added with factor Y constant. Concentrating

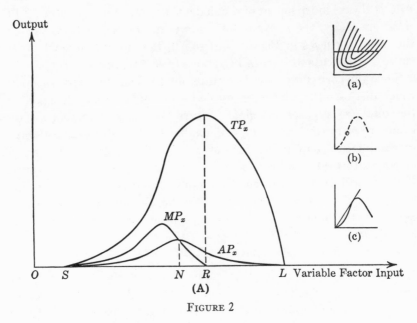

FIGURE 2

our attention on the pins inserted into this cross cut of the production function, we observe that the figure that would evolve would resemble curve TP_x in Figure 2A; where we measure total output on OY and quantities of factor X on OX. The height of the total-product curve TP_x, would be zero until at least some minimum amount of X, say OS, was combined with the fixed Y; no isoquants, not even the portions outside the ridge lines, would cross this segment of the chart field. TP_x would rise and reach its maximum at that quantity of X located at the ridge line OB for the constant amount of factor Y; TP_x would thereafter taper off as further amounts of factor X (amounts of X outside the ridge line OB) were employed.

On the same field we can draw an MP_x curve showing the marginal physical product of X (the additions to total output made by a further unit of X) while Y was constant. Symbolically,

$$MP_n = TP_n - TP_{n-1},$$

where n refers to the amount used of factor X.

Likewise, an AP_x or average-physical-product curve can be sketched, where

$$AP_n = (TP_n/n),$$

with n being the number of units of factor X employed.

To ascertain the MP_x and AP_x values we would thus have to know, as our basic data, the relations between the amount of the variable factor hired and total output. Given this information, MP_x and AP_x follow immediately. The first four columns of Table 4 contain an arithmetical statement of these relations.

TABLE 4. Output from Ten Acres of Land with Varying Amounts of Labor

Number of men (X)	Total product (TP_x)	Average product (AP_x)	Marginal product (MP_x)	Acres cultivated per man	Total acreage in excess of or below 1 acre tilled per man	Total product with 1 acre tilled per man	Marginal product of total excess or deficient acreage (MP_y)
·7	66	9.4	—	$1\frac{3}{7}$	$7 \cdot \frac{3}{7} = 3$	70	−4
8	79	9.8	13	$1\frac{1}{4}$	$8 \cdot \frac{1}{4} = 2$	80	−1
9	90	10.0	11	$1\frac{1}{9}$	$9 \cdot \frac{1}{9} = 1$	90	0
10	100	10.0	10	1	$1 \cdot 0 = 0$	100	0
11	109	9.9	9	$\frac{10}{11}$	$11 \cdot \frac{1}{11} = 1$	110	+1
12	116	9.6	7	$\frac{10}{12}$	$12 \cdot \frac{2}{12} = 2$	120	+4

Geometrically, each MP_x point can be derived by drawing a tangent to the TP_x curve above the particular amount of factor X in which we are interested; the slope of the tangent would denote the value MP_x, since in this case the tangent measures the rise in output with an increment in the use of factor X. Thus

$$\Delta Y/\Delta X = \Delta TP_x/\Delta X = MP_x.$$

When the tangents are rising the MP_x would be rising. At the amount of factor use at which the gradient of the tangent was steepest, MP_x

would be a maximum. In terms of the isoquants, when MP_x is rising and the tangents to TP_x increasing, as indicated in Figure 1c, the isoquants would be closely bunched, because a smaller ΔX is required to expand output by one unit. As MP_x falls we can infer that the isoquants of successive outputs are farther apart.

AP_x can also be deduced geometrically by directing a vector from O to any point on TP_x in which we are interested; dropping a perpendicular from TP_x to OX, and dividing the vertical TP_x amount by the horizontal OX quantity, we obtain the AP_x. Merely by noting whether the gradient of the vector is rising or falling as we direct it to successive TP_x points, we can determine whether AP_x is rising or falling as the amount of variable factor use increases. When the vector drawn from O is just tangent to TP_x, as in Figure 1c, then $AP_x = MP_x$. At this point AP_x is a maximum, the reason being that AP_x will rise only when $MP_x > AP_x$ and will fall when $MP_x < AP_x$. When the two are equal, AP_x is neither rising nor falling, so that we must be at the peak of a bell-shaped AP_x curve, for only at the peak is the curve not moving either higher or lower.

Relations between Total, Average, and Marginal Products

All three curves, appropriately lettered, are shown in Figure 2A. AP_x is a maximum, and $AP_x = MP_x$, when ON of factor X is used with the fixed amount of factor Y. At ON of X, when AP_x is at a maximum and equal to MP_x, it can be proved that we are at the OA ridge line in terms of the isoquant field: here the marginal product of the fixed factor Y is zero, operating neither to increase nor to decrease output. As AP_x is rising to the left of $AP_x = MP_x$, and assuming that factor Y though fixed is divisible, the marginal product of the fixed factor, MP_y, must be negative when less than ON of X is used with the fixed Y.

To indicate the proof by means of an illustration, let us examine Table 4, which contains some of the relations in the neighborhood of the maximum value of AP_x. Suppose that AP_x is at a maximum of 10 units of output when 10 men are used to farm the fixed acreage of 10 acres; each man thus farms 1 acre. Suppose also that when only 9 men are used, $AP_x = 10$, just as before; thus when each man farms $1\frac{1}{9}$ acres, the total output is the same as it would be if each of the 9 men concentrated on working 1 acre, allowing 1 acre to lie fallow. MP_y, or the additional $\frac{1}{9}$ acre of land beyond 1 acre per man—or a total of 1 acre of the 10 acres in our table—would have a zero marginal product. If more than $1\frac{1}{9}$ acres of land are cultivated per person, as $1\frac{1}{4}$ acres in our table, the excess land over $1\frac{1}{9}$ acres used by each individual would decrease output by 1 unit. The marginal product of land is thus *negative*. On the other hand, when 11 men work the land, AP_x falls off again to 9.9— this is the other side of the AP_x maximum on the bell shaped curve. Here with each man tilling less than 1 acre, average output is reduced: apparently MP_y is positive and total output could be expanded if each man had a little more land to cultivate. A rising AP_x, therefore, denotes a negative MP_y, while a falling AP_x implies a positive MP_y. When AP_x is at a maximum so that $AP_x = MP_x$, and MP_x is falling so that subsequently it lies below AP_x, MP_y is zero, neither positive nor negative. This, we know, is at the OA ridge line. It follows that if factor X were not available in an amount sufficient to render AP_x a maximum, it would be most sensible to utilize, with each unit of X, that amount of Y which would accompany X when AP_x is a maximum— one acre in our illustration. Allowing the rest of factor Y to remain idle would eliminate the negative marginal productivity of factor Y and guarantee that total output would be a maximum.*

Ultimately, MP_x will fall to zero. This will occur when TP_x reaches its peak; since MP_x is zero, TP_x fails to rise or fall, which implies that we are at the top of TP_x. Here AP_y (the average product of the fixed factor) will be a maximum, because AP_y, just as AP_x, is equivalent to TP_x/n, where n is now the number of units of the fixed factor Y; AP_y will thus reach its maximum when TP_x is a maximum, so long as Y is fixed. Hence for OR of factor X, in Figure 2A, TP_x is at a maximum. In terms of the isoquant field this must be at the OB ridge line, for there $MP_x = 0$. Thereafter if more X is added, X is a redundant factor: additional X without additional Y would *diminish* total output.

Analytically, the TP_x curve could be divided into three regions: (1) a first phase, ranging from the use of zero to ON of factor X. From OS onward, MP_x is positive, MP_y is negative, and TP_x, AP_x, and AP_y are rising; (2) a second phase, ranging from ON to OR of factor X. Both MP_x and MP_y are positive in this region, but AP_x is falling from its maximum and AP_y is rising to its maximum, with TP_x reaching its peak at OR; (3) a final phase, beginning at OR where MP_x is zero and thereafter passing through negative values. TP_x starts its descent at

---

* This presumes, of course, that factor Y, though fixed, is divisible. If Y is not divisible then all of it must be used. Nevertheless, as long as AP_x is less than a maximum we may infer that the same forces are at work affecting productivity as when Y is indivisible. It is to be noted that this entire statement of the change in output runs in terms of changing factor proportions. Emphasis on the scale of operations is reserved for the following section.

OR and AP_x continues its fall, with $AP_{\dot{x}}$ zero when TP_x is zero; AP_y reaches its maximum at OR but thereafter falls also. The only area, therefore, in which both factors have a positive marginal product is in the second phase, between ON and OR of factor X, given the fixed amount of factor Y. Neither AP_x nor AP_y is a maximum within these bounds, although AP_y does become a maximum at OR.

Areas of Factor Utilization

We might ponder over this diagram for its intimations on the ultimate selection and hire of factors, even though for the final answer to this query we shall need information not only on the marginal productivity of factors but also on the factor prices and product prices.

Consider first a simple case in which P_x, the price of factor X, is zero. Manifestly, with the fixed amount of Y, not more than OR of X would be employed. Analogously, given the market factor prices, so long as Y is hired in definite amount, not less than ON of X will be engaged to work alongside of the given amount of Y. For with less than ON of X, MP_y is negative, becoming zero at ON; hiring less Y would be more prudent. On these considerations the only area of rational factor utilization must be in the second phase of Figure 2A, where MP_x and MP_y are both positive and decreasing—in the area of "diminishing returns," for otherwise there is a negative MP for some factor. It is to be observed that in this region of rational factor hire, neither AP_x nor AP_y are at their maximum values, and, implicitly, $AP_x > MP_x$ and $AP_y > MP_y$. Factor choice is thus restricted to the area between the ridge lines, as between ON and OR of factor X in Figure 2A. This is as far as we can go in narrowing the area of factor hire; the exact selection will hinge, as stated, not only upon factor productivity but also upon factor prices and product prices.

RETURNS TO SCALE

Rather than vary one factor and hold others rigid in amount, as in the law of variable proportions, we can consider the variations in the physical productivity of factors as their joint use is expanded and output increased. This study is generally catalogued under the heading of the laws of "returns to scale."

Constant Returns to Scale

Suppose that output can be changed only by varying all factor quantities in exactly the same proportion—that is, increasing all of them by fifty per cent or doubling or trebling them, etc. Under these conditions, with a fixed proportionate variation in all factors, the proportionate increment in total output ought always be the same as that of factor use.* That is, a ten per cent increase in all factors ought to increase output by precisely ten per cent. With fixed and indivisible factors present, constant physical returns to scale in this sense are generally unobtainable. Holding the amount of certain factors constant, by increasing the variable agents by, say, ten per cent, will not insure an equivalent relative increase in output; the movement may instead be in greater or less proportion than the alteration in the amount of the variable factors.

The Elasticity of Productivity

The ratio of the proportionate change in output to a proportionate change in variable factors can be measured by the *elasticity of productivity*. Symbolically,

$$E_p = \frac{\Delta B/B}{\Delta X/X} = \frac{X\Delta B}{B\Delta X} \gtreqless 1,$$

where B represents output and X the initial quantity arrangement of variable factors; ΔB is the increase in output and ΔX is the absolute amount of equiproportionate increase in variable factors.† When a one per cent change in output accompanies a one per cent change in variable factors, so that constant returns to scale are indicated (implying normally the absence of fixed factors), the measure equals unity. With $E_p < 1$, there are decreasing returns to scale; returns to scale are increasing when $E_p > 1$. If E_p always exceeded unity, production would always take place in a stage of rising marginal products of factors as we augmented their use and advanced from one output level to another.

Aligning the concept to the isoquant field, straight lines emanating from O would denote that the variable factors X and Y are always added in a relatively fixed ratio; thus if $10X$ and $10Y$ were initially employed, $1X$ would be added for each $1Y$ as output expanded. In Figure 3, line OG assumes factors varied in a one-to-one ratio; according to the figure, the doubling of factors, from $5X$ and $5Y$ to $10X$ and $10Y$, results in a 100 per cent rise in output, from 30 to 60. Along OB, however, factors

---

* This implies a linear and homogeneous production function.
† Writing $E_p = (\Delta B/\Delta X)/(B/X)$, note that in the one factor case E_p depends on the ratio of marginal to average product.

are employed in a $10Y/4X$ ratio; doubling factors from this amount raises output from 30 to 70. On OH, the ratio is $3Y/10X$; doubling factors raises output to only 40 units from the previous 30. The value of E_p is thus different in each case. When isoclines and the expansion paths follow a line of equiproportional factor variation for some length, the elasticity of productivity can measure the composite factor productivity over this range of output. Also, if the production function is linear and homogeneous and there are constant returns to scale, with the constant-product curves being of the same shape, then the isoclines would be linear and the value of E_p would be directly applicable to the analysis of factor and output expansion. Whatever the production function, however, variations in E_p reflect the changing proximity of the constant-product curves; when $E_p > 1$, the constant-product curves are bunched closely together, while as E_p approaches zero, the constant-product curves tend to be widely separated in the chart field.

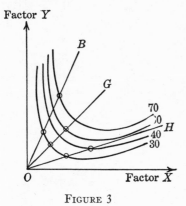

Factor Y

FIGURE 3

The E_p measure is seen to have limited applications when we recall that factor use follows an expansion path (which is generally curved) as output increases. If factor prices are constant the ratio of relative marginal products of the different factors (or of marginal products to factor prices) will also be constant; this is the condition of minimum cost. However, if we are in a sector of the isoquant field in which $E_p > 1$, all marginal products will be rising: the fact that expansion occurs by a disproportionate increase in some factors merely attests to a rise in their marginal products at a faster pace than that of other factors. If $E_p < 1$, then all marginal products are likely to be falling, with the substitution favoring those factors whose marginal products fall more gradually. The point that we shall need to comprehend shortly is that even though the ratio of marginal products to factor prices is the same for all factors at a *given* output level, this ratio, written as J, will alter with the output volume. If it rises, increasing marginal products are the rule; if it falls, decreasing marginal products are the rule. Thus, at each output level,

$$\frac{MP_x}{P_x} = \frac{MP_y}{P_y} = \frac{MP_z}{P_z} = J.$$

At 100 units of output these ratios are, say,

$$\frac{10}{\$1} = \frac{30}{\$3} = \frac{75}{\$7.50} = J = \frac{10}{1}.$$

At 130 units of output they may be

$$\frac{8}{\$1} = \frac{24}{\$3} = \frac{60}{\$7.50} = J = \frac{8}{1}.$$

The marginal-productivity ratio J has thus fallen from 10/1 to 8/1 as output rose.

Proportionality and Size in Returns to Scale

Returns to scale, it was averred, would always be constant if *all* factors were varied proportionately; the E_p was greater or less than unity only if there were some fixed factors present that could not be augmented in enlarging output. Diminishing and increasing returns to scale have thus been charged to a lack of proportionality among factors as output varies.

This view of productivity phenomena has been contested; it may be alleged that if all factors were diminished to one-tenth of their totals, output would be likely to fall off by more than 90 per cent because of the diminished opportunities for specialization and division of labor that are open to the reduced factor group. Essentially, even if factors were fully divisible, the methods of production and the arrangement of the work flow are not divisible. Operating alongside the influence of factor proportionality on output there are thus laws of *size*. As factor use grows, even though all factors are expanded proportionately, there will be a more than proportionate output expansion as the more numerous opportunities for the division of labor are exploited. Ultimately, since tasks can be subdivided too finely so that time is lost in waiting for the completion of other processes and tasks, the efficiency of size will yield to inefficiency, or operating economies to operating diseconomies.

If there are fixed factors, such as the stock of equipment, the size of the plant, or the capacity of the managerial group (who are unwilling to add to their numbers and to share their assignments with others) the E_p will achieve a maximum value. At this stage, due to the concerted forces of proportionality and size, the relative increment in output to a relative increment in the use of the variable factors is at its maximum. Thus even if *all* factors were varied proportionately, E_p would still, on occasion, exceed unity. If both of these elements cast their effect continuously, then the E_p ought first to rise as more factors are hired, reach a peak, and then decline.   At the E_p peak the J ratio of marginal products to factor prices would reach its maximum level.

FACTOR PRODUCTIVITY AND COSTS

The cost curves related output quantities to cost outlays.   The productivity studies of the law of variable proportions and the returns to scale stressed changes in the productivity of factors as output grew.   It is imperative that these separate analyses of factor productivity and cost movements be bridged and their interdependence underscored. Signifying economies to scale to mean falling average costs and diseconomies to mean the rising AC, we want to show that these phenomena can be explained by productivity factors.   Actually if we can extract the forces that determine MC, we have effectively explained the course of TC, TVC, AC, and AVC—for it will be the movement of marginal costs that accounts for their changes.

Starting with the simplest case in which several factors are fixed and one is variable, suppose that to increase output only more labor is required.   Writing W for the wage rate per laborer and ΔL for the amount of labor necessary to increase output by one unit, and MP_L, the marginal product of labor, then marginal costs are:

$$MC = W\Delta L.$$

But

$$MP_L \cdot \Delta L = 1;$$

therefore

$$MC = \frac{W}{MP_L}.$$

Thus, if the wage rate is constant, marginal costs will decline whenever marginal products rise, and will rise whenever marginal products fall.   If the marginal product of an additional laborer is 7 units of output, so that one man has to work but one-seventh (approximately) of the ordinary work-week to add but one unit to total output, and the weekly wage is \$70, then the marginal cost is \$10.   If the marginal product falls to 5, the MC will go up to \$14.   With one variable factor, therefore, falling MC implies increasing marginal productivity, while rising MC intimates diminishing marginal products.   Cost movements thus reflect the variations in marginal products.

As would be expected, a similar relation can be elicited for AVC. Writing L for the total amount of the variable factor hired, with W the wage rate and AP_L the average product of labor, with the subscript n denoting the amount of output, we have

$$A V C_n = \frac{TVC_n}{n} = \frac{W \cdot L}{n}.$$

But

$$n = AP_L \cdot L;$$

therefore

$$A V C_n = \frac{W}{AP_L}.$$

When the average product of labor falls because of diminishing (average and marginal) productivity, AVC will rise. It is a simple matter to deduce that at the output at which $MP_L = AP_L$, at ON amount of factor hire in Figure 2A, $AVC = MC$.

Marginal Costs with Several Variable Factors

This heading covers the case of one output and one variable factor. When there are n variable factors and still only one product, the proof that diminishing productivity means higher marginal costs is only slightly more intricate. Assuming there are three variable factors X, Y, Z, with their increase being $\Delta X, \Delta Y$, and ΔZ, their marginal products MP_x, MP_y, and MP_z, and their prices P_x, P_y, P_z, then

$$MC = P_x\Delta X + P_y\Delta Y + P_z\Delta Z.$$

But

$$\Delta X = \frac{n}{MP_x}, \qquad \Delta Y = \frac{r}{MP_y}, \qquad \text{and} \qquad \Delta Z = \frac{s}{MP_z},$$

where n, r and s are the fractions of the unit of output for which the respective increments in each productive factor are responsible. Therefore

$$MC = \frac{nP_x}{MP_x} + \frac{rP_y}{MP_y} + \frac{sP_z}{MP_z}.$$

But all the elements on the right contain the reciprocal of J, the condition of minimum cost for output advances by factor hire along the expansion path. Thus

$$MC = \frac{n}{J} + \frac{r}{J} + \frac{s}{J} = \frac{n + r + s}{J}.$$

Taking $n + r + s = 1$, as in the marginal-cost concept,

$$MC = \frac{1}{J} = \frac{P}{MP},$$

P/MP refers to the ratio of factor prices to marginal products.   Hence, as factor productivity falls, or the ratio of marginal products to factor prices decreases along the expansion path, marginal costs will rise. Obviously this last formula for marginal costs is but a generalization of the formula for the one variable-factor analysis, developed previously.

If expansion occurs by way of a proportionate variation of all variable factors, as in the E_p concept, then:

$$MC = P_x \Delta X + P_y \Delta Y + P_z \Delta Z.$$

But

$$\frac{\Delta X}{X} = \frac{\Delta Y}{Y} = \frac{\Delta Z}{Z} = \epsilon;$$

therefore

$$MC = \epsilon(P_x X + P_y Y + P_z Z)$$
$$MC = \epsilon TVC,$$

where ϵ denotes the proportionate variation in all factors and TVC represents the sum total of variable costs.   Recalling our E_p formula, we can write

$$E_p = \frac{\dfrac{\Delta B}{B}}{\epsilon},$$

$$\epsilon = \frac{\Delta B}{E_p B}.$$

Taking ΔB as equal to one unit, as in the marginal cost concept, we have

$$\epsilon = \frac{1}{E_p B},$$

and

$$MC = \frac{TVC}{E_p B} = \frac{AVC}{E_p}.$$

Thus as the elasticity of productivity equals unity, marginal costs equal average variable cost.

If productive factors are all heterogeneous so that we are debarred from drawing isoquants, isocosts, and the derived expansion path, then cost curves can still be used.   If the firm is intent on producing each output at minimum cost, it would hire first those factors for which the J ratio was greatest.   However, if several individuals of unequal skill are hired by the firm at the identical wage rate, with the most skilled persons employed first, the MC curve can be depicted as rising for what can also, in truth, be described as "diminishing returns."   This cause of rising costs must be distinguished from rising costs under the assumptions of homogeneity among vast numbers of factors.

Finally, in all of our discussion factor prices were presumed constant. If these should rise while marginal products are falling we have dual causes of rising MC. If they rise while the MP's are growing, there is a neutralizing of the forces to some extent. If MP rises while factor prices fall, there are two strong elements leading to decreasing unit and marginal costs.

PLANNING CURVES

The cost curves of Figure 1 in the present chapter were compounded from the phenomena of the expansion path. All along, however, we assumed that the firm already had a stock of fixed factors and that the important questions were those concerning the variable factors to be hired at each output level. There is still another problem to be explored: when the extrepreneurial group of the firm contemplates entry into a commodity field and plans to erect a plant and to equip it, it is faced with a choice in selecting not only the variable factors but also the fixed factors. At the planning stage, therefore, all factors are variable. Analytically, it would be possible to describe the production function for each possible "layout"—as we may describe the fixed plant and its equipment. We can cut through some of the details, however, by elaborating instead the average and marginal cost curves associated with each plant. Of course, in the final decision on the layout to be ordered we would have to know not only the costs of production with each plant but also the nature of market demand and price phenomena. But this phase of the study will be deferred for a while longer.

Alternate Layouts

Let us construe each point on the AC curves of Figure 4 as embodying the minimum average variable and fixed charges that the entrepreneur will strive to recover for each level of output before implementing a decision to enter the production field.

Suppose there is but one type of plant that can be constructed—other plant varieties are nonexistent although the particular plant may be duplicated. In Figure 4A, the average costs of producing with this layout is shown by the curve AC_1, which falls to a minimum at 500 units of output. If the firm, after appraising the profit potentialities and its access to funds, planned to grow to a size large enough to accommodate an output of 2,200 units per annum, it would seek to install four discrete

replicas of the original operating plant.   Hence AC_2, is a twofold projection of AC_1; average costs drop to a minimum at 1,000 rather than
500 units of output.   Similarly AC_3 is a threefold extension of AC_1, with
its minimum at 1,500 units, while AC_4 is a fourfold multiple, with its
minimum at 2,000 units of output.

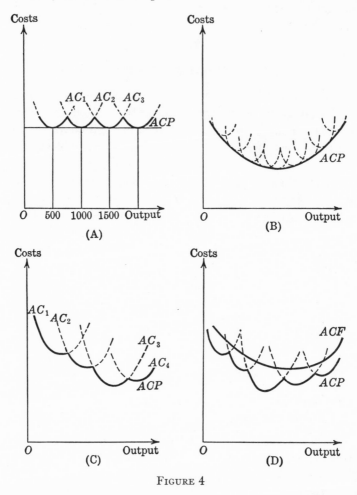

FIGURE 4

In contrast, in Figure 4B each U-shaped AC curve denotes a different
layout.   In principle we can surmise that there is an infinite variety
of plants, each with minute technical gradations, so that *at each level of
output* there is one particular plant and array of equipment which, if
used, would minimize production costs.   Although we have drawn only
those curves that are associated with plants which minimize costs at

some output level, innumerable other cost curves could be drawn higher in the chart field and assigned to plants that could be erected but that fail to obey this rule of minimizing costs at some output.

The Planning Curve

While each of the AC curves in Figure 4 is anchored to a particular layout or mass of equipment, by connecting the minimum AC points at each level of output, whatever their special cost curve origin and the implied plant, we derive what is termed a *planning* curve, the heavy lined ACP in Figure 4. The ACP curve, which is an envelope curve composed of minimal cost points, discloses the average costs of producing each level of output when the plant is still in the blueprint stage. If there are infinite varieties and gradations of plant, each point on the envelope curve can be abstracted from a different AC curve.* Contrariwise, when there are but few alternate types of layout the envelope curve will merge with an AC curve for some range of output before gliding onto a subsequent AC curve; the transition will occur at the point of intersection of the more "capitalistic" structure (an AC curve further to the right) with a less lavish capital plant. Thus wherever $AC_1 < AC_2$, the envelope curve follows the former path; commencing at the output at which $AC_2 = AC_1$ the planning curve follows the locus of the latter. Drawing ACP in this way, it is possible to derive a curve which is *marginal* to ACP. If the planning curve is discontinuous, following several of the particular AC curves, the MCP curve will also be discontinuous, coinciding with the individual MC curves until the ACP curve itself switches onto a new AC. The individual MC curves and the planning MCP curve compounded from them are not drawn in Figure 4. The principle of its construction is clear when we recall that each individual MC curve passes through the minimum point of the correspondent AC curve.

The planning curve ACP, to be sure, has a vitality only while the layout is still in the embryonic, conjectural, and planning stages. Once

---

* It is to be observed that the planning curve does not gather the minimum points from each AC curve, but only the minimum AC points for each output; there is a difference for by the time a minimum is reached on each particular AC, another layout may be less costly. The one minimum AC point definitely included on ACP is located on the AC curve whose lowest point lies closest to OX. As a tentative proof of the fact that the minimum point on each individual AC curve does not lie on ACP, we can consider that at each minimum AC point a tangent to AC would be horizontal. But if ACP is falling, the tangent to ACP at the same output would be falling; thus the points of horizontal tangents would not lie on ACP. For an amusing ancedote on this point, see the footnote reference (p. 36) of Professor Jacob Viner on the controversy between himself and his draftsman on the drawing of ACP, in "Cost Curves and Supply Curves," *Zeitschrift für Nationalökonomie* (1932).

a particular layout has been constructed the planning curve has only historical interest, a curiosity that is descriptive of the original cost potentialities facing the firm when it was pondering the several alternate production techniques. In Figure 4C, if the firm decides to install the plant responsible for AC_2, then after this plant is ready for operation AC_2 alone will be the relevant cost path.

Economic Change and Output Flexibility

If market phenomena, in the sense of demand and price, were always constant so that the same output level always guaranteed maximum profits, then the firm would select that block of equipment which promised to maximize profits or minimize the unit costs for a particular amount of output. Sometimes, however, in view of market phenomena it may be that output will fluctuate. In an unstable market a firm may, for these reasons, prefer a layout which although not least costly for any one level of output is yet so flexible that over any range of possible output its average costs are below those experienced with any other mass of equipment. For example, in Figure 4D, ACP is the planning curve moulded from the U-shaped AC curves, several of which are drawn in the figure. ACF, however, is also an average-cost curve, attributable to a single plant which, although more costly for any particular quantum of output than any of the layouts embodied in ACP, is still so adaptable that over a wide range of output its AC is less costly than with any of the plants comprising ACP. If output is expected to be volatile the plant implicit in ACF will be, in comparison to any of the layouts which comprise ACP, a superior vehicle for maximizing profits.

The Bases of Output Flexibility

The causes of the output flexibility divulged by the ACF curve of Figure 4D are worth pondering. If the firm expected to produce only one output volume in successive periods of time there would be one layout which would be more economical than any other. The plant would be so designed that it would be most efficient at this output level. It would comprise a particular mass of equipment requiring a definite number of individuals for its utilization; it would be relatively uneconomic for abrupt variations in production, when more (or less) men or more (or less) materials had to be used with it. Plant flexibility, in contrast, is largely the product of greater divisibility in the plant, achieved ordinarily by constructing numerous smaller but identical components, as smaller furnaces or duplicate wings of a factory, rather than a huge blast furnace or a gigantic conveyor-belt system that must be used as a unit or not at all.   When equipment is divisible, a substantial fluctuation in output may be handled without a sharp change in marginal or average variable costs.

Besides greater plant divisibility, output flexibility can also be secured by curtailing the volume of capital equipment employed per unit of output through substituting more of the variable factors for the fixed factors; if all factors were variable, marginal costs would always be constant for an identical composite of variable factors would always be hired in expanding output by one unit.   Usually, by limiting the installation of equipment and favoring the use of variable factors, AC should become more nearly constant as output recedes or advances.

THE ELASTICITY OF COSTS AND SUPPLY

Measures of the flexibility of output—that is, its responsiveness to cost and price phenomena—can be introduced at this point.   Consider first the concept of the elasticity of total costs, written E_c.

The Elasticity of Costs

The elasticity of total costs is defined as the ratio of the relative change in total cost to a relative increase in output.   Writing X and ΔX for the level of output and the increase in output respectively, and TC and ΔTC for corresponding total cost ideas, then

$$E_c = \frac{\frac{\Delta TC}{TC}}{\frac{\Delta X}{X}} = \frac{X\Delta TC}{TC\Delta X} \gtrless 1.$$

Rewriting and manipulating the terms, we have

$$E_c = \frac{X\Delta TC}{TC\Delta X} = \frac{\frac{\Delta TC}{\Delta X}}{\frac{TC}{X}} \gtrless 1.$$

But since

$$\frac{\Delta TC}{\Delta X} = MC \qquad \text{and} \qquad \frac{TC}{X} = AC,$$

then

$$E_c = \frac{MC}{AC} \gtrless 1.$$

E_c is thus defined as the ratio of marginal costs to average costs. When $MC = AC$, $E_c = 1$.   When $MC > AC$ and $E_c > 1$, we are to the right of the minimum AC point on our U-shaped AC curve.   When

$MC < AC$, with $E_c < 1$, we are to the left of this minimum point. Hence output is most responsive when $E_c < 1$. If $E_c = 1$ at every output level, then the MC curve would be a horizontal line, fused with a coincident AC curve; the TC curve would be a straight line running upward to the right from O. If MC rises steeply, as does a J-shaped curve, then E_c will take on infinite values, testifying to the difficulty of expanding output. In practice it ought not be too hard to ascertain the actual E_c values.

The Elasticity of Supply

As a companion measure to that of the elasticity of total costs there is the older and more familiar notion of the elasticity of supply (E_s). If we define a supply curve as showing the quantities offered for sale at the different prices, and (in the normal case) as sloping upward to the right so that greater quantities are offered for sale at higher prices, then the elasticity of supply relates the proportionate increase in output to a relative change in price. The measure may exceed or be less than unity. Thus:

$$E_s = \frac{\Delta X/X}{\Delta P_x/P_x} = \frac{P_x \Delta X}{X \Delta P_x} \gtreqless 1,$$

where X denotes the quantity of output and P_x the market price, while the Δ's refer to increments of each. Whereas the elasticity of total costs relates the ratio of the proportionate increase in the total costs of the firm to the proportionate increase in output, the elasticity of supply, for the firm, relates the relative output change to a slight proportionate price change. Supply offerings under competition will be shown later to depend upon the marginal-cost curve, in which case the supply curve will be reinterpreted as being compounded of the marginal-cost curves of the various firms.

In Figures 5A and 5B it can be proved that, geometrically, E_s is equal to the ratio MR/JR, where PR is drawn from OY as a tangent to a relevant point on the market-supply curve and extended upward in the chart field by the chord RS. The other points, as lettered, can always be located. When the ratio MR/JR exceeds unity, so that there is a relatively large output expansion with a slight price change, supply is described as elastic; when the ratio is less than unity but greater than zero, supply is termed inelastic, denoting but a slight increase in output in response to the price change. When the market-supply curve becomes horizontal, because the MC curves of each firm are horizontal, supply will be perfectly elastic, with the ratio MR/JR assuming infinite values.   If output is completely inflexible beyond a certain production, so that the supply curve is perfectly vertical, the measure becomes zero.

For a simple diagrammatic test of the elasticity of supply, draw a tangent to the point in question, extending the tangent until it intersects an axis.   If the tangent intersects OX supply would be inelastic, for this would imply that the tangent would intersect OY at a negative ordinate, as in Figure 5B.   If the tangent intersects OY at a positive ordinate value, supply is elastic, as in Figure 5A; if the tangent passed

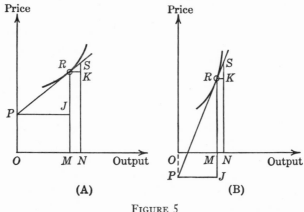

(A)   (B)

FIGURE 5

through O supply would be of unit elasticity: a relative change in price would expand output in the same proportion.   When the measure takes a negative value, because of a supply curve that falls to the right, supply price is decreasing; supply is overwhelmingly elastic.   The measure MR/JR is derived as follows.   By definition,

$$E_s = \frac{MN}{OM} \div \frac{KS}{MR} = \frac{RK}{KS} \cdot \frac{MR}{OM} = \frac{PJ}{JR} \cdot \frac{MR}{PJ} = \frac{MR}{JR},$$

for, by similar triangles,

$$\frac{RK}{KS} = \frac{PJ}{JR}.$$

The MR/JR measure reveals that even for linear supply curves elasticity will differ from point to point: in the upper reaches, whether the linear supply curve originates on OX or OY, the elasticity approaches unity; the E_s of an initially elastic linear curve would thus diminish, inasmuch as the addition to the numerator MR would be smaller than the addition to the denominator JR.   Conversely, for an initially inelastic linear curve the elasticity would increase, approaching unity in the limit.*   Comparing the elasticity of different supply curves at the same price height, so long as the tangents drawn to the separate curves emanate from the same point on OY, the elasticities will be equal. When the tangents to the curves are parallel at the same price, the curve farther to the right will have a lower elasticity.

BIBLIOGRAPHICAL NOTE

Besides the references of the preceding chapter, on the cost and total product curves, see the extensive exposition of G. Stigler, *The Theory of Price*, Chapter 8.   In shaping modern ideas on cost phenomena for the firm, the series of articles in the *Economic Journal* on the "representative firm" to which Sraffa, Young, Shove, Pigou, Robertson, and Harrod contributed, between 1926 and 1933, were rich and suggestive.   There is much to be learned from them even at the present time.   The elasticity of productivity is discussed in Allen, *Mathematical Analysis*, p. 263 and Carlson, pp. 17–21. Objections to the concept of "returns to scale" being viewed merely as a matter of factor proportions are indicated in Boulding, p. 492 and, at greater length in E. Chamberlin, "Proportionality, Divisibility and Economies of Scale," *Quarterly Journal of Economics* (February 1948).   Various concepts of diminishing returns are elaborated in G. M. Peterson, *Diminishing Returns and Planned Economy*.   Special studies of the production function and the law of variable proportions are: O. L. Williams, "Suggestions for Constructing a Model of a Production Function," *Review of Economic Studies* (1933–1934), and J. M. Cassels, "The Law of Variable Proportions," in *Explorations in Economics in Honor of F. W. Taussig*.   Economies of scale were further analyzed by A. N. McLeod, F. H. Hahn, and Professor Chamberlin in the *Quarterly Journal of Economics* (1949).

For the earlier and more important literature on the planning curve, consult M. F. W. Joseph, "A Discontinuous Cost Curve and the Tendency to Increasing Returns," *Economic Journal* (1933); J. Viner, "Cost Curves and Supply Curves," *Zeitschrift für Nationalökonomie* (1932), pp. 23–46; Roy Harrod, "Law of Decreasing Costs," *Economic Journal* (1931), and "A Further Note," *Economic Journal* (1933).   Also, the critical article of Professor Chamberlin on "Proportionality."   Plant flexibility is analyzed in the article of G. Stigler, "Production and Distribution in the Short Run," *Journal of Political Economy* (1939).

On the elasticity of costs, consult Allen, *Mathematical Analysis*, pp. 260-262 and, on supply, the thorough exposition of R. F. Fowler, "The Diagrammatical Representation of Elasticity of Supply," *Economica* (1938)

* This is amenable to simple mathematical proof.   Let k be the slope of a linear supply curve; the elasticity would thus be P/kX.   But k is equal either to $(P - a)/X$ or $(P + a)/X$, where a is a constant representing the initial height of the supply curve on OY. Ultimately a becomes extremely small relative to P so that $(P \pm a)/X$ approaches P/X. Thus the E_s measure approaches unity as P/X is substituted for k in the above measure.

Part II

MARKET BEHAVIOR

OF THE FIRM

Introduction

THE ANALYSIS OF DEMAND AND COST phenomena has provided a stepping-stone for investigations into the theory of price, for the market manifestations evolve out of the mutual interactions of consumers and firms. Considering the influence of the firm as paramount upon price, Part II is built about its equilibrium adaptation in various kinds of sales markets. Sometimes the firm cannot exert any perceptible influence on price; in other cases it can. In still other instances it is able to affect price but chooses not to do so. Hence we shall have to classify several types of market situations faced by the firm. That it is the actions of the firm which command the major share of the attention in the theory of price determination, constituting the bedrock of the analysis, is an important departure from older views according to which prices were conceived as a resultant of impersonal and mechanistic market forces.

Unfortunately, the question of classifying market positions is still an unsettled issue; it has aroused an intense amount of controversy in recent years. Perhaps this conflict was inevitable in view of the practically simultaneous appearance of the two epochal works, on the equilibrium of the firm in nonperfectly competitive structures, by Mrs. Robinson and Professor Chamberlin. Some of the discord may evaporate with the curative effects of time, considering the substantial harmony, in technique and results, by these two investigators. Rather than rekindle this still smoldering fire by yet another restatement of the respective positions, it would seem better, at this point, to confine ourselves to explaining only the mode of classification adopted for our own work. The price analyses to come treat of basic problems conceded by all.

Historically, from the seller's side, the presence of a large number of sellers offering a homogeneous product, with any one seller providing only a very small portion of the total output, has formed the backbone of the idea of competition. Professor Chamberlin has aptly termed this *pure* competition, while to others it is homogeneous competition or atomistic competition. As there are n firms in the field, where n is a very large number, and as the products are homogeneous, the elasticity of substitution between the firm's product and the products of the remaining $n - 1$ firms, is infinite. Hence any one firm that named a price higher than that of its competitors would see its sales slump to zero. At the market price its demand curve would thus be infinitely elastic. Also, as its production outpourings are but a minute portion of the total supply, either lowering its price below that of the rest of the market, or raising it above, would for all practical purposes fail to affect the sales of the other firms; the cross elasticity of demand between the firm's price and the sales of the other $n - 1$ firms (conceived as a unit) would be zero.* As the firm could not drive the other firms' prices up by withholding its output, and as it would be unnecessary to lower prices below the market level to secure sales, the firm would abide by the market price. Chapter 5 is devoted to the equilibrium problem of the firm selling under these circumstances.

Alternately, the firm may recognize that the elasticity of substitution between its product and that of other firms, is for many consumers less than infinite, with the exact degree of substitution contingent upon the relative prices. Here the firm is producing a commodity differentiated

---

* Triffin compares the atomistic firm to another firm so that the cross elasticity is infinite. I have criticized this position at another place.

from the rest; it now has a measure of market independence, for there is no longer a definite market-price ceiling above which its sales sharply and discontinuously shoot back to zero. If the cross elasticity of demand between its particular product and that of any other firm is nil, this situation can be described effectively as a case of monopoly. Not only is the firm's demand curve relatively inelastic, but the situation is devoid of any important interrelations between the price policy of the firm and the market behavior of other firms. Chapter 6 is constructed on these premises.

Conceivably, two (or few) firms may be producing a product that from the standpoint of consumers is homogeneous, so that the *MRS* between them is constant (and E_{ss} infinite). As n is now a small number, the supply offerings of any one firm may comprise a significant portion of the total; the cross elasticity of demand between the price policy of any one firm and the sales of the remaining $n - 1$ firms is finite. This is the characteristic problem of duopoly and oligopoly that comprises the subject matter of Chapter 7.

Similarly, the elasticity of substitution for consumers between the firm's product and that of other firms may be high but finite, rather than infinite, with the cross elasticity of demand between the firm and other firms also important. These instances are described as typifying monopolistic or heterogeneous competition, discussed in Chapter 8. Whenever the cross elasticity of demand is finite, as in oligopoly or monopolistic competition, we are in a network of circularity in market relations where the mutual interdependence of the respective firms must be stated.

The classification thus hinges upon the two criteria, of the size of the elasticity of substitution and the cross elasticity of demand. Schematically, the plan adopted can be represented in the following table.

TABLE 5. Market Positions

Market position	E_{ss}	$p_x E_y$
Pure Competition..........................	∞	0
Monopoly.................................	Finite—small	0
Duopoly—Oligopoly........................	∞	Finite
Monopolistic Competition..................	Finite—large	Finite

In both of the monopolistic situations, where the E_{ss} is less than infinite, the opportunity is open to the firm to enlarge its market by means of a sales campaign, as through advertising. This element furnishes the basis of Chapter 9. Similarly, because of a high cross elasticity of demand the firm may perceive the impracticality of a price reduction in advancing its sales because of the price retaliations of other firms; prospects of varying its product and modes of nonprice competition may appeal to it as more feasible methods of expediting sales. These phenomena are elucidated in Chapter 10.

Although most of the analyses of Part II are conducted with special reference to the firm, a buyer, in some cases, may dominate a particular market. If there are numerous sellers and but one buyer we have monopsony, or buyer's monopoly. Two or few buyers occasion duopsony and oligopsony patterns. The conjunction of one buyer and one seller recreates the traditional conception of bilateral monopoly. Problems of this sort provide the content of Chapter 11. Curiously, the classificatory problem from the buyer's side has largely been ignored, although many of the same intricacies that mark monopoly positions would undoubtedly obtrude. The lack of devotion to these problems can be attributed to the intuitive belief that pure monopsony structures are less prevalent than monopoly structures. To balance out the discussion of Part II, and modify the typical hypothesis that different firms producing a homogeneous technical commodity are significantly influenced by even trivial price changes on the part of other firms, Chapter 12 deals with the geographical separation of firms and the spatial interdependence of prices. Besides contributing some realism, this analysis opens up some new matters.

We shall have to make reference to static, stationary and dynamic equilibrium, and to long- and short-run equilibrium. As these terms are usually as germane to one market structure as to another, we might clarify them here, to indicate the usage intended. It is not a breach of faith to confess that equilibrium concepts are always unrealistic. And yet, however repellent such abstractions are to our sense of reality, the analysis is incomplete until it depicts the final position towards which individual markets, and the economic system, are impelled by the underlying forces.

Briefly, static analysis abstracts from time. The demand curve and the cost curves are taken to refer to the same time interval. Although there may be a past, future periods are disregarded, blacked out. Perhaps it may better be termed single-period analysis. The stationary state, on the other hand, envisages constant and repetitive supply and demand forces through time. Economic life is not really stilled: there is unvarying motion, with a constant output flow, constant consumer purchases, constant factor hire and constant factor incomes.* In dynamic analysis, change in the taste, income, and productivity data is of the essence: in a dynamic temporal equilibrium sequence, in each time interval the new changes are equilibrating. This involves a study of multiple time intervals.

The concept of long and short periods is due to Alfred Marshall. To Marshall, whether price problems were of the immediate, short-run, or long-run variety revolved about the nature of supply. When supply consists of a fixed stock of goods, there is an immediate market price problem. Regarding supply as a rate of flow from existing equipment or "facilities"—the productive resources within the industry—the price problem is viewed as a short-run phenomenon. Allowing more time, so that the stock of equipment and the number of firms could grow or contract, the price problem is a long-run conception. The construction thus has little to do with clock time; instead, it is erected upon the degree of fluidity in production adaptations.

Allusion will also be made to the concept of comparative statics. In this type of analysis, it is assumed that a (slight) change in demand or supply has occurred and that the system responds to the movement, frictionlessly clicking into equilibrium. The task then is to depict the final influence of the change, tracing the differences between the equilibria and ascribing these to the variation in the determining data.

A BIBLIOGRAPHICAL NOTE ON MARKET CLASSIFICATIONS

The relevant literature on the classificatory controversy consists of the following titles. The main works are of course those of Professor Chamberlin and Mrs. Robinson, in *The Theory of Monopolistic Competition* and *The Economics of Imperfect Competition* respectively. In Chapter IX of the later editions of his book, Professor Chamberlin summarizes his views and describes the controversy. See also his "Monopolistic or Imperfect Competition?," *Quarterly Journal of Economics* (1937). Mrs. Joan Robinson, in "What is Perfect Competition," same journal, (1934), can be said to have set the classificatory cauldron to boil; Professor Chamberlin replied to this article in 1937. Following this there appeared Nicholas Kaldor's "Professor Chamberlin on Monopolistic and Imperfect Competition," and the reply of Professor Chamberlin, same journal (1938). See also P. M. Sweezy, "A Note

---

* Professor Pigou has characterized this model as the stationary flow equilibrium, to emphasize the attribute of motion. *Employment and Equilibrium*, Chapter 10. To Professor Schumpeter it is the "circular flow" economy. (*Theory of Economic Development*, R. Opie, trans., Chapter I.)

on the Definition of Monopoly," same journal (1937); Felix Machlup, "Monopoly and Competition: A Classification of Market Positions," *American Economic Review* (1937).   One comparative study of the distinctive features of the conceptual schemes of the two chief participants was promulgated by Horace G. White, "A Review of Monopolistic and Imperfect Competition Theories," *American Economic Review* (1936).

A stimulating and relatively new approach was advocated by R. Triffin, *Monopolistic Competition and General Equilibrium Theory*, Chapter III especially.   Some criticism of his ideas is presented in my article on "The Classification of Market Positions," *Quarterly Journal of Economics* (1942); Dr. Triffin's reply is in the same issue.   E. F. Beach has suggested some additional criteria to accompany Triffin's classificatory scheme in "Triffin's Classification of Market Positions," *Canadian Journal of Economics* (1943).

A condensation of older ideas on the subject of monopoly and competition appears in H. L. Moore's volume on *Synthetic Economics*, pp. 13–15.   See also the comments of Henry Schultz in a review article, *Journal of Political Economy* (1937), pp. 262–265.

CHAPTER 5

Pure Competition

In PURE COMPETITION THE FIRM IS conceived to be unable to influence market price. Supposing the firm strives to maximize its profits, the first market problem is that of the firm acting to dispose of the most profitable amount of its fixed holdings at the externally determined market price. Next, the problem is that of producing with its present facilities the most profitable output volume, while through time the firm must reach a decision on installing the volume of equipment and producing the amount of output that promises it maximum profits. These several aspects of the adaptation of the firm under competitive conditions will be discussed in this chapter. In each phase of the investigation (since the individual firms selling the same commodity comprise an industry, which can be defined without ambiguity or arbitrariness) we shall also be interested in the equilibrium of the larger group as well as of the firm. Concepts of stable and multiple equilibria, as well as the notion of general equilibrium, will also be developed.

FIXED STOCKS OF GOODS

The first of the equilibrium analyses is that in which supply consists of a fixed stock of goods. The analytic problem is to depict the conditions of equilibrium for the firm and for the industry.

Equilibrium of the Individual Seller

As a simple problem in the theory of exchange under pure competition, let us suppose that an individual comes to the market with commodity Y and wishes to trade Y in return for commodity X. Being but one buyer among the numerous buyers of X, and one of the multitudinous sellers of Y, the individual is presumed to be powerless to influence the terms of the trade.   The quest on is that of ascertaining the number of units of Y that will be proffered and the quantity of X that will be purchased at each of the possible price ratios.

The indifference curves and the price-consumption line can aid us in solving the problem.   The indifference map expresses the individual's preferences for the two commodities.   Assuming his stock of commodity Y to be OM, his income or purchasing power consists of OM of Y.   Rotating several linear price lines from point M on the vertical axis, the price lines would indicate the purchase possibilities with respect to X and Y at the several prices; that is,, the amount of Y that is *retained* by the individual can be regarded as a market purchase of Y by the seller *from himself*.

At each possible exchange ratio the sales and purchases most satisfactory to the seller will be those quantities indicated at the point of tangency of price line and indifference curve, with the difference between the original OM amount of Y and the equilibrium amount of Y comprising the quantity exchanged at the market rate of exchange for commodity X.   When the market exchange ratio varies, and a series of price lines thus emanate from point M, the locus of the price-consumption line appears, describing the amounts of X bought and the amounts of Y retained (and also sold) at the successive prices.   If commodity Y is a superior good which the seller could not afford to consume when its price (and thus his income) was relatively low, or if X is an inferior good, as P_x falls the price-consumption curve may curl up toward OY, revealing that the seller will offer fewer units of Y as its exchange value rises.   This is tantamount to a smaller supply being offered at a higher price and is explicable in terms of a strong negative income effect for commodity X with a positive income effect for Y.

Rather than the seller trading his commodity for another one, the firm's typical problem is to exchange its holdings of goods for money. If we measure the goods on the vertical axis, and fix this quantity at OM, and measure amounts of money along the horizontal axis, indifference curves for goods and money can be created.   For each possible P_y (where $P_x = 1$) a price line can be rotated from M to a point on OX representing the maximum money sales proceeds for OM of Y at the going P_y.   The amount of the sales offerings of Y can be observed at each tangency point of price line and indifference curve.   Following the course of the price-consumption line, thereby learning of the amounts of Y unloaded at each P_y, the familiar supply curve of the firm can be elicited.   If the indifference curves between the Y commodity and money form vertical lines, indicating an infinite rate of substitution of money for the Y commodity and implying that well-being can always be raised by a pecuniary enhancement, then regardless of price the full Y commodity will be sold. The firm's supply offerings at the various possible prices will be constant, equal in amount to OM; the firm's supply curve will be perfectly inelastic.

Market Equilibrium; Fixed Stocks of Goods

Leaving the individual analysis and turning to the market equilibrium where stocks of goods are fixed, if we postulate tastes, incomes and

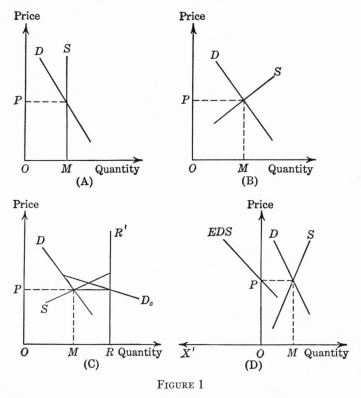

FIGURE 1

other prices as given, the demand quantity of commodity X for each individual at each P_x can be read off at the tangency points of the system of price lines to the successive indifference curves. By totalling the quantities wanted by each individual at each successive P_x, we can construct the market-demand curve. For the market to be in balance the price must equate the quantity demanded, D_x, and the quantity available, S_x; if sellers' demands for their own commodity are nil, the equilibrium price for the sale of the full stock must evoke a demand quantity for just that amount, neither more nor less. If sellers have their own demand at the respective prices, a supply curve can be built out of the quantities that they wish to dispose of at each price; the difference between the quantities offered and the full stock on hand will measure their withholdings at each price, evidencing a preference for the goods rather than for the money and other goods obtainable from the sales proceeds. Familiarly enough, the intersection of the demand and supply curves indicates the equilibrium price at which quantities wanted for purchase and quantities offered for sale are equal. (See Figure 1B.)

Individual and Market Equilibrium Conditions

Whatever the price and quantity sold, so long as consumers and sellers are informed of the going prices in the numerous markets and are impotent individually to affect market prices, the marginal rates of substitution among each pair of goods will equal the ratio of prices among the commodity pairs. This relationship must obtain at the equilibrium price, for it prevails *at each price point* on the demand curve for, say, commodity X (which thus also contains an implicit demand for commodity Y). In marginal utility doctrine, this condition of consumer equilibrium is expressed in the equiproportionate ratio between marginal utility and prices at each possible price, as

$$MU_x/P_x = MU_y/P_y = \cdots MU_n/P_n = R,$$

where MU refers to the marginal utility of a commodity, and R is the additional utility of an increment of income (money). Shifts in consumer expenditure will develop whenever this condition is unfulfilled, so that the position cannot be one of equilibrium.

In short, these are the dual conditions of market equilibrium under competition: (1) the market condition of an equality of the quantities supplied (S_x) and quantities demanded (D_x) at a common price, and (2) the individual conditions of equivalence between price ratios and marginal rates of substitution. Each consumer accepts the market price as a datum and orders his own purchase plan to conform to the price structure; in so doing the aggregate of consumers shape the market-demand curve and, with supply (which is also compounded of individual elements) determine the market price. Price, a datum to each individual participant, is thus a variable for the market.

Diagrammatic Illustrations

These ideas may be illustrated diagrammatically. In all of the diagrams of Figure 1, and in all supply-demand diagrams, prices are conventionally measured vertically and quantities horizontally.

Curve D represents the market-demand curve, denoting the aggregate quantities wanted by all consumers at each price. In Figure 1A, supply is perfectly inelastic, implying that sellers want to discard their full stock OM regardless of price; being devoid of any taste for the good they prefer money to any quantity of it. The supply curve is thus rigid, pursuing the path S above the output quantity OM. Market price must settle at OP, for if but one price is to rule this is the only price that will clear the market without a remainder of supply offerings or demand quantities.

Some flexibility of supply offerings is indicated by the supply curve in Figure 1B; depending on prices, sellers will offer varying portions of their total holdings. At each price some quantities will be withheld, either in the thought of more favorable future prices or because at the successive prices, the stocks withheld are preferred by the sellers for their own use compared to the additional income obtained from the sale of their full holdings. As OP is the only price at which $D_x = S_x$, it is the sole equilibrium price position, assuming that sales occur only at a single price within the time interval.

The facts implicit in the supply curve of Figure 1B are repeated in another form in Figure 1C. The total stock of the commodity on hand is OR; a vertical line RR' is drawn through this amount. The curves D and S are drawn on the same premises as before. But at each price there is added to the market-demand curve the "own demand" of sellers; in amount this is always the lateral difference between the total supply quantity OR and the quantity reflected on the supply curve S at each particular price. Mounting the sellers' demand upon the market-demand curve (the buyers' demand), we derive the *communal-demand curve* for the commodity, the DD_c curve of Figure 1C. This will intersect RR' at the price OP: quantity OM will be sold to buyers while MR will in effect be purchased, retained by sellers for their own use.* Besides disclosing that the supply curve is an inverted type of demand curve the analysis also reveals that each

---

* A communal-demand curve drawn on this basis is likely to have some strange "kinks" if the supply curve bends backward due to a positive income effect for the good by the sellers. The phenomenon of supply as reverse demand is often referred to as the "reversibility" of the supply curve. The sellers' own demand is also called the "reserve prices."

consumer will be able to command a greater stock of any good, and improve his own well-being, the closer the market-demand curve lies to the ordinate axis or the less the commodity is valued by other consumers. According to Figures 1B and 1C, sales will be numerous, and *consumer* well-being higher, the lower the sellers' valuation of the stocks they possess.*

Figure 1D describes the *excess* demand, or supply, of buyers, or sellers, at each price height. When the S_x quantities offered exceed the D_x quantities wanted at some price measured horizontally, the locus of *EDS* (the excess demand-supply curve) lies to the left of the vertical axis. When $D_x > S_x$, the *EDS* quantity will lie to the right of OY, while if $D_x = S_x$ the *EDS* curve will cross OY. Although *EDS* is drawn as linear in Figure 1D its actual shape will depend on the nature of the D_x and S_x curves. The locus of *EDS* also corresponds to that of DD_c in Figure 1C but the excess D_x or S_x quantities are now measured from OY rather than from the RR' line denoting the available market quantity.

The Equilibrium Position

In summary, let us review the results when the market equilibrium condition of $D_x = S_x$ is not satisfied. If the same situation tended to repeat itself through time, and if at the market price there is excess demand, price will tend to go up as buyers strive to acquire more of the good and as sellers perceive higher price opportunities. With excess supply, it is the sellers who scramble to regulate their inventory position. Neither position would be able to endure and price would have to yield. Only that price which equated the quantity offered and the quantity demanded could equalize the D and S forces.

VARYING SUPPLIES OF GOODS

In the second of our competitive analyses supply is regarded as a flow, with the amount of goods that sellers proffer for sale conceived as a variable, a resultant of the productive process. The amount of fixed factors engaged by the firm, which includes the stock of equipment, is posited as a datum. The expansion of the firm is thus limited to the hire of variable factors. Imposing this restriction on the firm, and if the number of firms is simultaneously held rigid, then the ultimate

---

* Thus to Pareto the tastes of other consumers are an "obstacle" to the want-satisfaction of any one consumer (*Manuel*, pp. 155, 175). See also, Irving Fisher, *Mathematical Investigations in the Theory of Value and Prices*, pp. 44–51.

supply facilities of the industry are immediately bounded. In short, the initial analysis is confined to a firm possessed of fixed equipment faced by externally determined product and factor prices; the object is to describe the output volume that will be prepared for sale, assuming that the firm endeavors to maximize its profits.

The Output Equilibrium of the Firm

If we overlook any nonpecuniary motives, the equilibrium output of the firm is the output volume at which profits are a maximum, for when profits are at their peak the firm will be relieved of any incentive either to accelerate or curtail its output flow, but instead will seek to maintain its production schedule. In principle, whether it be pure competition or monopoly, it will always be profitable to expand output whenever the addition to total revenue exceeds the addition to total costs caused by the output increase. Alternately, it will be lucrative to contract production when the total revenue drop is less than the dent in total costs. The change in TR is of course simply the marginal revenue, MR, while the movement in TC is obviously MC. Hence, whenever $MR \gtrless MC$, production plans will be rearranged. Maximum profitability, on the other hand, entails that $MR = MC$.

Recalling our formula for $MR \ (= P - X\Delta P)$, under pure competition where the firm can sell additional quantities of output without influencing market price the $X\Delta P$ portion of the formula vanishes, so that $P = MR$. The condition for maximum profitability of the firm is thus elongated under pure competition to the statement that

$$P = MR = MC.$$

This is the necessary condition of output equilibrium under pure competition on the presumption that the firm seeks to maximize its earnings. Generally, we can refer to it more succinctly as $P = MC$. It must not, however, be interpreted to mean that each entrepreneur consciously thinks in marginal concepts. Our condition is, instead, a property of the maximum-profit position. If profits are at a maximum under pure competition, whatever the computations are that led the firm to this output position, marginal cost *will be equal* to price.

To make sure that the output volume is one of maximum short-period profits rather than minimum losses, there is a supplementary proviso that must be attached, namely that price also exceed average variable costs.* Thus the full condition for maximum short-period

---

* This also guarantees that marginal costs are rising. If $MC = P$ while marginal costs

profits under pure competition may be written as

$$P = MR = MC \geqq AVC.$$

If the AVC curve sits everywhere above market price, the $(P = MC)$ position would be one of minimum losses rather than maximum profits. On a rising MC curve the full condition can be satisfied only to the right of the minimum AVC point. Through time, for the firm to remain in business under the ruling ownership and not succumb via bankruptcy, thus impairing the original capital investment of its owners, fixed costs must also be recovered. Otherwise, even if the firm continued production with its current equipment, its plant is unlikely to be replaced as it depreciates. The longer-period equilibrium would thus require the substitution of AC for AVC. In the following analysis this restriction engendered by the longer view will be waived.

Diagrammatic Illustration

To illustrate these relations, MC and AVC curves are drawn in Figure 2A along with a price line PP', which is indicative of a market

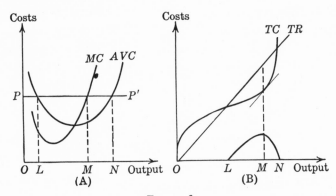

FIGURE 2

price external to the firm and beyond its control. Output would thus be OM, for at any other output level the firm would fail to maximize its profits. Producing less than OM, the OP addition to total revenue of a further unit of output would exceed the MC addition to total costs: it would be profitable for the firm to step up its output rate. Beyond OM, where $MC > OP$, the firm would deem it prudent to curtail its production schedule. OM, therefore, is the equilibrium output; at

---

are falling, the position would be one of minimum profits, rather than one of maximum profits or minimum losses.

this output volume the impulse to advance or contract production disappears.

At all outputs greater than OL and less than OM the supplementary condition of equilibrium is satisfied; namely, $P > AVC$. As short-period profits occur at all outputs between OL and ON, this condition by itself would hardly afford an unequivocal directive for the most profitable production policy, since it leaves the most profitable output level undefined; in contrast, as long as $P > AVC$, then the $P = MC$ point does indicate immediately, under pure competition, the most profitable of all output levels. When $P < AVC$ at all output levels the firm would withdraw from production entirely. The difference $P - AVC$ at the $P = MC$ output can be regarded as the unit earnings available to meet fixed costs and profits, while the product $OM(P - AVC)$ can be viewed as the total earnings that can be allocated for profits and fixed charges. If we draw in the AC curve, which includes the long period fixed charges, we can see that this would not affect the equilibrium output. So long as $P > AC$ at output OM, fixed charges will be covered.

Solution by Means of Total Revenue and Total Cost Curves

It has been shown that it is uninformative, so far as the position of maximum profits is concerned, to advocate that the firm produce an output at which $P > AC$; inasmuch as this is true at numerous outputs, this statement would leave the solution overly determinate. Another frequent error is to suggest that the firm ought to produce the volume of output at which its AVC (or AC) is a minimum. The fallacy can be detected when we realize that the aim of the firm is to maximize its profits rather than to minimize its unit costs. The output indicated at the minimum point on the AC curve will be the most profitable one only if market price is at the minimum AC level so that $MC = P$ at the minimum AC point. AC will then be tangent to PP' at the output at which $P = MC$.

The output of maximum profits can also be described by TR and TC concepts and curves. The problem can be posed as one of rendering

$$TR - TC = \text{maximum.}$$

In Figure 2B, as price to the firm is constant, TR is linear and rising.* TC, of normal form, is also included. Subtracting the ordinate differences of these two curves, the total-profit curve, the LN path, is also drawn. This reaches its maximum at output OM, although profits are

---

* For each price another linear TR curve can be drawn.

noted between output volume OL and ON. Following the course of TR and TC it can be shown that at M output the slope of TC is the same as that of TR, signifying that $MR = MC$ and also, in this case, that $P = MR = MC$. This is a characteristic of maximum profitability, whether the businessman makes his computations by subtracting totals, or calculates first unit profits and then total profits, or thinks in marginal terms. If profits are maximized then $MR = MC$.

Rather than drawing only the TC curve, we could also insert the TVC curve in Figure 2B. As the TVC curve is parallel to that of TC, at OM output its distance from TR would be greatest and its slope would be the same as TR, indicating that $MC = MR$. Translating this in commonsense terms, we can observe the subordinate role of fixed costs. For insofar as a firm maximizes the difference $TR - TVC$ it will garner the largest sum possible for covering TFC and for distribution as profits. As TFC is the same whether output is zero, one unit, or an infinite amount, TFC cannot influence the most profitable output position. Movements in TVC, however, with those of TR, are decisive in this respect.

Equilibrium Factor Hire

The condition of equilibrium factor hire for the firm selling in a competitive market is also worth elucidating. Essentially, it is an alternative mode of expressing the output equilibrium condition for the firm, because when we have determined the factor hire the output volume is implicitly determined, and vice versa.

As in the earlier expansion-path analysis, factor prices are assumed constant. Variable factors, it was concluded, would be hired at each output in the amounts indicated along the expansion path. Consequently, at each output level we have

$$\frac{MP_a}{MP_b} = \frac{P_a}{P_b}, \quad \text{and} \quad \frac{MP_a}{MP_c} = \frac{P_a}{P_c}.$$

Alternatively,

$$\frac{MP_a}{P_a} = \frac{MP_b}{P_b} = \frac{MP_c}{P_c} = J.$$

Multiplying each marginal product by the market price of output, P_x, we have

$$P_x \frac{MP_a}{P_a} = P_x \frac{MP_b}{P_b} = P_x \frac{MP_c}{P_c}.$$

Terming the product $P_x \cdot MP$ the *marginal-value product* (abbreviated MVP), it will pay the firm, under competitive conditions, to hire additional factors so long as their marginal-value product exceeds their price, or whenever the last set of ratios exceed unity, for then the factor will add more to the value of output than to total cost. Hence if $MVP_a > P_a$, more of factor A will be hired.* Conversely, if the marginal-value product lies below the factor price, some units of the factor will be released. Maximum profits thus require an equality of MVP_a and P_a or a value of unity for the preceding ratios.

But this entails that $P = MC$. In proof, we add the numerators and then the denominators of the last set of ratios. If we do so, the ratio of numerator to denominator will be unchanged. Thus:

$$\frac{P_xMP_a + P_xMP_b + P_xMP_c}{P_a + P_b + P_c} = \frac{P_xMP_a}{P_a} = \frac{P_xMP_b}{P_b} = \frac{P_xMP_c}{P_c}$$

If we select an amount of the several factors sufficient to produce but one unit of output, so that

$$MP_a + MP_b + MP_c = 1,$$

then

$$\frac{P_x(MP_a + MP_b + MP_c)}{P_a + P_b + P_c} = \frac{P_x}{P_a + P_b + P_c}.$$

When the sum of MP's and the ratios of value products to factor prices is unity, then

$$P_x = P_a + P_b + P_c.$$

But the left-hand component is simply the market price, while the elements on the right comprise marginal costs. Thus, when the marginal-value products coincide with factor prices, $MC = P$.

Market Equilibrium

Building on this idea of the output equilibrium of the firm we can deduce the market-supply curve. Whatever the market price may be, we now know the output volume that will be rendered by each firm. Guiding the horizontal price line PP' of Figure 2A parallel upward or downward would reveal that output volumes greater or less than OM would be offered in the market as the market price fluctuates. The

* As MVP is equal to the marginal product of the factor multiplied by the selling price of the product, when other factors are fixed the MVP curve is the marginal-product curve of Figure 2A, Chapter 4, transformed in the chart field only by the market-price multiplier.

MC curve is thus literally the firm's supply curve under competitive conditions.*

This condition will be true of each firm. By aggregating at each price the quantity offerings of the individual firms we can construct the market-supply curve: this is compounded out of the lateral output distances on each firm's *MC* curve at each particular price. It should be recognized, however, that this unique association of the market-supply curve and the aggregate of the individual-firm *MC* curves is valid only on the maximum-profit hypothesis and in stationary conditions, or with anticipations that price will remain unchanged; for then, whatever the price, the firm will produce its maximum-profit output volume and proffer all of it for sale on the belief that the price will persist. Another attribute of this market-supply curve that must be stressed is that each point on the supply curve now refers to a rate of production per unit of time and that at each market price $P = MC$ for each firm. Previously the supply offerings came from existing stocks at each price; now each price is conceived to evoke a particular quantity of output. Construed as representing output flows, a new vitality is imparted to the supply curve, enhancing its use in the more realistic problems.

With the lateral sum of the *MC* curves shaping the aggregate market-supply curve, the condition of market equilibrium when supplies are variable and buyers and sellers are numerous can be summarily described. Figure 1B contains the appropriate diagram: market price is located at the ordinate height of the intersection of the *D* and *S* curves. But whereas the earlier price analysis pertained to the equilibrium price of a fixed stock of goods, the system has now been opened to output flows: each price point is conceived to precipitate the corresponding rate of production on the supply curve in each unit of time, while each point on the demand curve details the amount of purchases at that price over the same time interval. Thus the $D_x = S_x$ position refers to an equality in the rate of purchase and production over the same time span. However long or short we draw our time interval, so long as conditions are stationary the annual *D* and *S* curves will be twelve-fold projections of the monthly curves, and fifty-fold extensions of weekly curves, etc. Allowing for some flow variation, such as weekly or seasonal movements within the stationary continuum, the

---

* A firm holding part of its output for its own consumption can be viewed as *buying* at the market price.

stationary time period ought to be so chosen that each later time length is a replica of the preceding one.

The condition of output equilibrium for the firm has been shown to require $P = MR = MC$, while that for the industry entails that $D_x = S_x$, or that the flow of output from all firms at a particular price equals the rate of purchases of all buyers. In order for the output decisions of firms to be consistent with the market equilibrium it must be presumed that all firms estimate in advance, as the basis for their output volume, the price that does rule later as the equilibrium price for the industry. If other than the market price is expected, and production plans executed on these estimates, even though it is conceivable that the equilibrium price for the industry is achieved the individual firms will not have been successful in their forecasts and will alter their output volume, despite the fact that the underlying cost and market-demand conditions are unchanged through successive periods.

VARYING AMOUNTS OF EQUIPMENT

So far the analysis has been confined to the output equilibrium of existing firms. Besides neglecting the entry of new firms the analysis has been silent on the matter of the current firms' augmenting or depreciating their equipment mass. In introducing these elements we are immediately thrust into long-run price analysis. Whatever the time length of our supply curve, the output forthcoming at each price appeared from a particular equipment array. Comparing this supply curve with one pertaining to a similar time length in the further future, there are opportunities for firms to penetrate the field or to depart from the industry, to augment their facilities or to allow them to deteriorate. Alterations in the plant facilities of the industry will exert a profound influence upon the supply curve. In general, an expansion in the number of firms and in the stock of ready equipment ought to push the supply curve to the right. Price, through time, ought to fall unless there is an expansion in demand. The converse propositions would also be valid. To show this is to embark on the third of our price analyses.

The Maximum Layout: Stationary and Competitive Conditions

Let us study the problem as it presents itself at its inception to a firm that is considering the equipment volume that is most profitable prior to ordering its erection. At this stage we assume that the product price in the output sector pierced by the firm is subject to pure competition and that, as conditions are stationary, the firm envisages that this price will remain constant.

Recalling our planning curves of Figure 4, Chapter 4, we can superimpose on any of the diagrams a horizontal line to depict the level of market price. Typically, profits will be maximized at the output and for the layout at which the *MCP* curve intersects the price line. It would be to the entrepreneurs' advantage, therefore, to erect the layout indicated on the *ACP* curve at the $P = MCP$ output. If the *ACP* is discontinuous, there may be several intersections of P and *MCP*; we would then be interested in the one equality conveying maximum profits. One further restriction must be injected in order that the size of the firm under pure competition is not indeterminate, namely, that the *ACP* curve be of U-shape, reaching a minimum and then rising. Figure 4A is thus precluded from consideration at this stage. Figure 4B contains the valid illustration.

Manifestly, even under competition the layout chosen may be "larger" than the plant that minimizes *ACP*. The minimum *ACP* point is important only because new firms would renounce their efforts to penetrate the field unless price promised to exceed this minimum level. But if price was expected to be permanently higher than this minimum *ACP* sum, conceivably with a larger layout a larger profit sum could be amassed. But this would entail that other firms are unable to enter and select the equipment consonant with the minimum *ACP* point, and thereby drive down market price while securing a permanent niche for themselves in the field. Hence the selection of an equipment volume or layout that is larger than that embodied in the minimum *ACP* point foreshadows differences in entrepreneurial abilities, or opportunities, or mistaken calculations in the entry plans of other firms.

The planning curve has been linked to a firm considering entry and building a new plant. Some of the analysis might pertain to a firm already operating and possessed of productive facilities but pondering whether it should augment (or diminish) its stock of equipment. The problem of organizing a new firm and building completely anew involves a movement from zero plant to a positive plant size; the problem now is that of altering the plant size. In developing this aspect of the analysis we must assume that one of the *AC* curves that moulds *ACP* is already a reality, and that the successive *AC* curves evolve from the combination of new facilities plus old. Starting from any of the *AC* curves in Figure 4, Chapter 4, if we include the old plus new capital costs (besides all other costs) in the new AC curve that lies to the right of the old, if total profits with the new plant exceed those with the old the expansion will be warranted. As an alternative formulation of the problem, if new capital charges on borrowed sums are excluded from the cost calculation (although depreciation is included), and if the additional earnings with the additional equipment exceed the rate of interest, the installation will commend itself. The effect of the plant construction, however, will be to shift the entire AC curve.

Entry Equilibrium of the Industry

There is a further aspect of the theory of competitive entry that ought to be unraveled—namely, the conditions of equilibrium with respect to entry. Normally it is declared that the entry of additional firms will cease when the new firms are unable to earn "normal" profits. Including normal profits as a long-period cost (and thus assuming them to be contained in the cost curve), when the current number of firms are earning normal profits the U-shaped AC curve of firms acting under the rule of competition will be tangent to the price line, as in PP' Figure 2A, Chapter 5, with the tangency occurring at the minimum AC point.

Again we run into the chronic antithesis—that existing between the expected and the actual, between estimates and events. It may be that new firms cannot earn normal profits so that, by objective criteria, we can declare that the industry is in equilibrium. Yet if the equilibrium condition is invoked in order to describe the conditions under which entry will cease, the current level of profit normality is irrelevant; for so long as entrepreneurs of new firms *believe* that a profitable level of earnings will ensue, they will not cease their efforts to enter. Contrariwise, the facts may disclose abnormal profits. Nevertheless entry may be stifled through ignorance, erroneously pessimistic forecasts, or impediments in the loan markets.

Judged therefore, by the number of implemented decisions to enter, the industry may suffer perpetual shocks and chronic instability as entrants endeavor to carve a spot for themselves in the field despite subnormal profits of existing firms. Or an immanently normal profit structure may be destroyed and transformed into losses by the endeavors of new firms to penetrate the field. Hence the concept of equilibrium, in the sense of an absence of inherent forces that attract new firms and new entrants, is not amenable to objective description in terms of an absolute level of profits. In the usual version the industry will be in equilibrium when only "normal" profits are being earned. But this entirely overlooks the motives underlying entry, the mental attitudes and prognostications of entrepreneurs. Rather than being susceptible to meticulous arithmetical calculation, everything hinges on the vision of the individuals who appraise the future prospects in the diverse fields. Situations that would be unattractive to most bystanders might still act as a powerful magnet upon others. Or, whatever the truth of actual profit opportunities, if individuals are dubious of their ability to earn profits, entry will be delayed and numbers in the field will be "normal" and in "equilibrium," entirely aside from the actual facts on profits. Objective criteria would be meaningful only in a stationary world where the future was expected by all interested participants to remain unchanged and where unfolding events proved the correctness of their prognostications.

Exit as a Subjective Phenomenon

Just as the level of profits that invite entry is a subjective phenomenon dependent on forecasts, the forces conditioning the exit and the economic demise of a firm are likewise mental estimates of the future. There are, however, certain differences; for when a firm is in the conjectural stage its ability to enter depends not only on its profit forecasts but on its capacity to command capital funds, something usually taken for granted in the literature. Once in the field, however, the firm will continue production so long as sales proceeds can be made to exceed at least total variable costs by a margin equivalent to earning prospects on the current market value of the fixed equipment in an alternative field. Even if earnings are "normal" or "subnormal," in the sense that a given entrepreneur does not feel prospects are conducive to his entry if he were again faced with the opportunity of coming into the field, the level of earnings at which the same individual will leave the field is probably lower. The expected level of profits that fosters entry is probably greater than the sum that precipitates exit.

Pure Competition and Entry

The matter of entry must not, however, be confused with that of the purity of competition. As long as there are innumerable buyers and sellers of the product acting individually rather than in concert, a purely competitive price will be the upshot. If homogeneous entry into the field is possible, and if new firms do embrace the opportunities, the effects of the entry of innumerable new firms will betray themselves in a rightward shift in the supply curve and thus in a fall in market price and in profits of firms already ensconced in the industry. The entry then can be associated with the degree of perfection of the equilibrium and competition; it is superfluous, however, to the concept of pure competition. Likewise, if present members of an industry dissolve and disappear, closing out their productive activities, unless the exit is on such a scale that the remaining sellers are too few for competitive price making, the exit also is irrelevant for the concept of pure competition. Questions of the opportunities for homogeneous entry, of the obstructions placed in the path of new firms, of aversions to and preferences for heterogeneous entry, will have their implications on the level of prices, the level of profits for the contemporary firms, and on the nature and variety of goods produced to satisfy consumer wants. For if homogeneous entry is blocked while heterogeneous entry is unfettered, new firms will resort to the production of imperfect rather than perfect substitutes. If we agree to categorize the perfection of competition by examining the conditions respecting entry, any obstacles to new firms, whether they be psychological or objective, will occasion imperfections in competition. The equilibrium can then be described as one of pure but imperfect competition.

The Irreversibility of Supply

Whatever the forces which provoke it, the expansion of the stock of equipment within the industry will shift the entire market-supply curve; the effects of the additional equipment on the economy will linger until it wears out and disappears from the productive scene. Thus as equipment expands in response to a rightward shift in the demand curve, say from D_1 to D_2, the supply curve in Figure 3B is successively dislodged to S_1, S_2, S_3. Connecting the various points of intersection of each D and S curve we derive the "long-run" path of adjustment of supply to demand, represented by the curve RN. This need not be a continuously upward-sloping curve, for as new firms enter (or old firms expand) production costs may fall; the curve RN of Figure 3B is but one possible picture of falling long-run supply price. If after its initial growth the market-demand curve shifts leftward because of a sudden aversion to the product, so long as the equipment is on hand S_3 will be the relevant short-period supply curve. As the stock of equipment in the industry is likely to depreciate and be withdrawn from the field in a manner different from the order of its introduction, RN is unlikely to represent the path of contraction. Hence *RN*, the long-run supply curve, is "irreversible" as compared to the reversibility of each *S* curve that portrays the price-quantity relations for both expansion and contraction with the existing array of equipment. Each point on *RN* should be interpreted as the "long-run" output if the corresponding price is perpetuated.

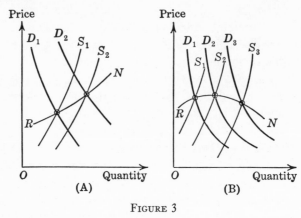

FIGURE 3

External Economies

Undoubtedly it is perplexing to find that *RN*, the long-run supply curve, is downward-sloping. When we study this phenomenon we see that it is attributable to very special causes. For example, there appears to be little reason why resources required by the firms decline in price as the industry widens; the contrary would appear to be the more logical result. Moreover, if factor prices altered, *all* short-period supply curves would move rightward—not only those attributable to the new entry. Conceivably, however, as the industry expands a host of specialist industries may come into being to service the common needs of this industry. Perhaps, because of indivisible agents, demand for these specialist services may have been too small before the industry growth to permit any firm that catered to the trade to operate profitably. This may explain the falling long-run supply curve. Following Marshall, to whom the concept is due, we designate these cost changes as "external economies." Diseconomies can be charged to rising factor costs due to the more intensive demand for productive factors.

STABLE AND MULTIPLE EQUILIBRIA

After the study of equilibrium positions, questions of the stability of the equilibrium relationship and the possibility of multiple equilibrium values invite our scrutiny. In the stability analysis we inquire whether the system contains forces strong enough to restore the equilibrium relationships when either output or market price accidentally deviates from the $D_x = S_x$ equality. Fascinating though it is, the stability study is not an end in itself. Instead, by exposing the recuperative forces in the system when once the structure is pushed slightly ajar, we ought to discover how the economy responds at least to minor shocks in the form of slight changes in either the D or S data. Unless the system can right itself for small disturbances, in the guise of nonequilibrium prices and quantities, while the underlying forces are unaltered, there can be little assurance that an eventual $D_x = S_x$ position will be forthcoming when there is a real modification in D and S. The stability analysis thus constitutes an introduction to economic dynamics. We shall examine only the condition of stability of particular markets; if we locate each point on the market demand and supply curves on the hypothesis of equilibrium in other markets, this is the sole inquiry that we need undertake.

There are two possible minor disruptions to the equilibrium that we shall want to unravel; generally we can deal with them simultaneously: (1) a shock to the equilibrium structure by way of a price slightly above or below that indicated at the $D_x = S_x$ point; (2) output slightly in excess or smaller than the quantity reflected at the $D_x = S_x$ position. Briefly, the equilibrium will be perfectly stable if both the slight price or quantity disturbance sets forces in motion to restore the original $D_x = S_x$ price-and-output pattern. It will be completely unstable if, after either shock, the immanent D and S forces urge the system ever further from the initial $D_x = S_x$ point; it will be but imperfectly stable if movements in one direction are self-correcting while a departure in the other direction renders the system unstable. For a system in neutral equilibrium the new price-output location will perpetuate itself; the initial dislodgment invokes neither recuperative forces to recover the original position nor a further oscillation to a new point of rest.

Stable Equilibria

As we visualize the conventional downward-falling D curve and upward-rising S curve, an accidental price fall from the equilibrium price while the $D_x = S_x$ output continued to be offered would release forces strong enough to restore the equilibrium price. As $D_x > S_x$, or as there is excess demand at the lower price, the market pressures in a free market would drive the price upward. An increase in output would also carry its own corrective; the supply price would exceed the demand price for this larger output volume, and the fall in price and consequent disappointment of sellers' expectations would restrain future output, thereby serving to reestablish the earlier equilibrium. Analyzing a price rise or a decrement in output would also disclose stabilizing tendencies. We conclude, therefore, that the normal D and S field, with the demand curve downward-falling to the right and the supply curve upward-rising to the right, will presage a perfectly stable market.

Unstable Equilibria

A complete reversal of the normal position of the S and D curves, in Figure 4a, is the most obvious illustration of a completely unstable equilibrium. A rise in price while output is at the $D_x = S_x$ level will reveal an excess demand; despite the apparent market shortages at the higher price the subsequent decreased production would only intensify the rising price tendencies. Similarly, for an initial price fall the departure from $D_x = S_x$ would involve unsold stocks; despite the excess supply and falling price pressures, each fall in prices would only extend the excess-supply position and further unbalance the situation. Like results follow from either an increment or decrement of output. Quixotically, if both D and S have the same directional slope, as in Figure 4b, with the D slope steeper than that of S, the equilibrium will be fully stable for an output dislodgment despite the incongruous D curve, for at an output in excess of the equilibrium quantity, although market price will rise, there is excess supply, which would drive the price back, while below, for less than the equilibrium output, there is excess demand. However, if price, rather than output, accidentally rose or fell for the equilibrium output quantity, the results would be destabilizing. If the demand curve is of normal form while the supply curve falls, as in Figure 4c, the instability arises from an output departure from the equilibrium level. For a price fall, with the equilibrium output, there is, however, an excess demand, working to raise price, while for a price rise there is a deficiency of demand. Thus there may be price stability with output instability, or price instability with output stability.

Neutral Equilibria

Figure 4A contains an example of neutral price equilibrium; $D_x = S_x$ over the full price range P_1 and P_2. Any price in this area is possible and so the actual market price is indeterminate: neither a price rise nor fall would stir any recuperative forces. As an increase in output would drive price below P_1 while a decrease would lift it above P_2, price and output shocks also lead to independent results in this case. As an example of an output rather than a price indeterminateness

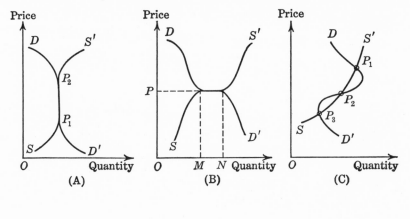

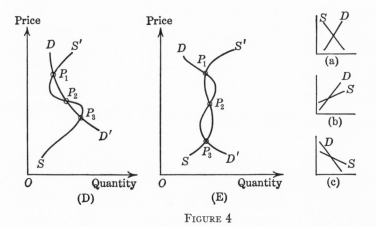

FIGURE 4

an alternate neutral equilibrium is portrayed in Figure 4B; for an output change the system is in neutral equilibrium between OM and ON, while for price movements it is stable.

It is easy to draw rather grotesque curves that purport to evidence instability. But the display of diagrammatic elegance is unconvincing unless we have reason to suspect that it represents some reality. For whatever comfort it may render, we can conclude that whenever the income effect is normal on the demand side, or whenever negative I

effects for one portion of the consuming public are counterbalanced by positive I effects of the remainder of the consumer body, the normal D curve will describe the course of market demand; from this side the stability conditions will then be fully satisfied. Analogously, when each firm's MC curve is rising because of diminishing productivity, stability from the cost side will ensue. When personal services are sold a positive income effect from those providing the service is a prerequisite for stability and the normal rising supply curve.* When these conditions are not satisfied the market may be either partially or entirely unstable.

The Correspondence Principle

Symbolically, the condition for perfect stability developed in this section can be written as follows. Denoting the excess D or S at a price P as D_E and D_p for the difference of demand and supply price for some output quantity X, then for perfect stability with respect to price and output dislodgments, we must have

$$\frac{\Delta D_E}{\Delta P} < 0, \tag{1}$$

$$\frac{\Delta D_p}{\Delta X} < 0. \tag{2}$$

With perfect stability both values are negative. From $D_x = S_x$ a fall in price must raise the excess demand, and an increase in output must widen the gap between supply and demand price. To be sure that price movements or adaptations in other markets do not derange the equilibrium position in the particular market, a price movement in some other commodity Y must not alter the excess demand for commodity X. Thus

$$\frac{\Delta D_E}{\Delta P_y} = 0.$$

If the equilibrium is perfectly stable, with D and S curves of normal

* Although a rising market-supply curve is usually likely, it is possible for the volume of services rendered to decline as price (and thus producer's real income) rises. Sellers may consume part of their own product, which they could not afford to do at a lower price and low income; in the field of labor, workers may prefer more leisure at a higher hourly wage rate to exerting the normal quantity of effort, thus decreasing the number of hours worked. For example, if an individual's demand for money is relatively fixed, an increase in wage rates may decrease the amount of labor available, because each wage earner would want to work fewer hours. The complaints against absenteeism in war industries in 1942 may have been attributable in part to the swollen wage rates in these fields. In principle this is evidence of a strong positive income effect for leisure and relatively small income demand for more commodities. The supply curve, where hours of work are measured on the horizontal axis, would tend to turn back to the vertical axis. (See SS' in Figure 4D.)

form, we can be sure that if D shifts to the right with S unchanged, P will rise and sales and output will be greater. Likewise, if S shifts to the right, with D unchanged, P will, in equilibrium, be reduced but sales and production will be enlarged. The stability analysis thus conveys some meaningful information relevant for comparative statics where only equilibrium positions are being analyzed and compared. A problem of dynamics, however, is that of tracing the path by which the new equilibrium is reached, and emphasizing the time required before the new balance obtains. Building on these ideas it becomes possible to regard the stability analysis as an excursion into dynamics. If we write ΔP for the change in price, and Δt for the passage of time, assuming that the equilibrium is perfectly stable, devoid of tendencies to fluctuate through time, then

$$\frac{\Delta P}{\Delta t} = 0.$$

Thus the stability analysis is revealed as an exercise in dynamics. In dynamic processes the value of this ratio will normally be other than zero; this congruence between economic dynamics and stability analysis has been termed the *correspondence principle*.*

Multiple Equilibria

The examination of neutral equilibrium disclosed some instances of multiple equilibrium. It is useful to pursue this analysis further, for it portends certain indeterminacies and certain elements of arbitrariness in even the competitive order. Figure 4C furnishes an illustration, with an abnormal backward-bending D curve typical of inferior goods. The normal supply curve, SS', thus intersects it at the three points P_1, P_2, P_3.

All three positions satisfy the equilibrium condition $D_x = S_x$. Depending on the price arrived at, the chain of substitutes and complements will be differently affected in this overdeterminate situation. Stable equilibria, however, are located at the extremities, at prices P_1 and P_3. At either P_1 or P_3 an increase in price would render $S_x > D_x$, while a slight fall would leave $D_x > S_x$. At P_2, on the other hand, a slight accidental price or output movement would set in motion a train of events that could not be deterred short of P_1 or P_3.

Multiple equilibria might also be ascribed to an abnormally shaped supply curve cutting a normal demand curve; Figure 4D is illustrative.

* P. Samuelson, *Foundations of Economic Analysis*, Part II.

Suppliers, perhaps, prefer leisure to income; consequently at higher prices they offer fewer services. Stable equilibria for slight price or output changes obtain only at the end points, P_1 and P_3, where an accidental rise in price would reveal an excess supply quantity and would exert pressure for a return to the original equilibrium position. When, as in Figure 4E, both D and S are abnormal, the end points are stable for a price rise but not necessarily for a (slight) output modification; for the latter the price adjustment might shuttle between P_1 and P_3. Parenthetically, it is to be observed that an abnormal S curve must, in its uppermost region, revert eventually to normal form as income opportunities become immensely attractive to present suppliers or to new suppliers entering the output fold. Much the same may be said for the lower stretches of the D curve: new lower income classes enter as buyers while previous purchasers can, with but a slight outlay, obtain a large amount of the commodity and by substituting this commodity for other products of even remote substitutability, they can free income for diversion to other "superior" goods.

GENERAL EQUILIBRIUM

The analysis of the equilibrium of supply and demand forces in particular markets can be extended to the entire system; so long as we are convinced that there is an equilibrium position for each market under the assumption that other markets are in balance there must be, under the assumed conditions, a total equilibrium for the entire system. The analytic method of focusing attention on one market while ignoring ramifications and repercussions in other markets is generally called *particular equilibrium analysis*, in contrast to *general equilibrium analysis*, which adumbrates the conceptual possibility of the simultaneous equilibrium of prices, purchases, and outputs in all markets besides demonstrating the interrelations between the separate markets.*

Few would quarrel with the proposition that an equilibrium between decisions to offer certain quantities for sale and decisions to purchase an identical quantity at the same price is possible in particular markets— in the sense that the price that sellers are willing to accept (while continuing to produce the same quantity) tends to equality with the price that consumers are willing to pay. That there is a balance between production and expected sales is attested by the fact that new

---

* What has been termed *particular equilibrium analysis* also goes under the name of *partial equilibrium analysis*. But there is nothing "partial" about the equilibrium; it is but a limited view of the system. Thus "particular" seems to be the more appropriate term.

output is generally sold, with unplanned inventory fluctuations being fairly small. And although this is but indirect and extremely tenuous evidence of economic order and competitive balance—for the world we know has its fill of both competitive and monopolistically determined prices—there is good reason to suspect that an approximate balance of expected and actual prices and outputs would be commonplace in particular markets in a completely competitive world, especially if the more violent swings of the business cycle were eliminated.

Presumably we might be ready to concede that particular equilibrium analysis divulges some fundamental tendencies in the economy, the end-results of market processes that secure a balance. But we are much more reluctant to concur in the view that all markets are in balance simultaneously; admitting the tendency in individual markets is still a long way from subscribing to the proposition for all markets simultaneously, over any period or even any moment of time. But once we acknowledge that in each particular market and in each sector of the economy that there are certain equilibrating forces at work, there is no sensible reason to shrink from the view that the entire system, or a good portion of it, can settle down in an equilibrium of supply and demand. In this light the abstraction and "famous fiction" of the stationary state is not without interest, for it describes the price and output tendencies within the entire economy over (short) periods of time when the fundamental data remain as postulated. Nevertheless, whatever violence the idea of general equilibrium does to our sense of reality, and even if we entirely reject it as an artificial image of the economic world, it is still incumbent upon us to demonstrate the conditions that need to be satisfied for the general equilibrium of production and consumption, and to explore the interdependence among markets.

Adjustments with. Successive Markets

Just as we draw D and S curves for commodity A, we can do the same for commodities $B, C, D \cdots$, etc. There are, however, certain complications. First, separate supply curves, with their cost-curve basis, can be drawn in each particular market; unique cost curves can be drawn for each firm so long as equipment is constant and input-output relations and factor prices are known.* For the demand curve

---

* There is a slight complication for nonintegrated output; we can assume either that prices of products purchased by one firm for use in its own output are constant, corresponding to the assumption of constant factor prices, or that (since all cost curves are known)

in each market, whatever the prices of all other commodities we can ascertain the quantity wanted of any particular commodity at each price.   Thus if we assume that only one good, commodity A, and another good, R (which is the money commodity) exist in the community, we can ascertain the quantity of A wanted at each price; the difference between the expenditure on A and the initial money supply of the purchasers corresponds to their demand for money which, added to the money receipts and initial holdings of sellers, equates the total demand for money to the total stock of it.   The equilibrium P_a for A can thus be deduced, P_r (the price of a unit of money in terms of itself) being simultaneously unity. R is thus the numéraire commodity, the standard of value in terms of which A is computed.   Introducing commodity B, and holding the money stock constant, there will be some repercussions in the A market: at each successively lower P_b, there will, say, be less of A wanted; for each possible P_b, therefore, we can draw a full demand curve for A and obtain the interlocked equilibrium price for that good, on the assumption that the B price is an equilibrium price. Allowing for a reciprocal variation in P_b with ΔP_a, thus recognizing the mutual interdependence among the two prices, we can fit that set of prices that equates $D_a = S_a$ and $D_b = S_b$.   As we introduce additional commodities, markets previously adjusted will be affected and their prices will have to be realigned; each price will affect every other price. Thus if through a change in demand one price varies, all of the interdependent prices will be shaken.   It is plausible to suppose that there is a set of prices for the system that will equate supply and demand in each of the markets, rendering excess demand or supply zero.   This will be the general equilibrium price configuration.*

If the demand for each commodity were independent of prices in other markets, or if consumer evaluations of alternate modes of expenditure were not a fact, the analytic problem would be enormously simplified; each S and each D curve could be drawn quite independently of other prices, and particular equilibrium analysis would secure its final sanction.   Its retention is most plausible, therefore, when each individual is spending but a small portion of his income on any one commodity for which there are no close substitutes; lower prices of the

---

the price of intermediate output is determinate at every output level of the product-using firms.

* It is conceivable that more than one price set will satisfy the simple equilibrium conditions—that there are multiple general price solutions.   We noted that multiple equilibria are possible in particular markets.

more remote substitutes would then scarcely compress the expenditure in any particular market. Similarly, if each purchaser modified his expenditure on a commodity only slightly as its price altered, and if each consumer transferred expenditure to or from a different commodity in response to price changes, the hypothesis of market independence would indeed be serviceable although it would ignore some very definite (if small) interrelations.*

Mutual Interdependence Illustrated

The process of mutual adaptation of prices to a consistent equilibrium can be illustrated, for the two-commodity case, by a pair of reaction curves; if the equilibrium relationships hold between all pairs of commodities they must be typical of all commodities simultaneously. In Figure 5 the price P_y is measured along the vertical axis and P_x, the price of commodity X, is measured along the abscissae. Selecting at random any arbitrary price of Y, we can locate a point on the chart field corresponding to the P_x which, in the light of the given P_y, establishes equilibrium in the X market. Plotting a series of these points, each time imposing a new P_y, we can draw the curve $_yP_x$, showing

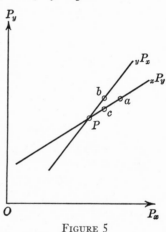

FIGURE 5

the variations in the equilibrium price of X as P_y fluctuates. If we take X and Y as substitutes, as the typical relationship in the system, each time that P_y rises P_x ought to move higher, since the demand curve for X shifts rightward, raising the price of this commodity. These being less-than-perfect substitutes, however, the coefficient of price interdependence, $\dfrac{P_y\Delta P_x}{P_x\Delta P_y}$, ought to have a positive value below unity, and so the elasticity of this curve ought to be less than unity. If the interdependence is extremely small then the $_yP_x$ curve will appear as an almost vertical line. It will usually originate on the horizontal axis, for even if P_y is zero, there will be a positive P_x.

Similarly, assuming P_x as the independent variable, a curve $_xP_y$ showing the equilibrium P_y values can be constructed, with properties

---

* It is not only the existence of taste interdependence but also the fact that entrepreneurs draw from the common pool of productive factors that gives credence to the notion of general equilibrium.

analogous to those of $_yP_x$. The coordinates of the point P, where the two curves intersect, denote a set of mutually consistent prices that are conducive to simultaneous equilibrium in both markets. At a P_x in excess of the equilibrium value, that implicit at, say, point a, the resulting P_y would be such as to drive P_x to that level implicit in point b. But this would provoke P_y to the level at c, etc. Each successive price adaptation thus draws the system closer to the mutually compatible price relations at P.

The Equations of General Equilibrium

Rather than rely on the verbal proof that general equilibrium is conceptually possible, the mathematical proof rests on the demonstration that for each price that is to be determined we have an equation. If the number of equations is equal to the number of unknowns then the results are deemed to be determinate; the counting of equations gives evidence that there is a set of prices that can establish simultaneous equilibrium in the several markets. Other properties of the structure of equations, such as the demonstration that the equations permit of only a unique set of prices, are regarded as a problem mainly of mathematics rather than of economics. The economic interpretation is often fairly simple.

If there are $(n + 1)$ goods in the economy, and if we select one commodity as money, as the standard of value (*numéraire*) in terms of which the prices of other goods are stated, then the price of this $(n + 1)$th good is unity: one unit of it represents one unit of "money." Thus for this good,

$$P_{n+1} = 1.$$

Letting b denote any one of the n commodities, for each of the n goods remaining we have a demand equation of the form

$$D_b = D_b(p_1, p_2, p_3 \cdots p_n),$$

a supply equation of the form

$$S_b = S_b(p_1, p_2, p_3 \cdots p_n),$$

and implying an excess demand equation of the form

$$E_b = D_b - S_b = E_b(p_1, p_2, p_3 \cdots p_n).$$

For the n commodities, there are n equations of this sort. The system is in equilibrium when the price configuration is such as to render the excess demand for each commodity, or the E_b equations, zero. When the excess demand for each of the n commodities is zero, then the demand and supply of the *numeraire* or standard commodity must also be equal; the excess demand for it must automatically be zero. For if each person has bought or sold the quantity of n goods that he wants to acquire or dispose of at the market price, he has simultaneously disposed of or acquired the quantity of the standard commodity that he wants to obtain at the market prices. Although the equations written above pertain only to the market structure, other equations could be written for the individuals comprising the market, showing the equalities that would have to be satisfied for both maximum individual satisfaction in consumption and maximum profits for the firm in production.

SUMMARY

The chief topics of this chapter were the demonstration of the equilibrium output of the firm under pure competition, following which was an exposition of the market supply curve as compounded out of the cost curves of individual firms. The competitive equilibrium was then redefined as entailing an equality between the rate of flow of purchasè and production at the market price, or at the quantity at which demand price and supply price were equivalent. The stability analysis and the general equilibrium concept were but supplementary aspects of this basic analysis of the market behavior of the firm.

In surveying the ground covered, it is appropriate to remark on certain of its implicit assumptions. In the output equilibrium of the firm it was presumed that the aim of the entrepreneur was to maximize pecuniary profits. As shown earlier, this also presumes that the entrepreneurial effort accompanying greater output is a costless psychological phenomenon. Undoubtedly this is in error. Conceding the irksomeness of organizing greater output volumes, it is unlikely that the $P = MC$ output will be forthcoming if to the left of this output amount the valuation of leisure exceeds that of the extra income to be derived from the greater production. Conversely, if the entrepreneur derives pleasure from production, even though profits are thereby diminished output would transcend the $P = MC$ profit-maximization norm. We may infer that the latter conduct will be relatively rare compared to the inertia checking output below the profit-maximization level.

Manifestly, auxiliary motives for other than the $P = MC$ output position would thus not be absent even under pure competition. We shall be able to distill many more reasons for nonmaximum profit output under monopoly; hence we may defer the formal presentation of the theory of nonpecuniary profit maximization until the ensuing chapter.

Another hypothesis vital to the theory is that the firm is able to command enough financial resources to equate MC to P, granting the absence of nonmaximum profit motives. Now even if all markets were purely competitive, in the sense that nowhere in the economy could a firm influence price, this hypothesis seems unwarranted. Before output can be produced, materials must be purchased, and variable factors must be paid in advance of the sales of their output. In fact, even fixed costs must usually be paid before the output is sold and cash received. Even if interest rates were competitively determined, there might still be barriers to the firm's borrowing the amounts appropriate to its profit maximization. With borrowing conceived of as entailing the sale of securities (that is, promissory notes of one kind or another), the market lenders may refuse to purchase the offerings of the particular firm. Lack of finance thus becomes a stringent limitational factor indeed. A theory of competitive output equilibrium that presumes unlimited borrowing opportunities, ignoring the obstacles in the way of securing funds to float the maximum profit output volume, is surely incomplete. Although we do nothing to repair the deficiency currently, it is well to note it and to be explicit about it. Pure competition in factor markets and product markets, while access to funds is limited, is an insufficient guarantee of the $P = MC$ output volume.

Analogously, in the theory of plant selection it is generally assumed that the firm is able to command whatever financial resources are necessary to enable it to order the volume of equipment that will maximize its profits. Merely stating this as the implicit proposition is sufficient to throw it under a cloud. Pure competition in selling products and hiring factors would never assure, by itself, access to funds for all entrepreneurs. Although more work remains to be done to demonstrate the economic significance of these limitations, it is an easy matter to see that they may prevent the erection by a new firm of the $P = MCP$ layout and restrain the $P = MC$ output tendencies of an active producing unit.

BIBLIOGRAPHICAL NOTE

For the theory of value under competition, with the stress laid upon the equilibrium of the industry, the great *Book V* of Alfred Marshall still commands universal respect. The theory of exchange, as one aspect of this analysis, is elaborated in the modern work of Hicks, Chapters IV and V. Also, J. Mosak, *General Equilibrium Theory in International Trade*, Chapters I and II. For the theory of the firm under competition, much the best treatment is to be found in the monopoly studies of Chamberlin and Mrs. Robinson. Most of the argument has by now been incorporated in the main stream of economic analysis, available at the textbook level.

The elucidation of supply as inverted demand, and the communal demand curve, was originally developed with typical thoroughness by P. H. Wicksteed in *The Commonsense of Political Economy* (L. Robbins, editor), Vol. II. The analogous concept of seller's reserve prices as accounting for the shape of the supply curve was formulated by H. J. Davenport, in his *Economics of Enterprise*, pp. 48–52.

An excellent account of the forces provoking entry and exit is given in the two-part article by F. Machlup, "Competition, Pliopoly and Profit," *Economica* (1942). On the stability of equilibrium, besides the chapters in Samuelson, there are Hicks, Chapter V; O. Lange, *Price Flexibility*, Mathematical Appendix; Lloyd Metzler, "Stability of Multiple Markets: the Hicks Conditions," *Econometrica* (1945); and the readable resumé in M. Reder, *Studies in the Theory of Welfare Economics*, Chapter IX. A discussion on Marshallian lines is given in A. C. Pigou, *Economics of Welfare* (4th edition), pp. 794–795. Marshall's own statement appears on pp. 345–346 of the *Principles*. Besides Marshall's own work and that of Pigou on the concept of external economies, see Howard S. Ellis and William Fellner, "External Economies and Diseconomies," *American Economic Review* (1943), as well as the older article by Allyn Young, "Increasing Returns and Economic Progress," *Economic Journal* (1928).

The history of general equilibrium theories is described in G. Stigler, *Production and Distribution Theories*. For a verbal statement of equation counting, see Hicks, pp. 59–61. Also, G. Cassel's *Theory of Social Economy*, Chapter IV. Mathematical analyses, as I. Fisher's *Mathematical Investigations*, A. L. Bowley's *Mathematical Groundwork of Economics*, as well as the older works of Walras and Pareto and the more recent statements of Hicks, Lange and Mosak, contain the equilibrium equations. A criticism of the monetary aspects of the older equations, and further references, will be found in Don Patinkin, "Relative Prices, Say's Law, and the Demand for Money," *Econometrica* (1948). A valuable development of his views is contained in a later article in the same journal (1949) on "The Indeterminacy of Absolute Prices in Classical Economic Theory."

CHAPTER 6

Monopoly

IN THIS CHAPTER WE BEGIN OUR studies of monopoly markets. So long as a firm produces a commodity regarded by consumers as distinct from other products, the door to monopoly pricing is open. The seller—or, impersonally, the firm or income-maximizing unit—will perceive that its demand curve departs from the horizontal and that its sales are a function of the price named. To forestall the characteristic features of monopolistic competition, the degree of market interdependence between the firm's product and that of any other firm is assumed to be virtually nil. It will then be the entrepreneur's privilege to name that price which maximizes the firm's income; no longer is it merely a matter of producing to sell at a price determined by the external, impersonal forces of the market. The task of price policy that devolves upon the entrepreneur will be a matter as vital from a profit standpoint as that of economical resource management. Using this as the main theme, we shall introduce at a later stage the likelihood and consequences of nonpecuniary motives.

A methodological comment is in order at this point. To impart a comparative flavor to our results we shall assume that the firm whose pricing policy is under scrutiny was formerly adjusted competitively, equating MC to P, and now undertakes to wield its monopoly power by proclaiming a price more productive of profits. This is the method of comparative statics. This approach is warranted not only because of our familiarity with the $P = MC$ pricing model but because it enables us to detect immediately some of the economic derangements caused by monopoly pricing. An unqualified analysis of monopoly price policy by one firm divorced from the concept of general competitive equilibrium, and extrapolated to the case of n firms, implies ultimately an entirely monopolistic world. More realistically, our procedure assumes that the world is partially competitive, with $P = MC$ firms

134

not uncommon, and partly monopolistic. This is closer to the facts, a more rewarding field for study.

Initially, aside from the monopoly-pricing venture we suppose that other conditions are unchanged: consumer tastes and incomes, factor prices, and input-output data are presumed constant. Also, the number of firms, the variety of outputs, and the stock of equipment of firms remain as before. Most of these hypotheses will be shelved as the analytic structure is opened.

Monopoly a Matter of Opportunity and Not of Motive or of Size

It should be underscored at the outset of our inquiry that monopoly — pricing is a matter not of motive but of opportunity. The objective of the firm is to maximize its earnings, whether it is selling in a competitive or a monopoly market. The difference is that under competition the firm is impotent to alter its market price, so it accepts the fact and adjusts its behavior in the light of it. Under monopoly the firm enjoys the power to name its sales price. In this sense, all firms would like to be monopolists, but in the nature of things such aspirations cannot be realized in certain fields. Nonetheless, the motives are the same—the pursuit of maximum profits and the diversion of as large a flow as possible of the income stream to the firm. Under competitive conditions the fulfillment of this objective through pricing policy is denied to the firm. Profit ends are the same for competitors and monopolists; means of fulfillment differ.

A corollary of this proposition is that it is an error to insist that monopoly is purely an aspect of the size of firms. Large firms, in industries that can absorb but few large firms, are likely to be monopolists.* But monopoly is not an attribute of the capital strength or productive capacity of the firm. Small firms, measured in terms of either volume of employment or the asset value of plant and equipment, may well be monopolists in the fundamental sense of price power. Small monopolies of this sort may, in the aggregate, cast a greater economic spell than the industrial giants whose price policies are open to public scrutiny and responsive to public feeling, and for whom it is thus often incumbent to moderate their price exactions. But the strength of these patterns can be appraised only by empirical inquiry: our remarks, however, should set our perspective, to focus on price policy rather than size. Size is frequently a source of productive economy; it would be a hollow improvement, say, to correct monopoly-

* Or oligopolists, as we shall later describe them.

pricing firms and practices only to replace them by the diseconomies of small scale production.

By the same token, the enormity or insignificance of profits has little to do with the notion of monopoly, even though the two are so frequently confused in public railing at monopoly. Large profits may accrue under pure competition. Conversely, the number of worthless patents and copyrights are legion; the losses of business firms with acknowledged monopoly power are also common. One proposition that might safely be made respecting monopoly and profits is that if demand is such as to assure profits to firms that price according to competitive formulas, then profits would be even greater with monopoly pricing. If production is unprofitable under competitive arrangements it may still be profitable under monopoly. But this is as far as we can go. It is far-fetched, however, to describe monopoly as a guarantor of profits.

MONOPOLY EQUILIBRIUM

Monopoly price and output can be portrayed neatly and summarily as a result of the insight afforded by the marginal revenue curve.

The Condition $P > MR = MC$

In pure competition the firm can sell as many units as it cares to at the going price; its demand curve is a horizontal line at a price height corresponding to the market level. Price (or average revenue) and marginal revenue are, to the firm's way of looking at them, identical. Recalling our formula for MR, since the $X\Delta P$ component is zero in pure competition, $MR = P$. Equilibrium output is then determined by the relation $P = MR = MC$. A monopolist, on the other hand, will perceive that the demand curve confronting him possesses some inelasticity so that $P > MR$ (for $P = MR + X\Delta P$, where ΔP is not zero). Lacking a settled market price to which he must conform, the monopolist must choose both the output and the price that maximize his income.

A demand curve D_1 and the corresponding MR curve are drawn in Figure 1A along with a curve of constant marginal costs. Our guiding principle is that a firm able to name its price will accelerate its output flow, and hence lower price, so long as the additions to total proceeds (MR) exceed the additions to total cost (MC). The equilibrium condition for the maximum price-output adjustment is still $MR = MC$, the equality of the increment to costs and sales proceeds. As $P > MR$, the complete rule becomes $P > MR = MC$. In Figure 1A this would be at output OM and price MP_m. As a supplementary condition once more, total revenue must exceed the total costs—either the full total costs or the full variable costs, depending upon the time length under discussion. In terms of the average concepts, $P \geqq AC$. Curiously, AC bears no determinate equilibrium relation to MC; P, however, must always exceed both AC and MC. As another contrast to the competitive equilibrium, in which MC was rising and greater than AC, now MC may even be falling (and AC necessarily falling) at the $MR = MC$ intersection. More will be made of this point later.

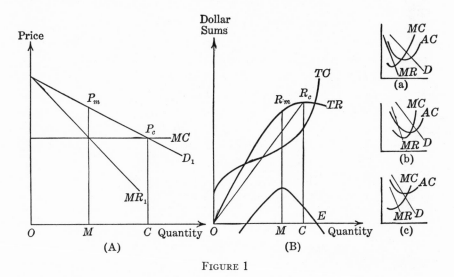

FIGURE 1

The condition for maximum profits is thus as before, that $MR = MC$. The difference is that under pure competition $P = MR = MC$, and therefore the equation of $MC = P$ is identical with $MC = MR$. Under monopoly, at the equilibrium output $P > MR = MC$. That P exceeds MR under monopoly is, of course, attributable to the fact that $X\Delta P$ is a positive sum, greater than zero. As an implication of this analysis, if a monopolist wanted to dispose of a fixed stock of goods, which either cost nothing to produce or which were irreproducible, the price that yields maximum profits would maximize total revenue; from earlier considerations, MR would be zero and E_d would equal 1.

The monopoly equilibrium can also be depicted by total cost and total revenue curves, as in Figure 1B. Monopoly equilibrium will be at output OM, where a tangent to TR is of exactly the same slope as a tangent to TC. The rate of change in total costs and revenue being of the same order evidences an equality of MR and MC. Once more the relation $MR = MC$ stands revealed as a property of the output of maximum profits, whether businessmen think in these categories or not. The vertical spread between TR and TC will of course be greatest at this output, denoting maximum profits: hence the profit curve E, also drawn in the figure, reaches its maximum value at this output. Competitive equilibrium, meaning merely a $P = MC$ price, would occur at output OC where average revenue equalled marginal costs. Consequently, a vector from the origin to TR above OC would be of the same slope as a tangent to TC.

It will be convenient, hereafter, to refer to the output at which $P = MC$ as the competitive output and to refer to the $P > MR = MC$ position as the monopoly output. Generally, no harm will be done in this use of terms. However, with but one firm in the field, any use of the term competition is a misnomer; a single firm would scarcely have any incentive to produce the $P = MC$ output. The reference to competition is intended only to convey that $P = MC$, and it is not to be construed as signifying that if the monopoly firm were decomposed into multitudinous atomistic units and pure competition evolved, hat the aggregate MC curve of the industry would be a rigid and unimpaired projection of the monopoly firm's MC curve.

Decreasing AC and Monopoly Pricing

In Figure 1A, MC was portrayed as constant; the AC curve was omitted completely from the discussion. Under pure competition, with a U-shaped AC curve, positive maximum profits would emerge only if $P = MC \geqq AC$. Under monopoly it was declared that a unique and consistent equilibrium pattern of AC and MC is lacking, except that both had to be less than price.

Consider Figure 1a. Market demand is such that $MR = MC$ at an output at which AC is still falling. Consequently in equilibrium $P > AC > MC$. In Figure 1b, not only is AC falling at the output of maximum profits, but also MC. Again, $P > AC > MC$.

In both Figures 1a and 1b, $P > AC$ at the intersection of the demand curve and the MC curve. In Figure 1c, however, if a firm, by desire, accident, or legal compulsion, produced the $P = MC$ output, then $AC > P$ and losses would ensue. Short of subsidies or charitable intent, a firm could not engage in business very long under these circumstances. Although we could still term the $MR = MC$ output as the monopoly position, the "competitive" output would have to be redefined as, perhaps, the $P = AC$ output level, short of philanthropy or subsidies.

The declining AC was demonstrated earlier to be a consequence of the laws of proportionality and size in factor use. Insofar as it is proportionality, generally it will be attributable to the presence of indivisible or "lumpy" equipment. If demand is so limited that by choosing equipment of the most economical sort in the light of market demand only one firm (or few firms) can exist in the field, then monopoly or oligopoly will be the upshot. Even without limitations on entry, the numbers in the field will be too few for competitive pricing. A rightward shift in demand can, conceivably, rid the commodity sector of its monopoly aspects.

Equilibrium Factor Hire

As an alternative condition of output equilibrium for the firm under competitive conditions we described the condition of equilibrium hire, namely, the equality of the factor's marginal value product and its price. Let us formulate the corresponding rule for monopoly.

At each output level, as before,

$$\frac{MP_a}{P_a} = \frac{MP_b}{P_b} = \frac{MP_c}{P_c} = J,$$

where the numerator refers to the marginal products of factors and the denominator refers to their prices. Multiplying each factor's marginal product by the marginal revenue derived from a further unit of sales, and terming the result the *marginal-revenue product*, we have

$$MR\frac{MP_a}{P_a} = MR\frac{MP_b}{P_b} = MR\frac{MP_c}{P_c} = MR \cdot J.$$

As before, it will be profitable for the firm to expand its hire of factors until the factor's marginal-revenue product equalled its price. But this equality, or a value of unity for the $MR \cdot J$ ratios, involves $MR = MC$. For, by taking

$$MP_a + MP_b + MP_c = 1,$$

then

$$\frac{MR(MP_a + MP_b + MP_c)}{P_a + P_b + P_c} = \frac{MR}{MC} = 1.$$

OUTPUT RESTRICTION

It is important to assess the possible magnitude of monopoly output restriction as compared to a $P = MC$ price policy. The degree of restriction will depend on the shape of the cost-and-demand curves in the region between competitive and monopoly output.

The Demand Curves

In an earlier chapter it was observed that the MR correspondent to a convex market-demand curve intersected a line parallel to OX at an

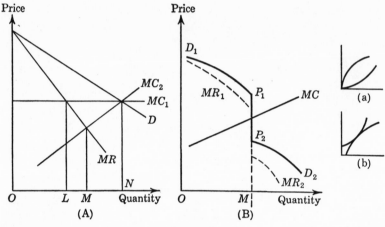

FIGURE 2

abscissae distance less than one-half the intersection of the same parallel line with the demand curve.* Viewing the parallel line as a curve of constant MC, the conclusion now is that, with a convex demand curve and constant MC, monopoly output will be less than one-half the competitive total, evidencing a really serious degree of output restriction. On the other hand, when the demand curve is concave the monopoly output would approach more closely the $P = MC$ norm; it will at least exceed one-half the competitive level. For a linear demand curve and a constant MC curve, monopoly output is precisely one-half the $P = MC$ total. This last case is shown in Figure 2A; OL is the monopoly output and ON is the competitive level. Thus the curvature of the demand curve is an important determinant of the degree of monopoly output restriction and consequently of the height of monopoly price.

* See above, p. 41.

Clearly, if numerous buyers are very sensitive to a price change from the ruling market price, with a rise of ΔP_x driving them to buy a wide array of substitute products, and a fall of ΔP_x attracting custom from the entire commodity field, then the market-demand curve will be extremely elastic in the region of the market price; this will serve to enforce what amounts to a competitive adaptation of $P = MR = MC$ despite the fact that the full demand curve for the firm is not perfectly elastic. A number of price-conscious buyers can accomplish the competitive result even if the demand of other buyers is inelastic. Recalling the earlier formula,

$$\frac{P}{MR} = \frac{E_d}{E_d - 1},$$

it is clear that as the elasticity is larger, marginal revenue approaches price.

The *MC* Curves

So much for the demand curves: there seems to be little more to be said on an abstract, general plane of analysis. We could, of course, examine various mathematical curves but until we found a market to which they applied they would confer little in the way of economic knowledge. Instead, let us consider the effects of the *MC* curve on output restriction. Assuming the demand curve to be linear, like D_1 in Figure 2A, on drawing the relevant curves it can be seen that when *MC* is constant the degree of output contraction will be more serious than when *MC* is rising between *OL* and *ON*, assuming both *MC* curves intersect *D* at the same point.

From the standpoint of comparative output totals a combination of (fairly) constant costs and a convex demand curve threaten the gravest departure from the $P = MC$ position. The conjunction of a concave demand curve and a rising *MC* curve should cause a lesser output derangement. Likewise, if the constant *MC* curve lies above a rising (linear) *MC* curve until the $P = MC$ output level, the concave-demand-constant-*MC* configuration will push output closer to the competitive norm than the convex-demand-rising-*MC* pattern.

Relaxing the linear *MC* assumption and examining the canoelike constellation in Figure 2a, it is clear that the lower wing (the convex sector), is conducive to output expansion while the upper branch exerts a strong contractionist pull, at least over the range drawn. If the positions of the curves were reversed, as in 2b, the conclusions would have to be modified.   Strictly speaking, the concavities and convexities of MC are devoid of significance until we fix the position of the cost curve with respect to a demand curve.

Equality of Monopoly and Competitive Output

Occasionally, monopoly output may coincide with the competitive level.   For example, envisaging a perfectly inelastic demand curve, monopoly and competitive output would be fully equivalent.   There could be, however, a substantial divergence between the prices: the competitive price ought to equal MC so long as the latter was constant or rising; if falling, price would amount to AC.   The monopoly price would, in principle, reach the highest point on the inelastic demand curve.*

A less obvious case is depicted in Figure 2B.   For the moment we need not probe too deeply into the cause of the inelastic kink at output OM: under oligopoly conditions we shall have a plausible explanation for it.   Meanwhile we may regard it merely as a firm's demand curve with sales being elastic just above the P_1 price height although the firm's sales are almost completely insensitive to a price fall until P_2; as MC intersects MR at OM, competitive and monopoly output converge.   The $P = MC$ price, however, is located at the intersection of MC and D_1, while monopoly price will be at P_1.   Because of the discontinuity in MR, it appears, in this case, a little far-fetched to describe the equilibrium as one at which $MR = MC$; a slight alteration in the statement is called for, namely that to the left of the maximum-profit output, $MR > MC$ and to the right, $MC > MR$.   In all but discontinuous cases, therefore, $MR = MC$.   Similarly, if the firm is producing its maximum output so that its MC curve becomes vertical and perfectly inelastic at this output, while MR is greater than MC, a similar alteration is required.   At the capacity output, the gap between MC and MR will usually be less than when output is to the left of the capacity volume; but these modifications to allow for discontinuities are common-sense interpretations of the formula.

PRICE AND OUTPUT INTERRELATIONS

Let us briefly consider the reverberations in the rest of the economy consequent upon the monopoly price policy of the firm under review.

* Perfectly inelastic demand, at least for more than a small range, is inconsistent with the basic assumption of the indifference system which presumes substitution among commodities and rejects the hypothesis of an absolute desire for one good to the exclusion of other goods.

We can assume that prior to firm A's shift from a $P = MC$ price to a $P > MR = MC$, all firms were in competitive equilibrium, with a $P = MC$ adaptation for each firm.   Let us set out some of the immediate repercussions of A's monopoly price innovation even if, under our special assumptions of monopoly, the impact effect on any single other firm is small.

Substitute-Complementary Relations

A price rise, we have learned previously, will invite a transfer in demand to substitutes: they should rise in price while complementary goods should fall.*   On the simplest view, assuming unity aggregate elasticity of consumer expenditure, the higher the arc elasticity of demand for commodity A from the competitive to the monopoly price, the more likely it is that alternate outputs will expand and their prices will rise, for there is now less expenditure on A's output and more on other goods.   If the arc elasticity is low and inelastic, suggesting a greater expenditure on commodity A despite the higher monopoly price, other prices and outputs will fall, a price decline entirely ascribable to the monopoly pricing.

Normally, if substitutes are available the arc elasticity of demand should exceed unity.   Thus the demand and output of other goods will expand as A prices monopolistically.   If the diverse firms to which demand is transferred adhere to a $P = MC$ policy their prices will rise only if their MC curves are rising: the general output expansion will be more limited the less elastic are their MC curves.   If the other firms to whom demand is transferred are themselves monopolists, even with constant MC curves in these firms their prices will tend to rise.   Manifestly, there is increased output and employment in the rest of the field to set off against the monopoly diminution.   Over the whole field, however, the tendency will be toward higher prices.   Consumer money incomes constant, and neglecting the diversion of income to monopoly profit recipients, the implications for relative well-being need not be labored.

Extension to N-Monopoly Firms

The results so far are quite unimpressive.   The number of firms are unaltered, one firm prices monopolistically and the effects are widely diffused, with increased output elsewhere to balance off against the

* In view of the unpredictable income effect, rather than speak of substitutes and complements we should stress that for some goods the cross elasticity will be positive and for others, negative.

monopoly contraction.   But when we assume that the new monopolist is not one firm but innumerable independent firms producing dissimilar commodities, the analysis attains a new significance; the sum total of the little bits of monopoly contractions may be of major significance, urging the general equilibrium further from the competitive price-output configuration.   It would be erroneous to conclude that from the standpoint of want-satisfaction the economic importance of the alternate output expansions exactly offsets the monopoly contractions. Even if the employment total, as an index of aggregate output, is maintained, the monopoly pricing will disrupt the relative division of income and the composition of aggregate output.   It is in the relative distortions of the output structure that monopoly pricing works its own special havoc.

MONOPOLY PRICING AS AN INDIRECT TAX

Some added insight into the nature and consequences of monopoly pricing can be derived by comparing it to an indirect tax, such as a sales tax or excise tax per unit of output levied under competitive conditions.

Monopoly Pricing as an Indirect Tax

In Figure 3A, suppose D is the demand curve and MC the supply curve under competitive conditions.   The competitive price would

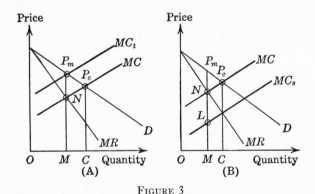

FIGURE 3

then be P_c and output, OC.   Suppose a unit excise tax was imposed equal to NP_m per unit; the new supply curve under competition would be lifted to MC_t and price would finally settle at P_m, with output falling off to OM. The price rise would equal $P_m - P_c$ and the output diminution would equal $OC - OM$.

Modifying our hypothesis, we can visualize MC as the marginal-cost curve of a monopolist, and D and MR as the demand and marginal-revenue curves, respectively. Obviously, under monopoly conditions output will advance only to OM and price will be fixed at P_m. But these are precisely the results that would ensue under the imposition of a tax in competitive circumstances. Monopoly pricing can thus be likened to an indirect tax with the important distinction that the tax proceeds, in amount $OM \cdot (P_m - N)$, are amassed by the monopolist as income rather than being deflected to the Treasury as a tax collection.

A Device to Secure Optimal Output

To carry this analysis a step further, an ingenious use of subsidies has been suggested to ensure the $(P = MC)$ output and price which at the same time fails to enrich the monopolists.* In Figure 3B, if we draw D, MC, and MR, the competitive output would be OC and monopoly output, OM. In these circumstances if a subsidy of NL per unit of output was granted to the monopolist, it would lower the marginal-cost curve to MC_s. As MC_s intersects MR at OC, output would go to the latter level and the competitive price immanent in the real data would be announced. After this output level was achieved the subsidy could be recouped, via an appropriately designed income tax, in an equivalent amount; as the most profitable output is not affected by an income tax, output would stay at the OC level. Undoubtedly the suggestion is more provocative than practical, although during World War II subsidies such as those on meat, together with heavy rates of excess profits taxation, tended to operate in the same way, so that the scheme is perhaps not as fanciful as it might have once seemed. Nevertheless an economy intelligent enough to apply the device would possess the wisdom to eliminate monopoly pricing by more straight-forward processes if this were deemed salutory.

MEASURES OF MONOPOLY POWER

To impart some precision to the concept of monopoly power, the following measures have been devised. They pertain solely to the particular firms practicing monopoly pricing or output restriction. The first measure stresses the discrepancy between MC and P as an indicator of the price distortions attributable to monopoly power.

* Mrs. Robinson, p. 163. The suggestion is credited to Mr. Robinson.

The Discrepancy $P - MC$

The measure suggested by A. P. Lerner which has since gained fairly wide currency, is grounded in the divergence between price and marginal costs. Thus

$$M_L = \frac{P - MC}{P},$$

where M_L is the degree of monopoly power, P is the price and MC, marginal costs. When $MC = MR$, the typical monopoly equilibrium, the measure is equivalent to the reciprocal of the elasticity of demand, $1/E_d$.

Obviously, the measure could be extended to encompass all deviations from the $(P = MC)$ equation, as in cases of pure competition but imperfect foresight where entrepreneurs fall short of the optimal result. In some circumstances, as with a rising demand curve or unwitting overproduction, the measure may be negative; intentionally or not MC may exceed P. Normally, the measure will fluctuate between zero and unity. When $MC = P$ the numerator (and hence the deviation from the competitive result) would be zero. At the other end, for costless output the measure will become unity, indicating the ability of the seller to charge a price for a free good.*

The Difference $(P_m - P_c)$

For many purposes a more apt comparison than that between P and MC would relate monopoly price (P_m) and competitive price (P_c). For the latter purpose, Lerner's measure fits perfectly for the one case of constant marginal costs; it breaks down when the MC curve either rises or falls.

A provisional measure of the discrepancy between P_m and P_c can be constructed on the assumption that demand and marginal-cost curves are linear in the region between the monopoly output and the competitive figure. Although this is a serious limitation it does afford some idea of the possible price distortion. Thus,

$$P_m - P_c = \frac{(X_m b_1{}^2)}{b_1 + b_2},$$

---

* One weakness of the measure would be its failure to distinguish between Cournot's illustration of plentiful mineral water flowing without cost and Marshall's manna of hard stones, limited, valuable, costlessly produced, but irreproducible.

where X_m is the monopoly output while b_1 and b_2 represent the numerical values of the slopes of the D and MC curves, respectively.*

Clearly, when b_1 is zero—as in infinitely elastic demand—the difference between P_m and P_c is zero. On the other hand, the larger the slope of the demand curve relative to MC, or the more inflexible the demand curve, the greater the divergence of the two prices; with perfectly inelastic demand the difference between the prices is enormous. Also, a rising MC curve beyond the monopoly output tends to keep the two prices more closely aligned. When marginal costs are constant, b_2 is zero and the divergence of monopoly and competitive price then depends on the exact slope of the demand curve.

It is wrong, of course, to pretend that the D and MC curves will in fact be linear. Should the demand curve be convex downward, and the MC curve be linear, the measure will overstate the discrepancy; it will understate the gap if D is linear and MC is concave. Where both curves are convex, exaggeration is again likely, while if both are concave the difference will be understated. Suitable diagrams can be drawn for all these cases. Dispensing with analytical finesse in the face of factual ignorance, an even rougher approximation might often suffice; it might be surmised simply that P_c lies midway between P_m and MC.

A Measure of Output Restriction

Frequently we will want to have some idea of the relative extent to which monopoly output falls below the competitive level. A measure couched in terms of the divergence of P and MC is uninformative on this aspect of the equilibrium.

A relative measure of the output difference X_c and X_m, for linear curves, works out neatly in this case. Thus,

---

* To derive the formula, simply equate a linear demand to a linear MC curve, then solve simultaneously for the competitive price (P_c) and output (X_c):

$$X_c = \frac{a_1 - a_2}{b_1 + b_2}; \qquad P_c = a_1 - \frac{b_1(a_1 - a_2)}{b_1 + b_2}.$$

Likewise, deriving MR and equating MC to MR for monopoly behavior,

$$X_m = \frac{a_1 - a_2}{2b_1 + b_2}; \qquad P_m = a_1 - \frac{b_1(a_1 - a_2)}{2b_1 + b_2}.$$

Subtracting P_c from P_m and substituting for $(a_1 - a_2)$ we derive the result stated in the text. In all this, a_1 and a_2 refer to the demand and cost curve intercepts on OY. The measure based on linear curves is suggested by Bowley, *Mathematical Groundwork*, p. 60.

$$\frac{X_m}{X_c} = \frac{b_1 + b_2}{2b_1 + b_2},$$

where b_1 and b_2 have the meanings assigned to them previously. For costless output, or for production under constant MC conditions, b_2 is zero and X_m is thus exactly one-half the X_c amount.* A steeply rising MC curve will lift the ratio, bringing X_m somewhat closer to X_c.

SPECIAL EQUILIBRIUM CASES

It is instructive to consider some special cases of monopoly equilibrium, such as those in which supply and demand are interdependent and the phenomena of rising demand curves as well as instances of multiple equilibria.

Interdependent Supply and Demand

The analysis of the maximization problem of the firm is generally predicated on the supposition of supply and demand being independent functions. From the standpoint of the economic system, however, it is an old proposition that both cost and demand phenomena are interdependent: the classical statement of this truth was embodied in what became known as Say's law of "supply creating its own demand." Sometimes, however, the assumption of independence, even from the standpoint of the firm, is misleading. Though it would be false to suggest that illustrations of interdependence of demand and supply for the firm abound, they are not uncommon; employees may, for example, purchase from the firm some of the goods which they help produce, purchases which would not be made if they were not employed by the firm. Or they may buy standard items in a company store; the firm would certainly assess the importance of such factors when hiring personnel. For the moment we shall evade the latter type of multiproduct problem and concentrate only on the former.

In Figure 4A the demand curve d_1 is the market purchase schedule even before the firm starts producing. As it makes one unit of output ready for market, the d curve shifts to the right—to the new position d_2—because either those engaged in its production now have income with which to buy the product, or through the knowledge acquired in its production they have become conscious of its existence and wish to own it, thereby supplementing the original market demand. A second unit of production would give birth to d_3, etc. Working with linear demand curves and a rising marginal-cost curve, which implies that more wage

* See pp. 140–141 above.

earners are hired at the given wage rate to produce further units of output, the lateral distances of the d_1, d_2, d_3 $\cdots$ curves will spread further apart as production expands.   To ascertain the sales price of one unit, we would seek it on d_2 at the ordinate above the abscissae of one unit of output.   For two units, on d_3, three units on d_4, etc.   Con-

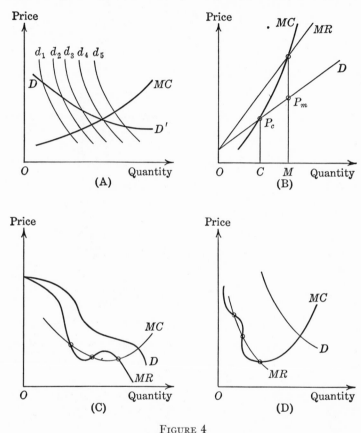

FIGURE 4

necting these actual demand points for the corresponding outputs, we trace out the curve DD' which describes the effective market-demand relations from the standpoint of the firm.   To determine the equilibrium price and output, a curve marginal to DD' would have to be drawn and equated to MC.

There are many twists that we might give to the d_1, d_2, d_3 $\cdots$ field, depending on the particular circumstances of each case—or more aptly, the discontinuous gyrations in demand; for the general case the preceding analysis should suffice.

Rising Demand Curves

Earlier we referred to rising demand curves for commodities of "conspicuous consumption," where consumers were prone to buy more at higher rather than lower prices. This is a reversal of the fundamental notions of demand: rather than prices being dependent upon quantities offered and wanted, quantities wanted become dependent upon prices. In Figure 4B the demand curve is D, while MR and MC have the customary meanings. Monopoly pricing in this peculiar environment is unquestionably conducive to larger sales and output than a $P = MC$ policy: in this one case our usual norms are upset. There seems to be no dispute, however, that no matter how irrational the procedure appears to an outsider the consumers themselves regard their well-being improved by the "high-price distinction" conferred upon them. Steps to lower prices will decrease the "well-being" of those afflicted with a high-price psychosis.

Aside from the Veblen case, a few other instances of rising demand curves can be developed. The backward-falling demand curve which may accompany inferior goods will be recalled. If goods that follow this pattern are also subject to monopoly, the resources in these fields may well exceed the competitive level; this will have to depend on the exact position of the two curves. Rising demand curves can also evolve from the interdependent supply and demand constructions of the preceding section; the sole requirement is that the demand points on the succeeding demand curve lie above the demand points for the preceding volume of output. It might happen that as more workers are hired and employment prospects brighten, there is a strong element of "sympathetic consumption." In all of these instances of rising demand curves, resource utilization will be pressed further when prices are adjusted on monopoly rather than competitive criteria.

Multiple Equilibria

Corresponding to the possibilities of multiple equilibria in a competitive order, several points of intersection of MR and MC curves are also conceivable.

In Figure 4C the slope of the demand curve veers sharply from points of higher to lower to higher elasticity, perhaps because at certain prices a new layer of market demand is uncovered, with lower-income groups entering the market discontinuously; unable to purchase automobiles, say, at $2,000, they suddenly find the purchase attractive at $1,500, so that there will be a marked extension of demand at this last price. At

$900, say, another substantial income tier is tapped. Examining the diagram, and the diverse $MR = MC$ positions, we see that the end points are positions of stable equilibrium while the intervening $MC = MR$ point is a minimum and an unstable position. Which end point yields maximum income will, of course, depend upon the precise shape of the MR and MC curves. Figure 4D describes an even more likely market relationship, in which marginal costs fall irregularly until they finally turn upward. Here, too, the end points are stable while the middle $MR = MC$ equality is a minimum position; a movement in either direction will swell profits.

NONPECUNIARY MOTIVES

Our analyses have relied for their solution upon the fundamental assumption of the pursuit of maximum pecuniary profits. Although it is probably accurate as a general principle of business conduct and as an indicator of the ultimate results, the shortcomings of this assumption are commonly acknowledged; no one will dispute the contention that it fails to describe all the facts. Public utility corporations, for example, are prohibited by law from applying the maximum formula; the modifications called for in the analysis ought at least be outlined. Besides conscious restraint from the maximum rule, it is also true that to attain the maximum-income position, economic subjects must be capable of performing the proper computations. Ignorance and incompetence are all too rife; a brief quizzing of a business man on the effect of taxes and fixed charges upon his behavior will generally corroborate this fact. Among the practices that may be cited as exhibiting flagrant violations of the maximum rule are retail markups and full-cost pricing, both of which will be treated briefly.

Although motives would not be lacking for producing an output other than that at which $MC = P$ under pure competition, there are very many more compelling reasons under monopoly for the superficially anomalous policy of $MC \gtrless MR$, even though it involves the sacrifice of some immediate monopoly profits. Occasionally, even actual losses may be sought, braved with complete equanimity. In a competitive regime firms would seldom have the purpose or the temerity to invite losses.

Some of the factors that may impel a monopolist to forego the maximum current pecuniary income may be listed briefly. For one thing, "just price" notions often prevail and condition price policy, invoking a "fair" price code rather than a price of maximum consumer exploitation.   Or the monopolist may be anxious to deter the market inroads of producers of substitutes.   Or the policy may be designed to forestall government regulation, or to retain consumer good will.   Or, being human, entrepreneurs may, despite the monopoly power of their firms, like to boast of their output level and of their productive prowess, contenting themselves with a "fair" rather than maximum profit.   Or, rationally, the entrepreneur may be deterred by the additional entrepreneurial output exertions incident to procuring additional profits. Another element that we shall develop later is the fact that current losses may be planned to influence consumer tastes for the future, at which time a more thoroughgoing monopolistic price policy can be instituted; there would never be any rational basis for comparable action by an atomistic firm selling in a competitive market.   Whatever the particular forces are that prompt a departure from $P > MC = MR$ pricing, price and output will deviate from that implicit in the maximizing principle.*   This must not be overlooked in deriving propositions and drawing comparisons between the monopoly world and a competitive organization.

Graphic Analysis

Whatever the motives may be that guide the monopoly firm, they may be epitomized in a system of indifference curves.   Measuring profits or money income vertically and output horizontally, there is associated with each combination of income and output a certain amount of irksomeness, an apprehension of potential competition, or perhaps a governmental regulation, or a certain welfare attitude of a fair price, etc. Each indifference curve will connect a series of income-output combinations representing a definite preference level; at each point along each curve the marginal rate of substitution between output and income can be computed, while the ascension from one curve to another denotes successively higher preference levels.   According to a convex figure, such as that shown in Figure 5a, an entrepreneur will substitute output for income at a decreasing MRS: the concomitant advantages of enlarged production—perhaps the prestige of a large production volume, or the fear of government punitive action with restricted output, or the sales losses to market usurpers at higher prices—outweigh the pecuniary losses of profits consciously foregone by output expansion.   Output

---

* When output forces predominate, the monopolist will be less reluctant to lower price the more elastic are the demand and supply curves, for the profit position will then be rather well maintained despite the lowering of price.   See Bowley, pp. 25, 60.

forces then dominate. If we draw the locus of a profit curve on the same diagram, found by subtracting the total receipts from the total costs of each output, it will, in general, be bell-shaped with the maximum height at the $MR = MC$ point, as in Figure 5b. Equilibrium will be found at the point of tangency between the profit curve and an indifference curve, for this will be the highest level of well-being open to the firm. This is shown in Figure 5c. Output, when the output-income indifference curves are convex, will exceed the quantity shown at the simple $MR = MC$ equality reflected at the top of the profit bell, for the tangency is now to the right of the summit of the profit locus (circled in

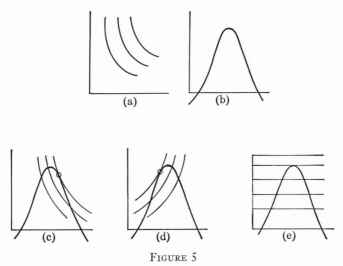

(a)

(b)

(c)

(d)

(e)

FIGURE 5

5c). Conversely, the entrepreneur may find additional output irksome and may prefer the peace and quiet life associated with less output: only the prospect of increased profits can move him to produce more. Here the indifference contours are those of 5d, so that contractionist forces predominate. As restraining forces are in the saddle the equilibrium output lies below the amount indicated at the equation of MR and MC.

Even under competitive market conditions where the firm is unable to affect price, the profit locus would also assume a bell shape; given the indifference field for the relations between income and effort we can determine whether expansionist or contractionist motives predominate. Extending these ideas, the type of indifference system visualized in the conventional assumption of the pursuit of maximum pecuniary profits, translated into profit-output indifference contours, assumes indifference curves that are parallel to OX, as in Figure 5e, so that the entrepreneur is motivated solely by profits, regardless of the effort and output entailed: the *MRS* between effort (and output) and income is not only constant but always zero.   The entrepreneur is depicted as utterly indifferent between small- and large-scale production, not even deeming his labors the more arduous because of greater production.   On this postulate the point of tangency between the indifference lines and the profit bell must be at the top of the latter curve, where *MR = MC*.   Interpreted in this way, it would appear that the behavior implicit in the Fundamental Assumption is but a special case that probably errs in indicating the output even under inherently competitive conditions. Invoking the Fundamental Assumption does illuminate the business mechanism but it must be regarded as exemplifying not the whole facts but only an important first approximation.

There is one other direction in which the sharp edge of the Fundamental Assumption must be tempered.   Just as the assumption of the pursuit of maximum pecuniary profits explains less than the full facts, it was disclosed earlier that for each level of output the firm may fail to hire the minimum-cost factor combination.   Just as profits can be reduced through price restraint, they can also be lost by uneconomic factor hire.   The minimal total-cost curve may thus fail to describe the actual cost path of output expansion given a disinterested and non-pecuniary entrepreneurial attitude.*

Pricing in Regulated Industries

Probably the best illustrations of nonmaximum pecuniary forces under monopoly can be drawn from the field of regulated industry, where, for a variety of reasons, competition is ineffective or the state has been impelled to place the field under its regulatory surveillance. Invariably the price policy of the public utility is moderated toward the end of "fair" profits rather than maximum (monopoly) profits; non-maximization precepts are legally implanted by law to guide the adaptation of the firm.   Springing from the countless controversies and law suits, the rule of regulation is encompassed in the phrase "reasonable return on prudent investment."

Using this as the broad directive governing regulation, there are two major problems involved here: (1) first, "prudent investment" must

---

* Some writers often contend that competitive markets must compel the adoption of minimum-cost methods of operations through the pressure of entry and profitability. But this argument is shaky in fact as well as in principle.   Competitive price making and homogeneous entry are by themselves insufficient to ensure minimum cost modes of production.

be determined. There is no need, for our purposes, to discuss the endless snares encountered on this route; the typical nightmare of the regulatory authorities concerns the appropriate valuation of non-marketable capital assets. (2) After the prudent investment is determined, there is the need for concurrence on the volume of earnings to which the firm is entitled in order to obtain a "reasonable" return on the fixed investment. Ultimately, this is a matter of deciding on a price which promises to secure "reasonable" earnings; the price approved by a regulatory commission must be sufficiently high to create a reasonable return on investment out of the difference $X(P - AVC)$. But the line separating investment and variable costs is itself frequently a murky one. Still, if the utility property is valued at a sum V, then the ratio $X(P - AVC)/V$ must promise a "reasonable" rate of return. The rate problem is further complicated by the fact that the regulated firm produces more than one output.

Visualizing the usual D, MR and MC curves, and deriving from them the profit locus alluded to in the previous sections, we can state that if all the information were at hand it would be a simple matter for the regulatory commission to approve of that price which allowed "reasonable" earnings. Whether this requires the monopoly price, the competitive price, an intermediate figure or even one higher than the monopoly price or lower than the competitive price is, a priori indeterminate.* Conceivably, only the monopoly price may insure reasonable earnings although occasionally, even the competitive price might exact more than the "fair" earnings so that the only tenable price, according to the legal directives binding the regulatory body, will lie below the $P = MC$ level.

Full-Cost Pricing

Practical men are often impatient with the economists' view of business men adjusting marginal costs and revenues. Instead, they contend that industrial firms ordinarily estimate their average cost and add to it for "good measure," a sum to guarantee "reasonable" profits.

The allegation of the pervasiveness of this practice raises several issues. Analytically, it conceives: (1) demand to be completely inelastic and the production scale to be rigidly fixed for then entrepreneurial costs, to which a "fair" profit is added, would be unique; (2)

---

* Despite the indeterminateness, it is strange that public utility writers almost invariably suggest that the regulated price is normally intermediate between the monopoly and competitive figure.

the conception may visualize the firm as always preparing goods to order, or always operating at capacity so that the supply curve is completely inelastic.   Otherwise AC fluctuates with the level of output so that price and output policy entails estimations of demand, not of costs alone.   Once we concede some elasticity to demand and costs we are thrown back to some mode of connecting MC and MR, but recognizing irrationality—calculating incompetence—and nonpecuniary pricing motives.   As another avenue of full-cost pricing, if, despite fluctuating demand, the AC curve is flat so that average costs are constant, the firm may adhere to its "full-cost" price.   But for any *given* demand conditions, the full-cost pricing would represent either irrationality or nonpecuniary motives.   Obviously, after prices are named they must equal profits plus other costs: "full costs" are undoubtedly facts of arithmetic.   But they are not a theory of price determination; there is no explanation of why the "full costs" change or why they are larger rather than smaller, or why prices are sometimes *below* costs.

Whenever either demand or the MC curve is inelastic, it is a matter of indifference from the standpoint of economical resource allocation whether a high or low price is charged: output will be the same in either event, with only the income distribution among sellers and purchasers affected, having some secondary reverberations in other markets.

Retail Markups

A concrete discussion of price making demands some comments on retail markups which seem so remote from either competitive or monopoly price theory.   Briefly, markups are the retailer's description of his practice of price making, of determining selling price by adding, say, ten per cent of the cost price paid for merchandise.   Visualizing an urban department store, a policy of maximum price making would counsel that each division of the store cover at least its full separable expenses, including the direct variable cost of sales help, wrapping paper, floor space having an alternative use value, and store room and warehouse facilities, where these must be specially rented or where they have valuable alternate uses.*   Normally, as the merchandise is purchased at a single price for resale, the major component of MC is constant; if variable "merchandising" costs were zero the buying prices would represent

---

* Ultimately all divisions compete with one another for store locations. Bids by individual departments would depend upon neighboring counters; substitute and complementary profit maximization relationships abound.   See pp. 328–334.

the full height of MC. When the selling costs are rising, the MC curve will be upward-rising. Fitting a demand and MR curve into the picture the maximum price can be computed. After computing maximum price in this fashion, obviously the difference between sales price and cost of merchandise can be termed a "markup." Viewed superficially, merchandise cost appropriately "marked up" has determined price. But this fails entirely to explain the differences in markups in different stores and departments of the same store, or why markdowns and clearances are common phenomena. Undoubtedly business men are often confused on the best mode of securing maximum profits so that instead of engaging in minute cost calculations they may employ a rule-of-thumb *average markup*, in the belief that a typical variable cost accompanies each unit of sales. If the intersection of the marked-up cost curve and MR occurs to the right or left of a more rational cost calculation, a reconsideration of pricing policy would be remunerative. In this sense the average-markup procedure is irrational, for the markup tactics are ill suited for the attainment of the maximum profits which they seek.

BIBLIOGRAPHICAL NOTE

On the theory of monopoly price the volumes of Chamberlin and Mrs. Robinson are preeminent. Among the other specialized books, there is Robert Triffin's *Monopolistic Competition* and William H. Nicholls, *Imperfect Competition Within Agricultural Industries*. Two of the better articles are: R. F. Harrod, "Doctrines of Imperfect Competition," *Quarterly Journal of Economics* (1933), and J. R. Hicks, "The Theory of Monopoly," *Econometrica* (1935). There is also the volume *Monopoly*, by E. A. G. Robinson, in the Cambridge Economic Handbook Series. A criticism of the $(MR = MC)$ condition on the basis of cost-curve discontinuities, with $MR > MC$ at the firm's capacity output, has been voiced by W. J. Eitemann in his "Factors Determining the Location of the Least-Cost Point," *American Economic Review* (1947). See also the comments of R. L. Bishop and W. W. Haines, same journal (1948).

A discussion of the degree of monopoly restriction is contained in Chapter 11 of Mrs. Robinson's book. A. P. Lerner's measure of monopoly power comes from his article, "The Concept of Monopoly and the Measurement of Monopoly Power," *The Review of Economic Studies* (1933–1934). The following may be cited as representative of other suggestions for measures of monopoly power: the late Henry Schultz, in essence, multiplied Lerner's measure by x/X, where x referred to the output of the firm while X was that of the industry; but this measure is redundant when the "firm" is the "industry"—that is, when there are no products perfectly substitutable for the firm's output. See review article, "The Theory of Free Competition," *Journal of Political Economy* (1937), p. 264. Similarly, R. H. Whitman suggests merely using the numerator of Lerner's measure, $P - MC$, as an index of monopoly power, arguing that the absolute changes here are most important to the business man as an indicator of his control over the market. This modification does not involve a matter of principle, for it advocates an absolute rather than relative measure; the measure should of course be determined by the particular purpose to be served by the index. "A Note on the Concept of 'Degree of Monopoly,'" *Economic Journal* (1941), pp. 202–203. See also the reply of M. Kalecki, same journal (1942). Alternately, in view of the availability of accounting records, a comparison of price and average costs is suggested as an index by Joe S. Bain in his article, "The Profit Rate as a Measure of Monopoly Power," *Quarterly Journal of Economics* (1941). As a more novel departure, K. W. Rothschild devises a measure based on the comparative slope of a demand curve for the firm's output when other prices are constant, as against other prices fully adjusted to its price policy. This technique appears to be too artificial to be useful; one curve or the other will be relevant, but not both. See, however, "The Degree of Monopoly," *Economica* (1942). Professor E. Mason has been a major critic of Lerner's measures; the issues in this dispute involve the entire matter of the relevance of theoretical analysis. See "Price and Production Policies of Large Scale Enterprise," *American Economic Review* (1939), Supplement, p. 61.

M. Reder, in his "Inter-Temporal Relations of Demand and Supply Within the Firm," *Canadian Journal of Economics and Political Science* (1941), deals with supply-and-demand interdependence. On multiple equilibria, see Mrs. Robinson, pp. 57–59. On nonpecuniary motives, besides the articles of Scitovsky and Reder noted at the end of Chapter 3, see B. Higgins, "Elements of Indeterminacy in the Theory of Non-Perfect Competition," *American Economic Review* (1939), as well as his note and that of E. S. Lynch in the June 1940 issue. A. J. Nichol, in "Monopoly Supply and Monopsony Demand," *Journal of Political Economy* (1942), argues for the abandonment of the MR and MC apparatus because of its failure to include nonpecuniary elements, advocating instead the indifference-curve technique. For a general methodological criticism of the fundamental assumption of profit maximization, see T. W. Hutchinson, *The Significance and Basic Postulates of Economic Theory*, Chap IV.

More recent statements of regulation in the public-utility field are Irston Barnes, *The Economics of Public Utility Regulation* and Emery Troxel, *Economics of Public Utilities*. The subject of valuation is exhaustively treated by James Bonbright, *The Valuation of Property*, 2 vols.

Current interest in the full-cost theory of pricing was aroused by the article by R. L. Hall and C. J. Hitch, "Price Theory and Business Behavior," *Oxford Economic Papers* (1939, No. 2). A similar questionnaire study of businessmen's views on pricing is in Clive Saxton, *The Economics of Price Determination*. Recently the controversy was brought to a head in the articles by R. A. Lester, "Shortcomings of Marginal Analysis for Wage-Employment Problems," *American Economic Review* (1946), and Fritz Machlup, "Marginal Analysis and Empirical Research," same journal (1946). The respective replies and rejoinders are in the 1947 volume, along with the article of G. J. Stigler, "Professor Lester and the Marginalists," same journal, same year. One of the rare studies on retail selling is Arthur Smithies' "The Theory of Value Applied to Retail Selling," *Review of Economic Studies* (1939).

CHAPTER 7

Duopoly and Oligopoly

WE CONSIDER NOW THOSE CASES of circular interdependence, of duopoly and oligopoly, where two or more firms produce perfectly substitutable goods and each individual firm is able to influence, but not determine, the price of the commodity it sells. Here too—as numbers are presumed too few for the competitive result—in the final equilibrium, $P \neq MC$. But the analysis takes many peculiar turns.

In our duopoly and oligopoly analyses, we suppose that the firms comprising the market are producing an undifferentiated, perfectly substitutable good. Each seller, to hold any part of the market, must at least meet the price of his competitor.* It might be protested that there is nothing new here; that for each duopolist or oligopolist the price policies of other firms could be subsumed in the demand curve for the firm on the hypothesis of full price and output adjustment elsewhere. There is this consideration, however, that explains the special status accorded these problems. In the ordinary monopoly problem we concern ourselves with the equilibrium of the firm, elaborating the repercussions on the rest of the system and contrasting the monopoly interrelationships with the competitive balance. But now, besides the intellectual fascination in discovering how two closely related sellers reach a mutually satisfactory equilibrium, there is the important fact that a market-demand curve can be drawn, so that it becomes pertinent to contrast the adjustment of two firms with monopoly or competitive-pricing patterns under common ownership of the several individual plants.

This much of the discussion might be anticipated to prepare us for the often inconclusive results of the present chapter: briefly, we must not be

---

* That is, unless the "low"-priced seller rations sales, thereby leaving some custom for others even at higher prices. If the commodity can be profitably resold by those who purchase in the lower-price market, ultimately only one price can prevail.

surprised to learn that from an a priori standpoint the solution of the price problem is indeterminate, in the sense that there are *multiple* solutions. When one firm must look to the actions of another, and must weigh several alternative reaction patterns to which it in turn must respond, there are just too many eventualities, all depending upon the forecasts made and the actual reaction chain. Games of chess (the usual simile goes) can be played in many ways, depending on the strategy, psychology, and prescience of the participants. Without more information we cannot predict which of the manifold paths will be traversed; all that we can do is to lay out some prospective developments and leave it to empirical study to isolate the model which best represents a particular market situation. Hence, to say that duopoly problems are indeterminate is to say that they are overly determinate, that there are too many potential solutions. Whether an equilibrium will be reached, its exact content when reached, and its stability will depend entirely upon the special data of the particular market environment.

Before we become submerged in these problems, it should be underscored that so long as ultimately $P > MC$ the usual strictures on monopoly pricing apply, whatever the minutiae of the particular equilibrium solution.

OUTPUT FOLLOWERS

Suppose first firm B's output is known to firm A together with the full curve of market demand: both are so much data to A. As a further simplification B, say, intends to sell the full quantity of output that A expects him to produce, to preclude the possibility of B's withholding supplies depending on price. As an additional simplification we assume output is costless, as in Cournot's mineral spring.* Market demand is assumed to be linear, as D_m in Figure 1. Competitive output for costless production is thus ON while, if there was but one firm, monopoly output would be OM, or $\frac{1}{2}ON$. B, we postulate, produces an amount equal to $\frac{1}{2}OM$, one half the quantity that a monopoly combine would offer for sale on the presumption that A would do the same and that the maximum aggregate profit obtainable would be shared equitably between them. Knowing that B will sell $\frac{1}{2}OM = KN = \frac{1}{4}ON$, this quantity must be subtracted laterally from the market demand curve in order to ascertain A's maximum sales possibilities at each price. Doing so, the results are reflected in the curve D_r, which can be termed a *reduced* demand curve for firm A's output.

* This is the celebrated problem of Augustin Cournot, *Researches into the Mathematical Principles of Wealth*, N. T. Bacon, trans., Chapter VII.

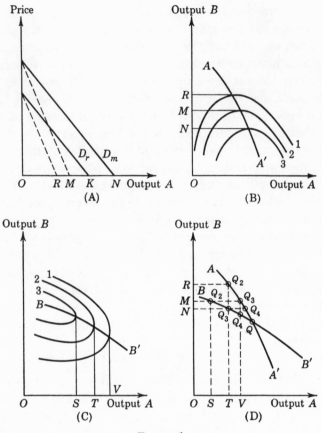

FIGURE 1

The Equilibrium Solution

Adjusting its output policy to the D_r sales curve, by the usual principles A's output will settle at $\frac{1}{2}OK$ or $\frac{3}{8}ON$. Total output in this case would, therefore, equal $\frac{5}{8}ON$, thus exceeding the monopoly figure by one fourth. The combined output, on the assumptions we have made, surpasses the simple monopoly level.

On the same linear market-demand assumptions, one case that is of interest is that in which B produces $\frac{1}{3}N$ where N is the competitive output volume. Therefore, A will produce

$$\tfrac{1}{2}(N - \tfrac{1}{3}N) = \tfrac{1}{3}N.$$

In this event each produces the same amount of output and the combined duopoly output is $\frac{2}{3}N$, while the monopoly output volume is but $\frac{1}{2}N$.

This analysis is relevant whenever B's rigid production or sales plan is announced, known, or predicted by A. Inasmuch as A accepts B's output as a datum and adapts accordingly, A is described as an *output follower*. Clearly, if A underestimates B's output, with the distance KN of Figure 1A actually understating B's production, total output and, presumably, sales will move even closer to the competitive level. Conversely, when A, in planning, exaggerates B's output, total production may fall short of even the monopoly quantity. For example, assume that the competitive output is 8 units and the monopoly output is thus 4 units, since the demand curve is linear and costs are zero. If A assumes B will produce 6 units, then A will produce but 1. If B actually produces but 1, then the combined output is 2, which is 2 units less than the monopoly volume.

Reaction Curves

If from the market-demand curve, as in Figure 1A, we deduct each possible output of B, we can thereafter find A's maximum profit output for each corresponding B quantity. If we list all these related quantities, a *reaction curve* for A can be derived. Let us develop this device more systematically, for it will be found to have many uses.

In detailing the full theory of the reaction curve, let us measure B's output along the vertical, and A's, on the horizontal axis. Curve 1 in Figure 1B is a *profit-indifference curve* for A, consisting of all outputs of A that, in conjunction with outputs of B leave A a fixed amount of profit. Curve 2 indicates profits somewhat greater than those depicted along 1, and curve 3 indicates still higher profits. Hence a system of profit contours can be formed with profits ascending as we approach the OX axis under the mantle curve 1. The lower contours are more profitable for they assume lower output by the B firm.

Drawing lines parallel to OX from R, M, and N to denote a given output of firm B, and noting their tangency to the profit-indifference curves, we can extract the successive outputs of firm A that yield A maximum profits. When we connect these various points by a continuous line, A's *reaction curve* appears, lettered AA' in Figure 1B. This curve discloses the locus of the most profitable output adjustments of A to each and every B output. It is negatively inclined, for (aside from complementary goods) as B's output diminishes it is profitable for A to extend its own production. Its gradient should be less than unity, implying over its course a smaller expansion by A than B's contraction. The reaction curve AA' can also be constructed by subtracting laterally from the market-demand curve all possible outputs of B, and thereafter observing A's maximum adaptation to the reduced demand curve.

Likewise we can derive a similar reaction curve for B, based on B's adjustment to A's output. B's profits rise as the contours approach the vertical axis in Figure 1C. If the two firms are vastly different in size, with B the smaller firm, then A's reaction curve will be rather steep, uninfluenced by B's output which is presumed almost constant. B's reaction curve, however, will be of the sort pictured in Figure 1C, ranging about a lower production level than A's output.

The Equilibrium Solution

The reaction curves reveal the equilibrating tendencies when both A and B act as output followers, each assuming that the other's output of the previous period, say, will continue into the forthcoming market period. Drawing only the reaction curves AA' and BB' in Figure 1C, suppose that B's output was OR, and A's output was OS. In the subsequent period OT will be produced by A and OM by B—points Q_2 on the reaction curves in the figure. In the third period, the outputs will be, respectively, ON for B and OV for A,—the points Q_3 on the reaction curve. Then each will advance to the Q_4 points until finally their successive adjustments will carry them to the intersection of the reaction curves at point Q. Here, at the "Cournot" point, the equilibrium balance will be stable, for, once attained, neither firm will have any incentive to depart from it—under the assumptions made thus far. The firms being of equal size, the respective outputs at the Cournot point should be the same, since the output equation of MC to the MR on the reduced demand curve of each firm should be identical. For the linear-demand case, and costless output, each firm ought produce $\frac{1}{3}X$, where X is the competitive output, or a combined duopoly total of $\frac{2}{3}X$.

The special, and strange, premises of this argument need not be labored. It is almost inconceivable that entrepreneurs, seeing their predictions of continuing behavior on the part of their rivals falsified time after time, are nevertheless so unimaginative and obtuse as to impute this behavior pattern to their rival each time. Hence we do well to scrutinize some alternate and more plausible hypotheses.

OUTPUT LEADERS

As one possibility, B may act as an *output follower;* A may know this and may therefore hasten to produce that quantity which evokes such a

reaction in B as to maximize A's profit. Firm A may then be designated as an *output leader*. In Figure 2A, BB' is firm B's reaction curve,
which is known to A. The output of maximum profit for A will then
appear at a point of tangency between A's family of profit contours and
the reaction curve BB', at point N in Figure 2A. All contours above 1
would be less profitable for A; in seeking the more profitable lower con-

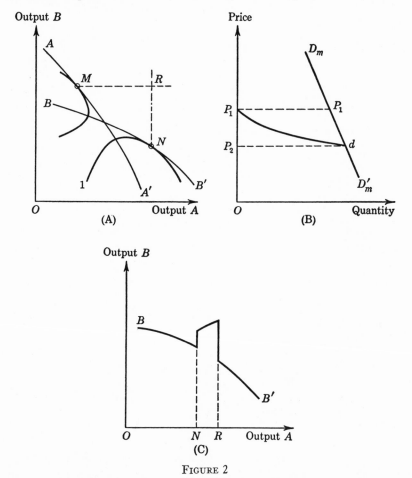

FIGURE 2

tours, as A fixes an output greater or smaller than indicated at point N,
B's output reaction is such as to place A on a less profitable contour, one
higher in the chart field than that with index 1.

The output-follower-output-leader pattern is, therefore, perfectly
determinate. If we visualize the problem in terms of the market-
demand curve, A could subtract laterally at each price the amount that
B would produce, starting at the monopoly price that B would name for

zero output by A. To illustrate, in Figure 2B, D_mD_m' is the market-demand curve; with zero production by A, B will produce P_1P_1 units and sell them at B's monopoly price OP_1. As A produces one unit, two units, etc., driving the price down, B's production will contract according to a plan which, we assume, is known to A. The effective reduced demand curve for A is thus P_1dD_m'. Firm A is in a position to determine its most lucrative output opportunity by forcing B's response. Of course, if B is a large firm which hardly responds to output changes in A, so that BB' is fairly flat, nothing that A can do is likely to alter the aggregate output, so that the analysis borders on that of output dependence.

Indeterminateness with Contending Leaders

Suppose that B vies with A for output leadership. Say that firm B, like A, has witnessed and amassed information on A's production policies and tries to avail itself of this knowledge. Just as A endeavors to produce the output indicated at N in Figure 2A, B will seize upon the amount noted at point M. Consequently, the combined output culminates at point R. This is obviously unprofitable to both firms; a revision of anticipations will undoubtedly follow. The final equilibrium settlement is indeterminate pending more data on the new reaction pattern. Thus, although the output-follower-output-leader case converges to a determinate equilibrium, when two output leaders contend for the leader position, a reversal of policy and acquiescence on the part of at least one firm to play the other's game is ultimately in order—unless both are willing to deprive themselves of the greater profit opportunities available to a meek follower.

A mixed configuration might also be sketched. For the most part, B may be content to act as an output follower, while A is the acknowledged leader. But B may refuse to be goaded beyond a certain output; rebellious, it can threaten retaliatory price warfare. B's reaction curve, which we assume known to A, is the discontinuous locus BB' in Figure 2C. Until an output ON of A, B's reactions are normal: there is a less than unit decrement in B's output for every unit output increment of A. Should A insist on an output between ON and OR, B may essay one last stand, whether the final results be noble or ignominious for itself. By increasing its production substantially, market price will be forced down. Firm A will thus have to weigh carefully the consequences of an output decision in this area; the price fall may be more than the firm relishes or is able to withstand. Beyond OR output by A, however, B may refrain from combatting it with a precipitate output expansion of its own, for the ensuing losses which it will suffer itself may be regarded as too severe, so that BB' resumes approximately its normal course.

Parenthetically, it might be observed that the output leader will probably have to wait at least one period before its market policy bears fruit in generating the appropriate output response on the part of the follower. A display of output firmness will, in time, secure its reward.

Conjectural Variations

We might explore some further samples of conjectural variations—as A's guess of the estimated reaction of B to its own output policy is termed. Conjectural variations refer to the attempt of firms to predict the behavior of their rival so as to render their own output adjustment profitable.

It was shown that if both A and B expect each other's previous output to be repeated in the subsequent market period, an equilibrium is eventually attained. Contrast this with the results forthcoming when each seller presumes that the other is altering its previous output level, without being certain of the direction. Thus on the basis of the output in the first period, A expects B to expand in the second period and B expects A to contract. After the second period is concluded both may be surprised—B pleasantly and A adversely— for the output expected by A of B may be less than B actually produced, while A's output, on the other hand, falls below B's expectations. As A prepares to contract his output again because of B's expansory proclivities, he may impute some knowledge of his behavior to B and thus A may foreshadow a further increase in B's output. In contrast, B might have been astonished to see the initial recession in A's output; not quite comprehending it B might merely extrapolate this output of A for the forthcoming periods, dismissing the thought that A will curtail his operations further.

This is likely to mean indeterminateness, as both firms strive to anticipate the forthcoming behavior of the other. Enduring equilibrium cannot prevail unless the respective forecasts are eventually realized and adhered to. Even if forecasts of rival's behavior are accurate, the equilibrium will not automatically perpetuate itself, for revisions in anticipations can unloose a completely new cycle of fluctuations. Only when the ex ante forecasts are compatible with events and have some durable base will the duopoly adjustment be at all stable.

It can be observed that if the output of A expected by B is exaggerated, then B's production for the period will be, in retrospect, entirely

too small and the market price too high.   Demands for substitute products would be stimulated.   Conceivably, the output expected by *A* of
B, and vice versa, may surpass the actual behavior; duopoly output
might then fall short of a combined monopoly level.   An exceptionally
large output, exceeding even the competitive volume, and due to each
firm minimizing, ex ante, the other's production, is likewise not beyond
the realm of possibility.

Cases of "bluff" tactics can also be included within the scheme; one
firm may overproduce in one market period in order to instill a spirit of
caution in the rival's production policy for subsequent periods.   Winning strategy requires that each firm include in its own conjectural variations the full response that can be induced in the other firm's output,
whatever the technique for doing so happens to be.   Stultifying problems may also be envisaged.   Each firm may give the other the impression that it is going to produce the competitive output volume.   The
upshot may be that both abstain from producing.

MARKET-PRICE ASSUMPTIONS

The exposition of duopoly theory so far revolves about the assumption that however output decisions are reached the full quantity
produced is released for sale in the given market period.   This is a
restrictive hypothesis.   Firms can sell from, or hold for, inventory; if
carrying costs are prohibitive they can destroy part of the output if to
do so is more profitable than enlarging sales.   To understand these cases
involves not output but *market-price* hypotheses.   Assuming that firm
A announces the price and is thus the *price leader*, the assumptions with
respect to market price policy comprise at least three distinct types: (1)
A knows *B* will follow his (*A*'s) price policy whatever the direction,
whether up or down; (2) *A* knows *B* will not follow a price rise above
some level but will meet any price fall; (3) *B* will follow upward price
movements but will object to downward price revisions below some stipulated level; if *A* should try to enforce such low prices *B* will retaliate,
say, by a ten per cent price cut for every one per cent lowering by *A*.
Supplementary assumptions can be made in each case; until we explicitly disclaim it we assume that *A* possesses full knowledge of how *B* will
act.*

---

* This analysis should be applicable to "open price" industries and to many real world
cases; for one firm usually initiates a price movement; others follow with a minor or major
time lag.   Simultaneous action seems to be a more dubious hypothesis; when it occurs it
probably evidences collusion rather than spontaneous behavior.

Complete Price Follower

When A knows that B is a complete price follower, if both firms are of approximately the same size the price should finally settle at the monopoly level, for this figure should maximize each individual profit share. If we assume a linear demand curve and costless output, and if we include the proviso that as price is the same and both firms are the same size they share the market equally, then if the market-demand curve D_x intersects OX at N, the demand curve for firm A will be $\frac{1}{2}D_x$, cutting the OX axis at $\frac{1}{2}ON$. The MR curve of A's demand curve will cut the OX axis at $\frac{1}{4}ON$. This is the most profitable sales volume for A; on our assumption, it is also B's sales. Total output is thus $\frac{1}{2}ON$, or equal to the monopoly amount.

Precisely the same consequences would ensue if the millions of farmers selling under conditions of atomistic competition complied with the lead of one of their number in raising price. It is the advantage secured by not joining the movement when others agree to withhold supplies that prevents monopoly pricing practices from becoming even more pervasive; with everyone anxious to dispose of more output at the higher (monopoly) price the price is driven down to the competitive level.

Downward Price Follower

If A knows that B will follow any downward price revision from some presumed level, say OP_1 in Figure 3A, but would never go higher, A's demand curve would resemble the discontinuous path $P_1d_2d_3d_4$, where $d_1d_2d_3d_4$ represents one half of the market-demand curve; the latter would be A's demand curve if B was a completely servile follower, but sharing the market equally with A at identical prices. In the light of

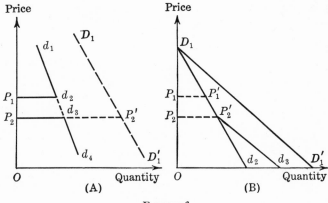

FIGURE 3

B's behavior, A's MR curve runs from P_1 to d_2, then drops precipitously. Although the solution will actually depend on the exact shape of the MR and MC curves, there is a strong likelihood in this case that price will stick at OP_1; certainly it cannot go higher.   Oddly, if A's MC intersected P_1d_2 to the left of d_2, then firm B would fill more than one half of the market demand quantity.   The outcome thus depends on the level of OP_1 and the reasons for B's attachment to it; it may be a monopoly figure for the combined pair, or it may be either lower or higher.   If costs have risen while B is wedded to a past price (and historical levels do color much of the business man's thought) the final figure may not depart too severely from a competitive price height.

Price Cutting

Rather than merely follow downward, B may threaten to cut price by ten per cent if A dares even a one per cent price reduction below a certain level, say OP_1.   Figure 3A describes this situation.   If B was a complete price follower, the reduced curve $d_1d_2d_3d_4$, one half the market curve D_1D_1', would be A's demand.   As it is, A's curve follows d_1d_2 and then darts back to P_1, for as A names a price even fractionally below OP_1, B cuts to OP_2.   Thereafter, if A meets the OP_2 figure, and even lowers price further, B may merely meet the new price cut.   Should B refuse to sell below a price of OP_2, A's demand would spurt out and then coincide with the full market demand curve.   The demand curve for firm A is thus $d_1d_2P_1P_2d_3P_2'D_1'$.   In this event price would in all likelihood settle at OP_1.   Once more, the proximity to competitive or monopoly price is likely to depend upon the price height at which B's obstreperousness asserts itself.

Limits on B's Sales

Another duopoly variation is outlined in Figure 3B: D_1D_1' is drawn as the full market-demand curve.   If B always concurred in A's price policy, D_1d_2, which is $\frac{1}{2}D_1D_1'$, would appear as A's demand curve, with the remaining half of the market demand quantities supplied by B. A may perceive, however, that B will not assent to a price above OP_1, so that if A should list a higher price B would capture the full market.   Further, knowing that B's full supply quantity equals the abscissae amount P_2P_2', A may reason that at a maximum B can share the market equally only down to a price of OP_2.   Subtracting this amount from the market demand curve D_1D_1' at prices below OP_1, we can define A's demand curve as the discontinuous path $P_1P_1'P_2'd_3$: A's price will settle at the maximum profit position along this path, which is likely to be at or between OP_1 or OP_2. If B withholds some supplies from the market at prices below OP_1, refusing to participate in the price cuts, $P_2'd_3$ will assume a concave form, with d_3 approaching D_1' asymptotically.

Contesting Leadership

The argument of this section has been predicated on the supposition that firm A (the price leader) knows the reactions of firm B (the follower) and thus, by a suitable choice of price policy, can induce B to implement A's price pronouncement. This supposition is akin to the output-leader analysis. If B is obdurate and cannot be provoked from a given market price, firm A can influence B only if it announces a lower price. Then B must either yield or lose all its custom—unless A refuses to fill all orders at the lower price. When A does not care to lower the price, A is the effective follower.

It remains to clear up which firm will be the price leader. Here too, unfortunately, the air is charged with indeterminateness. In certain market structures one firm, not necessarily the largest one, may be the acknowledged leader to whom all others look for the price key. Tradition and little else may govern the relationship. The leader may estimate the price most lucrative to itself, on the basis of a sales analysis of other firms at each potential price. Barring an acknowledged leader to whom all eyes are turned, if the practice is to post prices simultaneously then the lowest priced firm will immediately be the leader, with the others having to conform after a longer or shorter time lag. In the interim, however, the normal distribution of sales may be upset. Hence it will be to the interest of each firm to form their price estimates on the assumption of the lowest possible level that may be declared by the others or risk the loss of immediate sales. If prices are posted, with some time lag separating the announcements of the individual firms the later decisions will in almost all cases have to at least meet the previous low price, even if this was not originally intended, or go lower—but not higher unless the other firms are expected to raise price in short order. In general, even if the price pronouncements are not made exactly simultaneously, the firm that proclaims the lowest price must, in the particular sequence, be adjudged the leader, setting the pattern for the other firms.

Financial Strength and the Role of Inventories

One inference that may be drawn from this analysis, and that emphasizes some unwholesome aspects in fields of small numbers, is that a disproportionately larger firm—one able to supply a greater quantity at a given average cost—and possessed of superior financial resources,* will have a preponderant influence upon price, merely through its ability to instigate a session of price cutting of longer or shorter duration.   A smaller firm (measured in the comparative terms of the output volume of minimum AC) or one that is financially impotent, would be unable to counter the threat.   Contrariwise, where both firms are of approximately the same size there appears a new motive for inventory holdings, namely, to ward off a rival's price-cutting propensities with the retaliatory weapon of sizeable inventories.   The costs of an excessive inventory carry-over may be less than the cost of acquiescence to downward price revisions.

A few remarks on kinks or sharp corners in demand curves and the level at which they are found are in order.   Often these features can be assigned to the entrepreneur's faithfulness to an old historical price and, through inertia and friction, to a reluctance to change.   Perhaps long-run estimates of "spoiling the market" in the future by a current change have a bearing.   Seeking a more rational explanation, perhaps when A raises his price B may refuse to follow because of a high degree of output elasticity, with production taking place under relatively constant or even falling marginal-cost conditions.   New entry into the field might also be facilitated at but a slightly higher price; A's price rising tactics are thus opposed by B.   A converse set of reasons would account for the hostility to a price fall.

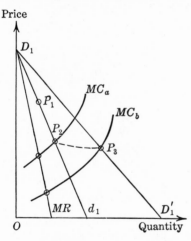

FIGURE 4

A COST-CURVE SOLUTION

The effects of duopoly on the demand curve, and through demand on price, have been labored.   Costs have been virtually ignored.   One suggestion of a unique and determinate solution of duopoly problems for firms of dissimilar size has centered about disparities in cost curves.

In Figure 4, $D_1 D_1'$ is the market-demand curve and $D_1 d_1$ is the demand curve confronting each firm, on the assumption that both charge identical prices and supply one-half the market. MR is mar-

* To be defined more precisely below, pp. 174–178.

ginal to D_1d_1. MC_a and MC_b are the marginal-cost curves of firms A and B respectively.

A Special Case of Conjectural Variations

Considering these relations, suppose A possessed the power to name market price with the one proviso that the sales were shared evenly. It would announce a price of P_1, for at the output corresponding to this price its profits are maximized. On the other hand, if we visualize A's average-cost curve (not drawn), if A's minimum AC equals P_3, say, A will not offer any output at all below this price.

Firm B's MC curve intersects the MR curve at a price within the P_1P_2 range. Sharing the market equally, B would post a price somewhere in this range; thus, it is argued, as B's price is lower A will have to conform to it. Further, it is contended that so long as the price named by B does not drop below P_2, at which $MC_a = P_2$, A will produce and provide for one half the market demand. But if price fell blow P_2, but above P_3, A would equate MC_a to market price, and serve less than one half the market-demand quantity. B's demand curve, therefore, is $D_1P_1P_2P_3D_1'$; it will adapt itself to this curve and name its market price pursuant to usual profit-maximization principles. Hence, it is averred, B will inevitably emerge as the price leader.

The flaw in the analysis is that it assumes that A will submit tamely to B's market price and will sell precisely the amount B proposes for him. To demonstrate its lack of generality, suppose B posts a price in the range P_1P_2 and produces an output equal to one half the total of market demand. If A *correctly predicts* B's production, and subtracts it laterally from the demand curve, A would produce more than the amount mentally allotted to him by B. The defect lies in its neglect of A's output independence and conjectural prescience on market price. B could inspire obedience to its price policy only through price-cutting tactics whenever A failed to submit to its plan of "collusive conformity." But if B imposes its price through intimidation it is superfluous to emphasize the shape of B's or A's marginal-cost curve. Fundamentally, this duopoly solution relies on B's knowledge of A's reactions, which thereby moulds the demand curve $D_1P_1P_2P_3D_1'$ for B. The argument is a special version of the theory of conjectural variations.

ECONOMIC WARFARE

We pass now to issues of economic warfare. Economic warfare can be distinguished from duopoly proper in that its aim is to lower prices in order to drive a rival from the field.   In price-cutting campaigns, in contrast to warfare, the aim is more limited—to secure a greater volume of sales or to punish rivals for certain price actions, but not to compel them to abandon the field.   Economic warfare as a means of reducing numbers in the field also belongs to the theory of entry and exit; merely the occasional brandishing of the big stick is apt to render entry extremely uninviting.

Successful Warfare and the Durability of Equipment

Discerning its rival's intentions, a firm about to be assaulted may submit without a struggle; foreshadowed losses will often breed a docile attitude, and the quietude of an alternative output may well be preferred.   Nevertheless, while its equipment remains as a productive entity its mere presence constitutes a damper on the monopoly price, for some part of the market could be regained whenever the price went high enough to make the foray lucrative.   This raises the extremely important question of whether forcing a firm into bankruptcy accomplishes the ends of battle.

Let us say that because of the struggle the defeated firm undergoes reorganization proceedings, which may entail new ownership and new management, with the claims of old owners and creditors reduced, but that its plant and equipment do not pass into the hands of its belligerent opponent.   Hence, regarding the firm as a bundle of equipment, it will be preserved as a going entity despite the changes in ownership rights. Unless it regards discretion as the better part of valor, production with its equipment will cease only when the bellicose firm makes it impossible for any management to cover average costs, including in the latter the costs of all factors that have alternate uses.*   This condition goes far beyond the legalistic phase of bankruptcy.

Cost Assumptions

There are two sets of vital assumptions in analyzing the problem of economic warfare.   The first pertains to the cost structures of the contending firms, while the second has regard to the financial strength or the capital positions of the dueling firms.   In developing the diverse

---

* Full contractual overhead costs would have to be included in the curve of average costs to indicate the price the firm would receive for each output level in order to cover its full operating charges.   But remembering that revisions of contracts are constantly made (and would have to be made after bankruptcy), only the lowest sum that would be accepted by factor owners needs be included in the relevant "longer-period" *AC* curve.

cost assumptions we shall at first postulate identical financial strength for each firm, both of whom produce identical commodities.

Assume first that the attacker A possesses the cost advantage, interpreting this to mean that the minimum point on firm A's AC cost curve lies below that on B's cost schedule. The cost structures are represented in Figure 5A. D_1 is the general market-demand curve for the commodity; the cost curve AC_a belongs to firm A and cost curve AC_b to firm B. Least-cost outputs are, respectively, at OL and ON. Examination of the diagram makes it evident that B can be driven from the

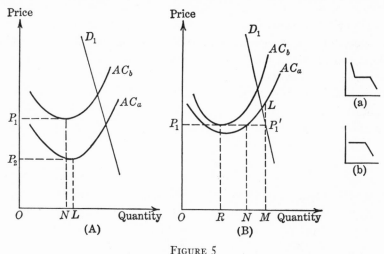

FIGURE 5

field without any loss to A, for by announcing a price slightly below OP_1, (the minimum point on B's cost curve) A can envelop the entire market while escaping any loss to itself. B can produce only by impairing its capital position and foregoing the more lucrative alternate uses of factors under its control.

The cost structures depicted in Figure 5B are more probable. Here, although A's least-cost output is below B's, the entire market demand cannot be filled by A except at a price below the minimum AC_b, unless A is willing to accept losses on its part. Unless A consciously welcomes the loss to render production unprofitable for B, B can produce and remain in the field.* For A to supply the full market at a price below B's minimum cost would involve a loss of at least LP_1' per unit for itself.

---

* B might produce the minimum-cost output even though actual sales in any period do not warrant it, holding as inventory the unsold portion of output from one period to another, perhaps producing a by-product in the interim idle periods. Of course, carrying charges would have to be included. See below, p. 411.

Actually B, the besieged, could punish A and impose greater losses upon it by producing some quantity and driving the price lower still.   So long as B stays at or to the left of its point of minimum costs, while A is at a cost point to the right of its minimum, A's total losses on the greater volume might be so overwhelming as eventually to threaten it with bankruptcy.* If B simply announced that it was willing to sell an amount OR at a price equivalent to OP_1 and A, pursuing its objective of overwhelming B, announced a lower price, the ultimate upshot would be that A itself would be forced from the field.†

Conceivably, A can drive B from the field in this second case without serving the full market.   Suppose, at a price just below OP_1, which is B's minimum cost, A agreed to sell all the output that it could produce without loss to itself, amount ON in Figure 5B.‡   Then a demand quantity slightly greater than NM, at a price slightly below OP_1, would remain unsatisfied and open to B.   Unless this border of demand, or the demand schedule which is left for B after A's "rationing" policy at the lower price, is tangent to or lies above some portion of B's cost curve, B would have to succumb because of its inability to sell profitably, and the A firm would accomplish its purpose§.

Assuming similar cost structures, with the minimum AC being identical for each firm, in order to render production unprofitable to firm B, the A firm would have to declare its willingness to sell at a price below its own minimum AC.   Warfare would be a costly business and eventually A itself would have to fall, on the hypothesis of equivalent financial strengths and sideline pricing by B at its minimum AC level.

Finally, the cost advantage may lie with B.   In Figures 5A and 5B, AC_a now belongs to firm B and AC_b to A.   Formidable losses would be in the offing for A in attempting to capture the field; it could not hope to succeed but would fall vaingloriously, because whatever losses B might suffer, A's losses would always be commensurately greater.   Thus it is only when a decided cost advantage is possessed that an attacker can compel a rival with relatively equal financial strength to desist in its productive operations.

* Recall in this connection our postulate of equal financial resources.

† This kind of announcement by B which does not result in sales of the particular product, while it occupies itself say, with by-products, might be called "sideline" pricing.

‡ The A firm would have to insure that the goods went into the hands of final consumers to avoid the growth of secondary markets.

§ The demand schedule facing B would be discontinuous; in 5a there would be a horizontal segment at OP_1 for at this price B could share the market with A.   If the upper portion of the demand curve allowed profitable output to B, A would have to offer more than ON units for sale at OP_1.

Financial Strength

It is time to discard the hypothesis of equal financial resources. Suppose first that the balance of financial strength, including in the latter both cash and the ability to command cash by borrowing or disposing of other assets, lies with the attacker. Possessing a cost advantage along with financial strength, it should be able to bully its way into sole dominance, depending of course on the margin of its financial resources. Even if it is at a cost disadvantage, it may still succeed if its financial strength is adequate for, so long as it can withstand losses, and is willing to do so, it can make the field unprofitable for its rival. Should preponderant financial strength reside with the besieged *B* firm, barring extreme cost advantage to the attacker, *B* should be able to weather most economic warfare campaigns.

Thus we can appreciate the crucial role of financial strength in economic warfare. Undoubtedly vast financial disproportionalities can insure victory and dominance in the field. Still it is only a sharp cost advantage that is likely to be permanently successful in deterring rivals from challenging a firm's position and, by each conflict, weakening it. For suppose a firm is defeated despite economically superior equipment; if it announces that it will always fill orders at its minimum cost, the financially strong firm will incur chronic losses; it will never receive an opportunity to exploit its monopolistic position and sooner or later it too will dissolve and disappear. Because of these fears, business firms are likely to prefer some form of price and sales collaboration rather than embark lightly upon economic warfare; irretrievable decisions that can launch a costly internecine strife will be carefully weighed.

But evidence is plain that the financially strong firm may eventually become the sole monopolist seller for, after the first success in a test of strength it may acquire the equipment of the bankrupt firms at "bargain" prices. It thus buys its way into a monopolist position.* New entrants, thereupon, have to compete with a firm that, in a period of struggle for the market, does not have to plan to recover interest and amortization charges on its capital investment—costs that must be included by new entrants on a parity with wage and material costs.

Cost Interdependence

We have presumed throughout that the aggressive and aspiring monopolist concentrated upon forcing price below its rival's costs in

---

* We thus acknowledge implicitly the importance of access to wealth and loan markets, which may debar an economically superior firm from competing on equal terms with one

order to expel the latter firm from the field. Precisely the same result might be accomplished by a policy designed to lift the rival's costs above the sales price.

Let us say that the *A* firm, looking beyond the throes of battle, desires to keep price rigid at the historic level in order not to "spoil the market" for the future, realizing that even a temporary low price will make consumers hostile to a later price rise. If there are certain strategic factors of production required by the rival firm, the bellicose firm could contract for all the factors itself or bid up their price so high as to inflict losses upon the rival *B* producer if the latter emerges as the successful bidder for them. After the latter's bankruptcy, however, if the aggressive firm is still confronted with potential challengers its demise through bankruptcy is also likely.

A single firm could seldom buy enough versatile homogeneous factors of a large factor class as to raise their price and make production costs prohibitive to a new entrant. This suggests that in carrying out its policy a firm will generally concentrate upon heterogeneous factors as operative keys for action. If substitute agents can also be employed they too may have to be blocked to the rival, by contract, hire or a bidding up of their price. The particular resource owners would be the principal beneficiaries of the contest between the warring firms.

MARKET AGREEMENTS

The probability is strong that overt collusion will be the upshot in fields of small numbers. Price-follower-price-leader, output follower, and, generally, all passive market patterns are a tacit form of collusion, rather than an explicit act of connivance for restrictionist ends. Their effectiveness may, however, be as sure as a straightforward agreement among the participants. Let us discuss briefly some types of collusive agreements that may be sought to introduce order in oligopoly markets.

Output Agreements

One obvious form of agreement covers the output level of each firm over a future (usually the annual) period; all too frequently the participants protest with an air of injured innocence when it is suggested that they conspire to fix price. Price, it would be demurred, is left to the

---

inferior economically, but with capital market contacts and a superior liquidity position comprised of readily saleable assets.

"market." Manifestly, the relevant analysis in these circumstances is that of pricing a fixed stock of goods—that is, the market quota.

If the restrictionism accomplishes its ends the monopoly output level may be approached—assuming the agreement covers a perfectly substitutable good for which a full market-demand-and-supply curve can be drawn and competitive and monopoly outputs contrasted. In general, if each firm knows the output permitted to others, and assumes they will produce it, this quantity can be subtracted laterally from the demand curve; the firm can then calculate whether it should produce its full allotment, or less, or seek to exceed it. If the full allotment covered by the agreement forced the MR of the reduced demand curve below the MC for that output, the firm would be anxious to cooperate; it would even seek to restrain its output below the permissable levels and proclaim it as an act of "voluntary" abstention if this is allowed under the terms of the original concurrence. Similarly, it would experience a strong urge to expand its output and surpass its quota if, for the production of the latter amount, $MR_r > MC$. The success of the agreement for the full market comprising all the firms is thus likely to depend upon: (1) whether each firm is fully apprised of the total output quota; (2) whether estimates of the market-demand curve are uniform; (3) whether for all firms $MR_r = MC$, so that they could be trusted to abide by their quota quantities, neither to surpass them nor fall below. If $MR_r > MC$, and the firms retain some freedom of output action after the quotas are assigned, the analysis tends to coincide with the earlier discussion of the output dependence case.

The bases of quota assignments are literally legion, though in practice either historical norms or percentages of imaginary capacities seem to exhaust the ingenuity of the architects of restrictionism. Nonetheless, whatever the totals subscribed to, unless the agreement contains clauses providing for an enforceable system of punishments for breaches of contract, and of rewards for compliance, the arrangement is likely to disintegrate unless in each firm $MR_r = MC$.

Price Agreements

Price agreements are at least a frank approach to the monopoly objective without the equivocation of "orderly output" agreements; for the moment we presume that the agreement fails to include output. The price may likewise be a historical one, or it may be deemed "fair," or it may be sanctioned by law, or appear most profitable, etc. If each member complies, a sort of pseudo-competition evolves; for each firm will

detect that the demand curve facing it is perfectly elastic at the stipulated price. In contrast to the perfectly competitive case, where the
market-demand curve turns downward at an output far beyond
the economic capacity of any one firm, each firm now discerns that the
demand curve has a sharp corner, at its maximum sales quantity at the
stipulated price, at an attainable output level; this is shown in Figure 5b.
At this point of discontinuity, we learned earlier, MR is likely to be
negative.

If in each firm of the member group the MC curve cuts the MR curve
directly under the demand-curve discontinuity, the full market demand
at the conspired price will be served. If the gap between P and MC is
extremely large, and if this is true in each firm, there is a likelihood that
a lower price and extended output would prove profitable for the full
market. Quality improvements, selling pressure, surreptitious discounts, and price shading are all likely to appear as each firm tries to
expand its share of the market. If the gap between P and MC is narrow, higher prices may prove profitable. If the MC curve cuts the
horizontal price line to the left of the discontinuity, higher prices are
probable, with all firms concurring. If the avenue of higher prices is
closed, the individual firms caught in this particular predicament may
refuse some custom or ration its sales; or, if the firms are honor-bound
to fill all purchase requests, we have curiously enough a situation in
which MC > P.

This is probably all that we need say about collusion, at least on a
general plane: each output and price scheme is likely to have special features of its own which must be treated individually, for they are the
product of the arts of compromise and business diplomacy for which
general principles cannot be advanced. Moreover, the degree of durability and compliance is always a nebulous and indefinite matter. Still,
so long as the result is a price policy in which $P > MC$ for each of the
participating firms, the usual strictures leveled against monopoly will
apply.

Coalitions and Compensations

In addition to overt collusion, there is always the possibility of coali-
tions among certain members to drive others out of the field. Forms of
economic bribery, consisting of compensations by one firm to another to
deter the firm from lowering price or to induce it to increase price, are
also within the realm of strategy and execution. Many possibilities
exist; it is always profitable to make "compensatory" payments when

the amount of profit to be gained exceeds the amount of disbursements to be made.   But the amounts and direction of payment are vague and indeterminate, depending on the individuals who play-the oligopoly game, their resources, their prospective profit gains, and their personal psychological traits.   Furthermore, since such payments may be traceable, prosecution under the antitrust laws would appear to be a powerful deterrent to their universal adoption even though the economic forces invite their use.

DUOPOLY INSTABILITY

Stability in monopoly markets in stationary conditions of demand and cost requires that for each firm $MR > MC$ to the left of the equilibrium output, and $MC > MR$ to the right: running beyond the $MC = MR$ output level will reduce pecuniary income in precisely the same way as falling short of this output.   The latter production level will therefore tend to be maintained.

In contrast, under duopoly even in fundamentally stationary supply-demand conditions, one seller or both may alter their adjustment policy in the quest of greater profits.   As one firm's behavior will depend so much on what it expects of its rival, and as both may move simultaneously from any adjustment already reached, each position is at best unstable: each adjustment has been aptly described as of the "cat and mouse" variety.*   Each firm's movements will provoke the other; neither will stir without prejudging what the other will do.   As the profit balance may be radically transformed by the mutual action patterns, any stability postulates become extremely tenuous; they could be posited only if one firm's output was unalterably rigid or its mental processes prejudiced against even a consideration of change.

The Temptation for Corporate Consolidation

Even besides the instability inherent in the perennial forecasts of the rival's conduct, there is one additional item that renders suspect any solitary stable equilibrium solution of the duopoly problem.   Manifestly the firms cannot help but apprehend the mutual interactions of their policies and their complete interdependence for a profitable life.   Ultimately the appreciation of their common interest in a monopoly policy would tend either to foster collusion of an overt kind or to encourage efforts towards a consolidation of the firms and reorganization of the field.   Even abstracting from combination, the agreement may evolve

* E. A. G. Robinson, *Monopoly*, pp. 24–30.

by mutual consent, through intimidation in the form of warfare or in the form of bargained compromise in a live-and-let-live-let's-be-friends atmosphere.

A duopoly field, therefore, contains elements of perpetual instability, with prospects for a continual regrouping in a way not typical of firms in a competitive or monopoly structure where the individual firm's demand curve is unaffected by the actions of any other single (or few) firm(s). A monopoly reorganization of a former duopoly field would eliminate the oscillations that appear to be inherent in duopoly. In a world in which dynamic changes incessantly interrupt the stationary flow, the manifestations of duopoly instability are undoubtedly lost in the sea of change; they are likely to be of only minor importance as compared to the effects of shifts in demand and costs.

Extension to Oligopoly

After this survey the argument can be readily extended to oligopoly configurations of three or more sellers; assumptions of precisely the same type utilized in the duopoly analysis are again suitable. Normally, it can be surmised that each seller lumps together the output of all other sellers, treating them as one—a procedure that simplifies and imparts greater determinateness to our solutions. Firms probably do view their rivals in this way, observing most intently the projected plans of the larger rivals and compounding them with the probable policies of smaller firms.

The output-follower case can be treated briefly. A small firm of a compact oligopolistic group is likely to act according to our output dependency postulates. Viewing the probable outputs of other firms as a datum the firm plans its output policy. Recalling the case of zero costs and linear demand, we can state that if there are 100 firms in the field with 99 firms each producing $\frac{1}{101}X$, (X being the competitive total of output) then the remaining firm will tend to produce:

$$\frac{1}{2}\left(X - \frac{99}{101}\right) = \frac{1}{101}X.$$

Total output for the 100 firms will thus be $100/101$ of the competitive amount. If there are 1000 firms it will be $1000/1001$, and if 1,000,000 firms, $1,000,000/1,000,001$ of the competitive amount. As the number of firms increase, the approach is closer to the competitive position.

Output-leader roles will probably only devolve upon the larger firms of the oligopolistic group. The principles are as before: if two or more firms embrace this course simultaneously, it will probably culminate in an unsatisfactory profit level for each until at least one of them succumbs to a follower role.

Price leadership, which can be associated with output dependence, presupposes adherence by others, the price followers. The price leader will have to compute the quantities that others will unload at each price before appraising the most profitable figure. If the firm is a small one, any attempt at price leadership, apart from institutional structures in which others are guided by the small firm by tradition or by some ingrained reason or other,* is generally doomed in advance. The small firm cannot succeed, for one thing, in inducing a price rise by withholding output. On the other hand, its output quantity of minimum average cost would probably be too small to press price downward.

In the output-dependence case it was seen that with larger numbers total output approached competitive levels more closely. Another reason for expecting prices more closely approximating competitive norms with oligopoly, despite several larger firms in the field, would be the knowledge of each of the larger firms that as they withheld production to force up prices, smaller firms, individually too small to affect output substantially, would take up the slack: the smaller firms would thus be the prime beneficiaries of the output restraint and price-raising proclivities by the larger firms.† The larger firms will conclude that the slightly higher price, after small firms had filled in the void with their own sales, would be an inadequate recompense for their own substantially reduced sales volume. Consequently, unless the production capacity of small firms is fairly rigid and inelastic, or unless an output policy can be imposed upon them, the price-raising propensities of the large firms will be severely circumscribed.

As oligopoly also involves assumptions as to rival's price or output policy, and as many of the firms may modify their plans simultaneously, the instability noted for the duopoly model will have a counterpart here. Overt or tacit collusion and combination of some portion of the field is a likely development, presaging a more markedly monopolistic structure. But this control can be perpetuated only if new entry and expansion by smaller firms can be blocked.

* As is possibly true of gold, silver, or foreign-exchange dealers where historical factors may introduce a traditional leadership element having almost the sanction of law.

† In a sense this may happen when one country attempts to control the output of its own producers without power to control other producing areas; for example our cotton program and the impetus given to Brazilian growers.

BIBLIOGRAPHICAL NOTE

The theory of duopoly goes back at least to Cournot, who wrote in the 1830s. As indicative of the modern literature on duopoly the following might be cited: Allen, *Mathematical Analysis*, pp. 204–206, 345–347; Chamberlin, Chapter III; A. C. Pigou, *The Economics of Stationary States*, pp. 92, 94, 101; A. Smithies, "Equilibrium in Monopolistic Competition," *Quarterly Journal of Economics* (1940); T. Kristensen, "A Note on Duopoly," *Review of Economic Studies* (1938); George J. Stigler, "Notes on the Theory of Duopoly," *Journal of Political Economy* (1940); W. Leontieff, "Stackelberg on Monopolistic Competition," same journal (1936); an expository article by E. J. R. Heyward, "H. von Stackelberg's Work on Duopoly," *Economic Record*, Australia (1941). For a more philosophical discussion of oligopoly solutions, see K. W. Rothschild, "Price Theory and Oligopoly," *Economic Journal* (1947). As a sample empirical study, see G. J. Stigler, "The Kinky Oligopoly Demand Curve," *Journal of Political Economy* (1947). On the discontinuous demand curve typical of many duopoly solutions, there is the important note by P. M. Sweezy, "Demand Under Conditions of Oligopoly," *Journal of Political Economy* (1939), and the articles by M. Bronfenbrenner, "Applications of the Discontinuous Oligopoly Demand Curve," same journal, 1940; also C. W. Efroymson, "A Note on Kinked Demand Curves," *American Economic Review* (1943). A recent survey is provided by H. Gregg Lewis, "Some Observations on Duopoly Theory," *American Economic Review*, (1948), Supplement, and the surrounding discussion.

The recent volume of John Von Neumann and Oscar Morgenstern, *Theory of Games and Economic Behavior*, breaks new ground in this field. Introductory articles to their massive and monumental work are: O. Morgenstern, "Oligopoly, Monopolistic Competition, and the Theory of Games," *American Economic Review* (1948), Supplement; J. R. N. Stone's review article, "The Theory of Games," *Economic Journal* (1948); C. Kaysen, "A Revolution in Economic Theory?" *Review of Economic Studies* (1946–1947); L. Hurwicz, "The Theory of Economic Behavior," *American Economic Review* (1945); J. Marschak, "Neumann's and Morgenstern's New Approach to Static Economics," *Journal of Political Economy* (1946). Also, the seminar on this volume, reported in *Econometrica* (1949).

The idea of conjectural variations is attributed to R. Frisch. See Hicks, "The Theory of Monopoly," *Econometrica* (1935), p. 14, and Allen, p. 347. The suggested cost-curve solution of duopoly is due to T. Kristensen. The discussion of economic warfare follows that in my own article, "Price Cutting and Economic Warfare," *Southern Economic Journal* (1942).

CHAPTER 8

Monopolistic Competition

THE MONOPOLY CONCEPT REVOLVED about a firm producing a commodity for which perfect substitutes were non-existent and, as a secondary condition, the lack of any substantial market interdependence between the firm's price policy and either sales or prices of other commodities, so that this aspect of the structural adaptation could be ignored. Under monopolistic competition the first condition is retained, while the second restriction is abandoned; the cross elasticity and the coefficient of price interdependence are so large that to omit these interrelations is to miss a vital part of the problem. The analysis is thus reminiscent of the duopoly relations of the preceding chapter, with the distinguishing proviso being that now the interdependence is presumed to be between sellers of imperfect rather than perfect substitutes. Some of the impediments to entry that serve to explain the multiplicity of products and the heterogeneity of competition will also be considered. The peculiar dilemma of monopoly and innovation constitutes a final topic for this chapter.

PASSIVE AND ACTIVE REACTIONS

The circle of interdependence was quite definite for perfect substitutes; it is more difficult to prescribe similar bounds for differentiated products. In the oligopoly group the firm was in complete competition with firms producing the identical commodity, but a clear gap in the chain of substitutes separated it from the remainder of the structure; now, however, the firm finds its bearing only relative to the full system. To throw a cordon about any two (or few) firms and to denote their relations as duopolistic (oligopolistic) is always arbitrary, defensible only because of a presumed higher elasticity of substitution of their goods or cross elasticity of demand than between either of them and other commodities at roughly the going price ratios and aggregate income level. Of course we can isolate from the full system any number of firms whose mutual study appears remunerative, examining their interdependence while overlooking their relations with the rest of the structure, calling the exhibit a problem of monopolistic competition. This will do as the formal extenuation of our procedure. It is feasible to fix our sights somewhere and get some results for closely related firms, rather than to abandon the project on fastidious perfectionist grounds of incompleteness because it evades some side relations.

Our main analytic distinction is between structures of passive and active reactions. Thus B is a passive price follower if, after A has named his price, B regards it as immutable and proceeds to adjust MC to the MR of its new forthcoming demand curve. This assumption is similar to the output-dependence and price-follower cases. In contrast, a combatant price leader will not acquiesce so supinely if it is dissatisfied with A's price. Instead it may, through price pressure, strive to compel A to alter its ways: by lowering P_b sufficiently, the announced P_a can be rendered unprofitable to firm A. Although the B firm's MC will probably exceed its MR, during the course of the struggle it refuses to sanctify A's price but takes measures to force A to revise it. In short, the passive price-follower pattern relies on entrepreneurial estimates of asymmetry; the coefficient of price interdependence, with P_a the independent variable, is thought by A to be positive. With P_b the variable, however, whatever price is named by B, it is believed by B that the A firm will hold fast its own price. Differences in the size of the firms would be an adequate reason for the belief in asymmetry.

There are some structures, however, that do not fit neatly into this scheme. For example, suppose the B firm adheres to its old price despite the change in P_a, even though its new $MR \gtrless MC$. B reacts neither actively nor even passively—on our definitions—but quite inertly. Also, the B firm will react passively to some price movements of A and vehemently and actively to other price changes. This does destroy any straightforward, rigid, empirical application of the scheme. Actually the passive or active designation ought to be withheld until the particular price relations are specified.

Passive Reactions

The theory of passive reactions for two closely substitutable goods, A and B, can be clarified by means of a pair of interrelated demand curves. In Figure 1A, suppose firm A originally announces a price of OP_1. The demand curve for firm B is thus D_1 in Figure 1B. Realizing its impotence to influence P_a, firm B equates its MC to the MR correspondent of D_1. Firm B's price thus settles at P_1' and sales at OM'. Once P_b is known, the demand quantity of A at price OP_1 is also determinate, at OM. As A raises price, to OP_2 say, the demand curve for B moves out to the right, to D_2. For simplicity, assuming constant marginal costs in firm B, indicated by MC_1, and recalling the formula relating price and

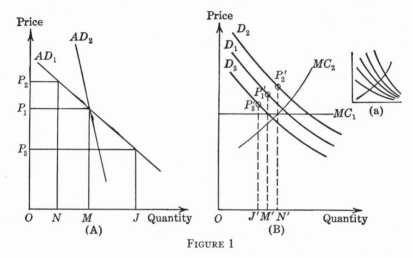

FIGURE 1

marginal revenue; we can write

$$P = MR \frac{E_d}{E_d - 1};$$

then

$$P = MC \frac{E_d}{E_d - 1}.$$

Since, at the same P_1' price as formerly the elasticity of demand will be smaller on D_2 than on D_1, the price of firm B will rise, to P_2', with sales at ON'. A's sales become ON. Whereas A's sales must fall off in given conditions of demand, if P_b rises less than proportionately, B's sales may even increase, despite its higher price, as some of A's former purchasers swing over to buy from B^*. The effect on B's sales can be decomposed into its loss of custom because of its higher price (P_a unchanged) and its increase in custom due to the demand shift from A as P_a rises. If A and B were formerly serving disproportionate parts of the market, with A being larger though having a substantial body of price-sensitive customers, then almost certainly $ON' > OM'$.

Conversely, if A lowers price to OP_3, the demand curve for B will fall

---

*The conclusions are provisional for they depend on the exact shift of the demand curve. Figure 1B is only one illustration.

back to D_3.   Price in B will descend to P_3' with sales at OJ'. A's sales will advance to OJ.   If B's price fall is less than proportionate to A's, then B's sales may narrow while A's market expands.   Conceivably, the sales of both A and B may expand at the lower prices named by the respective firms.   As P_b is determinate once P_a is announced, and as A's demand quantity is then determinate, the full demand curve for firm A, AD_1 in Figure 1A, can be constructed.   On the basis of this demand curve A will name the most profitable monopoly price.   Once A does so, it settles the demand curve evolving for B; then P_b and B's sales are determinate, as well as A's demand quantity.

If the marginal-cost curve for the B firm is rising, as is MC_2 in Figure 1B, then with curves to the right of D_1 price will be higher than P_2'. With demand curves to the left, as D_3, the price will be lower than P_3'. The demand curve for A will be relatively inflexible, as illustrated by AD_2 in Figure 1A.   An interesting conceptual possibility is that in which P_b's price may be constant despite A's price maneuvers even while B's marginal cost curve is rising.   As MC is lower with a backward shift in B's demand curve, for a constant price the demand elasticity must be higher.   The converse holds for a rise in D_b.   In these circumstances the demand curve for A literally degenerates into one drawn on the assumption of other prices constant.

Thus with passive reactions, for both firms $MR = MC$, the difference being that one firm's (A's) demand curve is drawn on the basis of other prices varying with each P_a, and B's demand curve on the basis of other prices being constant.   The higher P_a will drive B's demand curve to the right; the dislodgment will be greater the higher the interdependence at each price ratio, tending to raise P_b.   Sales will expand more in B as B's marginal cost curve approaches the horizontal, simultaneously checking the magnitude of the coefficient of price interdependence. Firm A can thus induce any of several price reactions in B; it will be A's task to extract the price configuration that is most profitable to itself. If B's MC is falling, so that a ΔP_a actually *lowers* P_b, the demand curve for A will be extremely elastic in the upper reaches, mitigating the chances of a price rise by firm A.   By and large, if firm B produces an item that is complementary to that of A, most of the foregoing analysis can be reversed, with D_b shifting to the left as P_a goes higher.

Active Reactions

Undoubtedly the assumption of passive behavior encompasses a good part of the economic field and is an intelligible type of relationship among monopolists producing close but not perfect substitutes.   The analysis takes a more novel turn when B, disgruntled with A's price moves, disregards the equation of MR and MC and bends its efforts to compel A to name a price more satisfactory to himself, to B. Generally, B will seek a higher P_a. Its energies will be directed towards creating for itself a demand curve further to the right, thus securing greater sales. Some of the implications of this relationship can be unraveled by an appeal to an earlier diagram.

According to our demand-curve analysis, the shape of the demand curve for A rests on the diverse assumptions made of B's price movements. For comparative analysis the starting position might be taken as the $P = MC$ position of each firm. Referring to Figure 1, Chapter 2, this can be taken as implicit at point P for firm A. If B realizes that A can be urged to modify its price policy through cutting P_b disproportionately— or threatening to do so— for any P_a below P, the demand curve for A will be of the discontinuous form D_1PD_3 in Figure 1, Chapter 2, as compared to D_2D_2', predicated, say, on proportionate price movements in P_b to any change in P_a. A may well eschew a contest that is unprofitable and instead adhere to the price indicated at P. In view of the discontinuity of the demand curve, at P, $MR = MC$. It will always pay B to react actively by price cutting, if in so doing it can enlarge its profits by forcing other firms to restore their former prices or desist from lowering them. In marginal terms, B's sacrifice of present income, based on a *given* P_a, will be justified so long as the subsequent additions to income through A's revised (higher) price policy outweigh the current income loss. Retaliatory price cuts will be self-defeating beyond this point. After the weapon is once employed the mere threat of retaliatory future price cuts by B to price changes by A can decide A's price policy. Nevertheless, B must prepare to implement its policy whenever A fails to be intimidated by the mere threat of a price war.

Thus, to represent the equilibrium under monopolistic competition for firms selling differentiated products; for the A firm we draw its demand curve on the basis of full adjustment elsewhere; for the B firm, we draw its demand curve on the assumption of A's price as a datum. When B is passive it will equate MC to the MR curve forthcoming on the basis of P_a constant; for both A and B, $MC = MR$; when B is an active respondent, its $MC > MR$ during the period of conflict so that P_b is lower than the maximum monopoly price on the basis of the given P_a. If B reacts actively to a new P_a, then D_a is discontinuous and, at the P_a named, it is likely that $MR_a < MC_a$, while $MC_b > MR_b$, making the particular price unattractive to both firms.

Conditions of Active and Passive Reactions

Departing from the purely formal plane of analysis, passive reactions are likely whenever the B firm is so remote from A as to dispel any illusions of influencing the latter significantly by a counter price cut; this condition is, of course, very close to our definitional image of monopoly, and largely evades the peculiar problems of monopolistic competition. Perhaps B is convinced of A's adamancy to either guile or temporary price pressure; it would then be futile for B to launch an active but temporary price-cutting policy.   More lasting conflict might be unsatisfactory to B on contemplation of the disparity in financial strength or in cost conditions, and thus the potential losses in any protracted session of economic warfare.   Active opposition is probable when the markets are so closely intertwined that there is a sharp fall in B's sales if B does not meet A's price fall proportionately while, if it does, it can only maintain but scarcely augment its previous volume of sales: the general "market" demand, so far as B visualizes it, is believed inelastic, with the primary effect of a fall in P_a being a fall in P_b without any real enlargement of sales.*   The demand-curve family that confronts B, based on the different P_a prices, tend to converge at low prices or fan out more at low levels of sales than at high, as in Figure 1a.   We can conjecture that as P_a and P_b both fall, the income effect on demand is fairly nil and the substitution effect is also small, so that purchasers flock to buy more remote substitute products although they are very responsive to changing price relationships between P_a and P_b.   As a condition for active reactions, B must also believe in A's amenability to a display of resistance.   Financial strength figures to be a factor of the utmost importance in determining whether a firm's reaction is of a passive or active variety; the firm will hesitate to launch even a temporary price struggle unless it can withstand the early losses and forego those profits that are immediately within its grasp despite A's objectionable new price policy.

Warfare and Differentiated Products

The analysis of economic warfare, earlier conducted on the assumption that A and B sell perfectly substitutable commodities, is simplified

* It might be objected that if B's sales are insensitive to a price fall, A's demand will also be inelastic, thus checking A's price experimentation if B allows price to fall roughly proportionately.   Two explanations are possible: (1) either A or B may be mistaken as to the degree of demand elasticity, with A imbued with the idea of elasticity and B obsessed with the fear of inelasticity; or (2) as the products are dissimilar, if B appeals to a higher income class it may lose the sensitive, price-conscious purchasers if it fails to cut price while failing to gain any important additional custom when it does slash its sales price.

when the products are differentiated. For A to banish B from the field it will be necessary for A to dictate a price that moves D_b at all points under B's curve of average costs. It is conceivable that some consumers may be so attached to B that despite A's strongest efforts the demand remaining to B may be large enough to accommodate it and enable it to subsist in the field. In the duopoly relations of perfect substitutes, given a more satisfactory cost position and adequate financial resources, the aggressive firm could always bend its rival to its will, pushing it from the field if it set its mind to do so.

MUTUAL INTERDEPENDENCE

Just as for output reactions, it is possible to draw *price-reaction curves* to picture the process of mutual price adaptation. They are analogous to the output-reaction curves of duopoly theory and are a further extension of the curve relations depicting the general equilibrium interdependence of two commodities under the competitive hypothesis. Under monopolistic competition, prices rather than outputs constitute the direct connecting links between markets. In Figure 2A, equal-profit contours for firm A are drawn, with each point on a curve indicating the price P_a that, given the associated P_b, allows a given profit level. The individual curves tend to be circular: at the same P_b, multiple values of P_a might yield identical profit results or vice versa. Only the lower portions of the curves are drawn on the figure. As we move up the field to higher contours, A's profits rise, for as P_b goes higher, purchasers are deflected to A's market and, at the same prices as before, A's demand curve is further to the right and profits higher. Similar profit contours can be drawn for B. As before, the minimum points on each profit curve can be connected and A's price-reaction curve, AA', elicited. As the point of tangency between a horizontal line from each P_b and the profit contours indicates the P_a of maximum profits for each P_b, the price-reaction curve relates A's price adjustments of maximum profits to the various possible P_b prices. Normally, it should rise to the right, for as P_b goes higher a rise in P_a ought to enhance A's profits; ultimately, however, it will become perfectly vertical, for a further price rise in A will be unprofitable despite the lift in P_b. The reaction curve BB' can be constructed in the same way. The separate price reaction curves AA' and BB' are placed in juxtaposition in Figure 2B.

Imagine that A knew B's reactions, and was literally apprised of the BB' curve. A would name the price indicated at point a, which is the highest possible point of tangency between BB' and A's profit contour system. In the same way, if the *B* firm was the price leader, able to proclaim a price and induce *A*'s reaction, it would announce the price indicated at *b*.

There is a spurious paradox here: apparently, each firm is better off as

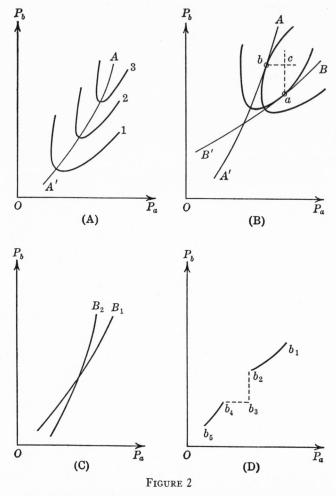

FIGURE 2

a follower than as a leader, for when *A* is the leader its profits are indicated by the profit contour through point *a*, which is on a lower contour than that running through *b*. This seems fantastic; it is incongruous that a firm that knows the reactions of its rival will not profit as a consequence. These anomalous results are ascribable to drawing the reaction curves in such a way that P_a always rises in sympathy with P_b (and vice versa), implying that the profit contours wind endlessly up the field

When we recall that the profit contours are circular, it appears, manifestly, that P_a will not follow P_b continuously upward, for a higher P_a will divert demand, if not to B, then to the rest of the product field, and reduce A's profits.   But this must mean that at some P_b there is a P_a of higher profits than any other position in the chart field; thereafter an advance to a profit contour higher in the field actually denotes lower profits.   The apparent greater profitability at point b, the follower position for A, is therefore readily explicable: that b is higher on the field than a does not signify greater profits at the former point.

Price Leadership

If both A and B vie for price-leader positions, announcing prices simultaneously in an effort to induce the appropriate reaction of the other, the final equilibrium would have to be the result of a new series of adjustments, because the a and b positions of Figure 2B are mutually inconsistent.   The momentary price relationship would be at c if both firms pursued their projected price policy on the assumption that the other would respond along the path of the reaction curves.   Ultimately market behavior is likely to be revised, perhaps with one becoming the leader or both followers.

Let us suppose that A acquires the leadership and estimates that B's price-reaction curve is as B_2 in Figure 2C.   Suppose this view is wrong, that the actual reaction curve is B_1.   Unless the price indicated at the intersection of B_1 and B_2 is named by A, the price is unstable, for A's anticipations will be discovered to be erroneous in short order.   Somehow or other A must locate on B's reaction curve for market equilibrium.   By experimenting with his price policy, A will learn not only his own demand curve but also the reaction curve B_1.

The preceding price-reaction curves describe instances of passive price reactions.   Active reactions are implicit in a curve of the form $b_1b_2b_3b_4b_5$ in Figure 2D.   Apparently, as A tries to lower price from the level implicit at b_2, P_b will fall precipitously from the ordinate value at b_2 down to b_3.   If A announces a price between b_2 and b_1 B's reactions will be normal.

Mutual Determination

In the leadership pattern one firm was depicted as a price innovator and the other as a follower, a pattern that appears to have a counterpart in many real situations.   Sometimes both duopolists will accept the price of the other as a datum, adjusting to it rather than surmising that

the rival's price will be modified by its own price; each assumes, erroneously, that the other's price is constant as its own price and sales vary.
Implicitly, each firm presumes its demand curve is drawn on the hypothesis of other prices constant, while actually the demand curve should be
conceived on the assumption of other prices varying as the firm alters

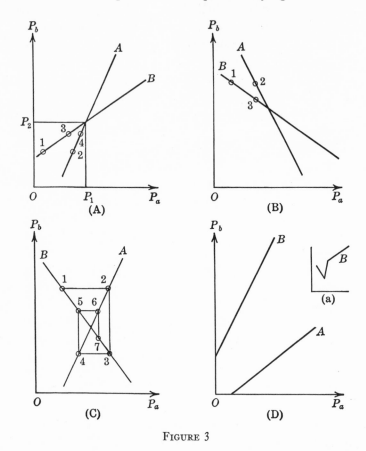

FIGURE 3

price.   In describing the equilibrium path, which is an outgrowth of the
mutual adaptations, the price reaction lines are again helpful.

In Figure 3A, curve A is the reaction curve of firm A, and curve B is
the reaction curve of firm B.   Price equilibrium is possible only at prices
OP_1 for A and OP_2 for B.   With the P_b at point 1 indicating B's original
price, and the P_a at point 2 indicating A's original price, on the assumption that the going prices of the other firm would be named, B will move
to 3 and A to 4, etc., with the movements leading ever closer to the equilibrium price at the intersection of the curves.   The analysis resembles

the equilibrating movements for output followers in a regime of undifferentiated products. Probing the implications of Figure 3A, both firms are apparently producing under conditions of rising marginal costs; as P_b rises P_a rises. In Figure 3B, both firms are producing under conditions of falling marginal costs; here too the movements are equilibrating. In Figure 3C, B is producing under conditions of falling MC while A operates under rising cost conditions. A mutually satisfactory equilibrium is still possible as the numbered points along the adjustment path indicate. In all these cases, at the intersection of the two curves the demand curve of the firm, erroneously conceived as drawn on the basis of other prices constant, is intersected by the real demand curve which is of the other-prices-adjusted variety; point P on D_1D_1' and D_2D_2' could be just such a point.* The MR curve determining the firm's output behavior is associated with the demand curve drawn on the other prices constant hypothesis.

If reaction patterns followed the course of Figure 3D, equilibrium is impossible. At each price named by B, A names such a price as to encourage B to raise his price; then A proceeds once again to do the same. The curves depict the absurd spectacle of both firms pushing skyward in their price policy—presumably despite the total disappearance of buyers!

Hence when each of the closely interdependent firms acts as a price follower and merely projects the rival's previous price, the prices indicated at the intersection of the price-reaction curves are mutually compatible. More generally, when each firm believes that the other's price is fixed independently of its own, the price equilibrium ought to be determinate.

Complementary Goods

When the A and B commodities are in complementary relationship we have another variety of interdependence among differentiated commodities. In the complementarity cases we can choose either price or output hypotheses, although an analysis in terms of price seems more general. In Figure 3B, reaction curve A shows A's response to any given P_b, while B's reaction curve to any P_a is the B curve. In general, a fall in B's price should evoke a less-than-proportionate rise in P_a, and vice versa. As before, an equilibrium is possible at the prices shown at the intersection of the two curves. Profit contours can also be inscribed onto the figure; as A's profits will increase with a lower P_b, a profit contour closer to OX will signify higher profits for A.

* Figure 1A, p. 32.

Follower-leader patterns can also be disclosed for complementarity; if *A* knew *B*'s reactions, *A* could name the price most profitable to himself; indeterminateness is likely if both insist on playing the leader's role. If one firm, *B* say, is willing to take vigorous and active steps to implement its price policy its reaction curve might resemble that of Figure 3a. Firm *A* would be almost compelled to accede to the price indicated at the point of discontinuity at which *B*'s reaction curve sharply rises.

ENTRY AND HETEROGENEOUS COMPETITION

Leaving the realm of price interdependence, let us consider some of the factors responsible for the heterogeneous competition among firms with monopoly power, with or without circular interdependence. The causes of the multiplicity of products can be ascribed in part to the factors that impede entry. If all obstructions to entry vanished, each spot in the commodity belt would be occupied by as many firms as felt they could earn satisfactory profits at the particular station in the commodity universe. There would be commodity diversification in that innumerable commodities would be produced. But when entry into a field is irrevocably sealed, with new firms unable to duplicate an existing product, or when entry into known places on the commodity belt is clogged by one cause or another, then the opportunities of new firms to wrest profits from the environment are contingent upon their ability to devise new products, substitutes of better or worse degree for products currently remunerative. Of course there would be much of a heterogeneous flavor even if all barriers to penetration were whittled away; new firms testing their ingenuity would profit by stealing a march on the remainder of the firms in creating new products. Yet as soon as profitability was proven, a host of imitators would appear. Thus, although there is always an urge to innovation and differentiation in the commodity world, this urge is intensified and the diversity of the commodity belt multiplied by the obstructions to entry. Individuals normally content to be imitators are compelled to become superficial innovators when opportunities to duplicate are closed to them.

In merely broaching the topic of impediments to entry, it is assumed that potential entrants surmise, perhaps wrongly, that there are profitable spots in the commodity chain to which they aspire and to which they are denied access. Knowledge and desire are thus imputed to a latent entrepreneurial group. Ignorance and disbelief in the potentialities will of course deter entry, but in these circumstances there is little further to be said. An impediment can be alleged only if there is an initial desire to appear in some sector of the commodity field on the basis of current knowledge. But monopoly itself may sometimes be attributed to an undue pessimism constraining new firms from embracing opportunities in the commodity chain that would prove profitable to more optimistic spirits. Some of the uncertainty and misgivings, suspicions of consumer hostility and aversions to new products, might be allayed through repeated testimony of the facts on profits by detailed and punctual earning reports by firms currently in the field.

Foundations of Monopoly Power

Let us summarize the chief methods by which entry is impeded. The more durable causes of monopoly power can be confined to a few distinct classes of phenomena, although their disguises are legion. To enumerate: (1) there may be consumer resistance to the products of new firms, despite technological superiority or technical identity with present goods; this resistance is often a consequence of consumer ignorance, inertia or bias. Because of these factors the demand curve for current firms will be less than perfectly elastic. Although these barriers may be vulnerable over time they doubtlessly hinder effective competition. (2) Demand may be too small, in the light of technological facts, to support more than one (or few) firm(s). This factor looms as the basis of the "natural" monopolies, of which public utilities afford the common illustration. (3) Certain types of output are contingent upon the possession of rare skills or unique natural resources. Control over a natural resource, such as iron ore, may establish a *strategic* monopoly foothold. Financial domination of security and loan markets may serve the same purpose. (4) Legal privilege and restraint may exist. Although numerous firms can be supported in a particular industry, entry is blocked through public policy. State-licensing schemes, patent and trade-mark laws, public-utility franchises exemplify the principle. Also, the state may arrogate certain productive functions to itself; state tobacco and liquor monopolies immediately come to mind. (5) There may be physical terrorism and violence. Threatening newcomers with physical punishment may dampen their enthusiasm for entry. Apart from the notorious episodes of the Prohibition Era, American industry has largely been free of these more pernicious practices, which is a testimony to the law-abiding nature of the citizenry and the strength of the legal processes. (6) There may be economic coercion. Price wars, trade-union boycotts, dealer boycotts, denial of access to capital markets, and collusive compensation constitute important limitations upon entry. (7) Collusion and combination may establish monopolies. Bribery of a newcomer may also suffice to bar entry. But these phenomena will be only of transitional importance unless accompanied by a deep-rooted monopoly force. Many of the situations that can be classified within these groupings are frequently characterized as frictions. They cannot legitimately be dismissed as ephemeral phenomena in view of their tenacity and power of survival.

Advertising, be it noted, is important as a cause of monopoly only insofar as it wins consumers and stiffens resistance to substitutes or implants a trade-mark advantage impeding homogeneous competition. Because advertising relies upon the accompaniment of (1) and (3) above, it is not entitled to separate status as a creator of monopoly power. Numerous concrete illustrations can be cited for all these causes. Undoubtedly among the myriads of monopoly manifestations there are cases that almost defy classification; generally the salient characteristics will be found amid the list of our several categories.

Usually the same forces that permit only one firm to flourish in a particular sector of the industrial belt can also be cited as an explanation of the small numbers of duopoly and oligopoly.

ENTRY AND PROFITS

As another aspect of the monopoly world, consider now the plant layout that will be chosen by a firm operating in a monopoly market. Once the demand curve is envisaged, whatever the price premises for alternate products subsumed in its drawing, given the planning curve of average costs, the problem is determinate. After this demonstration we shall examine the concept of a general equilibrium of profitless monopoly even though all the other symptoms, aside from monopoly profits, mar the equilibrium landscape. It is plausible to construe this residue as the characteristic of monopoly, with monopoly profits merely one of the features of impure competition.

The Monopoly Installation

When the plant is in the conjectural stage, monopoly, inherently, does nothing to affect the ACP curves of Figure 4, Chapter 4. However, we are no longer entitled to draw the horizontal price line indicative of a competitive, externally determined market price; instead it is a demand curve that ought to be poised as a counterweight to the ACP curve. If we insert the D and MR curves in the diagrams of Figure 4, Chapter 4, the equipment implicit at the equation of $MR = MCP$, where $P > MR$, will be the maximum layout open to the firm.

Analytically, the theory of monopoly plant selection runs parallel to the competitive theory of installation in much the same way as the earlier analysis of monopoly and competitive output. But there are some deeper implications: just as competitive output could never be to the left of the minimum AC point on a U-shaped cost curve—while in monopoly structures it might be—this arrangement is also conceivable when we consider the ACP curves; the intersection of MR and MCP may occur to the left of the minimum ACP output. Under competition this would violate the fundamental equality of $P = MCP > ACP$.

Hence there are a dual set of forces operating to restrain output in a particular monopoly market: (1) the volume of equipment installed by the particular firm is smaller than if price were adjusted on a $P = MCP$ basis or, where this is impossible, on a $P = ACP$ relation; and (2) after the equipment is installed, output is less because of the monopoly behavior than it would be if the firm, with the equipment on hand, proceeded to equate P and MC. Curiously, as the firm erects too small a layout there is underinvestment in the field; as the layout that it does install is underutilized, there is excess capacity, measured by the difference between the $P = MC$ and $P > MR = MC$ output volumes. Against this output restraint of the firm, however, must be set the expansion of substitute outputs to fill the void as demand is transferred to them by the monopoly pricing practices.

Profitless Monopoly

Let us suppose that heterogeneous entry is universal, that firms must always, in piercing the commodity belt, offer a new product for sale; also, that the repercussions on the demand of existing firms, while small, are still positive. The old firms will be denoted as A, B, C, while R is the new entrant. After firm R is organized as a heterogeneous (if remote) competitor, the effect would be to dislodge the demand curve of firm A and push it to the left. This may engender the strange result of a price rise in P_a; because of falling average cost in the production of A, it may be that a higher P_a is alone profitable after the transfer of custom to firm R. As more and more new firms make their appearance in the commodity cosmos, with limited inroads on the established firms by each new firm, in the limiting case it may be that the final demand curve for a typical older firm, as A, is just barely tangent to A's average cost curve, so that profits are nil even though P_a is higher than before.* Despite the disappearance of profits, the other symptoms of monopoly remain— too many firms, too many products, too many entrepreneurs and too low

* This is Professor Chamberlin's celebrated theorem.

a level of output by each firm and thus, too high a level of average costs, with each firm operating to the left of the minimum AC. Also, there is too much equipment, with simultaneous overinvestment in the entire field compared with the underinvestment and underuse by each individual firm. Furthermore, if the individual entrepreneurs can supervise a larger output level than they are producing, they too must be described as underemployed. Just as the monopoly profits of the firms already in the field are dissipated by the inroads of new firms, a new entrant may seek a place in the field and strive for a footing even though its prospective demand curve is just barely tangent to its estimated ACP curve.

To elucidate the profitless-monopoly situation by way of monopolistic competition rather than monopoly, suppose that new firms are created in response to monopoly profits offering substitutes of a better or worse degree. Rather than countering the entry by a sharp price reduction, the existing firm(s) may passively acquiesce to the new competitor, accepting its price as an unalterable datum, and adjusting their position by equating MC to the MR of the new, contracted demand curve. Price may well be higher than before the entry and profits smaller. Ultimately, as the shock of each new entry dislodges the existing firms' demand curves further to the left, a position may be reached where the demand curves are just tangent to AC. Only at the price indicated by the point of tangency is there any prospect of successful operation; at this output and sales volume, at which $P = AC$, the fact of tangency implies that $MR = MC$, so that $P = AC > MR = MC$.

Envisaging entry into all those commodity sectors in which $P > AC$, so that the demand curves of all profitable firms are constricted until they just touch the AC curves, it is possible to conjure a model in which monopoly pricing prevails but which, because $P = AC$, is devoid of monopoly profits although with all the other features of monopoly action. But this image depends on the ability of new firms to concoct product varieties which entice demand solely from firms enjoying excess profits. Occasionally this profitless equilibrium has been portrayed as the long-run monopoly equilibrium, analogous to the normal profit equilibrium of perfect competition. Entry in both worlds will cease, it is claimed, when profits are normal.

We shall scrutinize this view in a moment. Meanwhile we can agree that the analysis itself is engrossing and important, indicating: (1) that the major consequences of monopoly may be present even without abnormal profits, and (2) that many firms may well be operating to the left of the minimal AC point so that unless demand is increased, shifted from other firms perhaps, a universally competitive price policy is impossible without many firms dropping out of the system. As a further implication, each commodity and its output volume is produced at an uneconomic high cost with some factors being negatively productive —otherwise AC would not be descending.*

That all the characteristics of monopoly may pervail without excess profits, which is puzzling at first sight, is amenable to commonsense interpretation. Many monopolies are notoriously unprofitable; for example, witness the fact that many items are patented but are never exploited. It is apparent that many items can be produced (barely profitably) only because of the suppressed competition and monopoly pricing. Profitability, then, is not the hall-mark of monopoly; it is only one, and not always the most important, of its consequences.

Limits to Profit Absorption

Monopoly profits could be annihilated only if new firms could penetrate the curtain of consumer resistance and absorb custom from going profitable firms. When we consider that a new firm will usually attract custom not solely from one substitute product but from the vast commodity network, the unreality of the profitless-monopoly conception is manifest. As consumers spend on the new good there is a transfer of expenditure from a wide array of goods rather than from one alternate and particularly close substitute. Although some consumers will purchase the new good because the older *functional* variety failed to accommodate them at the prevailing price, usually the demand curve for the new commodity will be compounded of many transfers of demand. Once we acknowledge that the substitutionary relations among goods differ for each consumer, it is futile to argue that new goods can always be created to reduce demand and profits of only profitable commodities. Good substitutes may be devised in some cases; it may be more difficult in others, and quite impossible for still other goods. Either technical limitations, or the animadversions of consumer tastes, may successfully defy commodity emulation. Whatever the reason, the prevailing monopoly profits may be substantial and enduring, diffused in disproportionate amounts among the several firms.†

Sometimes it is argued that entry anywhere in the commodity chain will drain off the abnormal profits. For even in the monopoly case, it is

* Above, p. 81.
† See the restatement by Chamberlin, 5th edition, pp. 201–202.

averred, new firms will siphon demand from the innumerable present commodities, reducing the profits of each going firm.   Even after concurring in this view, it still represents a vast logical leap to conclude that by further entry the abnormal profits of firms insulated by a strong preference fence will be whittled down.   As new firms poke through somewhere in the system, the burden may fall largely on firms barely managing in the struggle for existence; further entry may drive them from the field and only faintly affect the firms enjoying abnormal profits. The mere removal of some firms formerly on the profit periphery may even swell the abnormal profits of those whose profit surpluses were originally alluring to newcomers.

This must not be construed as signifying that profit opportunities do not encourage commodity innovation; they do.   But we should hardly be astonished to learn of the persistence of abnormal profits, for it would be unreasonable to expect them to be consistently eliminated by every clumsy imitative maneuver.

MONOPOLY AND PROGRESS

Progress is a matter of change—although the converse would not always be true.   Economic progress, in the main, is marked by either change in the commodity varieties or in technological processes of producing the known commodity types.   Once new equipment has been conceived, or a new product devised, the entrepreneurial promotional measures to place it on the commodity belt will undoubtedly be quickened if the innovators enjoy sole right to exploit their creation by sealing off entry and exercising the unitary monopoly powers within their grasp. It would be wrong to conclude that innovation would vanish from a fully competitive world; in the time lag between the innovator's first actions and the entry of imitators an important volume of profits may be amassed.   Even after the appearance of homogeneous competitors the equation of MC to P may leave an excess of P and AC adequate to cover depreciation and warrant the replacement of equipment.   Indubitably then, there would be innovation if homogeneous entry prevailed. Merely the prospect of earning a (subjectively) normal level of profits on a new commodity, rather than subnormal earnings on old, will be conducive to measures to introduce a new product variety.   But it is true that many products just profitable on a $P > MR = MC$ policy will not be lucrative on a $P = MC$ pricing stipulation.   Both the order of commodity innovation and the diversity of products in a monopoly pricing system are likely to depart significantly from that obtaining in a competitively pricing universe.

This is the dilemma of monopoly. For, by stimulating innovation and accelerating the pace of progress, monopoly has some wholesome aspects. For resource allocation, as manifest in the relative amounts of production, the results deviate from those that would be experienced in a competitive world. We would have to separate and weigh these elements in considering the welfare aspects of the diverse modes of price behavior.

As a final word on the monopoly-equilibrium adaptation, we ought to note that under monopoly, just as under pure competition, the ability of any firm to make its most profitable adaptation, of $P > MR = MC$ with existing equipment, or to erect the most profitable layout, hinges upon its ability to command the requisite money sums for these adjustments. This assumption ought to be made explicit.

In all these problems dealing with fields of small numbers, with their "games aspect" and indeterminacies, it is worth noting that pecuniary compensations among firms, besides the cat-and-mouse market policies, may make their appearance. In principle, compensations are latent between producers as a means of inducing suitable price policies; while in entry, the intruder may, when his intentions can be discovered in advance, be forestalled from implementing his plans by a suitable payment. But this process, besides running afoul of the legal processes, may well be a costly one; hence it is not, by itself, likely to be permanently successful in protecting a going firm from the encroachments of others.

BIBLIOGRAPHICAL NOTE

The emphasis on the interdependence of markets under monopolistic competition, and the concept of profitless monopoly, is largely the contribution of Professor Chamberlin. Other articles on interdependence are listed in the note at the close of the preceding chapter. Aspects of the interrelations among demand curves are elaborated in my article, "Foundations of the Demand Curve," *American Economic Review* (1942). Because of these interrelations, and a belief in the normal presence of a mass of price sensitive consumers, Alfred Nicols has argued recently that the firm's demand curve is likely to be extremely elastic, making practically imperative a $P = MC$ adaption for the individual firm. See "The Rehabilitation of Pure Competition," *Quarterly Journal of Economics* (1947).

A recent plea for more prompt and complete reporting of corporate profits to facilitate the birth of new firms, and an argument for more efficient operation of the price mechanism is contained in the brief volume by businessman H. S. Dennison and economist J. K. Galbraith, entitled *Modern Competition and Business Policy*, which also contains a reaffirmation of older views.   The literature on monopoly practices and large-scale enterprise is mountainous. An admirable and fairly recent empirical study of monopoly practices is A. R. Burns, *The Decline of Competition*. The various TNEC studies provide a mine of information on complex cases of monopoly behavior. Most of the material still awaits effective synthesis although some steps in this direction were taken by G. Stigler, M. M. Bober, M. Abramovitz, and M. Watkins, "Papers Relating to the Temporary National Economy Committee," *American Economic Review* (1942), Supplement.   Also, D. Lynch, *The Concentration of Economic Power*.   Obstructions to entry are discussed in Chapter VI of Corwin Edwards, *Maintaining Competition*.

CHAPTER 9

Selling Costs

SALES OUTLAYS MUST BE INCORPORATED into our study as an additional attribute of a monopoly world and determinant of the equilibrium of the firm. Advertising expenditures constitute the most interesting, though not the sole, manifestation of sales outlays. The use of salesmen, public-relations expenditures, and gifts to purchasing agents, are all to be included as sales outlays. Most of this chapter, however, will view sales outlays as synonymous with advertising. It is not an exaggeration to say that the procedures of advertising simultaneously accomplish commodity homogeneity and heterogeneity. To encroach on the market preserves of other sellers, the firm must demolish the notion of a sharp differentiation of other products from its own. Advertising with this objective will restore a larger degree of substitutability among goods and of market homogeneity. In the same act, however, the firm must inculcate an attitude of the superiority of its own product, to instill in consumer consciousness the idea of a greater heterogeneity than exists in fact. Whatever the motives, it is the ubiquity of these outlays and their ramifications on costs, demand, prices, and sales, which make imperative the segregation of this monopoly model from a monopoly world devoid of sales pressures.

Furthermore, in a regime where advertising flourishes we cannot be unmindful of the fact that advertising fits rather awkwardly into the concept of a social order in which productive resources are deployed strictly according to consumer desires; advertising operates to reshape desires, even after we have conceded that some advertising campaigns are notoriously unsuccessful. The traditional portrayal of the economic process, of producers acknowledging the inviolateness of consumer tastes, and adapting to them, is not wholly accurate. Resources are not merely adapted to given consumer ends; instead, tastes are partially shaped to producer ends.   The diversion of resources to consumer ends depends upon the receptiveness to sales appeals and the entrepreneurial ingenuity, initiative and imagination in creating them. Although this observation modifies our views on the motivating forces of economic activity, it is by no means tantamount to the conclusion that all sales pressures are inexorably baneful.   Ultimately, advertising must be considered as a venture in political liberty, an exercise of the right to influence the opinions of one's fellow men.   Advertising is analogous to education in that the purpose of both is to increase or modify knowledge and thereby influence the individual's sense of values; yet it differs from education in that it is a one-sided appeal rather than an intellectually complete presentation of the facts.

Advertising is usually associated with the impersonal sales appeals. Often the same objective of influencing purchase decisions is sought through direct contact with prospective buyers.   Letters, house canvassing, and trade salesmen are illustrative; their object is to create a favorable sales climate.   Although in the ensuing analysis we generally discuss advertising outlays, the personal selling pressures can similarly be included in the concept of selling costs.   Sometimes the precise line of demarcation between selling and production costs is difficult to draw; still, the idea of producing to fill an existing scale of preferences, and of activities devoted to modifiying the preference structure, is clear in principle and acted upon in practice.

Although conceptually discrete, it is not easy to divorce the theory of advertising from that of entry and the legal protection accorded sellers by trade-mark laws enacted to safeguard their infringement.   Motives for advertising all but vanish in an atomistic competitive world where entry was open to all, for only a fraction of the benefits, an amount quite disproportionate to the aggregate advertising outlays, would redound to the favor of the firm incurring the expenditure.   Consequently it is only the legal protection against commodity trespass in conditions of demand expansibility that provides the sustenance for the familiar fabric of the advertising world.   Cooperative advertising of the tamest sort, by an industry in an "Eat More Bread" or "Drink More Milk" campaign, would flourish under atomistic competition.   Even then it would be undertaken not by a single firm but by the united group—a monopolistic type of organization combined to differentiate·the industry's product from all the rest.

It is likewise hazardous to separate the study of advertising from the theory of product variation.   In the light of the subjective definition of a commodity adopted earlier, we observe that as advertising alters consumer valuations it literally places a new product in the commodity belt. Puristically the logic of this view is unassailable, yet for our present purposes it may be questioned.   As we are anxious to detect the special influence of sales outlays on a given commodity chain, we can distinguish advertising from other costs of producing a *technical* commodity, defined from the seller's standpoint, and witness its ramifications.   Only if the technical commodity variety is indefinable, and if advertising costs are inseparable from other costs, would we have to treat sales outlays as merely a special aspect of product variation.

ADVERTISING AS A PRODUCTIVE AGENT

Earlier, a distinction was made between output factors and income factors.* Both factors are paid for because they are productive of income to the entrepreneur.   The output factors have a marginal physical product with a sales value; sales outlays, as an income factor, are incurred not for the physical productivity of, say, a \$1,000 expenditure block, but because with the outlay either the demand quantity at any given price can be expanded, or the demand price for any output quantity can be raised, with either extension contributing to entrepreneurial profits.

Considering the several types of sales outlay, such as billboards, daily newspapers, weekly newspapers, magazines, radio time, etc., let us seek the conditions under which a further expenditure will be lavished on one sales medium rather than another.   Writing $\Delta X_1, \Delta X_2, \Delta X_3 \cdots \Delta X_n$, as the increase in sales at a given price from advertising media 1, 2, 3 $\cdots n$, and $\Delta A_1, \Delta A_2, \Delta A_3 \cdots \Delta A_n$ as the additional sum of expenditure on the various forms of advertising, where each ΔA represents, say, a block sum of perhaps \$1,000, then further sales expenditure on sales agent 1 (say newspaper space,) will be preferred to medium 2 (say radio time,) if

$$\frac{\Delta X_1}{\Delta A_1} > \frac{\Delta X_2}{\Delta A_2}.$$

Just as marginal physical products, at any given level of output, had to be proportionate to factor prices, for any aggregate sum of sales expenditure, the equilibrium condition for the sales increase for each outlay must be

$$\frac{\Delta X_1}{\Delta A_1} = \frac{\Delta X_2}{\Delta A_2} = \frac{\Delta X_3}{\Delta A_3} = \cdots \frac{\Delta X_n}{\Delta A_n}.$$

* Chapter 3.

There is thus a strong analogy in the hire of income and output factors.　These remarks also help us in distinguishing selling costs from production costs.　Production costs for any given output quantity are those minimal sums imperative in readying a commodity for sale, even if the demand price for the output quantity is zero.　Thus the output quantity must have a form, time, place dimension, and a mechanism for transferring possession.　Given the demand price for each unit of the commodity mass defined in this fashion, additional cost outlays designed to raise the demand price can be classified as a sales outlay rather than a production outlay.　Any change, of course, in the physical dimensions of the commodity, or location or time availability, will likewise affect the demand price.　But once these dimensions are isolated, however vague and faint their boundaries are, then other cost outlays fall naturally as sales sums.　It is as if, from the seller's viewpoint, we can impute separate dimensions to the commodity, represented by the symbols A, B, C, D, $E \cdots N$.　Symbol A might denote the form of the good, B its location, C its time availability, D its provisions for transferring title, E delivery, F terms of payment, G newspaper advertisments, H radio time, etc.　Expenditures by the firm on some of these elements fall naturally as production costs, and others fall as sales costs; some of the magnitudes will defy classification according to these simple criteria.

Diminishing Returns to Advertising

As advertising expenditure aims at changing tastes, ideally each increment in the sales outlay should dislodge the demand curve, pushing it to the right.　It is tempting, and it probably bears some degree of verisimilitude, to cite a law of diminishing returns to advertising.　But it would have to be so burdened with qualifications as to belie its status as a valid working principle; the subject affords abundant scope for empirical investigation.　The thought would be expressed in some such way: as constant increments of advertising expenditure are made, the demand curve is dislodged laterally to the right by ever less significant amounts.　Or, more precisely, at any given price the additional sales quantities wanted diminish as further increments in sales outlay are incurred.　Assuming market price, and the total sum expended on advertising (A), and the total sales (X) as data, if we let ΔX_n and ΔX_{n+1} represent the increase in sales, and ΔA and ΔA_{n+1} the increase in advertising, then

$$\frac{\Delta X_n}{\Delta A_n} > \frac{\Delta X_{n+1}}{\Delta A_{n+1}}.$$

Thus if total sales are 1,000 units and total advertising expenditure $10,000, and ΔA is $1000, the ratio may be, say, 100/$1000. If sales are 1100 units and advertising outlay $11,000, the ratio may fall, say, to 95/$1000. It would signify that the measure of the elasticity of advertising,

$$E_a = \frac{A\Delta X}{X\Delta A},$$

ultimately approaches zero.

The substance of this law could be sought in either of two premises: (a) that the initial increments of sales outlay immediately attract the groups most receptive to the new education, so that additional sales expenditures influence less interested groups; or (b) even if the entire group is immediately bombarded with the first sales plea, successive sales expenditures that canvass the same audience are less effective in evoking additional demand, for to induce them to buy more of the advertised product involves an increasing sacrifice of other products: there is a type of decreasing marginal rate of substitution (or increasing rate of resistance) in operation, rendering the demand curve more rigid.

Irregularity in Response to Mental Stimuli

A first qualification to any stubborn adherence to this "law" is that the efficacy of an advertising campaign is dependent largely on the general size of the block sum allocated to the purpose rather than to minor increments or decrements about this total. For example, there is seldom any way of knowing when advertising—or any type of education, for that matter—will strike firm root. Minute gradations are likely to make only a feeble impression, while a $10,000 "increment" of expenditure from a zero level may have a marked result. The next few increments, by amounts even as large as $250 each, may fail to arouse any additional desires at all until a total sum of say $17,500 is reached. Demand may then suddenly spurt sharply and vigorously to the right. Interminable discontinuities of this nature undoubtedly conspire to complicate the maximizing effort of the firm. Probably all that can be safely concluded is that in any geographical area (given the rest of the data) and beyond a certain expenditure, diminishing returns to "education" will probably prevail, depending upon the income position of the audience, their receptiveness to sales promotional devices, and the perspicacity and discrimination of entrepreneurs in waging the sales campaign. Sometimes, even the assumption that demand curves will move laterally and invariably to the right when more advertising expenditure is lavished is not unequivocally warranted.   For example, an intensive campaign to popularize a certain item may actually offend upper-income groups without engineering a compensating improvement in the demand from lower-income groups.

SELLING-COSTS EQUILIBRIUM

Let us diagnose the profit-maximization problem of a firm expending outlays for advertising.   If we visualize D_1 as the demand curve prior to the inception of the advertising program, and MC as the cost curve exclusive of any sales expenditure, the monopoly equilibrium will settle at the usual $MC = MR_1$ output position.   Introducing advertising outlays, D_1 now moves out to a new position, D_2.   Once more the equilibrium condition must be satisfied, but this time of $MC = MR_2$.   The advertising allowance will repay itself if the new *net* revenue—the sales receipts over and above production costs—exceed the old net revenue by more than the sales outlays.   In the final equilibrium not only will $MC = MR$ in the usual sense along given MR and MC curves, but the addition to total profits derived from creating a new demand and MR curve will equal the incremental selling outlays.   For introductory purposes the dual equilibrium conditions may be stated as

$$P > MR = MC, \tag{1}$$
$$\Delta R = \Delta A, \tag{2}$$

where MC is exclusive of any sales outlay, ΔR is the additional profits created by the demand-curve shift, and ΔA is the additional sales expenditure to move the demand curve to a higher total-profit level. Thus:

$$\Delta R = (TR_2 - TC_2) - (TR_1 - TC_1),$$

where for both total revenue and total cost quantities, $MR = MC$, with the difference between them being that different demand curves generate the TR_2 and TR_1 sums.   Advertising outlays are omitted from the TC totals.

In terms of factor hire the conditions also imply, that just as factors are used so that marginal revenue products equal factor prices, so that further profitable factor use is impossible, the marginal receipts from an increment of advertising is equated to the cost of a unit of advertising. Thus

$$\frac{MRP_a}{P_a} = \frac{MRP_b}{P_b} = \cdots \frac{\Delta R_1}{\Delta A_1} = \frac{\Delta R_2}{\Delta A_2} = \cdots 1.$$

Sales Contours

In view of the new equilibrium dimension, that involving marginal selling costs and marginal profits, the diagrammatic analysis is more intricate than heretofore. We first employ an indifference-curve technique to resolve the equilibrium problem when advertising becomes a variable of market policy. On the chart field of Figure 1A, dollar sums of total production revenue and total selling costs are measured vertically, while price is the variable on the horizontal axis. Production revenue is defined as total sales revenue minus total selling costs.

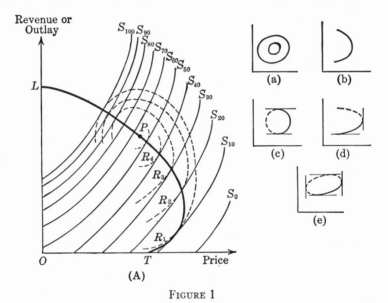

FIGURE 1

The S curves describe sales contours; each coordinate along a curve, such as S_{10}, for example, indicates the various ways in which 10 units of output can be sold. Either sales outlay* can be increased and price raised, or price can be lowered and outlay decreased. Obviously, whatever the price and advertising outlay, production costs along the locus of a particular S curve are the same. Assaying the vertical distance from, say, S_{40} to S_{50}, or from 40 to 50 units of output, the curves are further apart than from S_{30} to S_{40}.* This is a tacit embodiment of the fact that stimulating sales by a given absolute amount, at any stipulated price, can be accomplished only by a growing amount of advertising expenditure, a manifestation of the law of diminishing returns to sales outlay.

---

*In the upper regions. This need not be the case at all prices in view of the irregularities in returns to sales outlays.

In the upper reaches the S curves taper off and become parallel to OY, for despite higher sales outlays, sales cannot be enlarged by raising price. The arrangement of S curves may also be construed as signifying that at any volume of sales outlay, greater absolute decreases in price are necessary to expand sales by a specified amount; demand is thus pictured as less sensitive in the very lowest price ranges after lower-income levels are once tapped.   The S curves closer to OY represent, of course, a higher output level, for at any sum of sales expenditure the sales volume can be expanded only by a price fall.   Though our family of sales contours exemplifies a reasonable general hypothesis, these contours must not be construed as signalizing an immanent law of the data for all markets.

Production Revenue Contours

Production revenue (PR) contours are also inscribed in the figure. Each PR curve relates the various combinations of price and selling cost that yield the same production revenue.   To eliminate any obscurity a numerical illustration will help: if at a price of \$1 and sales expenditure of \$50, 100 units of output can be sold, then production revenue is:

$$PR = TR - A = \$100 - \$50 = \$50,$$

where TR is (as always) total revenue, and A is total selling costs.

The PR field, when fully drawn, tends to have a circular multivalued shape because, by and large, the same production revenue can be derived from innumerable price and advertising combinations; there are literally no bounds to the curvilinear design that might be woven. Assuming that the same PR sums are released by only two prices at each advertising outlay or only two sales outlays at each price, the field would be circular, as in Figure 1a.   Somewhere in this PR curve family will be a point circle that will contain the sales price and sales-outlay combination of maximum production revenue.   If the demand curve and the market responsiveness to advertising are continuous, all circles outside the maximum PR circle will connect price and sales outlay combinations of smaller production revenue.

Just as production theory was simplified by eliminating those portions of the isoquants outside the ridge lines, much the same treatment can be prescribed for the production revenue contours.*   Thus of each circular PR contour, the left-side portion of the full curve can be dropped, leaving an arc, as in Figure 1b, as the sole valid portion of the contour, omitting the segment of the curve that evidences a lower price

* Above, Chapter 4.

at each sales outlay; for greater sales and larger output, with a given production revenue, will foreshadow a minimum rather than maximum profit position. Hence this portion of the PR contours can be deleted: all values to the left of the points at which the tangents to the production revenue contours become parallel to OX can be erased. (See Figure 1c). If the production-revenue curves were perfect circles we would be left with dual sales-outlay totals for each price, as in Figure 1b, but without dual prices for each sales outlay.

One of the dual sales outlays at each price can be eliminated in the same way. Their multiple value denotes that at each price both higher and lower sales outlays leave as a residue the same production revenue. But the higher sales outlay is presumed to evoke a greater volume of sales at the same price and thus entails more output while leaving the same PR; the upper portion of the contour, the broken line in Figure 1d, describes minimum rather than maximum profit positions. Consequently the only portions of the production-revenue contours that are of interest for the maximization problem of the firm are those to the right and above a horizontal tangent parallel to OX, and to the left and below a vertical tangent to OY, as in Figure 1e. The dashed line that completes the contour is economically irrelevant.

The Equilibrium Adjustment

Typically, the production-revenue contours should resemble the sales contours; each production-revenue contour will rise positively with an increase in sales outlay and price. The relevant PR field is drawn in Figure 1. Moving up from the R_1 contour onto R_2, the PR level is raised, for at each given sales outlay the lower price will increase sales and, will, when demand is elastic and TR rising, increase production revenue until the MR along the given demand curve is zero; thereafter PR will decline. Hence all PR points to the right and to the left of this maximum-price point will foreshadow lower levels of PR. With this information, we can construct each PR contour. But only to the right of the maximum PR contour (the point contour P in Figure 1) will the PR contours be of normal form; to the left of P the contours will appear in the convex form that we have decided to suppress.

To solve the equilibrium problem, the most profitable way of selling varying quantities of output is indicated at the points of tangency of the S and R contours; the tangency position reveals the maximum PR obtainable for the output volume. At these points the change in production revenue for a small change in price is exactly equal to the change in sales outlay for a given sales volume with the same change in price.

Thus

$$\frac{\Delta PR}{\Delta P_x} = \frac{\Delta SO}{\Delta P_x},$$

and therefore

$$\frac{\Delta PR}{\Delta SO} = \frac{\Delta P_x}{\Delta P_x} = 1,$$

or

$$\Delta PR = \Delta SO,$$

where SO = sales outlay and ΔP_x = the change in market price. This last relationship essentially is an alternate formulation of the second of our earlier statement of the dual equilibrium conditions. Wherever sales and production-revenue contours intersect, less than maximum production revenue is returned for each output level. Literally, the tangency points ferret out the smallest output for each total production revenue, permitting profits to be maximized at these points. Connecting the points of tangency we trace out TL, a *sales path,* which describes the most profitable way to expand sales.

The most profitable price-and-selling-cost combination must lie between T and P in Figure 1, for only in this range does total production revenue increase as sales (or output) increase; beyond P, total production revenue falls off despite a greater sales and output volume. It will be more remunerative to concentrate on advertising expenditure rather than on price-cutting in order to expand sales if the sales line is steep; if the slope of the line is gentle, lower prices are preferable. On the segment of the TP line that curls up in the same direction as the S curves, a concerted sales effort and price rise will be most effective in enlarging production revenue and profits.

Finally, to determine the equilibrium sales outlay and the equilibrium price, and implicitly, the volume of output, the point of maximum profits along the *sales path* must be isolated. To ascertain this position, which reflects the output-price-sales-outlay combination of maximum profits, we recall that each sales contour refers to a definite output and hence to a definite production cost, while each PR contour describes the absolute amount of production revenue; performing the implied subtraction we extract the maximum profit position. In marginal terms it must comply substantially with the conditions already stipulated: (1) moving on the sales line from tangency position to tangency position, a relation between MC and MPR is implicit. At the maximum position marginal production revenue equals marginal production costs, or

$MC = MPR$, where MC excludes sales outlay,* and (2) at each price (or sales volume) the marginal sales outlay equals the marginal increment of production revenue at that price (or output).

A Demand-Field Device

Another method of illuminating the equilibrium adjustment involves an extension of the demand-and-cost-curve diagrams. In Figure 2, D_1D_1' is the original demand curve prior to any advertising outlay at all. The average production-cost curve is lettered in the customary way, AC. Equating MC to MR, though we omit the latter curve to avoid encumbering the diagram, the firm's output rests at OM and its price at P_1. Suppose that some advertising expenditure is undertaken and that the new demand curve settles at D_nD_n'; if we adjust MR_n to MC, the output becomes OR and the price P_n, and so on. For each advertising outlay there is a new demand curve to which the maximum adaptation is made. All this is familiar; there is nothing to detain us so far.

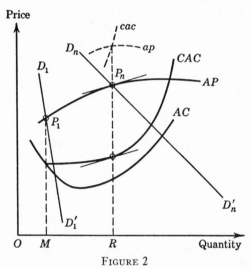

FIGURE 2

When we connect the various prices denoting maximum profits, as $P_1 \cdots P_n$ on the separate demand curves associated with the different advertising outlays, the curve AP of Figure 2 is born. Adding on to each AC the unit advertising outlay required to create the individual demand curves from which the AP points are extracted, we trace out the curve CAC. Thus the lateral distance CAC minus AC indicates the advertising outlay required per unit of sales for each maximum price adjustment at which $MC = MR$, or for the prices and sales amounts reflected in the curve AP. Inasmuch as production costs ultimately rise, and as advertising encounters areas of increasing resistance, the CAC curve must rise. Conversely, as price must eventually fall in order to increase sales despite huge sales outlays, the AP curve must

* This involves $MC = MR$, but also something more—for the production revenue, as output and sales outlays are increased, is computed from successive demand curves.

finally turn down; the two curves must thus sometimes cross, with CAC eventually lying above AP.   The maximum profit equilibrium will be found at that output at which the lateral distance $AP - CAC$, multiplied by their common output abscissae, is greatest, or where the area of an inscribed profit rectangle is greatest.

Alternately, as in equilibrium the additions to total revenue through advertising equal the additions to both total advertising and production costs, curves cac and ap, which are marginal to CAC and AP, can be drawn and their intersection noted: the curves will intersect at an output at which the slope of CAC equals that of AP, at output OR in Figure 2.   Here the additions of total revenue will equal the additions to total costs, where the latter include both production and sales costs. Simultaneously, the individual marginal equations—of the direct marginal revenue equal to marginal production costs, and the marginal profit attributable to a marginal sales outlay equal to the marginal sales outlay—will be satisfied.

Advertising Dependent on Price Policy

Although the geometrical apparatus of Figure 2 is readily comprehensible, running as it does in terms of familiar concepts, it suffers one major defect from which the indifference-curve technique is singularly free—namely, the assumption that the advertising campaign is independent of any specific price policy.   Implicitly, each marginal expenditure on advertising was presumed to shift the *full* demand curve, enabling the firm to choose the price most advantageous to itself, that at which $MC = MR$ in this new state of demand.   Unheralded, too, was the hypothesis that the sales campaign was unique and definite, with greater advertising expenditure permitting a more extensive geographical area of potential consumers to be bombarded with the same sales appeal or a given area to be cultivated more intensively with the greater sales outlay.

Very frequently the sales outlays are built around a declared sales price so that on undertaking its selling campaign the firm relinquishes its freedom, temporarily at least, to charge the most profitable price in the new demand environment.   Rather than a full demand curve being created by each sales outlay, the advertising expenditure simply extends the volume of sales at the advertised price from their initial level at zero sales expenditure.   The effective demand curve to the firm is thus literally a perfectly elastic horizontal line at the stipulated price.

The affirmation of a specific price as part of the advertising campaign would not occasion any special difficulty if the same type of sales appeal is made regardless of sales price, or if there was but one sales plan feasible or conceivable. But if the preparation of the sales campaign is contingent upon price, directed to advertising media which appeal to separable income groups regarded as potential consumers at the successive prices, then it is not possible to draw a family of normal demand curves and extract the appropriate AP points, as in Figure 2, after the $MR = MC$ equation at each level of advertising. To illustrate, if a low sales price of say \$1 is contemplated, the sales appeal to the likely group of purchasers will have to stress functional performance rather than the atmosphere of distinction and exclusiveness that will have to be underscored if the product is to sell at \$1,000. Reminiscent of competitive-price analysis, when the advertising places stress on market price or when the appeal is made with some price in view, both the demand and marginal-revenue curve to the firm merge into one.

Clearly, the indifference-curve technique is admirably suited to handle this new aspect of the problem, for each point on the sales contours can be interpreted as embodying the advertising appeal calculated to sell the maximum output *at each price* for *each sales outlay;* it does not require the stipulation that the sales campaign is unchanged despite an altered price and total sales outlay. Let us see if we can surmount this new difficulty with the aid of more familiar demand-curve constructions.

Suppose that a lump sum is allocated to finance the sales campaign, based not on any deliberate calculations of the most profitable volume of sales expenditure, but as a percentage of the previous year's profits. The demand curve at the advertised price would spurt out as a horizontal line to the right, to a sales total representing the market purchases at the ruling price. Conceivably, to fill the full market demand quantity at the advertised price might carry marginal production costs well above price. If the firm refuses to push production this far it may have to resort to some unobtrusive form of rationing; if it agrees to accept all orders at the stipulated price we can be sure that its advertising expenditure has been excessive or that its market price is too low so that it will have failed to maximize its profits. Contrariwise, the lump-sum advertising outlay may leave price well in excess of the marginal production costs for the purchase quantity at the fixed price. Here the advertising outlay is too small for profit maximization.

Let us develop the equilibrium conditions for a firm whose sales program is attached to a definite price policy. In Figure 3A, D_1 is the firm's demand curve prior to any advertising whatsoever and MR_1 is the correspondent marginal revenue curve.   As always, MC is the curve of marginal production cost.   In the absence of any sales expenditure OM would be the monopoly output.

If the firm advertises at and adheres to a market price of P_1, its relevant demand curve is P_1P_1'.*   If we subtract *the marginal sales outlay*—the outlay necessary to expand sales by one unit—from P_1P_1',

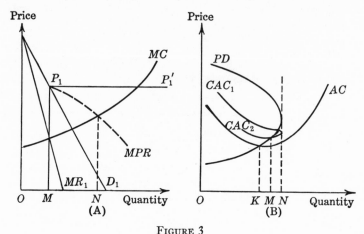

FIGURE 3

the sum remaining will be marginal production revenue (MPR).   Thus

$$MPR = P - MSO,$$

where MSO is the marginal sales cost.   If we connect the successive MPR points they will form the curve indicated in Figure 3A, on the assumption that there are diminishing returns to advertising.

Manifestly, at price P_1 the equilibrium sales volume is at ON, where $MC = MPR$.   Stopping short of this output, or selling more, will leave $MC \gtrless MPR$.   The full equilibrium condit on is

$$P = MC + MSO,$$

or

$$P - MSO = MPR = MC.$$

As in all monopoly problems, therefore, $P > MC$, where the latter embodies only production costs.   As the diagram indicates, if MSO is small (say, practically nil), with the advertising accomplished by infor-

---

* Conceivably, after the sales outlay is expended the firm might retract on its promise to sell at the advertised price.   The new demand curve would be of normal form at the level resulting from both initial tastes and advertising unless resentment to these tactics repelled prospective purchasers.

mation passed along by consumers, MPR will practically coincide with P_1P_1' and production will be pushed literally to equality of MC and P. This might also be the adjustment position if the firm allocates a fixed sum to advertising that stresses a particular price. This is an interesting conclusion for it seems to be a not uncommon behavior rule.

To calculate aggregate profits we would have to superimpose a curve of average production (AC) and average sales costs (ASC) for each sales volume on our diagram and summate the two into a combined average cost, as CAC. Total profits would then be the difference between total sales proceeds, or $P_1 \cdot ON$, and total production and sales costs, calculated by multiplying the CAC at ON by ON.

By drawing a similar diagram for each price we could then compute the total profits at each price selected as the vehicle for advertising, and then extract that combination of price and advertising outlay which maximized profit. At very high prices the firm would probably find few buyers; lavish sums spent for advertising would be wasted; the most profitable sales volume at a very high price might thus be extremely small, due to the enormous ASC required for extending sales. Conversely, because of rising marginal production costs it would pay to spend very little on advertising at extremely low prices. Given the tastes, the efficacy of advertising at each price, and the cost conditions, if we isolated the most profitable sales quantities at each price and placed them in juxtaposition on the price-quantity coordinates of Figure 3B, a new and peculiar member of the widening family of demand curves would emerge. This is the PD curve of Figure 3B; each of its points represents the sales quantity that the firm undertaking advertising outlays attached to each price would seek in view of both marginal production and marginal sales costs. It may be called the *profitable demand* (PD) curve. In the upper and lower reaches PD would probably turn back to the OY axis. We could mount the AC curve, representing average production costs, on the same diagram. It then becomes necessary to add to AC the average advertising costs incurred to sell the most profitable sales volume at the stipulated price. Since PD is multivalued there would be two advertising sums at each sales volume, although the average advertising cost expended to sell a given sales quantity at a lower price will be below the sum required to sell the same quantity at a higher price.

Immediately we can ignore, as devoid of profit significance, all those PD points that lie beneath AC, for to sell any of the sales quantities at sales prices below AC will fail to recover even production costs. To the left of output OK, at which $AC = PD$ we need, therefore, to add to AC only the average sales outlays incurred to create the upper segment of PD. Doing so, the CAC_1 curve is traced, with the difference $CAC_1 - ACP$ representing average sales outlays for the corresponding amount of sales at the PD prices.

Beyond OK output, each of the multiple PD values exceeds AC. Up to a sales volume of OM, however, selling at the lower price fails to cover CAC_2, which contains ACP plus the selling outlays necessary to sell the quantities between OK and OM at the lower of the PD prices. Only after a sales volume of OM must a real decision be made between charging the lower or higher sales price for the identical sales quantity. This alternate choice continues until the sales total ON; beyond this sales volume profits will not be maximized if the advertising appeal is attached to a specific price. Indicative of this the CAC curve has been broken at ON.

When we once have the PD and CAC curves, the remaining problem is to derive the maximum price, sales quantity, and advertising expenditure from among the multifarious potential equilibrium positions. Curves marginal to PD and CAC_1 (and CAC_2) can be inserted; their intersection would reveal the sales volume, price, and unit advertising outlay of maximum profit. The equilibrium condition would be that at each price $MPR = MC$, and, for a change in price, the increase in total revenue must exceed the increase in both total production and total sales outlay. Similarly, we could inscribe profit rectangles between PD and CAC_1, with the rectangle of maximum area being indicative of the most profitable price, sales, and advertising position.

RETALIATORY CROSS-ADVERTISING AND PRICE CUTTING

The equilibrium analysis has been confined to the firm initiating the expenditure, and thus fits most properly into our monopoly analysis; when we widen our sphere of reference to include market interdependence there are other interesting configurations to be unraveled. Let us scrutinize some of the possibilities.

Briefly, there are three sets of reaction patterns to consider: (1) other firms can respond passively or actively, but only in terms of price policy, to the advertising outlay of the firm; (2) they can reply with an advertising program of their own; (3) they can answer with a product-variation measure designed to neutralize the inroads of the first firm's advertising. Only the first two forms of behavior will be discussed; defense through product variation will be deferred to the following chapter. Assuming some advertising originally by all firms, and writing A_1 and ΔA_1 as the sales outlay and outlay increment by firm 1, and ΔA_2 and ΔP_2 for advertising and price changes by a firm influenced by it, in the first case we have

$$\frac{A_1 \Delta P_2}{P_2 \Delta A_1} \gtrless 0,$$

and in the second case,

$$\frac{A_1 \Delta A_2}{A_2 \Delta A_1} > 0.$$

Advertising and Price Interdependence

Let us pretend that for several reasons competing firms prefer not to imitate the advertising program with an advertising campaign of their own but accept it as a datum. Thereupon the only problems that concern us are the reverberations of firm A's sales-expenditure policy on the rest of the price structure.

Conceivably, firm A's advertising policy may be wholly unsuccessful so that, contrary to expectations, its demand curve remains frozen at the original position. Here the sole effect consists of a transfer of income from monopolist to advertising agency; there will be some effects in the economy so long as the expenditure pattern of the new income recipients for finished goods does not exactly coincide with that of the former monopoly-profit recipients.

Normally the policy will be successful in a profit sense. Demand may be shifted to the firm at the expense of: (1) certain definite commodities—"near" substitutes; (2) more remote substitutes or the whole commodity chain; (3) individual propensities to consume may increase so that the added expenditure is against saving.* There can, of course, be some overlapping in these relationships, or a combination of effects.

The second case, which is a throwback to the monopoly hypothesis, may be disposed of summarily: it furnishes a sound reason for passive reactions by affected firms when firm A embarks on a sales program. For when A's advertising affects only distant substitutes, with present customers of near substitutes remaining attached to existing firms, it is also probable that there will be a diversion of demand from the vast commodity field to the proximate substitutes for the advertised good. The awakening interest in the commodity class will be conducive to the

---

* There are some implications here for the level of employment and the interest-rate structure.

sale of higher-priced substitutes, and for less-affluent income groups, to lower-priced grades. The firm's advertising will therefore benefit all of the nearby firms. Unless the enlarged demand enables the firms to exploit latent productive economies, prices of the chain of goods favorably affected by the switch in tastes will evidence some rising tendencies; if the shift in demand has made inroads in the markets for some particular commodities, their prices will be depressed. If savings margins are alone contracted, only rising-price pressures are in the offing. Apart from the price and output ramifications, income is now earned in the advertising profession, a new occupation, and their demands for finished goods now appear as part of the equilibrium structure.

Active Price Reactions

More frequently the shift in demand will affect a nearby chain of substitutes. This will probably signalize market inelasticity of demand for the commodity "class," inasmuch as the new purchasers of firm A's goods are habitual purchasers of similar technical varieties from competing sellers. Either they may maintain a discreet silence, persisting in their previous price policy in the belief that the demand transference is but an ephemeral phenomenon, or they can retaliate through either a price fall, an advertising policy of their own, or by a minor variation in their own product, publicising perhaps some mythical attribute. In the latter event the advertising will have caused a reorganization of the commodity belt for the entire interdependent group.

If the nearby firm (or firms) do reply through price action we are confronted once more with a problem in monopolistic competition. As the products are differentiated, and the advertising has presumably shifted its demand curve, the firm advertising need not join in the game of price cutting, especially if in embarking on the original sales outlay the firm is presumed to have weighed these responses. If the competing firms do reduce their prices so that their previous volume of sales is largely maintained, unless new demand is drawn to the advertising innovator from decreased savings or from remote substitutes, the advertising outlay is unlikely to be remunerative: there will be lower prices within the field, except perhaps for the firm pursuing the active sales policy, with a portion of the normal earnings of the group now being deflected to the advertising agency by the aggressive selling firm.

Price cutting is likely to be the retaliatory weapon with which to bludgeon an obstreperous firm that insists on advertising a commodity for which the demand over the entire commodity class is inelastic and insensitive even when all firms advertise, so that the aggressive firm's sales expansion is to the detriment of a few "near-by" firms. As for the nonadvertisers, they may have no other recourse, for production may be completely unprofitable after the transference in demand.

Retaliatory Cross Advertising

Visualizing the monopoly case where the expanded demand after advertising is siphoned from the vast commodity field, suppose that all firms employ advertising as an instrument of sales policy. In this event the sales of the firm are a function not only of its own price and all other prices but of its own sales outlays and those of other firms.* Conceivably, after the full round of advertising, demand curves may be in exactly the initial position—not an inconceivable contingency when the interplay of cross advertising is accredited its due weight. The sole beneficiaries of the selling program would be the advertising industry to whom there now accrues what would otherwise become monopoly profits. Normally, some demand curves will be distended to the right and others pulled to the left, when advertising becomes an instrument of sales policy; the entire configuration of prices, income, and output will be affected. If the universal advertising campaigns merely reduce saving propensities there need not be any significant disruption of particular price and output fields, at least in conditions of underemployment; instead, the employment and output structure will be enlarged.

It may be surmised that retaliatory cross advertising will not be the typical response of neighboring sellers unless the enlarged demand for the advertised product occurs at their expense. It is of course conceivable that firms formerly dormant will also advertise because of the prestige associated with selling a "nationally advertised" product: nonpecuniary motives are strong here and imitation will have its enthusiasts. But rationally, counter-advertising appears as a weapon of defense only when market injury is experienced from the sales appeals by rival firms. After the retaliatory sales campaigns there are the several likelihoods that (1) the original sales positions will be restored; (2) the countering firm's position will be improved; (3) its market share will be not quite recovered; and (4) for all the firms of the group a demand improvement will occur at the expense of more remote substitutes or savings.

Hence firm A must evaluate, when preparing a sales campaign,

* Thus $x = f(P_1, P_2 \cdots P_n; SO_1, SO_2 \cdots SO_n)$.

whether the B firms will or will not follow suit.   If they do, and if the original sales positions are (practically) restored, we see a strange idiosyncracy of competitive cross advertising: the sole beneficiary is the advertising fraternity.   This is largely true in the other cases; the minor emendations to the analysis can be filled in mentally.

Advertising to Prevent Price Cutting

Rather than advertising being conceived as either an independent phenomenon or as a counter measure to a sales program of a rival, it may be designed to fend off the price-cutting tactics precipitated by a competing firm.   If both A and B are of vastly different size, with B much the smaller, it may be that firm A, visualizing the market demand as inelastic, poses no objection to a price rise by B.   If the commodities are heterogeneous, with P_a constant, the demand curve for B would be of normal form for a P_b price rise.

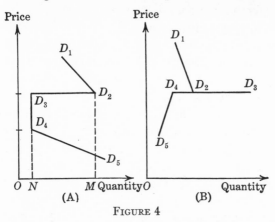

FIGURE 4

For a P_b price fall, A may reply by an extensive advertising campaign destined to expand the total market custom and siphon demand from B.   With this onslaught, B's sales dwindle from OM back to ON.   Thereafter B cannot increase its sales unless P_b falls below OP_2.   The demand curve for B thus assumes the extremely flighty $D_1D_2D_3D_4D_5$ drawing in Figure 4A.   Firm B will be under strong economic compulsion to name the price indicated at the elastic demand stretch D_3D_2.

In a similar vein, firms A and B may be selling conventionally priced but imperfectly substitutable commodities, with the normal price indicated by the ordinate height of the $D_4D_2D_3$ horizontal line in Figure 4B. At prices above the normal figure for the commodity class, B's sales may fall off precipitously, so that its demand curve in the upper area is as $D_1D_2D_3$.   If B tries to lower price below the market figure, rivals may resist by advertising, rather than reducing prices, imparting to firm B a reputation for purveying a "cheap" and inferior product variety.   The discontinuous curve $D_1D_2D_3D_4D_5$ depicts the facts described. B will deem it the better part of valor to conform to the price convention.

ADVERTISING AND COSTS

At least a brief comment is expected on the ancient conundrum of whether advertising raises prices. In the light of the oligopoly background a simple answer is impossible; the problem is indeterminate for it contains several concealed assumptions. In the one case in which demand curves after advertising remain as they were before, prices are obviously unaffected.

When advertising greatly extends the demand for a commodity there is a presumption that through time the price will be higher. But this is almost irrelevant; price will always be higher when demand for a product increases; the sole possible objection is that now the demand shift is "inspired" rather than "spontaneous." The issue here concerns the ethical right to advertise rather than the fact of a higher price. The only apparent exception to the rule that advertising, with the ensuing demand expansion, raises price—excluding advertising at the original price before advertising—is when AC is falling; the new demand may facilitate a price fall. This last case cannot be ignored, for widespread economies of scale are often obtainable only after demand is augmented. If the demand shift also occurs to the disadvantage of a specified list of other commodities, unless their outputs are also marked by decreasing AC, their price should also fall.

Another way of examining this problem is to consider not only the effects of advertising on prices in a system where they are first introduced but in a system from which they are withdrawn: we can speculate on the consequences if suddenly all sales outlays were declared to be illegal. If nothing further happened, if tastes moulded by *past* advertising were to be unaltered, then prices should be essentially uninfluenced. In the longer future, as tastes deviate from the pattern they would assume when subjected to sales pressures, the relative price structure would reflect these facts of a more somber world. Products normally unadvertised should be relatively higher, with those goods whose demand relies more strongly upon sales expenditure selling at relatively lower prices: this envisages rising MC curves. But, in general, it is not possible to advance an unequivocal answer in terms of price relationships, for the forces influencing tastes would differ in nature and intensity. Undoubtedly the major readjustment would devolve upon the advertising field itself; as a supplementary matter price reductions through diminished demands for the normally advertised products would, to some slight degree, be counterbalanced by higher prices for periodicals and the disappearance of some publications from the social literature.

A Qualification for Nonpecuniary Motives

Although a priori conclusions on whether advertising raises prices must inevitably be vague there is one qualification that must be stated. Frequently, if firms voluntarily forego the full monopoly price and profits because of a variety of nonpecuniary motives, when pricing is undertaken with an eye to a "fair" volume of profits, rather than *maximum* profits, then advertising can be charged with raising prices. For with the removal of advertis'ng a firm whose demand curve is relatively unaffected by the sales outlays may find its profits unduly swollen by the retention of the usual sum of sales expenditures, so much so that its riches become a source of (say) political embarrassment. Making lavish advertising outlays, its ostensible monopoly profits can be dissipated, permanent "good will" created, and its hold on consumer demand irrevocably strengthened.   To the superficial observer, the pricing policy accompanied by sales outlays would appear as innocuous, as a guarantor of but "fair" and not extraordinary "monopoly" profits.   In instances of this nature the more extreme criticisms of advertising as a price-raising factor cannot be summarily denied.*   As borderline illustrations there are the wartime advertisements of firms which, despite the paucity of products to sell, made large outlays because otherwise the sums so spent would have had to be paid in taxes.   Normally, these sums would appear as profits.

Advertising and Profitless Monopoly

There are other directions from which advertising can be charged with raising prices.   Even arguing that advertising fails to affect demand curves, the combined average-cost curve, of selling and production costs, will be higher than if advertising costs were zero.   This would entail a higher financial investment in initiating an enterprise, operating as an impediment to firms deprived of easy access to capital markets.   As the financial scale of enterprise must be greater, this limitation upon entry

---

* As an illustration, consider advertising by milk companies, electric-power public utilities, and the public-relations advertising of corporations whose radio broadcasts can hardly influence the demand for their product or deflect business from a (nonexistent) competitor.

is a handicap to greater competitiveness. Higher prices ought to be the upshot. Diagrammatically, if we visualize the concept of profitless monopoly with demand curves just tangent to cost curves, the demand curves will now be tangent to curves of combined unit costs. As the average production-cost curve lies under the combined average-cost curve, even in the profitless-monopoly universe prices will be higher with sales outlays than without these costs. Interestingly, if firms were permitted to advertise but were compelled to subscribe to the $P = MC$ pricing formula, a firm producing under conditions of constant costs would never advertise.

Sales Outlays and Plant Selection

We can examine the influence of advertising on the size of layout. The solution follows established lines, with the only complication being that there are the alternate methods of forcing the demand curve rightward, by stressing a particular price in the sales campaign or merely conjecturing the demand-curve shift consequent upon definite sums of selling expenditure. Either the analysis surrounding Figure 2A or that accompanying Figure 3B will be the relevant one, with the AC curves now signifying ACP curves of average planning costs. The equilibrium price and output, and equipment implicit in the maximum-profit equation, can be located in the usual way. Assuming advertising does succeed, as a general rule, in expanding demand, then the ability to exercise sales pressure is responsible for the installation of a larger mass of equipment and, ordinarily, for a higher volume of output and employment than would occur with the suppression of these instruments of economic persuasion. The production expansion, as a long-run matter, can be viewed as a substitute either for involuntary unemployment, greater leisure, or greater output of staple, unadvertised commodities. Nevertheless, the plant size and output level will be smaller than if the same amount of sales outlays were incurred with $P = MC$ pricing.

In concluding this survey of sales outlays, a comment on the functions of salesmen is appropriate, for they are a ubiquitous element in our economic world. Order-taking is an indispensable, if routine, function in the economic system, an inevitable task to be performed in establishing contact between buyer and seller. Conversely, outlays on salesmanship duties proper, (the antithesis of order taking), are viewed as incurred partly as a good-will gesture in establishing a friendly atmosphere for the seller and thus in expanding the full demand curve through time, or as an immediately aggressive force to increase the firm's sales at the going market price. The cost of the selling organization must, therefore, be conceived in part as a form of advertising at a fixed price and advertising that is heedless of price. The appropriate equilibrium analysis for the firm, however, is likely to be that surrounding Figure 2, for the sales organization is likely to be visualized as involving a percentage of production costs for each sales and output volume.

BIBLIOGRAPHICAL NOTE

The path-breaking study of sales expenditures was made by Professor Chamberlin, Chapters V–VII especially. On the ethical aspects of advertising, see the little volume of A. J. Baster, *Advertising Reconsidered*. Also, the substantial study of Neil H. Borden, containing much material of interest, on *The Economic Effects of Advertising*. Further, the lucid essay by F. P. Bishop, *The Economics of Advertising*, and the analysis of E. A. Lever, *Advertising and Economic Theory*.

The indifference-curve technique for the resolution of the sales-outlay equilibrium is due to K. Boulding, *Economic Analysis*, first edition, pp. 581–587. G. Stigler, *The Theory of Price*, uses a modified technique, with output rather than price measured along the horizontal axis. For the treatment of advertising as shifting the full demand curve, see N. S. Buchanan, "Advertising Expenditures: A Suggested Treatment," *Journal of Political Economy* (1942). Also, J. P. Hayes, "A Note on Selling Costs and the Equilibrium of the Firm," *Review of Economic Studies* (1944–1945). Other informative articles are: Henry Smith, "Discontinuous Demand Curves and Monopolistic Competition," *Quarterly Journal of Economics* (1935) and, by the same author, "Advertising Costs and Equilibrium," *Review of Economic Studies* (1934). Also, the comment on the latter article by Chamberlin, "A Correction," same journal, 1944–1945, and E. K. Zingler, "Advertising and the Maximization of Profit," *Economica* (1940).

CHAPTER 10

Product Variation

Aᴛᴏᴍɪꜱᴛɪᴄ ᴄᴏᴍᴘᴇᴛɪᴛɪᴠᴇ ᴛʜᴇᴏʀʏ presumes that there is a diversified list of commodities produced, as A, B, $C \cdot \cdot \cdot M$, with each of the commodities drawn from an infinite number of firms. In this model it is plausible to omit the theory of product selection, for in stationary theory the commodity chain is fixed, limited to the M varieties, with new firms able to enter only in these product sectors and, in equilibrium, perceiving equal profit opportunities in all commodity directions. Stepping outside the stationary confines, the gains of even commodity innovation will be short-lived once we admit the universality of homogeneous entry. But if we envisage impediments to entry, the theory of product variation assumes a new significance: even trivial variations of old commodity types will be incessantly created, because differentiation (where there is the right to seal entry) may be handsomely remunerative. In the earlier discussion of profitless monopoly under heterogeneous entry, it was shown that to secure a profitable spot on the commodity belt new firms would have to devise close, if imperfect, substitutes for currently profitable commodity varieties. Similarly, new firms will sense an urge, especially in markets of circular interdependence, to sever the closely knit price cord by introducing a new product variety that can steal custom from other firms and mitigate, at least temporarily, the degree of market competition. Through time, however, other firms may be able to match the variation by product improvements of their own, disturbing the chain of market interdependence once more. One other motive for product variation ought to be underscored. To hasten obsolescence of existing commodity types and induce a new wave of buying by possessors of current varieties, firms will often perceive the advantage of bringing out a new style or creating a new fashion, and thus shifting the demand curve to a higher level. This is true of women's clothing as well as appliances and other durable goods.

229

In this chapter we describe first the greater degree of commodity diversification in a universe in which only heterogeneous entry is possible for new firms.   Then we discuss some consequences of the ability of going firms to vary their products as an instrument of market policy. These topics, though related, are not equivalent; the former assumes a widening of the number of firms and the enlargement of the commodity belt, while the latter presumes constancy in the number of firms but a reorientation in the commodity web.   The theory of nonprice competition can be developed as a sequel of either study.

COMMODITY DIVERSIFICATION AND SEALED ENTRY

As a partial proof of the proposition that commodity diversification in an economic universe in which only heterogeneous entry is possible surpasses that of homogeneous entry, it is instructive to consider a partially competitive case, where firms abide by the $P = MC$ rule but in which entry is obstructed, for example, by patent and trade-mark laws: this provides further corroboration that competitive pricing and entry are quite independent phenomena.

Heterogeneous Entry and Excessive Product Diversification

Although monopoly pricing is missing from this model, most of the other attributes of imperfection linger on.   As direct encroachments on existing product preserves are prevented, the gestation of a new firm signalizes the birth of a "new" product.   Normally it would repay the firm to devise a product so much like others that it could capture some of their demand while simultaneously instilling certain loyalties that would make consumers reluctant to shift to other products for minor price differences.   This then would be the goal of policy: to build concomitant identity and difference.   The impediments to entry would place a premium on ingenuity and improvisation in small matters rather than on important pioneering innovations, for merely trivial differences would enable new firms to penetrate the economic scene.   Further, the prospect of enduring profits to a successful innovation would encourage more frequent experimentation than with full freedom on entry.   A chance of gain would be less attractive if, when successful, it had to be shared with others while the contingency of losses had to be borne alone.

Although we have established the likelihood of a greater diversity of products, it is not clear whether this would comprise either an unmitigated waste or a positive benefit.   Everything hinges upon how wants are satisfied as a result; as entrepreneurs are provoked into experimenting, this spark of dynamism must be recognized as instrumental for progress. Consumers, however, are compelled to pay higher prices for the wares of the protected firm's product than would be necessary if others could locate in the field and proffer a perfect substitute; this would tend to reduce price if the existing firm is producing under conditions of rising marginal costs.

Barriers to entry are costly in other ways. The lack of a standardized final product may entail the use of different equipments; equipment costs are thus likely to be higher than if standard machinery were ordered by numerous firms. As a broader aspect of the same theme, as products differ productive processes will differ: supplementary industries will not grow as rapidly to service the common needs of the firms producing the commodity "type" as they would if practices were more highly standardized.* Although there may be a marked preference for the commodity of the firm first in the field, these higher-cost factors and the resulting higher price may alone enable new firms to secure a niche in the commodity belt despite inferior, imperfectly substitutable goods; with open entry, a homogeneous competitor could produce and lower the price of the superior good.

In sum, with open entry there would be product differentiation in that manifold commodity varieties would be produced. But there would be greater standardization and lower prices of certain commodities than under closed entry and $(P = MC)$ pricing. Diversification, with open entry, would be an outgrowth solely of consumer preferences for new varieties of goods that, in the light of price and cost relations, would be preferred to current commodity types. The coloring of the commodity chain would be explicable in terms of fundamental preferences and cost phenomena, rather than of prohibitions on entry.

MONOPOLY PRICING AND INNOVATION

Once we admit the possibility of monopoly pricing alongside that of sealed entry, there is even a stronger impetus to product innovation. Other things equal, innovations that are lucrative with competitive pricing will be even more remunerative on a $P > MR = MC$ pricing policy. Hence we can conclude that with monopoly pricing and closed-entry differentiation should be more complete and the commodity network larger than with sealed entry and $P = MC$ pricing: commodity varieties unprofitable under the latter formula may be profitable with the former.

The same conclusion could be obtained more conclusively in another

* These are Marshall's famous "external" economies. (*Principles*, p. 266.)

way.   If we are entitled to assume total employment is the same in the competitive and monopoly-pricing worlds, as the individual firm's price is higher and output smaller under monopoly pricing, there will be less employment generated by each firm. Consequently, for (approximately) the same total volume of employment there must be more firms and, as a consequence, there will have to be more entrepreneurs and a greater diversity of products; the ubiquitous advertising trappings of a monopoly model will also appear. The advertising itself, though not its volume, would be assignable to the protection accorded differentiation rather than to monopoly pricing as such.

The Order of Commodity Innovation

Besides innovations being more commonplace under monopoly pricing and heterogeneous entry, the innovations would not be introduced in the same order with monopoly pricing as with competitive pricing. A simple illustration will demonstrate this. Firm X, say, an aspiring entrant into the product chain, realizes that it is able to shut itself in from the encroachments of homogeneous competitors. Considering the product varieties, if it is subject to a $P = MC$ pricing mandate it will select that product and that layout which promised to maximize profits on this basis. Making similar profit computations, but now fortified with the right to name a $P > MR = MC$ price, it is likely to choose not only another layout but also *another differentiated product*. Assuming different average cost curves for commodities A and B, and combined with different demand curves for each good, as D_a and D_b in Figure 1, the A commodity with its relatively elastic demand is likely to appeal to an innovator under $P = MC$ pricing while, with monopoly pricing, the B commodity responsible for the more inelastic D_b curve will be selected as the more suitable profit vehicle. Commodity B may be ornamented with lavish accoutrements that confer prestige value but are without functional use, while item A may be unadorned but functionally serviceable.

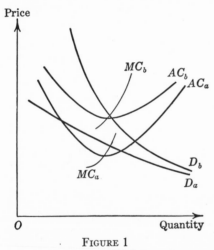

FIGURE 1

Thus there is the strong likelihood that the order in which commodities will be introduced in a world of $P = MC$ pricing will differ from that of a $P > MR = MC$ universe. Not only will the date of commodity innovation be different but the commodity universe itself is likely to take another hue, with products part of the one world excluded from the other. Undoubtedly some goods profitable with a monopoly pricing program will be unable to cover costs under a $P = MC$ pricing arrangement.

Patent Sealing

One problem not alluded to in this discussion is that of patent sealing, in which a firm registers patents not only upon the item it is producing but upon substitute varieties not in order to use the patents but to block their use by others and their encroachment upon what it regards as its legitimate preserves. The effect is of course to narrow the degree of market interdependence by roping off certain commodities in the chain of substitutes and instilling a gap by legal means. Pricewise, monopoly pricing can be instituted without the interference of the circularity that would otherwise obtain: prices ought to be higher and output of the general product class lower than with the prohibition of the practice of patent sealing. Commodity improvements or modifications that appeal to a diversity of tastes not satisfied by the current product type can be effectively suppressed by this device.

Some would contend that if the patents unutilized are for superior products then the monopoly firm itself will introduce them. But this argument abstracts entirely from the element of time and the role of "changeover" costs; an existing firm will have to weigh the losses occasioned by the abandonment of equipment which would become obsolete on the production of the new variety. A new firm would not be subject to the same restrictive calculations. Patents not for use but to prevent their use by others might be an important retarding influence depressing the level of consumer well-being, if the practice was shown to be widely pervasive.

INNOVATIONS AND PRICE REPERCUSSIONS

Let us now investigate the effects of the appearance of a new firm and a new item in the commodity belt upon the prevailing price structure. We can assume that the new commodity is priced according to competitive rules: the perturbations in the price structure, in kind if not in intensity, will be similar when the new product is subject to monopoly-pricing arrangements.

Inscribing consumer demand as a datum, with homogeneous entry and a new firm contributing to the supply of familiar commodities, there should be some downward pressure on price: although one new firm alone will in competitive conditions be insignificant, the downward tendency dominates. Price tends lower because existing firms have been pushing production too far into stages of decreasing marginal physical returns; the entry of the new firm with its new complement of equipment and entrepreneurship works to eliminate the higher cost output proffered by the existing firms.

The chain of price repercussions is more complex with heterogeneous entry and a new product being tendered by the new firm. Among the several possibilities, the new product might so siphon off demand from the current commodity types that the latter prices may fall. Some purchasers of the previous varieties might switch their expenditures solely to B, the new commodity, and omit A (their old commodity types) from their purchase budget; other consumers might apportion their expenditures between both A and B. In any event, the introduction of the new B good confers an undisguised benefit upon consumers. To those who continue to buy the A goods there is a direct enhancement of real income arising out of their price fall, while the very fact that (all or some) consumers include B in their purchase plan, despite the lowered P_a, indicates a preference for B and an improvement in well-being accomplished by the creation of the new good. A cogent argument can be adduced in favor of the innovation; consumers are better satisfied, inasmuch as the lower P_a accompanies the new B good.

A Conflict of Interests

Conceivably, the new B commodity may precipitate higher prices for some goods, such as C, in the commodity belt. The C goods, say, may be complementary to the new B commodity. For those consumers who purchase both B and C at the expense of A, there is an enhancement in well-being; for those on whom the appeal of the B commodity is lost, and who adhere to the buying of C as part of their consumption plan without purchasing any of the A commodities reduced in price there is a diminution in well-being as a result of the B good's appearing in the commodity chain.

Other causes of a rising P_c might also be cited. Frequently the demand curve for C may cross C's AC curve to the left of the minimum

AC point and hence may be too small to permit the equating of P and MC; only a $P > AC > MC$ price policy enables the firm to survive. Here a new innovation (which is a substitute for C) may, by driving the C firm's demand curve leftward, elevate its price. Or, if the new firm requires a relatively large volume of productive factors employed by the C firms, even if the final products of C and B are not closely related for consumers, their use of common factors may entail a cost increase and price rise whenever B strives to penetrate the commodity fold.

The fact that prices of current commodity varieties may rise on the appearance of a new product presages a real conflict of interests. Those who hold to the purchase of C despite the higher price are undoubtedly deprived of real income, compensated partially by the availability and the purchase of the B good. Those who would switch entirely to B, even if the original P_c prevailed, enjoy an enhancement in their real purchase position. In general, the well-being of one consuming group is augmented at the expense of another. Conceivably, we can visualize the B innovation attracting so much demand from C that the latter, unable to operate profitably, is supplanted by B and vanishes from the commodity field. Those former consumers of C's good, either repelled or unimpressed by B's variety, will suffer a diminution in well-being.*

A tentative answer as to the most preferable position might be sought on these lines. Perhaps after the introduction of B it is possible to recover from its purchasers part of their enhanced real income: earlier we observed that this enhancement is susceptible to a money measure.† Transferring all or some of this sum to those who continue buying C, the real income of the latter groups might be restored so that nobody will be injured by the innovations while others will benefit by the commodity nascence of B. The innovation and progress in commodity types would seem to have everything to commend it, especially if those who benefit from the *original* commodity scale cannot reimburse those who approve of the innovation in amount sufficient to deter them from promoting the change. Sometimes even a smoothly arranged income transfer and rectification, which averted individual wrangling and social contention, might be insufficient to compensate the consumers of the C good for the real damage caused them via the price rise. In this event the superiority of one equilibrium position over another could not be proclaimed with any real conviction. Only some convention, some

---

* When the firm is driven from the field by economic warfare rather than by generally acknowledged product superiority, the importance of this point becomes magnified.

† See Chapter 1.

noneconomic criterion, could be invoked to break the impasse.   The democratic principle of counting the numbers favorably affected and those adversely affected might constitute one standard.   Or we could ask how different income groups fared by the change and allow our biases to decide the issue.   But the advocacy of any of these solutions will be entirely arbitrary, consequent upon our personal predilections, whims, or social judgments rather than upon a standard of unequivocal benefit to all emanating from the particular structural change.

PRODUCT VARIATION

The foregoing sections dealt with the greater diversity of products accomplished by the heterogeneous entry of new firms instead of homogeneous entry.   An affiliated problem is that of a going firm in the commodity chain deciding to vary the nature of its product and abandoning its former position in the commodity belt.   Either the general preference of the consuming groups may have changed, making the production of a new variety of the former commodity type advisable, or the degree of competition and inroads by heterogeneous competitors may be conducive to a new commodity improvisation to relieve the tension of price interdependence.   Changes in relative costs, as compared to given demand functions, may also render a technologically superior design more economical than formerly.   Also, as stated earlier, the purpose may be to render existing commodity varieties obsolete in recognition of the fact that demand from new users is small and that, if current models are outmoded by the style change, demand can be enormously expanded—for example, by new fashions in women's dresses, new styling of automobiles, etc.   Finally, cognizance must be taken of nonpecuniary motives; the firm may strive to pioneer some new models mainly as a matter of prestige, feeling that perhaps in a longer future they may reap a profit harvest from their venturesome methods.   All of these factors can explain product differentiation by a going firm.

Differentiation and Maximum Profits

In essentials the problem of product variation by a going firm, in the sense of a departure from its customary product, is parallel to that of a new firm still in the planning stage, weighing which is the most profitable of all the alternative product types open to it.   The primary discrepancy is that as the firm already has its equipment it must consider profitability in terms of its current equipment, with additions, extensions, and modifications, rather than view the problem from the start as would a firm still in the planning stage and beginning operations anew. The commodity type most profitable to the one may not be the most profitable to the other: a commodity with smaller sales receipts and a lower sum of "change-over" costs will be superior to one with higher sales receipts but embodying a further lavish outlay for extensions to the existing stock of equipment.

The importance of "change-over" costs can be made more graphic by means of Figure 2. Assume the firm is producing commodity A currently and that for any of the several reasons listed it is now more profitable to produce either commodities B or C. In Figure 2, the curve D_b represents the demand for B, while the curve D_c represents the demand for C. Assuming a new firm were to be organized, the curve AC_1 may be the average-cost curve for producing commodity B. However, as the firm is already a going concern, AC_1 can be assumed to represent the actual unit costs of producing commodity C while, if the firm decides to switch to the production of B, unit costs are those shown

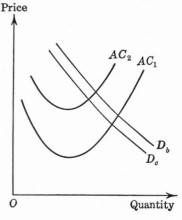

FIGURE 2

as embodied in AC_2: the firm must abandon some equipment and incur expensive equipment modifications besides covering capital charges on the abandoned facilities. In view of demand-and-cost phenomena a wholly new firm would thus undertake to produce commodity B, but the established firm would perceive the greater profitability of C.

The problem of implementing a decision to vary its product would, in general, have to be solved in the following way: imagine that there are N product types open to the established firm, each of which requires some modification in its layout. Average costs will thus always have to include the fixed charges on its present layout plus those on any plant additions plus the full variable charges. With costs calculated in this way, the question is to elicit the forces impelling the firm to select a K-th variety rather than any of the other $N - 1$ alternate commodity types.

For each of the N varieties we can visualize demand and cost schedules and assume that the firm announces the price and output that is most profitable for the commodity type.   If on the X axis we array the commodities according to their profitability, from the first possible commodity, A, to the Nth possible commodity variety, and measure profits on the ordinate axis, then the K commodity would touch the highest ordinate on the profit contour.   The marginal increment of profits for a product variation in either direction would be zero or negative.   If it were possible to conceive of the available commodity belt as being fully dense, in the sense that minute product variations—such as varying the size and weight of the package ever so slightly and shifting demand and cost curves but minutely—are possible, the equilibrium condition would reduce to one of an equality in the increase in total revenue and total costs.   The marginal revenue would be computed by subtracting maximum profit proceeds of producing commodities K and L, and total cost would be obtained by computing the change in total cost in the same way, as ensuing from a trivial variation in product.

If the commodity types are substantially discrete so that there are gaps in the commodity chain with the maximum total revenue and the maximum total cost of producing commodities A, B, C, D $\cdot$ $\cdot$ $\cdot$ being vastly different, then it seems best to abandon the concept of marginal-product variations and marginal-profit changes and instead to refer to the product selection being governed simply by the prospect of greatest profits among the available commodity alternatives.

Frequently the theory of product variation is discussed in a way that seems to imply that the firm is always engrossed in calculating whether or not it should vary its product.   No doubt these calculations are made, just as queries over whether plant expansion is merited or whether exit from the field is warranted are also in the entrepreneur's consciousness.   But once the plant has been constructed the firm will normally continue to produce its earlier commodity variety, and the commonplace decisions for it to execute are those of factor hire, product price, and quantity of output; commodity-variation problems are not brought to the fore as an everyday matter.   Among the notable exceptions are the practices of nonprice competition, which we describe shortly.

The Sales Function

Some aspects of the maximization solution implicit in the selection of a product by a new firm or product variation by a going firm can be clarified by the aid of some symbols and by the concept of the sales function.   Viewing a commodity, (for our immediate purposes) *from the sellers' standpoint*, we may say that it consists of a bundle of attributes that may be varied and profits thereby affected. The sales function x can thus be defined as follows:

$$x = x(P, p; A, a; C, c; W, w; T, t; D, d \cdots),$$

where x = sales of firm 1,

P = prices of all other products in the system,

p = price of product of firm 1,

A = sales outlays of all other firms,

a = sales outlays of firm 1,

C = "internal" contents ("quality") of all other products in the system,

c = "internal" contents ("quality") of firm 1's product,

W = "external" attributes (such as styling, design of container) of all other products in the system,

w = "external" attributes of the product of firm 1,

T = credit terms of sales of all other products,

t = credit terms of sales for the product of firm 1,

D = delivery terms of sales of all other products,

d = delivery terms of sales of the product of firm 1.

Of course, this breakdown of product attributes which firm 1 visualizes as influencing its sales is by no means complete; a more detailed decomposition of the C, W, T, and D concepts is certainly possible. However, it is within the province of the firm to alter any of the magnitudes indicated by lower-case letters; the factors indicated by capital letters are usually beyond its control. In earlier chapters we examined the relations between the firm's price policy and sales; in the preceding chapter we examined the relation between price policy, sales outlays, and sales. Now we consider some of the relations between price policy and the other variables of market policy.

Rather than write sales (x) as a function of price, selling costs, styling, quality, etc., it is often a simpler short cut to write profits (R) as dependent upon the sales receipts from each product, defined in terms of these variables, and from the total cost of producing each quantity of output, where the latter is also defined in terms of these specifications. Manifestly, the condition for maximum profits is that the increase in profits, ΔR, must be zero (or negative) for product movements in any direction, whether it be a variation in sales, in price, in selling costs, in quality, in external structure, in credit terms, etc. If this condition is satisfied for several different products the most profitable of all those products which conform to these maximization criteria is conceived to be chosen as the commodity vehicle about which production will be organized. There will be several commodities that satisfy these conditions only if there are gaps in the chain of variations.

Hence we have a long list of conditions, each equated to zero, which must be satisfied before the commodity selected can be adjudged the maximum. Thus, where each variation assumes other elements unchanged, we have

$$\frac{\Delta R}{\Delta x} = \frac{\Delta R}{\Delta p} = \frac{\Delta R}{\Delta a} = \frac{\Delta R}{\Delta c} = \frac{\Delta R}{\Delta w} = \frac{\Delta R}{\Delta t} \cdots = 0.$$

Each of the letters has the meaning already assigned to it. If there are changes in the external economic structure, in P, in A, in C, etc., then a new and varied product may become more profitable to the firm; the firm will, in general, be unable to influence these variables, for they are beyond its powers of control—except by strategem or economic coercion, as in structures of monopolistic competition. If the product does not lend itself to continuous and trivial modifications, then some of our ratio conditions for a maximum disappear; if it s not possible because of the chemistry of the ingredients to vary the internal composition, say, then Δc is simply nonexistent. Likewise, if terms of sale are regulated by law, then Δt vanishes. In either event the effect is to reduce the number of maximum conditions. Some of the more interesting problems arise when the firm finds it impossible, or impractical, for several reasons to vary its price. This gives rise to the phenomena of nonprice competition.

Diagrammatic Analysis

Some idea of the dimensions of the problem of product differentiation can be conveyed graphically. In Figure 3A, the curves R, S, T represent the average-cost curves of producing these commodities, all of which are close but imperfect substitutes. If the market price is held constant at OP, the quantity demanded of R is OL, of S, OM, and of T, ON. From the figure not only is unit profit on commodity T greater than profits on either R or S, but the total profits that can be amassed on T are also much more enormous. At the constant price, therefore, product T would be produced.

Yet when we permit not only product to vary but also price, relaxing the previous condition, then product R may emerge as most profitable. In Figure 3B, the full demand curves for the three products have been drawn: at a price of OP, points OL, OM and ON are the respective demand quantities for the three commodities, and are located as a point on the full curves.   In the lower price ranges the three curves may tend to converge; although product *T* enjoys more stylistic and quality embellishments than *S* which similarly is an improvement over *R*, as the price of each falls the demand comes largely from lower-income groups on whom the stylistic, rather than the functional, advantages are lost. Moreover, good *R* lends itself better to operating economies than either of the other two goods which, let us say, must always entail some skilled handicraft labors in order to impart their more distinctive features.

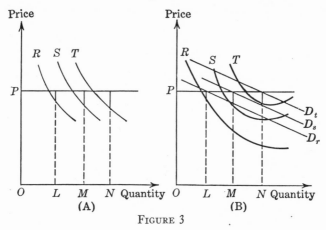

FIGURE 3

From a profit standpoint, therefore, considering the full cost-and-demand phenomena, commodity *R* will be produced.   Of course, this result stems entirely from the particular drawing.   If cost phenomena in *T* were more conducive to large-scale operations, T might still be chosen as the more appropriate market vehicle.*

From this analysis it is clear that it represents a profound degree of optimism to assert that the products on which productive energies are concentrated are those that evidence an undisputed technical superiority.   Instead, profitability will be the guide.   This is, however, not to suggest that technical superiority rather than preferences and costs *ought* to be the criterion.

NONPRICE COMPETITION

As in the other analyses of product selection, the theory of nonprice competition can be associated either with the entry of a new firm or a going firm which varies its product (perhaps to hasten the obsolescence

* Professor Chamberlin, in Figures 11 and 16 (pp. 79 and 95) draws the prototype of Figure 3A above.   But these curves should, for the true maximum-product solution, be accompanied by Figure 3B.

of commodity varieties already possessed by consumers) rather than price, because of the nature of the market structure and interdependence data.   Previously the entry of a new firm portended a price fall for goods in substitutionary relationship with the new product.   Although this is probably a valid generalization, in structures of nonprice competition the entry manifests itself in a greater variety of products with the price perturbations missing.   Let us analyze this situation.

If we assume that a new firm is organized to market a fairly close substitute for some current varieties of goods whose production is limited to one or few firms (in contrast to homogeneous entry in an atomistically competitive sphere where the new firm goes unobserved because there are already so many rivals), the new entrant is bound to excite and disconcert the present oligopoly members.   Ruling out any move by others to forestall entry by immediately lowering prices, after the field is reorganized we are once more amid a typical oligopoly problem, with greater numbers.   If the upshot was to lower prices, then the conclusion is warranted that consumer well-being would be enhanced.   However, there may be strong objections to lower prices; either a lower price will touch off a mutually disastrous price war or, as all recognize, total demand may be inelastic so that the policy will be injurious to all, including the price aggressor.   If the newcomer is a small firm able to satiate only a minor portion of the market, there is every reason for the old firms to persist in the price-maintenance policy.   Sales are redistributed with the new firm draining off custom from among the former members of the field, at a price perhaps below their price.

The truly interesting analyses in nonprice competition, however, are those in which the newly born firm introduces a differentiated but close substitute product for those of a close-knit heterogeneous oligopoly group, while adhering to the market level for that "type" of good.   As an illustration we may think of nickel candy bars, or $35 suits of clothes, etc.   Hence we have more varieties of the particular "class" of goods without any decrease in price.

There are innumerable ways in which demand and sales in the field may be redistributed.   The newcomer might siphon sales entirely from the older members of the closely knit group: if these inroads are important they may retaliate with price cuts.   Abstracting from this response, we can deduce that the reorientation of sales within the group will enhance consumer well-being, for their purchase of the new good (while other prices are unchanged) indicates that their wants are now better satisfied than formerly.

Besides draining off purchasers from within the group, the new firm may also thrive at the expense of a wide array of other products; consumers who were insensitive to the virtues of the former product types within the group may now be induced to buy the new innovation. Prices of all of the goods from which demand is deflected ought thus to evidence some downward tendency. Even if the price of the new innovation is higher than it might be with competitive pricing, the conclusion seems justified that consumer well-being is improved despite the nonprice competition. The suspension of price competition might thus lead to important quality advances. Existing firms will pose fewer objections to this form of competition than to price reductions, especially if market demand is inelastic; to the innovator the quality variation itself serves to protect it from a market onslaught in the form of mere price reductions by present sellers. It can be deduced, therefore, that where existing firms are reluctant to lower prices, and vigorously oppose a price fall, more frequent product variations are likely to be inspired than in circumstances in which price is freer to vary.

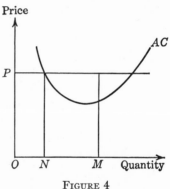

FIGURE 4

Nonprice Competition and Excess Capacity

Some implications of nonprice competition on excess capacity may be drawn. Suppose, in Figure 4, sales price is held at OP by firms in the field; AC represents the curve of average costs of a "typical" firm. At the ruling price, sales for each firm are OM. If new entrants are successful in winning consumers away from the former firms, and if the old firms persist in maintaining the price OP, their sales will slump back from OM toward ON. At a sales volume ON we have a profitless equilibrium position for each (or any) of the older firms. Obviously the result of the new entry is not to reduce prices but merely to redistribute sales, enabling consumers to some degree to be better served. It also leaves in its wake a rise in average operating costs for the firms previously intrenched in the field. This is an aspect of excess capacity, implying that with lower prices, a redistribution of sales, and the withdrawal of some firms from the field, the remaining facilities could be exploited more intensively, with general improvement in consumer well-being. To nonprice competition must be ascribed a role as a likely cause of excess capacity and uneconomic resource use.* Probably the same general conclusions on excess capacity can be educed in those cases, in which prices do vary after heterogeneous entry; the proof, however, would be more intricate.

Nonprice Competition among Existing Firms

Besides a new entrant having to subscribe to a ruling price for a particular class of goods, an existing firm may realize that it is caught in a rigid oligopoly price mesh and is unable to extend ts sales and avail itself of operating economies and greater profits through a price fall; the adamancy of existing firms may block this course. To extricate itself, it must either increase its sales outlays or proceed to differentiate its product anew relative to other commodities in the field. Figure 3A contains the relevant type of analysis. Thus when market price is stabilized we are likely to observe the spectacle of frequent changes in product types offered by existing firms eager to expand their share of market sales without destructive price wars. The innovation could only be charged as uneconomic when consumers would have preferred lower prices to "superior"products. Many of the innovations or improvements may be prized more highly than lower prices, especially when nonpecuniary motives are strong. Occasionally, because of peculiarities of the money system, such as the limited divisibility of the monetary units circulating or the aversion to holding small monetary denominations, consumers may prefer goods at customary prices (for example, chewing gum, candy bars, sandwiches, soaps, and even clothing) to the same goods at lower prices. In these situations quality improvements are undoubtedly commendable.

Fair Price Laws and Nonprice Competition

Nonprice competition has also been fostered by statewide adoption of laws permitting manufacturers to fix minimum prices of their wares at the retail level, ostensibly to outlaw "loss-leader" sales and "cut-rate" stores which arouse the antagonism of conventional retailers. Inevitably the results of price-maintenance practices must be to switch competition to a new channel in order to win sales and earn the liberal price spread conceded by manufacturers. In the retail trade the sales rivalry manifests itself in the form of increased services at the retail level, as longer credit terms, free delivery service, improved tone of the shop, surreptitious loss-leaders in the form of attractively priced menus in

* See the original argument in Chamberlin, pp. 104–109.

department-store restaurants, etc. As a result, goods bought at the retail level must be conceived as a hybrid composite of a technical good and "surrounding conditions of sale"; the effect must be to make the latter services more lavish and check lower prices.

It may be queried why manufacturers are anxious to prescribe fair prices. One reason is the socially perverse habit of judging quality by price; to preclude any possibility of their product's being stamped as an "inferior" good manufacturers are willing to accede to retail price fixing. Also, to perpetuate their position in the field, the retailer must be cultivated; unless retailers do accept their line (which is usually promoted by a liberal markup margin), their own productive endeavors will be frustrated. The arbitrament of the retailer is thus often more persuasive than the final judgment of consumers.

Some Forms of Nonprice Competition

It may not be amiss to catalogue some common forms of nonprice competition; some of the practices have aspects of discriminatory pricing while others might also be viewed as illustrations of pricing complementary goods. These features will be developed later.* Simple examples are those of a firm granting elongated credit terms or instituting a system of free delivery (within limits) to consumers, or the practice of granting samples and souvenirs to customers, or advertising "buy one at the regular price and get this (a quite different, perhaps unrelated good) free." The grant of liberal trade-in allowances may also be viewed as a variety of product differentiation and nonprice competition, where the standard price is overtly maintained but surreptitiously reduced through generous trade-in allowances. The publication of list prices from which discounts are universally granted to buyers can be viewed similarly; it maintains an aura of normalcy in the base price while allowing reductions to all consumers and discrimination in favor of some of them. Later it also lends itself more easily to plans to restore the "normal" price level by reducing the average discount level. Granting premium coupons to consumers is likewise a form of differentiation and nonprice competition. Undoubtedly an endless series of practices can be cited.

BIBLIOGRAPHICAL NOTE

Professor Chamberlin's work on product differentiation, Chapters IV–V especially, is the pioneer work on these problems. H. Hotelling in his sug-

* See Chapters 13 and 14.

gestive article, "Stability in Competition," *Economic Journal* (1929) likened the theory of location of firms to that of product selection, pointing out a whole host of analogies. See also M. A. Copeland, "Competing Products and Monopolistic Competition," *Quarterly Journal of Economics* (1940). S. Enke, "Profit Maximization Under Monopolistic Competition," *American Economic Review* (1941), and Hans Brems, "The Interdependence of Quality Variations, Selling Effort and Price," *Quarterly Journal of Economics* (1948) ought also be consulted. P. M. Gregory, "Fashion and Monopolistic Competition," *Journal of Political Economy* (1948) treats fashion as a form of product differentiation designed to accelerate the rate of obsolescence of many varieties of goods, especially clothing.

A list of practices of nonprice competition is provided by S. Nelson and W. G. Keim in "Price Behavior and Business Policy," Temporary National Economic Committee, Monograph 1 (1941). On excess capacity and nonprice competition, see also W. A. Lewis, "Competition in Retail Trade," *Economica* (1942). For some interesting remarks of a business man on the suppression of patents, see Samuel Courtcauld, "An Industrialist's Reflections on the Future Relations of Government and Industry," *Economic Journal* (1942).

CHAPTER 11

Buyer's Domination and

Bilateral Monopoly

Neither buyers nor sellers exert a perceptible influence on market price in the purely competitive framework. Derangements caused by monopoly were explained in the preceding chapters; there it was the sellers who violated the competitive maxims. But the price structure can also be controlled from the purchase side whenever buyers are in a position to dictate market price; the theory of monopsony embraces this set of phenomena as the analogue to monopoly from the buyers' side. Virtually the same classificatory issues that becloud the monopoly concept could be resurrected here.

The criterion of monopsony is the ability of the buyer to impose an effective price in the particular market. Lacking control over price, the purchaser may still wield some influence on price: the circular cases of duopsony and oligopsony conform to this pattern. Advertising outlays by purchasers may also appear in some monopsony situations. Though sellers are seldom bombarded with costly advertising campaigns designed to promote selling to a particular buyer, such maneuvers are not rare: witness the radio appeals of buyers of diamonds, old gold and used automobiles. Analogous to product differentiation, forms of purchase differentiation may also develop whenever buyers are few and are compelled to match one another's purchase price: some purchasers will grant sellers loans for future production, give the seller access to the legal and technical advice of the purchasers' staff, offer them gifts and, in countless other ways, make selling to them more attractive than sales to alternate purchasers who pay the same (or even slightly higher) prices. Nonpecuniary motives also guide purchase-price decisions; notions of a "fair" purchase price and of welfare solicitude for labor might be cited.   Obstructions to purchase entry can also be enumerated: through contracts for the full output of producers new purchasers may be frozen out of the particular purchase market.   Clearly, a striking parallel to the monopoly patterns can be discovered for the monopsony categories.

Not only do these monopsony patterns supplement the earlier array of monopoly structures but the dual forces may be combined in a single market so that the number of potential configurations is multiplied many times.*   To list but a few, there is first the venerable bilateral monopoly case, of one buyer confronting one seller.   Duopsony-monopoly, duopsony-duopoly, etc., may also appear.   To confuse matters further there is the not unlikely juxtaposition of monopsony in factor markets and monopoly in the sales markets.   Although it is not possible, nor desirable, to pursue all these market aberrations fully, the investigation will be complete enough to permit its refinement and extension to cover numerous situations likely in practical affairs.

MONOPSONY EQUILIBRIUM

While it was the demand curve, and the correspondent MR, which contained the heart of the monopoly solution, in monopsony the analysis turns about the supply curve (S) and its correspondent, the marginal supply curve (MSC).   Temporarily, to exclude problems containing both monopoly and monopsony elements, it is presumed that there are numerous sellers offering a homogeneous product.   On this hypothesis we can derive the marginal-supply curve.

The Marginal-Supply Curve

With one buyer among many, the market price is a datum and the market-supply curve, if thought about, would be envisaged as perfectly elastic: the price tags on merchandise in an urban department store are, to the buyer, immutable signposts of the terms on which alternatives are offered.   Poising the perfectly elastic supply curve, S, against the individual's demand curve, the purchases of the buyer at the settled price are determinate.   Immediately we may infer that, for monopsony, the S curve facing the purchaser must depart from the horizontal: normally, it will be positively sloped, rising with added purchases.   Corresponding to the notion of marginal revenue, where each additional unit sold made imperative a price fall per unit on the

* For an elaborate listing see John T. Dunlop, *Wage Determination Under Trade Unions*, Chapter V.

previous volume of sales, now a purchase expansion will lift the price paid on all units of smaller purchase quantities. The *marginal-supply price (MSP)* is thus stated

$$MSP = P_2\Delta X + X_1\Delta P.$$

In contrast to MR, where $X_1\Delta P$ was subtracted from $P_2\Delta X$, these two increments now represent an additive sum as long as the S curve rises positively with output.* The MSC curve connecting all the MSP points will, therefore, lie above the S curve, as in Figure 1a.

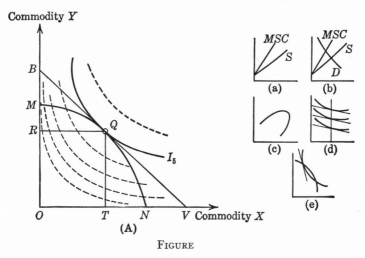

FIGURE

It should be remarked that MSC is not to be confused with the producer's MC curve. The market S curves are, ultimately, lateral summations of the individual producer's MC curves.† The MSC curve, in contrast, is a market reality solely from the buyer's standpoint: it is a curve of marginal supply price or marginal "cost" only when visualized through the eyes of the purchaser.

Monopsony Equilibrium

Given the demand curve, to wrest the equilibrium solution under monopsony is comparatively simple once the MSC curve has been

---

* Let P_2X_2 be the new expenditure and P_1X_1 the old, where $P_2 > P_1$ and $X_2 > X_1$. Hence

$$\begin{aligned} MSP &= P_2X_2 - P_1X_1 \\ &= P_2(X_1 + \Delta X) - X_1(P_2 - \Delta P) \\ &= P_2\Delta X + X_1\Delta P. \end{aligned}$$

When the supply price falls as purchase quantities increase, so that $P_2 < P_1$, the MSP formula resembles that of MR, and MSC lies *below* the S curve.

† See pp. 113–115.

extracted.   Mounting a demand curve D, and the S and MSC curves in the normal price-quantity chart field, the monopsony equilibrium occurs at the intersection of D and MSC, as in Figure 1b.   The condition of equilibrium is the equality $MSP_x = D_x$, with the subscript x denoting the equality at a particular output.   Below the intersection of the curves in the conventional diagram, the monopsony purchase volume is found on the horizontal axis, while the purchase price is located at the ordinate height corresponding to the supply point on S directly *below* the $D = MSC$ intersection: the monopsony price lies on S rather than on D or MSC.   Naturally, as MSC runs above S, the intersection of $D = MSC$ is to the left of the purchase volume at which $D = S$.   The important exception is of an industry producing in conditions of falling supply price, where the path of the S curve follows a normal D-curve course and the MSC curve appears *below S;* the $D = MSC$ intersection is to the right of the $D = S$ position and monopsony behavior portends an augmented sales volume.

As the supply curve is perfectly elastic and horizontal in purely competitive buying, then $X_1\Delta P$ is zero, so that $P = MSP$ and the supply curve merges with the marginal-supply curve.   As $S = MSC$, the intersection of S and D signifies that

$$D_x = MSP_x = S_x.$$

Monopsony Power

A measure of the degree of monopsony power (M_s) corresponding to the formula for monopoly power, can be written as:

$$M_s = (D_x - S_x)/D_x,$$

where D_x is the demand price for the quantity purchased and S_x is the supply price for the same volume.   The deviation $D_x - S_x$ is the ordinate difference of the demand and supply prices at the $D = MSC$ intersection.   Comparing this difference to the denominator, D_x, permits the measure to be employed in making market comparisons. When buying is purely competitive the measure of monopsony power becomes zero; it approaches unity with costless output for which sellers lack an alternative use but which, in view of demand, is not a free good. Other indices of monopsony control could be formulated to parallel the monopoly prototypes.*

* See Chapter 6.

MONOPSONY IN CONSUMER MARKETS

Once the demand curve has been drawn, the equilibrium solution follows in the manner described, with the D and MSC curves enabling us to pry open the answer. Yet when we ponder the monopsony adjustment, it appears that the demand curve pertinent to the theory differs, in the consumer market, from the ordinary demand curve.

For deeper insight, let us reconstruct the consumer-monopsony analysis in terms of the indifference system. Recalling the convex indifference maps, we note that the price line that was superimposed on the chart field was always linear, manifesting a constant price ratio P_x/P_y: in real terms it signified that the market facts compelled the sacrifice of a constant decrement ΔY to obtain the constant increment ΔX. The slope of the price (or budget) line was:

$$- \Delta Y / \Delta X = P_x/P_y,$$

leaving as the exchange relations along the price line:

$$- P_y \Delta Y = P_x \Delta X.$$

With P_x rising along the path of the positively sloped S curve following each ΔX acquisition, then the sum $P_y \Delta Y$ disgorged in payment for ΔX would mount as more X was acquired. Rather than the preceding relation, the situation would be

$$- P_y \Delta Y = P_x \Delta X + X \Delta P_x,$$

or

$$- P_y \Delta Y = MSP_x,$$

for ΔP_x is no longer zero. Rather than being linear, the budget line would instead become concave to the origin, for to procure a ΔX requires larger ΔY outpourings. If the S_x curve was negatively sloped, with MSC_x below S_x, then the budget line would be a convex contour resembling an indifference curve.

The Equilibrium Position

Our next concern is with the equilibrium position. The budget line embodies the external market facts while the indifference system displays the subjective taste attitudes. The two must be interlocked and balanced.

When prices were constant the condition of equilibrium involved the tangency of the linear budget line and indifference curve or, more fundamentally, equality between marginal rates of substitution and relative prices. For until the equality was established it would be possible to climb higher on the indifference map by diverting one's self of holdings of either X or Y. The same condition must prevail now: the concave (or convex) price line must be tangent to the indifference curve, occasioning the equality $MRS = MSP_x/P_y$, for otherwise the individual could enhance his level of well-being by a reshuffle of his holdings. Apparently the more gently the budget line edges out from OY, so that the decrement ΔY is small relative to the increment ΔX, the higher the ultimate level of well-being. When the concave dip of the budget line from OY is sharp and occurs immediately, connoting a sharply rising supply price for X, the monopsony potentialities are likely to be less remunerative—though more satisfactory than paying the full demand price for the self-same quantity of purchases.*

A graphic picture of the consumer monopsony equilibrium is furnished in Figure 1A; the concave curve MN is the budget line so that the purchase equilibrium is at Q, on I_5; OT of X will be bought together with OR of Y.

The Marginal-Demand Price

In indifference terms the monopsony analysis is hardly formidable. Now, we want to translate the mechanics of the adaptation into demand-curve terms. To contribute to the plethora of demand-curve concepts, still another demand curve is born, composed of the various MRS ratios of Y for X extracted from each of the points at which the budget line intersects the indifference map. To clarify the issues it is illuminating to follow the process of adaptation in detail until the tangency position is reached.

Using a linear budget line to elaborate the point, suppose that the individual has spent his full \$100 income on $100Y$ and now ponders the wisdom of reselling some Y to acquire some X. As a further simplification we can postulate that $P_x = P_y = \$1$, so that the slope of the budget line is

$$\frac{P_x}{P_y} = -\frac{\Delta Y}{\Delta X} = -1.$$

Also, $P_x = MSP_x$ and $P_y = MSP_y$, because for competitive buyers the market price is equal to the marginal supply price. Suppose that on the

---

* With sharply falling supply price, where P_x falls so rapidly as ΔX advances so that the total outlay on $2X$ units is less than on $1X$, the budget line will be of "horseshoe" concavity, as in Figure 1c.

initial indifference curve running through $100Y$ on OY, that the MRS of X and Y is

$$MRS = -\frac{\Delta Y}{\Delta X} = -\frac{10}{1}.$$

Hence to maintain well-being the individual would offer as much as \$10 to acquire $1X$: the *marginal-demand price* (MDP_x) for the first unit of X would therefore be \$10. Since only $1/10$th of a unit of X is necessary to maintain the level of well-being, and as a full unit of X can be secured by relinquishing $1Y$, the individual moves higher on the indifference hill by executing the trade.* On the indifference map the individual is now on the higher curve containing the coordinates $99Y$ and $1X$. The same problems arise now, for an exchange of $1Y = 1X$ can still be arranged. So long as the MRS of X for Y exceeds the $1/1$ market exchange rate, the transaction is advisable. If the MRS was now $8/1$, then the MDP_x for a second unit would be \$8 while the MSP_x ($= P_x$) would still be \$1. Manifestly, each exchange of ΔY for ΔX pushes the individual onto a higher indifference curve. With each exchange the MRS tends to be reduced until at the tangency position of

$$MRS = P_x/P_y = MSP_x/MSP_y$$

the one-to-one market exchange rate would equal the MRS ratio; for an added trade the indifference level would just be maintained and not improved. Beyond this point, assume that the MRS is such that $2X$ would be needed to overcome the loss of $1Y$; here the MDP_x would be but 50¢ while MSP_x would still be \$1, so that the purchase of further X is undesirable. Hence the indifference-curve equilibrium in demand-curve concepts is one where

$$MDP_x = MSP_x.$$

While the argument has been conducted in terms of a linear budget line, evidently the reasoning does not rely on such a line. If the budget line is concave the only modification is that now the market rate of commodity exchange is (as) MSP_x/P_y. So long as $MRS > MSP_x/P_y$ it will be preferable to part with the decrement ΔY to acquire the increment ΔX, with an equilibrium only when $MDP_x = MSP_x$, at point Q in Figure 1.

Two points merit further elucidation. At each indifference point

---

* See above Chapter 1. Commodity Y can of course be money, implying constancy of prices P_y, $P_z \cdots$

intersected by the budget line, whatever the shape of the latter, the MRS of X for Y, when translated into money terms, is the marginal-demand price (MDP_x), for it denotes the sum that the individual will offer at each indifference point on the budget line to acquire ΔX. In the competitive purchase market S_x is horizontal and perfectly elastic, enabling the MDP_x to be equated to market price.

As a second matter, as we move down the budget line, from point M in Figure 1A towards point N, it has been argued that each successive acquisition of X, accompanied by the loss of Y, lowered the MRS of X and Y and hence lowered the MDP_x. This requires some explanation, for hitherto the rule to which the indifference curves had to comply was one of a decreasing MRS along a *given* indifference curve, where real income was constant, but not from *one curve to another*, which introduces changing income levels into the picture. Normally, despite the income change, as Y was lost and X acquired the MRS of X and Y would fall. But there is no inexorable necessity here; conceivably, X may be more important in the consumption plan as income levels rise, so that the new MRS exceeds the old. This would happen if Y was an inferior good; the MDP_x sum would thereupon rise as the X holdings were augmented. Nevertheless, so long as MSP_x rose at a faster pace than MDP_x, an ultimate equilibrium is possible.

The Monopsony-Demand Curve

If we assume commodity Y to be money, and hypothecate a definite pattern for other prices, each MRS point intersected by the budget line indicates the sum of money—the marginal demand price—that will be surrendered for a further unit of X. Each MDP_x point is thus contingent on the exact combination of X and Y possessed. Plotting each successive MDP_x point on the price-quantity chart field, we elicit the demand curve appropriate for consumer-monopsony analysis. The assumptions of the full MDP_x demand curve are: (1) the initial income of the individual; (2) the preference system; (3) the price of Y (all other commodities); (4) the supply curve of X which, with P_y, shapes the course of the budget line, and finally (5) for each successive MDP_x point, the sums already expended on X and implicitly diverted from $Y, Z \cdot \cdot \cdot$ commodities; each demand point depends on tastes and the volume of expenditure already committed to commodity X. It is this last premise that distinguishes the MDP_x demand curve appropriate for consumer-monopsony analysis from the conventional demand curve. For the normal demand curve each demand point is independent of any previous commitment to spend an aggregate sum on X: each point can be extracted from the curve and enjoys a vitality even when divorced from the consecutive series of alternate points. Now, however, the points are not alternate likelihoods but an interrelated sequence; one point is meaningless without all of the others.

In short, in drawing the customary demand curve it is assumed that the buyer is confronted with a family of horizontal supply curves and, from the ensuing MDP curves attached to each perfectly elastic S_x curve, only the equilibrium-demand prices are isolated and combined into the continuous normal demand curve. Under monopsony the relevant demand curve is not compounded in this way: it comes from only one, rather than from a family of supply curves. Because of this discrepancy it will be convenient to describe the monopsony demand curve as an MDP_x demand curve.

The Marginal-Demand and Simple Demand Curves

It remains to demonstrate the relationship between the MDP demand curve and the simple demand curve. Extending the tangent to the concave budget line MN and I_5 in Figure 1 until it intersects the OY axis at B, and OX at V, we perceive that the OK purchase quantities of Y and OT purchase quantities of X would be bought only at an income level much in excess of OM, and at fixed prices equal to the MSC_x/P_y relation at Q. Holding income fixed at OM, so that both money income and P_y are constant, and radiating a linear budget line parallel to BV, we find that its point of tangency to the indifference system will normally be to the left of I_5, disclosing a demand quantity of less than OT of X at a fixed price P_x equal to the monopsony equilibrium MSP_x. This is just the hint we need of the relative location of the two demand curves: it affirms that at least to the left of the monopsony equilibrium the normal demand curve rests *below* the MDP demand curve.

As an exception to this rule there is again the constant marginal utility of money with respect to income; if the demand for X is completely inelastic with respect to income, the BV, and lower parallel price lines, are tangent at identical X, but at different Y quantities, as in Figure 1d. The simplification wrought by this hypothesis is evident once more: the MDP demand curve relevant for monopsony coincides with the simple demand curve. Likewise, if X is an inferior good the MDP demand curve may lie *below* the normal demand curve, at least near the relevant equilibrium phase: the higher indifference curves tend to be flat so that a price line emanating from M, but below and parallel to BV, would indicate more X purchased at low-income positions than at high-income positions.

This examination is sufficient to locate the relative positions of the curves in the neighborhood of the equilibrium $MDP_x = MSP_x$ price point. The proof over the full course of the two curves is more difficult. The MDP is determined by the MRS at each indifference level intersected by the (concave) price line representing actual market conditions. At each of the intersected MRS points a tangent can be drawn to the indifference curve, as in Figure 1e. Starting from OM, the fixed money income, a budget line parallel to the MRS tangent can then be projected; usually, the latter price line will be tangent to the indifference system at an OX quantity to the left of the point intersected by the concave budget line, indicating that the normal demand curve is located *under* the MDP demand curve. But beyond the equality of MRS and MSP_x/P_y, the MDP curve breaks precipitously, becoming highly inelastic for further purchases lower well-being. Only under duress would the individual purchase more X than indicated at the $MDP = MSP$ equilibrium. Although meaningless marketwise, if the MDP curve is extended, at very low MDP values the ordinary demand curve will lie *above* the MDP curve; the two demand curves will intersect when at some budget-line and indifference-curve meeting place the MRS tangent (extended) runs a linear course to point M.*

We must conclude that, as the demand curve appropriate for monopsony problems is distinguishable from the normal demand curve, it is improper to draw comparisons between monopsony and competitive-market purchases unless the convenient fiction of a constant marginal utility of money is explicitly imposed. That purchases would be greater if the monopsony price was externally announced and regarded by the monopsony buyer as immutable seems to be an accurate enough proposition; the analysis, however, has confirmed that the exact extent of the enhancement cannot be read off the chart field by glancing at a unique demand curve.

MONOPSONY AND THE COST CURVES

Strangely enough, the theory of monopsony price in factor markets is less formidable than in consumer markets; most of the preceding difficulties can be attributed to the fixity of money income: factor cost outlay is never limited in this way.† To trace the consequences of monopsony in factor markets, where the problem is more important and

---

* Simultaneously, the supply curve would intersect the ordinary and MDP demand curves for each point on the budget line is an implicit supply point of X (and Y). Consider Q in Figure 1A: to obtain OT of X, the individual must sacrifice MR of Y. Thus the supply price of X equals MR/OT.

† See Chapter 3, p. 61.

the situations more genuine, let us analyze the effects of a rising factor-supply curve on the expansion path, for once this is fixed then the derivative *TC*, *AC* and *MC* curves can be computed mechanically.

Varying Factor Prices and the Expansion Path

With a rising supply curve (S_x) of factor X, and P_y constant, the isocost will be concave. Writing MP_x and MP_y for marginal products, and MSP_x for the marginal supply price of factor X, we find the minimum-cost equilibrium volume of factor hire at the point of tangency of isocost

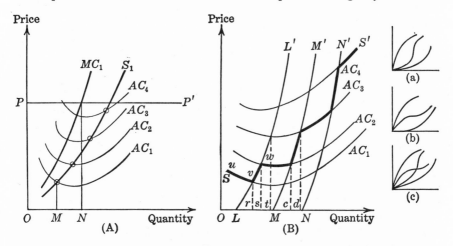

FIGURE 2

and a constant product curve, where

$$MRS = MP_x/MP_y = MSP_x/P_y.$$

With a greater sum spent on factors, with P_y and S_x posited, all that is involved is an upward transformation in the isocost; its shape is unaffected because Y must be surrendered at the same rate as before to obtain the same X quantity. The only fresh portion of the isocost is that lying to the right of the OX point at which the original isocost cut the horizontal axis; although formerly suppressed because of lower aggregate expenditure, and thus a lower maximum purchase of X, it now appears. This section of the isocost is likely to be steep, reflecting higher regions on S_x. Covering the isoquant map with a family of isocosts, the expansion path can be traced by linking the various points of tangency. As S_x is rising, with factor X becoming more expensive relative to Y, the expansion path will veer towards the upper ridge line, as in Figure 2a.

The reason for this contortion in the expansion path should be apparent.   Earlier, it was developed that when factor prices are constant the expansion path coincided with a definite isocline.*   Now, as P_x rises as more X is hired there are strong forces operative to discard X and substitute relatively more Y.   This explains the edging toward the top ridge line, crossing always onto new isoclines.   At the ridge line, despite the mounting P_x, more of X must be used when output expands, for MP_y tends to approach zero, indicating that the limit of the substitutionary process has been reached.   To balance out the analysis, when P_y rises relative to P_x as more Y is used, the expansion path approaches the lower ridge line, as in Figure 2b.   Placing the diverse hypotheses of factor price movements on the same isoquant field, the respective expansion paths form the hourglass figure of Figure 2c.

Monopsony and the Cost Curves

Each isocost, and thus each point on the expansion path, represents a definite output and outlay on factors; the implicit TC, AC, and MC values can thus be distilled.   Pending this task, let us examine some of the effects on the cost curves when monopsony pricing of factors is rife: as these aberrations are obscured in transplanting the TC, AC, and MC points from the expansion path, the cost curve apparatus will be examined more closely.

A family of AC curves are drawn in Figure 2A.   First, to expand output assume that variable factors X and Y must be used in fixed proportions; the curves are U-shaped, we can agree, because of the presence of a third fixed factor.†   Along each AC curve we postulate that factor prices P_x and P_y are constant.   Climbing from curve to curve, from AC_1 to AC_2 say, we presume that P_y remains unchanged while P_x increases, so that P_x is the parameter responsible for the curve family.

Commencing at output OM and curve AC_1, and thus the implicit P_x of curve AC_1, as output advances and more of X is hired in conjunction with more Y, P_x also rises; the relevant AC is situated on a higher curve.   For $1X$, say, the relevant AC point is located on AC_1; for $2X$, on AC_2, etc.   When we connect these average cost points, the locus S_1 appears, with each point on its path signifying the actual AC experienced at the particular output level.   Consequently it will be the S_1 curve that will be crucial in the firm's output calculations with a rising supply curve of factor X.   Drawing a curve marginal to S_1, as MC_1 in Figure 2A, we

---

* Chapter 3, p. 61.
† See page 75.

find that the output equilibrium in a competitive sales market involves the equality of MC_1 and P.* This is at output ON. To ascertain the AC at the equilibrium output we would have to glance at the S_1 point directly above ON or below the $(MC_1 = P)$ intersection. Observing the particular curve of the AC family through S_1 at ON, reflecting a constant P_x on AC equal to that paid in the monopsony equilibrium, and then drawing the MC correspondent of AC, we can draw a comparison between monopsony output and a competitive output based on an unchanging factor price P_x equal to the monopsony level. Apparently, if S_1 traverses a path to the left of the minimum AC points, the monopsony contraction will be more serious than when the S_1 course is to the right of the minimum point.

Substitution among Factors

Limited as the foregoing analysis is to fixed proportions of X and Y (like one man and a hoe, or one skilled plus five unskilled laborers for every output addition) it does, nevertheless, convey the correct impression. Normally, factors X and Y are substitutable and, through the substitution effect, the factor whose price has increased tends to be supplanted by relatively lower priced factors at each output level. The output effect, however, tends to sustain its use by operating to expand the employment of all productive factors as production is increased. If the output effect invariably exceeds the substitution force, then the previous analysis can stand, for with higher output, there is a movement from a lower to higher AC curve.

Let us deal with cases in which the substitution effect outweighs the output effect. In Figure 2B, at the P_x implicit in AC_1, suppose that $10X$ are used, along with definite amounts of Y, until output Or is reached. Beyond Or, if P_x remains constant more X will be demanded. On AC_2, in comparison, as P_x is higher the $10X$ are utilized until an output of Os is reached, with more Y replacing additional X between output $Os - Or$. On AC_3, $10X$ serves until output Ot is reached.

If we run the line LL' through the maximum outputs for which $10X$ are employed as P_x rises, the path LL' indicates that ΔX becomes economic to the right of LL' despite the higher price of X. Likewise, the MM' and NN' paths partition the AC curve system according to the

---

* The MC_1 curve resembles the Marshallian supply curves which differ from the U-shaped cost curves now in vogue. The suspicion has been voiced by Mrs. Robinson that the Marshallian curves are a composite of the two forces: (a) diminishing factor productivity as output expands, and (b) rising factor prices. See her penetrating article on "Rising Supply Price," *Economica* (1941).

identical maximum amounts of factor X implicit in the cost curves over the output range. Under fixed proportions, the LL', MM', and NN' paths become vertical lines.

Suppose that output is at Or. As output expands, if P_x were constant, more of factor X would be hired. As P_x rises it may be feasible to apply more of factor Y, holding X at 10 units. Soon, however, more X must be hired despite the higher price; the relevant AC path follows the course *uvw*, or *vw* between output Or and Os. Beyond Os, however, more X must be hired; the ΔX, plus the $10X$, will serve until an output of Oc. But the important point is that between Or and Os the output effect working to increase the use of factor X is dwarfed by the substitution effect, stifling its use in view of its price rise. If the lines of constant factor use, such as LL', have a very gentle slope, indicating vast substitutionary power, the output effect will be weak; if the factor use line LL' is practically upright, the output effect will be decisive. Assuming that the supply curve of factor X is such that P_x rises whenever the use of the X factor is expanded, the AC curve of output will follow the heavy-lined SS' staircase of Figure 2B. A curve marginal to SS' can be computed and rendered the effective-monopsony MC curve. In Figure 2B it would be discontinuous, merging with the separable MC curves attached to each of the AC paths in the family over outputs such as Os to Oc, then breaking off erratically as the SS' curve shifts on to a higher AC.

MONEMPORY

It is but an elementary extension of this technique to depict the equilibrium of a firm invested with monopsony power over one (or more) of the productive factors and monopoly power in the selling market for its product. Rather than designate this position by the hyphenated term "monopoly-monopsony," the term *monempory* has been suggested.[*]

Diagrammatic Analysis

The D and MR curves for final output are drawn in Figure 3, along with S_1 and MC_1, where the former are the market curves for the final output of the firm, and the latter curves are to be interpreted as in the last section. Monempory output of profit maximization, therefore, is at OM and price, at P_1 for these are the values at the $MR = MC_1$ intersection. The average cost of OM output is found on S_1 below the $MC_1 = MR$ intersection. Through this S_1 point a curve such as AC_2

---

[*] A. J. Nichol, review article, *Journal of Political Economy* (1943), p. 83.

can be drawn, denoting the AC path on the abandonment of monopsony pricing of factors, but with the factor price fixed at the monopsony level. MC_2 is marginal to AC_2. Let us appraise the separate output influences of monopoly and monopsony.

Removing monopsony pricing of factors, while retaining monopoly selling in final output, AC_2 and MC_2 are the relevant cost curves: the equilibrium would be at P_2 ($< P_1$) and output would be at ON ($> OM$). Similarly, with monopsony devoid of monopoly, output would be OK

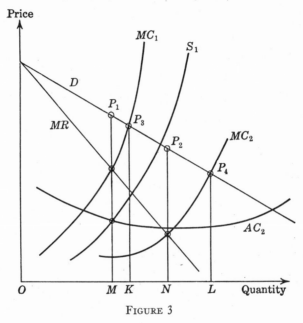

FIGURE 3

($> OM$); price would be P_3 (for here MC_2 intersects D). Deprived of both monopsony and monopoly power, price would settle at P_4, with output surging to OL: price would be lower and output greater than in any of the single-control cases.

This last position suggests the effects of a competitive adaptation. But we must be wary of hasty conclusions for, by using more of X in producing the greater output, there could be a rise in the price of the factor, so that the curve AC_2 is unstable; only if its rigidity were assured could the comparisons of fully competitive and monempory outputs be posited with confidence. As a further note, although monopoly in the sales market, without monopsony in factor markets, cuts output from OL to ON, while monopsony pushed it back to OK, supporting the inference that the monopsony structure was more deleterious than the monopoly relationship, this conclusion lacks any immanent necessity: the test of its validity hinges upon the exact shape of the MR and MC curves.*

Monopsony and Monempory Factor Hire

Equilibrium conditions of factor hire under monopsony and monempory can be stated succinctly, following the earlier competitive and monopoly models.†

Under monopsony in hiring factor A, but with competitive selling of commodity X, additional A will be hired until

$$P_x \cdot MP_a = MSP_a > P_a$$

or

$$\frac{P_x \cdot MP_a}{MSP_a} = 1,$$

and

$$\frac{P_x \cdot MP_a}{P_a} > 1.$$

This will also involve

$$\frac{P_x}{MC_x} = \frac{P_x(MP_a + MP_b)}{MSP_a + P_b} = 1$$

or

$$P_x = MC_x = MSP_a + P_b > P_a + P_b.$$

Under monempory, at the profit maximization output,

$$\frac{MR_x \cdot MP_a}{MSP_a} = 1,$$

and

$$\frac{MR_x}{MC_x} = \frac{MR_x(MP_a + MP_b)}{MSP_a + P_b} = 1,$$

with

$$P_x > MR_x = MC_x = MSP_a + P_b > P_a + P_b.$$

In contrast to consumer monopsony, the demand curve for a factor under monopsony is the same as the demand curve in competitive hire, inasmuch as the product price, the input-output ratios, and the prices of

---

* See J. Dunlop and B. Higgins, "Bargaining Power and Market Structure," *Journal of Political Economy* (1942), p. 13.

† Above, pp. 112–113, 139.

other factors are unchanged. The difficulty in drawing the demand curve of the consumer is occasioned by the consumer's having a fixed income sum to spend, while in factor hire this restriction is obliterated.*

Monopsony and Advertising

A few remarks may be injected on advertising under monopsony. These expenditures to shift the supply curve facing a monopsonist will normally accompany monopoly in the sales market—the monempory case. Advertising outlays to induce more sellers to deal with the buying firm will always be remunerative if the ensuing shift in the S_1 curve in the sales market, as by a fall in costs, enlarges profits by more than the sum of advertising outlays. Imposing continuity and decreasing effectiveness with further outlays in the advertising campaign, the equilibrium expenditure will be reached when the added profits attributable to the rightward shift in S_1 just equals the extra advertising outlay. To this equality there is, of course, the production equilibrium condition of $MC_1 = MR$. This is the kernel of the solution, although many of the intricacies of the theory of sales outlays abound here.†

Monopsony and Nonpecuniary Motives

As in monopoly, nonpecuniary motives will often influence a monopsonist in his purchase policy so that the full degree of monopsony power may not be exercised in any particular period of time. Once more this imparts an air of indeterminateness to any a priori solution. Motives for moderation and restraint in exploiting the monopsonistic position resemble the list enumerated for monopoly power: there may be mere inertia in using the power, ignorance of its full potentialities, or the monopsonist may have ideas on a "fair" buying price; or he may want to forestall government decrees and enactments or he may desire to foster future supplies, etc. Any of these reasons constitute a plausible

---

* A related monempory case is one in which numerous fabricators purchase a raw material sold by a monopolist and sell their finished output to a monopsonist buyer. To the individual firm caught in this cross-fire, a unique demand curve for the factor can be composed at each final product price. Depending on the factor price, the cost curve and the output equilibrium are determinate. Removing monopoly over the intermediate factors will cause the supply curve facing the monopsonist in the final market to shift rightward; with greater numbers in the final buying market and a higher final sales price, the demand curve for the raw materials will likewise move rightward. Inherently there is a struggle between the factor owners and final buyers, with the aim of each being to oust or dominate the other.

† Rothschild argues that "welfare" outlays of firms to attract larger and permanent working forces are an aspect of monopsony hire. See "Monopsony, Buying Costs, and Welfare Expenditure," *Review of Economic Studies* (Winter 1942–1943).

excuse for foregoing maximum pecuniary income in any single market period. In terms of indifference relations the equilibrium is determinate and soluble; the indifference relations between profits and factor hire are similar to the monopoly constructions. When we fit the profit contour on the same indifference field the tangency position depicts the combination of hire and profits that maximizes the preference level.

High-Wage Policies

There are many grounds on which to challenge the fundamental assumption of the pursuit of maximum profits. Empirical study might also disclose that firms with acknowledged monopoly power pay higher wages than their competitive brethren. It may be a consequence of social welfare concern on the part of the management but it may also mask other motives. Although the supply curve of labor is perfectly elastic to the firm, it views it as higher than its actual level; this can be visualized as a partial monopsony problem.

Paying higher than market wage rates will shift the firm's entire MC and AC curves up on the chart field, above the minimal levels. Consequently, in all the usual cases output will be reduced and sales price raised through the ostensibly benevolent policy. The implicit monopoly power, measured from the MC curve on which factors are valued at market prices, will probably be increased. From this point of view paying wages in excess of the market level is a form of monopoly profit sharing, with ramifications upon output. The members of the working force are made acquiescent, silent partners to the monopoly and thereby perhaps even vociferous champions on the management's behalf in defense of the price policy. This may be an inexpensive form of insurance for the firm, preferable to government regulation and a protection against potential "wage sweating" entrants whose offense consists of paying merely market wage rates.

DUOPSONY PROBLEMS

Duopsony and oligopsony denote markets dominated by two or more buyers respectively, but too few to nullify each firm's influence over purchase price. We could resurrect the reaction-curve apparatus and also distinguish between quantity leaders and followers, separating those instances in which the quantities that other firms buy are fixed as against those cases in which their purchases depend on one's own purchases. Only two simple cases of duopsony, however, are discussed.

Purchase differentiation analyses, by monopsonistic competitors, are by-passed.

Some Illustrations

As a first duopsony sample, firm A may expect firm B to purchase a fixed amount of the good. Admittedly this is a most unreasonable hypothesis, for with any insight at all A will know that B's purchases are not unrelated to price. Nevertheless we can examine this case in order to demonstrate the principle. Visualizing an ordinary market supply curve, and then subtracting B's expected purchases laterally

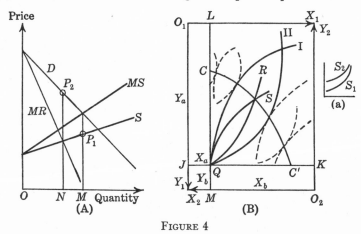

FIGURE 4

from it, we derive another supply curve, from which we in turn derive an MSC curve. With a linear demand curve representing A's demand, MSC intersects it at a higher price than would be paid to the sellers if A were the only buyer. The duopsony price, under the assumptions made, is more favorable to the sellers than the monopsony price.

As a more realistic hypothesis, A may feel, in view of B's demand, that there is a floor under the minimum market price. B's purchases, however, contract as supply price rises, tapering off and narrowing until they become zero, as in Figure 4a. Thus the supply curve confronting duopsonist A will be the S_2 curve on the left, with the lateral area between the curves signifying B's demand intake at the successive prices. Drawing an MSC to S_2, and following through to the final adjustment, if S_2 is fairly elastic the purchase adaptation would not deviate too far from the competitive price.

Rather than pursue duopsony situations through all their ramifications, so long as the demand price $D = MSP > S_x$, in the final adaptation the same remarks that pertain to all monopsony departures from the competitive price still apply. The sole difference is one of the degree of derangement of the structure from the competitive alignment. Further, besides elements of strategy in market purchase, we must again recognize the possibility of direct agreement between duopsonists and oligopsonists: collusion between firms or compensation of one participant by others to accomplish certain market results may be the outcome in fields of small numbers, with each firm able to influence the market price. Solutions of these "compensation" problems are, in general, numerous and inconclusive.

BILATERAL MONOPOLY

Bilateral monopoly—a monopsonist opposed to a monopolist—is an extreme case of conflicting interests, strength, and strategy.

In Figure 4A the demand curve D and the supply curve S are drawn. If the buyer was in a position to announce the price—a monopsony price —we could draw a curve marginal to S, as MS in the figure, and determine its intersection with D, indicating a price P_1 and output OM in Figure 4A. On the other hand, if the seller names the price we would have to sketch in the MR curve of D; market price now would be higher, at P_2, while output would be less—only ON. The nature of the price conflict is obvious. Price determinateness, therefore, is confined to the range $P_2 - P_1$; market price is limited to this range, for neither higher nor lower prices are profitable to either participant. If D represents a demand curve for an intermediate factor, and if the two firms mutually agree on price to maximize their *joint* profit, the output appearing at the intersection of D and S would be exchanged.* But this assumes harmonious attitudes and precludes either firm seeking to exploit the other's weakness in bargaining.

It is a commonplace in economic analysis that market price under bilateral monopoly is indeterminate in the sense that there are no a priori principles that enable us to judge precisely which price will be forthcoming in each case on the usual maximization hypotheses. It will depend upon compromise and strength and upon the bargaining ability of the participants—including the carrying costs of the seller, the threat of future competition, the nature of future demand and (for the buyer) the intensity of present demand, considerations of the future supply prospects, alternative sources of gratification, etc.

---

* Price could lie between the *average* supply price for this quantity and the maximum demand price, or in an all-or-nothing bargain, for this quantity. See the bibliographical references to Bowley, Fellner and Haley.

Contract Curves

The problem can also be analyzed in another way by means of contract curves derived from the indifference field.

In Figure 4B the usual indifference curves are drawn with their axes transformed. O_1 and O_2 are the origins and reference points for A's indifference map and B's preference field respectively. Furthermore, the axes are so chosen that the quantities jointly possessed of commodity X (amount X_a by A and amount X_b by B) equal the whole length of the unit line JK. Correspondingly, LM equals the total Y sum held (Y_a and Y_b). Through this device we are able to locate both individuals simultaneously at the common point Q on the combined indifference map.

For A, already at point Q, all equally preferred combinations are located along the indifference curve lettered I. For B the equal indifference combinations are along II. Seller A will be glad to trade as long as he moves up the field towards the O_2 origin. B, on the other hand, would want to mount up towards O_1.

Connecting all the points of tangency of the two families of indifference curves, whose members are traced in as dashed lines, the resulting locus is the *contract curve CC'*. The important property of the contract curve is that it connects the X and Y quantities at which the *MRS* for both parties coincides. Drawing a linear price line of any slope whatever through Q, and observing its point of tangency with some curve of A's and B's indifference system, we note that each individual could improve his real income by disposing of some Y for X or vice versa, until a point of tangency of the price line and the indifference system was reached. Varying the slope of the price line and connecting the series of such points of tangency, we trace out A's *offer curve QS*, and B's *offer curve QR*.* Appropriately enough, they intersect on the contract curve where a particular price line through Q is simultaneously tangent to both sets of indifference curves. This, we shall see, is the $D = S$ position.

So far, the contract-curve analysis has not elicited any new knowledge. Now, however, we are in a position to give the analysis a new twist and extract information unobtainable from the demand-and-supply-curve chart field. Suppose exchanges occur not at a single price but at varying prices, each unit being sold at a different price by new bargains between our individuals. Say that some units are exchanged at a given

---

*Concerning Y as money, A's offer curve QS is an implicit demand curve for each point indicates the sum of Y that will be sacrificed for an amount of X; QR would be an implicit supply curve, for each point indicates the total of X offered for a sum of Y.

price.   After the exchange, both A's and B's holdings fall within the possible area of exchange, within the shell formed between Q and the intersection of I and II.   If the price is favorable to B, the new position is on the offer curve QS.   Advantageous to A, on QR.   If the full quantities demanded or offered at the given price are not sold then some point outside the QS-QR circuit denotes the position of well-being.   Nevertheless the real income of both participants rises as compared to the initial position Q.

At the new location of the X and Y holdings, new offer curves similar to QS and QR can be constructed.   They too intersect on the contract curve; the way is therefore open for further exchange.   This is the significant point: no matter whether exchange takes place at one price, or whether there are several prices at which limited quantities are transferred, the final exchange must carry both participants to some point on the contract curve CC'.   The reason is that until the contract curve is reached the well-being of each individual can be augmented by further exchange; only on the contract curve is the MRS the same for both parties, for the same total stocks of X and Y, and equal to the ratio of market prices.   All subsequent movements from CC' will leave one party, or the other, or both, worse off than before.

Constant Marginal Utility of Money

The simplification wrought by Marshall's assumption of a constant marginal utility of money appears in this analysis too.   Commodity Y, in Figure 4B, is assumed to be the money commodity for both parties. Viewing the marginal utility of money as constant, we find that changes in the MRS ratio between X and Y are the result of changes only in the X holdings, never in the Y amounts.   Consequently the MRS equality is wholly contingent upon the relative distribution of X for, given the Y holdings of each, the MRS of X and Y will be the same whether A or B has more of the Y item.   The contract curve relating the consistent MRS ratios will thus be a vertical line.   If a price ratio equal to this MRS ratio is immediately named, the equilibrium holdings of X and Y are of course determinate.   Even if transactions are executed at several different prices, each of which are inconsistent with equilibrium, so long as the equilibrium rate of exchange is finally announced the total amount X transacted is the same.   Despite the numerous exchanges at prices incompatible with equilibrium, the indeterminateness in the real income position extends only to the final distribution of Y—the money commodity—between the individuals, never to X.*   Thus by choosing one commodity as money and introducing the Marshallian hypothesis, a greater degree of determinateness can be injected into the bilateral monopoly analysis.

BIBLIOGRAPHICAL NOTE

The theory of buyers' monopoly was restated and rechristened as monopsony by Mrs. Robinson.   (*Economics of Imperfect Competition*, Chapters XVII–XIX.)   A comprehensive survey of the theory, replete with hints for concrete applications, is contained in W. H. Nicholls, *Imperfect Competition Within Agricultural Industries*.   Dr. Triffin has advanced the terms heteropsony and homeopsony, circular or not, to fill the oligopsony categories. (*Monopolistic Competition and General Equilibrium Theory*, p. 143.)   For further aspects of the theory, and a critique of the conventional analysis, see A. J. Nichol, "Monopoly Supply and Monopsony Demand," *Journal of Political Economy* (1942).

Professor Hicks describes a curve analogous to the marginal-demand price curve developed in this chapter in his article on "The Four Consumer's Surpluses," *Review of Economic Studies* (1943).   On the effect of varying factor prices and monopsony hire on the expansion path, see Carlson, *Pure Theory of Production*, p. 38.   Bilateral monopoly and monopsony analysis, with special reference to labor markets, is discussed in W. Fellner, "Prices and Wages Under Bilateral Monopoly," *Quarterly Journal of Economics* (1947).

The literature on the theory of bilateral monopoly is extensive.   Among the more recent items is G. Tintner, "Note on the Problem of Bilateral Monopoly," *Journal of Political Economy* (1939).   Tintner also enumerates the conditions under which monopoly, monopsony, and competitive pricing merge.   Also, A. L. Bowley, *Mathematical Groundwork of Economics*, Chapter 1 and his "Note on Bilateral Monopoly," *Economic Journal* (1928), pp. 651–659.   Alfred Marshall furnished an earlier mathematical statement, *Principles*, Mathematical Appendix, n. XII, p. 485, working out the assumption of a constant marginal utility for money.   An interesting contribution is that of A. M. Henderson, "A Further Note on the Problem of Bilateral Monopoly," *Journal of Political Economy* (1940).   Henderson introduces cost considerations by measuring money amounts along one of the axes.   See also B. F. Haley, "Value and Distribution," in *A Survey of Contemporary Economics*, pp. 22–24.

---

* The amount of X transacted is thus the amount indicated at the intersection of D and S; the indeterminateness thus extends only to price.   See p. 266*n*.

CHAPTER 12

Spatial Interdependence

As an equilibrium problem of the firm, a relevant question concerns the area served by each seller. At this time we confine ourselves to the spatial price relations arising out of the geographical scatter of producers and consumers. The discussion will be conducted mostly in terms of the spatial price interdependence among technically identical goods, although occasionally we allude to the heterogeneous substitutes of monopolistic competition. Identical technical commodities separated in space are already imperfect substitutes, so that the one investigation should serve both worlds. Here too our remarks are only indicative of the problems and techniques, rather than being an exhaustive treatment of the varieties of geographical interdependence.

In retrospect, the preceding chapters can be described as embodying a simple locational pattern, with buyers and sellers clustered together, literally assuming away spatial aspects. Alternately, the analysis would be applicable in a world in which transport costs were zero and interest costs for the time involved in transport were nil. In these circumstances individuals are economically concentrated, however segregated they are in a geographic way. Transport costs are actually often negligible and, where substantial, they are constant and indecisive in short-period price movements.

THE EQUILIBRIUM BORDER

As a provisional hypothesis we postulate that all prices are quoted f.o.b. factory by sellers. Buyers thus pay the full transport costs from the seller's plant to their own doorstep. This seems to be the customary assumption in economic analysis.*

---

* See Marshall, p. 325. F.o.b.-factory pricing is also "mill pricing" and "works pricing."

Transport Costs and Demand Curves

Enumerated among the premises of the individual demand curve were the tastes, income, and other price data. If all prices are quoted as delivery free, a demand curve for X could be constructed for each individual; summating these laterally, we could compound the market schedule. If transport costs are say one penny per unit, then each buyer's demand curve would have to be reduced by this amount—one penny—subtracted from each demand-point ordinate. In miniature, in Figure 1a, if the continuous line represents the individual's demand curve in a world of free delivery, the lower dashed-line curve would form

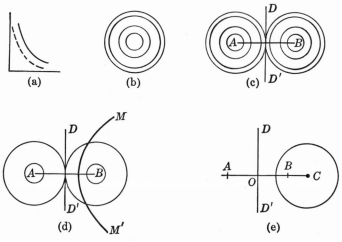

FIGURE 1

the effective demand curve under a regime of works pricing with positive transport charges. Obviously, the higher the transport charges the greater the reduction in the effective demand curve. An entire family of demand curves can be drawn in this way with each particular curve predicated on the same taste, income, and other price phenomena, with the distinguishing parameter consisting of the level of transport costs. Any lowering of transport costs would raise the f.o.b. demand curve confronting the seller.

For buyers living at the factory doorstep the individual demand curves for zero transport costs would be relevant. For those buyers located further away, with distance measured by transport costs, a lower demand curve would be appropriate. In this way the effective demand curve for each purchaser could be extracted until the full series of demand quantities for the entire market at each mill price was accumulated. In a regime of f.o.b. pricing, it would be a reduced demand curve of this nature that would govern a particular firm's price policy. A fall in transport costs would lift the market-demand curve in precisely the same way as a rise in the price of substitutes, an increase in income or a reorientation in tastes favorable to the particular commodity. The augmentation in demand would come from individuals in all geographical areas and not only from the more distant sectors. Of course, if transport costs are proportional to distance, after a fall of a penny per mile in the basic transport rates, the demand curves of those consumers located at a one mile radius would be elevated, in the ordinate sense, by one penny, while the demand curve of consumers located one thousand miles away would move up by $10 per unit. Consequently, changes in transport costs are likely to be potent in determining not only the geographical area served but the volume of sales within the area.

Let us elaborate the notion of the market borderland served by two firms in geographical competition. Suppose that firms A and B sell a homogeneous good at equal f.o.b. prices. Transport costs, we assume for simplicity, are proportional to distance in all directions. The problem is to demonstrate the spatial area covered by each firm under these assumptions.

Places of equivalent transport costs, on our hypothesis, are located on the circumference of a circle, with the firm enclosed at the center. Drawing a family of concentric circles, as in Figure 1b, we could depict buyers by points in the encircled field. When the points are on the same circle—at the same radius from the center—the full delivered price to each buyer is the same. If we draw a concentric locational pattern of buyers about firms A and B, and then connect the centers of each circle by a straight line, at some point between A and B buyers will deem it a matter of indifference whether they purchase from one firm or the other; these individuals are situated on the *equilibrium* border or the *indifference* boundary. With identical prices at works A and B, and transport costs proportional to distance, these individuals will be equidistant from each seller: in the concentric-circle pattern the equilibrium fringe will be found along a perpendicular to the line connecting A and B, such as DD' in Figure 1c, where DD' is precisely midway between A and B. Purchases by the individuals situated along DD' will be distributed at random, with A sometimes the source of supply and at other times B. Individuals to the left of DD' will deal exclusively with A, while those to the right will direct their custom to B.

For each pair of firms in the field we could draw a perpendicular, as DD', demarcating the areas of patronage. Surrounded on all its borders by firms equidistant from it, the A firm would be economically contained within a polygon whose sides would be the equilibrium boundaries; with an infinite number of firms the equilibrium border would form a circle. As they approached within the immediate vicinity of the A firm the latter would be enclosed in a point circle, after which consumers would not experience any advantage in buying from any one firm in the fully dense sales field.

Divergent Prices and Nonuniform Transport Costs

Visualizing firm A as lowering its price, so that $P_a < P_b$, individuals on DD' would no longer be indifferent as to the source of their purchases; there would be a deflection of demand from buyers along DD' to A. Curiously enough, the new isoequilibrium path will not move laterally, parallel and to the right of DD', but would follow the hyperbola MM' in Figure 1d. Firm B would retain all custom to the right of the MM' shield, protected by its geographical proximity. Between DD' and MM', A's lower price would attract demand and dominate the market. It is an interesting result that a discrepancy in f.o.b. prices, with transport costs equal and constant in all directions, would restrict the higher-priced firm to a sales area bounded by a hyperbola.*

Modifying the last hypothesis, when f.o.b. prices are equal while transport costs differ, it being more costly to transport from B than from A firm B's sales area would then be compressed within the walls of a circle, with the center of the circle (C) lying at a greater distance from A in the horizontal plane than the actual door of firm B: in Figure 1e the length $AO = BO$. In all areas outside the circle, in view of the transport savings to consumers, firm A will absorb all the custom.†

More irregular and amoebic shapes would evolve if we supposed that transport costs varied with factors other than distance—if, say, only railroad transport is available in one direction and only water carriage in the other, or if the rate structure is distorted by rules of thumb, custom and political pressure. If railroad rates are the same from point A to a full surrounding area, as in rates identical over a zone, the effect is as if all consumers within the area are located at the same point; rather than representing the consumers as located on a circle they would fall on a solid band.

---

* This can be proved rigorously by simple analytic geometry. See Allen, *Mathematical Analysis*, p. 81.
† Allen, p. 84.

An Alternate Diagrammatic Device

Let us examine an alternate and less cumbersome apparatus which affords further insight into the typical problems of spatial analysis. Rather than assume buyers and sellers scattered over the universe, suppose buyers and sellers are situated along a straight line, say on a national highway, as OO' in Figure 2A; prices can then be measured along either OY or $O'Y'$.

Writing A's price as OP, and B's as $O'P'$, with $OP = O'P'$ and transport costs the same per unit of distance from A or B, firm A will sell to

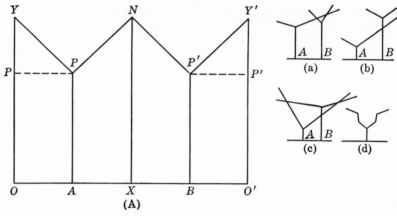

(A)

FIGURE 2

all buyers on its left who care to purchase at the f.o.b. price; B will likewise serve those on its right—those in its "hinterland." A will also secure the custom to the right of its site, those living on the right fork of its Y and out to X, where X is midway between A and B. Conversely, B will control the market to the right of X. The NX vertical cuts through the isoequilibrium spot separating the markets of the two sellers.

If P_a and P_b represent the prices at A and B respectively, and if R_a and R_b denote the linear east-west distance of a buyer from the A and B locations, with T_a and T_b the transport costs per unit of distance from each point, then the isoequilibrium fringe is given by

$$P_a + R_a T_a = P_b + R_b T_b.$$

Hence, if

$$P_a = P_b,$$

and

$$T_a = T_b,$$

then
$$R_a = R_b.$$

Expressed in words, the buyer on the equilibrium border is equidistant from A and B. If $T_a = T_b$ but $P_a > P_b$, it is likewise clear that $R_a < R_b$, that is, that the buyers on the equilibrium boundary will be nearer to A than to B. If $P_a = P_b$ and $T_a > T_b$, then $R_a < R_b$; buyers on the equilibrium border would again be located closer to A. If $T_a = T_b$, and if the delivered price from A to buyers located at B's doorstep is
$$P_a + R_a T_b < P_b,$$

then firm B's sales would be zero. If B's price corresponded with its minimum AC, then B would be driven from the field.

Discrepancies in Prices and Transport Costs

In Figure 2A the slope of the PY and PN arms of the Y stem AP is determined by the rate of increase in transport costs per unit of distance. If transport costs are zero the arms become perpendicular to PA, forming a T. If the f.o.b. prices are equal, and transport costs are the same from either A or B, the intersection of the elongated arms of the respective Y's occurs exactly midway between the firm's location, splitting the market area in two. This Y diagram discloses at all times the full price paid by a consumer, with the stem of the Y, measured on OY or $O'Y'$, depicting the f.o.b. price. The diagram also clarifies the market areas reserved for each seller under diverse price- and transport-cost assumptions. Although other firms can be located along our "highway," we assume that the spatial plane between A and B is unoccupied, because we are interested primarily in developing the sales interrelations in the "in between" area.

Symbolizing A's price by P_a, B's by P_b, and transport costs per unit of distance from A (or B) by T_a and T_b respectively, suppose $P_a = P_b$ while $T_a < T_b$, so that it is less costly per mile to ship a unit of the good from A than from B. As $P_a = P_b$, the stems $PA = P'B$ in Figure 2A; the slope of the Y arms, however, differ; the slope PN would rise less rapidly than $P'Y'$ in Figure 2A. Tracing out the full path, firm A would penetrate more than one-half the distance between itself and B, besides dominating the market area on the far right of B, confining B to a limited sales area on its left and a somewhat larger area on its right: the relations can be derived from diagram 2a which also assumes $P_a < P_b$.

Altering the assumptions, suppose $T_a = T_b$ but $P_a < P_b$: A will again extend sales to a border to the right of the midway mark between the two. So long as transport costs are the same, unless P_b exceeds P_a by a sufficient sum to enable A to undersell B at the latter's plant, A will secure markets only on B's left. If P_a plus transport costs from A to B results in a net price at B below P_b, then B would have to relinquish all its custom: it would be driven from the field at these price relations for the arm of A's Y would always lie below the arms of B's Y, as in 2b. Finally, if $P_a < P_b$, and $T_a < T_b$, A will gain most, if not all, of the custom in the entire market area, selling on both sides of B, perhaps compelling B to leave the field. It could likewise be demonstrated that if $P_a < P_b$ but $T_a > T_b$, A would supply part of the common market dividing the two while B's output would be diverted to buyers located at the extremities, deep in its own and A's hinterland, as in 2c. Hence, for control of neighboring market areas the mill price and thus, production costs, is of decisive significance but in "world" markets, transport costs are paramount. Ready access to the sea, rather than an innate commercial spirit, provides the explanation of the world trading proclivities of the dominant export-import countries.

Changes in Transport Costs

We might ponder the consequences of a change in transport costs. A proportionate fall, without any movement in f.o.b. prices, would leave the equilibrium border unaffected; a disproportionate movement, however, would create new boundaries. In terms of the Y diagrams, an equivalent transport cost reduction from A and B, while $P_a = P_b$, would leave the position of NX unchanged. But it would be wrong to conclude that the market demand curve will be unresponsive: the effective demand curve of each individual would be increased. Increased sales would be made by each firm, especially to the more remote regions where the burden of transport costs is greater. Further, in referring to Figure 2A, it has been implied hitherto that there were buyers spaced continuously along OO', and that there would be purchasers even at X. But the diagram must not always be interpreted in this way: although the people at X, for example, are indifferent as to the source of their purchase *if* they cared to buy at the prevailing f.o.b. price, this price figure might exceed any effective demand point on the individual demand curves. A fall in transport costs, therefore, might permit a fresh "in between" market layer—from A to X and B to X in Figure 2A—to be tapped by both sellers.

As a reduction in transport costs will always elevate the market demand curve, the f.o.b. price should ordinarily rise after a fall in transport costs. Nevertheless, only if market supply were completely inelastic, or the new MR curve intersected the MC curve at exactly the former output, would output be unaffected by the movement in transport charges. A rise in the f.o.b. price is likely to restrain the purchases of those in the immediate vicinity of the firm, with the result that the major implementation of demand would come from the outlying regions. This is an unexpected conclusion; the purchases of those near the seller's establishment would decrease and their economic position would deteriorate after the fall in transport charges.

It is interesting to reflect on the effect of transport costs that fluctuate in a way other than proportionate to distance; normal railroad schedules include special lower long-haul rates. In our Y figure if, after a certain distance from the f.o.b. point, transport charges move discontinuously the slope of the arms of the Y would break, as in Figure 2d. Whenever the rate falls as the mileage traversed increases, the average transport charge per mile is reduced and the economic separation of buyer and seller narrows: the handicap of distance is partially suspended and the disparity in delivered prices paid by buyers diminishes. If, apart from transport costs, there are economies of scale, then as transport costs fall the total number of independent producers of a particular commodity ought to contract; high transport charges from sectors in which goods can be produced more economically would permit many local firms to flourish despite higher direct production costs.

Our analysis so far has disclosed the forces determining the areas served by the respective firms under diverse price and transport cost assumptions. We have not analyzed the forces determining the individual prices of each seller nor the duopoly and oligopoly problems implicit in this analysis. As markets are interrelated, and as P_b will determine A's sales total and sales area at each P_a, and vice versa, each firm's price policy will be dependent upon the actions and responses of other firms. Some aspects of the analysis are developed below.

CONCENTRATION OF BUYERS AND SELLERS

Among the various spatial configurations of buyers and sellers and their significance for price determination, the simplest locational pattern is that in which both buyers and sellers are concentrated at one point; this virtually by-passes spatial phenomena. A second arrangement is that in which sellers are bunched while buyers are scattered over an area. This geographical structure might also typify conventional theory with the addendum that all individual demand curves are reduced by the sum of transport costs, for prices are presumed to be quoted f.o.b. at seller's location.   If buyers are dispersed but freight rates are the same regardless of locational differences, as are mail rates or zonal freight rates, all buyers in the same zone can be viewed as economically clustered at the same location.

Buyers Concentrated, Sellers Dispersed

A more elaborate analysis is necessary when buyers are concentrated at one spot while sellers are scattered over the area.   Envisaging a pinwheel, we can imagine the buyers constituting the hub and the sellers comprising the spokes.   On a macroscopic view, a city can be conceived as the hub and sellers, say farmers, dispersed in the hinterland.   Here we have an important image of reality, with the one flaw in the model being its disregard of the buyer's locational differences within the city. But often this is a minor item—for example, in fruit transported across the continent.

As the goods must be delivered to the conglomeration of buyers, free delivery and f.o.b. pricing practices ought to accomplish the same result: whether we deduct transport costs from the demand curves, or add them onto the cost curves, prices are unaffected.   Ostensibly, there is nothing detrimental to competition in this locational scatter of sellers: the one fresh point is that the level at which each seller perceives demand to be perfectly elastic may differ, depending upon the distance of the seller from the market.   Assuming goods are sold on a free-delivery basis, with higher transport costs the aggregate supply curve for the commodity will be lifted to the left and thus the market price will be higher.   Any reduction in transport costs will operate to lower price and increase sales; the larger sales volume will be enjoyed mainly by sellers situated in the more remote areas, beyond the former sales periphery. Sellers in the immediate market area, whose transport costs are practically nil, will suffer from the reduction in transport costs, for more distant sellers can offer greater quantities for sale at any delivered price— or buyers can go further afield at any mill price—thus tending to lower price to buyers.   The fall in transport costs that enables more firms to serve a market thus tends to increase the degree of competition in any given physical product.

Diagrammatically, if average costs of production are zero or constant, if sellers are located continuously along OO' in Figure 3A, and transport costs are constant per unit of distance, with the LX height representing the delivered price to buyers, all of whom are at X, the mill net price for each seller can be indicated by dropping perpendiculars from the sides of the isosceles triangle MLN.   The sellers barely able to sell in the market are at M and N where the distance $MX = NX$.   If transport costs were to fall, the arms ML and NL would slope more gradually, with M moving out to O and N moving out to O', as shown by the dashed lines in Figure 3a.   Delivered price would be lowered, and sellers adjacent to the buyer's location would be affected adversely.   In Figure 3a those

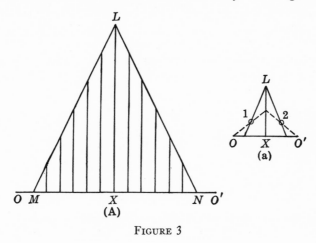

FIGURE 3

sellers located between point 1 and point 2 belong in this category; those outside this area would benefit from the transport cost reduction.

BUYERS AND SELLERS DISPERSED

The most realistic spatial configuration is that in which buyers and sellers are viewed as dispersed over the geographical area.   There are two key cases to unravel when sellers and buyers are separated in space: (1) instances in which the sellers' prices are completely unrelated, with a spatial hiatus of consumers served by neither firm; and (2) price policies are interrelated, with each firm sharing a common equilibrium border of consumers.   In the former instance, because of the facts of space and transport costs, despite the technical identity of the products each firm is in closer competition with sellers of commodities that are imperfect technical substitutes.   As we are interested primarily in exposing the market interrelations we can concentrate solely on two firms, for we are concerned to display the extent of the "in between" area of market contention: the area from A to B in Figure 2A.   As there are firms to the right of B and to the left of A, our problem is really one of oligopoly relations.   However, to diagnose some of the possibilities the simpler duo-poly (two-firm) analysis should be serviceable.

Prices Unrelated

To demonstrate the conditions under which P_a and P_b are completely unrelated, suppose P_a and P_b are at the minimum AC levels.   For sim-plicity also, assume $P_a = P_b$.   If $T_a = T_b$, then the equilibrium border is exactly midway between the firms.   But it may be that this position is unoccupied or individuals dwelling there are utterly disinterested in purchasing either the A or B commodity.   In the diagram of 4a, the region between CD is barren, without prospective purchasers even if P_a and P_b are at their minimum levels.   Firm A is thus wholly independent of its geographical counterpart, firm B, in price policy; its price is more sensitive to the prices named by sellers of differentiated goods produced in adjacent environs.   Manifestly, the assumption $P_a = P_b$ is irrelevant to this analysis: the vital matter is the absence of purchasers at X, in Figure 2A, when both sellers announce the minimum possible price.

Interrelated Prices

If there is a potentially common sales area when both firms name min-imum prices we have a budding duopoly problem.   It will, of course, be to the advantage of each firm to sell at a price above its minimum AC. Upon raising price both firms may find that their custom at the equilib-rium boundary dries up: the prospective purchasers withdraw in view of transport costs and mill price.   For all practical purposes this geograph-ical scatter and preference complex is devoid of the typical features of duopoly, for the atmosphere of struggle and strategy is missing from the final result.

Conceivably the firm's sales may be interrelated, with each firm shar-ing a common market, and yet an equilibrium mutually satisfactory to each is achieved.   In Figure 4A, suppose $P_1 = P_1'$, where both repre-sent the lowest possible prices, with the geographical separation midway between A and B, at X.   Firm A, however, (if we consider the cluster of buyers in its immediate vicinity and the nature of demand) may raise its price to P_2.   At this higher P_a price, firm B considers P_2' to be advis-able with $P_2 > P_2'$.   As transport costs are the same as before the slope P_2R' is the same as P_1R and $P_1'R$, the same as the gradient $P_2'R'$.   The new equilibrium fence is at X', rather than X.   By its higher-price deci-sion, firm A has forfeited sales within the area XX', with firm B filling part of this void.

In this spatial illustration, as in most duopoly problems, firm B will not object to a price rise engineered by firm A, for this will enhance its own demand and raise its own price and profits. Duopoly strife is imminent, however, when A endeavors to lower his price and encroach in a geographical area formerly served by B. B can either meet this attack and lower its own price correspondingly, thereby maintaining the previous geographical market division, or surrender some part of its market orbit, exploiting through relatively higher prices the more substantial groups of custom in its immediate vicinity. Market forays and

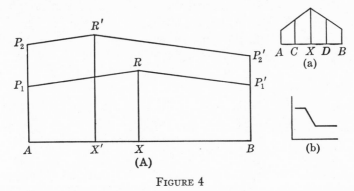

FIGURE 4

strategy, business conjecture and market instability—the common characteristics of duopoly—are likely to appear only when the border area between the firms contains a large cluster of buyers sensitive to a price change, and whose custom is necessary for the profitable operation of either firm. The purchase cluster also tends to invite the entry of new firms more conveniently located to consumers, for despite even a relative uneconomic cost position it can earn a livelihood through higher mill prices.

In view of the geographical transport-cost shelter, possessed by A and B, unless both enjoy similar cost and demand experience there is no reason to expect that identical prices, from the standpoint of profit maximization, will emerge. Yet it does come to be a matter of prestige, pride, and public relations—to forestall a drive for regulation—to meet the lower market prices of one's geographical competitor.

To envisage the firm's demand curves in this analysis, we can use the interrelated demand curve apparatus developed in Figure 1, Chapter 8. Firm B cannot estimate sales at any price without information, or a conjecture, on firm A's price. As A names a relatively higher price, B's demand curve is shifted rightward; for a lower P_a, D_b moves leftward.

Similarly, after the P_b is announced, A's demand curve is rendered determinate. For the final equilibrium, however, the prices named by each firm must be mutually compatible; A must be unable or unwilling to modify P_b further, and vice versa. If it was legitimate to assume P_b constant despite a fall in P_a, and if there was an important cluster of customers about the market borderland, a small price reduction by A would result in a significant expansion in its sales and a contraction in B's sales. Further P_a reductions, with P_b still constant, would cause a highly discontinuous and elastic demand curve for A and a loss of custom for B. Barring extreme differences in the size of the firms, B would be compelled to follow, in part at least, A's price fall. The latter's demand curve would then be much more continuous and far less elastic. Thus if P_b is constant, when

$$P_a > P_b + T_bR_b,$$

where the distance R_b is the full distance between A and B, A's demand quantity would become zero, whereas when

$$P_a + T_aR_a < P_b,$$

where R_a equals the distance from A to B, A's demand would merge with the full market demand, reducing B's sales to zero. The demand curve for A thus has upper and lower caps that are elastic, as in Figure 4b. It need not be labored that this result hinges on an assumption peculiarly inappropriate to duopoly models.

This discussion throws some light on questions of geographical market division and collusion. If firms agree to allocate geographical regions without concurring on price policy, the plan will be successful only if the geographical border agreed upon coincides with the economic border or falls in the vacant economic area served by neither firm. If the area allotted to A is to the right of NX in Figure 2A, then the plan will be defeated through surreptitious purchases, through intermediaries if necessary, from B. Hence geographical market sharing is likely to entail some degree of price collusion.

CENTRAL MARKET EXCHANGES

As a last pattern we might envisage buyers and sellers scattered indiscriminately in the plane but (perhaps for institutional reasons) with all trading being confined to a central market, as at a Fair or organized commodity exchange. Let us also assume that the actual physical transfers of property are also consummated at the market place.

Depending on numbers and products, the prices themselves in these circumstances will conform to the market structures described in earlier chapters. It requires little insight to perceive that if the goods are physically carted by the sellers to the market place there will ordinarily be some wasteful cross haulage of the good; for example, if purchasers dwell in the vicinity of the seller's establishment the transportation charges are twice the economic level. If only contracts are executed in the market place, and prices are quoted f.o.b. physical location of the goods, the uneconomic haulage can be eliminated.

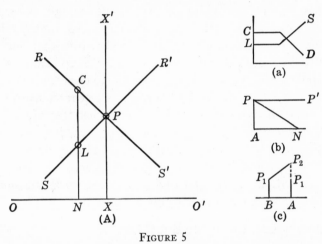

FIGURE 5

To illustrate suppose buyers and sellers are located along OO' in Figure 5A, while the market place is at X. Also, the goods are physically conveyed to point X, the organized trading mart, and that transport costs are uniform per unit of distance. Price at X is PX; depending on the distance to market the sellers located along OXO' receive sums per unit of PX minus their own transport charges: sellers' net receipts are shown on PS and PS'. Buyers, conversely, purchase at PX but then incur additional charges to carry the goods home. Hence sellers at N receive a sum NL net of transport costs, while buyers at N pay a unit price of CN. Obviously, if buyers and sellers execute the trade outside the market place, the price can range between LN and CN. It seems certain, therefore, that when the potential buyers are clustered about producers, in all but peculiar circumstances the buyers will purchase the products directly from the neighborhood sellers rather than waiting for the goods to be shipped to distant markets for sale and return carriage. In the local markets, the elasticity of supply and demand would be infinite at prices CN and LN because for a price below LN sellers at N would ship the full stock to X, while above CN the local buyers would buy at X and pay the return transport costs. The demand-supply diagram would thus resemble the miniature Figure 5a.

FREE DELIVERY

Before abandoning this venture into spatial price relations it is well to lift the assumption of all prices quoted f.o.b. Stores grant customers free delivery service, while manufacturers proclaim that they absorb freight charges; modern pricing practice leans strongly toward "free" delivery to buyers, with transport costs concealed among other costs and recovered through price proceeds.* Unless prices are quoted f.o.b. seller, there is always an implicit degree of price discrimination, favorable to some buyers and harmful to others as long as the freight costs in serving them are significantly different. It is a venerable proposition of economics that goods are fully produced only when they are in the hands of the final consumers, who are presumed to bear the full costs incidental to their production. In free delivery, market price will include the seller's expectations of the average transport costs accompanying each volume of sales, with buyers located near the seller's works bearing some of the conveying charges to the outlying areas.

Free Delivery and Profit Maximization

The volume of sales and the final prices to all consumers under free delivery will always deviate from the results achieved under f.o.b. pricing with one exception: when buyers are concentrated and sellers dispersed the net price to buyers should be the same whether prices are quoted f.o.b. seller with buyers paying the delivery tolls or "free delivery" is provided. Likewise, if transport costs are constant regardless of location, the mode of price quotation is a matter of indifference. Laying these instances aside, we need explain why firms should endorse free delivery practices. It is far-fetched to argue that the policy is pursued by each firm in imitation of the practice of other firms for, if there was not a more substantial reason for the practice, a firm that located near the free delivery competitors and sold f.o.b. terms could deprive the other firms of all the custom in the vicinity and compel them to modify their sales practice if their loss of custom was at all substantial.

---

* A given technical commodity delivered free is, of course, a different product from one sold f.o.b. factory. Free delivery thus represents a form of product variation that may be resorted to in order to escape the rigors of price competition.

Free delivery has its adherents because profits can be augmented by the practice. Ideally, the firm would compare its profits with f.o.b. pricing to the profit total with "free delivery." In the latter calculation there would be some new elements of fixed and variable costs, while the relevant market-demand curve would be the sum of the individual demand curves for zero transport costs; from the market-demand curve an MR curve could be computed and equated to a curve of marginal production plus marginal transport costs. The final profit calculation so computed would have to be compared to the f.o.b. total. Usually, free delivery and a unique final price to all will commend itself when demand is relatively inelastic in the adjacent areas and highly elastic in the outside areas. Conceivably, the free-delivery practice, by expanding the market periphery in conditions of decreasing production costs, might accomplish a lower net price to all consumers, wherever situated.*

Seldom will a firm commit itself to rendering free delivery regardless of the site of the buyer; generally the delivery will be restricted to an area, as the Eastern States, or a city, or a zone, etc. Profit calculations for each suggested geographical belt would have to be made and the firm would be impelled to select the price and delivery policy that maximized its earnings. Envisaging the problem as one of widening the geographic circle of operations, the firm would refuse to add another tier to its market expanse if net profits were reduced by extending the radius of the free delivery plan. In Figure 5b, if we view buyers as being located along AN, and PP' as the "free" delivered price, while the vertical difference of PP' and PN represents freight absorbed in serving customers away from site A, the firm would never push sales beyond point N. Free-delivery practices, we can surmise, should raise transport costs for the economy as a whole, for more consumers will utilize the "free" service, rather than acting as their own carriers.

BASING POINTS

The spatial analysis would be incomplete without some mention of the basing-point pricing practice, made familiar by the steel industry and long a bone of contention in this country. Its signal feature was that steel mills, regardless of locational differences, quoted their prices f.o.b. Pittsburgh, plus freight charges from the latter city to the purchaser's domicile.† Ideally, if each firm's site was a "basing point"—as it

* See pages 318–319 below for an analysis of price discrimination that reduces prices to all consumers.

† Actually there were several basing points, although Pittsburgh was the one most commonly proclaimed and was referred to as "Pittsburgh plus."

would be if all steel mills were actually situated in Pittsburgh—the pricing practice would consist of a mill net price plus freight charges incurred in delivery to the buyer, billed simultaneously as a composite amount rather than compelling the buyer to arrange for and pay a separate delivery charge.   Carried to its full logic, and ignoring surreptitious evasions of the practice, if a steel mill was situated directly alongside a buyer at some distance from Pittsburgh, the purchaser would have to pay the base price plus the "phantom" freight.   In terms of Figure 5c, if firm A situated to the east of Pittsburgh (where Pittsburgh is indicated by the letter B) adheres to this practice and if P_1 is the basing-point price, A will collect a sales sum per ton of steel from a buyer in its own environ equal to P_2, with the difference $P_2 - P_1$ representing an imaginary freight toll.   Manifestly, in areas west of Pittsburgh—to the left of B—any sales made by A would be relatively unprofitable, less lucrative than the identical sales made by firms in the same cost position located at or to the west of Pittsburgh.

Even in this brief analysis we can detect a valid criticism of the practice: it is alleged that the mode of price quotation involves an excessive amount of cross hauling.   For if all firms adopt the same base price, which generally was the prudent policy in view of the structure of competition within the industry, firms in Pittsburgh would reach out into areas adjacent to A, while firms at A might gain custom only to the east of Pittsburgh.   On the face of it, the market division and the cross haulage appear to be uneconomic.

Undoubtedly the practice was profitable to steel mills fortunate enough to obtain the business if their consumers were closer to them than to Pittsburgh—the importance of securing this trade would explain hidden price cutting and various elements of nonprice competition. Nevertheless it does not require much insight to appreciate the plaint that the objective of the practice was to enable the large firms about Pittsburgh to compete equally everywhere with all other steel mills despite locational handicaps.   With the prestige attached to their size and the guarantee of punctual delivery and quality production, they could obtain the more important selling contracts.   More significant in some ways, the continued adherance of all firms to the practice would obviate the need for the Pittsburgh giants to relocate their plants and sustain periodic capital losses on past investment after the growth of a new center of steel use or new natural advantages, such as sources of raw materials and labor supply, were uncovered.*

* Compare the remarks of the Federal Trade Commission referred to by A. R. Burns

Extending the analysis briefly to circumstances in which multiple basing points existed, insofar as a firm controlled certain sales by nonprice competition it could stipulate a basing point favorable to itself. Conversely, if it went far afield to gain its orders and had to sell at a basing-point price equal to that closest to the consumer, the seller would absorb an excessive amount of freight although this might be more profitable than lower sales and idle capacity and falling price. With multiple basing points and diverse cost-and-demand factors for each firm, the relevant query concerns the proximity of each of the common multiple bases and producing plants. As basing points become more numerous the situation approaches, in part, F.O.B. pricing.

BIBLIOGRAPHICAL NOTE

The literature on spatial competition, including both the theory of location and of geographical price interdependence, is mostly of recent origin and still limited. A volume that goes some way to close the gap is E. Hoover, *The Location of Economic Activity*. The article that aroused interest in these matters was H. Hotelling's "Stability in Competition," *Economic Journal* (1929). Among the recent writings the following can be noted: G. Ackley, "Spatial Competition in a Discontinuous Market," *Quarterly Journal of Economics* (1942); S. Enke, "Space and Value," same journal (August 1942); E. A. G. Robinson, "A Problem in the Theory of Industrial Location," *Economic Journal* (1941); and two articles by A. Smithies, "Optimum Location and Spatial Competition," *Journal of Political Economy* (1941) and "Monopolistic Price Policy in a Spatial Market," *Econometrica* (1941). On the Y diagrams, see the lengthy and recondite article of A. P. Lerner and H. W. Singer, "Some Notes on Duopoly and Spatial Competition," *Journal of Political Economy* (1937) and Smithies, "Optimum Location."

Basing-point pricing is still a live issue. Recently outlawed by court decision, it has its advocates in and out of Congress. The literature on the practice is voluminous. Among the later works containing further bibliographical material there can be listed A. R. Burns, *The Decline of Competition*, Chapters VI–VII; A. Smithies, "Aspects of the Basing-Point System," *American Economic Review* (1942); V. Mund, "Monopolistic Competition Theory and Public Price Policy," (same journal, same issue); J. M. Clark,

---

(*The Decline of Competition*, pp. 340 and 345). Also the quotation from the statement released by E. G. Grace, Chairman of the Bethlehem Steel Corporation, on the decision outlawing basing point pricing: "Large investments in processing plants are certainly placed in jeopardy." Benjamin Fairless, President of the United States Steel Corporation, was quoted as saying at a news conference that Pittsburgh would be the greatest sufferer, since the corporation's mills in the area would lose a competitive advantage in many cases. (*New York Times*, July 9, 1938).

"Imperfect Competition Theory and Basing-Point Problems," *American Economic Review* (1943), and "Basing-Point Methods of Price Quoting," *Canadian Journal of Economics and Political Science* (1938). Also, the TNEC study on *The Basing-Point Method* (1940) and the three-volume study of C. R. Daugherty, M. G. DeChazean and S. S. Stratton, *The Economics of the Iron and Steel Industry.* A most recent and exhaustive analysis is the volume by Fritz Machlup, *The Basing-Point System.* Also, articles by F. A. Fetter, "Exit Basing-Point Pricing," *American Economic Review* (1948) and J. M. Clark, "Law and Economics of Basing Points," same journal (1949).

Part III

MULTIPLE-PRODUCT FIRMS

Introduction

THE FIRM WHOSE EQUILIBRIUM adjustment we have examined produced but one product. This is, of course, a crude simplification of reality, for real firms usually produce a diverse array of products. In the ensuing two chapters we attempt to remedy the shortcomings of previous analyses in this respect. Chapter 13 is devoted to the natural and economic causes of multi-product firms, with the emphasis placed upon the cost interdependencies conditioning joint production. Some aspects of the theory of integration are also discussed. Chapter 14 discloses certain demand phenomena conducive to multiple-product production.˙ The topics that fall under this heading comprise a highly assorted list—discriminatory monopoly and monopsony pricing, pricing goods in substitutionary and complementary relations, and pricing goods linked in both production and demand.

CHAPTER 13

Cost Interdependence

RULING OUT ANY DEMAND INTER-
dependence for the products of the multiple product firm, in this
chapter we examine some aspects of the theory of cost interdependence;
the theory of integration can be tackled as part of this development.
The complication in multiple-product analyses is that normally the
expansion of one product will affect the firm's ability to produce other
goods. Envisaging its list of $A, B, C \cdot \cdot \cdot N$ commodities, the marginal-cost curve for any one product, such as A, is contingent upon the
quantities of $B, C \cdot \cdot \cdot N$ being turned out. If the production of one
good fails to influence the MC curves of other commodities, all of the
preceding analysis can be preserved intact even on recognition of multiproduct firms. Conceivably the firm may assign an entire factory
building, or an entire wing of a plant, to producing commodity A,
another to B, etc., thereby mitigating the common pressures on identical
productive facilities. In this event the assumption of independent
MC curves conforms very well with the facts.

If a firm does produce several products whose marginal-cost curves
and demands are independent, the condition of equilibrium for each output is, of course, $P \geqq MR = MC$. If we view the firm as the vehicle
for allocating factors among its several outputs, the relevant ratios to be
satisfied for each pair of outputs are

$$\frac{MR_1}{MR_2} = \frac{MC_1}{MC_2}.$$

In competitive sales markets the MR's, of course, coincide with prices.

As an analogous problem, firms will often erect independent plants for
a particular product variety, choosing to expand its layout horizontally,
with some geographic separation among plants, rather than enlarge its

facilities at a given site. Assuming that the identical product is sold in identical markets, it is clear that the volume of production in all plants will proceed until marginal production costs in each plant are equivalent; all MC's eventually will be equated to the composite marginal revenue, with the one proviso being that if marginal (and thus average) costs are falling in any one plant, output will tend to be concentrated there. Hence with a sharp fall in market demand there is a good likelihood that some plants will be kept idle, closed unless a by-product commodity type can be conceived. Production in several independent plants owned by a unitary parent firm can thus occasion a search for suitable by-product opportunities.

When we probe more deeply into the causes of joint production (as the multiple-product proclivities of the firm are termed), both natural causes and economic causes—the augmented profitability of the practice—can be distinguished. The line of division is often hazy; "natural" joint products can sometimes be produced separately but at enormously higher costs.

JOINT PRODUCTION

Joint products are those whose production is combined for natural causes. Illustrations are plentiful: there are the textbook examples of cotton lint and cotton seed, wool and mutton, zinc and silver, etc., produced in either fixed or variable proportions.

Just as the specialized literature becomes engrossed in the study of natural joint products, popular writings betray an affection for "by-products" and "waste" products. For example, soap is described as a by-product of meat packing. What is intended is that despite the major preoccupation with the slaughter of animals for meat, certain portions of the carcass are salvaged for other uses. Frequently the classification between by-products and main products is highly arbitrary. If we have become accustomed to classify certain firms as meat packers, then all but meat products are by-products. If prices move in such a way as to render the incidental outputs more valuable to the firm than its presumed major occupation—if, say, certain medicinal extractions from the cattle become more remunerative than the sales proceeds from meat—it would be more accurate to describe meat-packing as the by-product. But this is solely a question of suitable names; it is indubitably an instance of joint production in that several distinguishable outputs ensue from a unified series of operations.

Waste products, generally, are materials eliminated after a set of operations and are not necessarily valueless even in the form in which they first emerge. After further fabrication and refinement, the "waste" products may become an integral ingredient of final output. They are simply by-products, often conducive to further industrial integration.

Fixed Proportions: Competitive Conditions

The case of fixed proportions will serve as our introduction to the equilibrium adjustment of a multiple product firm. We commence with competitive sales markets.

If goods are producible only in a fixed ratio—for example, if two pounds of cotton seed are always and inseparably fused with one pound of cotton lint—the condition of output equilibrium assumes a slightly novel guise: marginal costs in competitive markets must be equated to the *sum* of the price proceeds derived from the independent sale of each commodity. Thus,

$$MC_{x+y} = rP_x + sP_y,$$

where r is the number of X units and s is the number of Y units which form the combined output. For simplicity, hereafter we assume $r = s = 1$. Modifications, where this is not so, are obvious.

It is interesting to unravel the effects of a rise in demand and price for one good (X) with the demand for the other good (Y) constant, where the goods are unrelated in consumption. The augmented joint proceeds after the higher P_x will stimulate further production of both products; the upshot will be that the increment ΔP_x leads to a decrement ΔP_y. In equilibrium, if the total output is to expand, the sum of the $P_x + P_y$ proceeds must be greater than before so that

$$+\Delta P_x > (-\Delta P_y).$$

Similarly, for a fall in demand for Y (with a lower P_y), and a rise in the demand for X (with a higher P_x), output will be augmented only· if the sum of the joint price proceeds is augmented.

Just as it is impossible to compute separable marginal costs for each product when they are produced in fixed proportions, it is likewise futile to endeavor to compute separable average costs. Hence the full competitive output equilibrium conditions are

$$P_x + P_y = MC_{x+y} \geqq AC_{x+y}.$$

Fixed Proportions: Monopoly Conditions

Continuing the discussion of fixed proportions when the firm is a monopolist in the selling markets of both X and Y, after the preceding exposition the solution of this problem is rather obvious: the firm will produce further units of the joint output so long as the combined marginal revenue derived from their sale exceeds their joint marginal cost. Equilibrium will involve

$$P_x + P_y > MR_x + MR_y = MC_{x+y}, \tag{1}$$
$$P_x + P_y > AC_{x+y}. \tag{2}$$

One point, however, should be set in bold relief. A monopolist will withdraw goods from any market in which marginal revenue is negative; it would enhance its profits by destroying or withholding the excess supply, depending on the cost of each maneuver. Unless this proviso is attached to the conditions stated, they could be construed as allowing marginal revenue to be negative in one market and positive, in the other, so long as their joint sum exceeds marginal cost. Thus, both MR's are to be positive and, for other than costless output, only one marginal revenue of the joint pair may be zero.

With this last qualification, our views on the consequences of an increase in the demand for one of the goods must be revised. Under competition this would always entail a fall in the price of the production complement. But under monopoly, only if the marginal revenue of the production complement is still positive will its price fall. Otherwise the monopolist will prefer to eliminate the excess output of the complement rather than deplete total income through its sale. Costs of destruction or withholding, however, will be weighed against the loss by sale.

Variable Proportions

We consider now the more intricate case of variable proportions under which commodity X must be produced in conjunction with Y, although the ratios of the fused production unit can fluctuate, with more of X produced in lieu of some Y or vice versa. The classic illustration is that of sheep bred more for their wool than for their meat, although it is not possible to displace either product entirely. In a sense, the aggregate output of the economy can be conceived as produced in variable joint proportions for with full employment producing more of one product will displace some quantity of another output. The peculiarity here is that it is technically impossible to abandon one product entirely.

Suppose that $10X$ and $30Y$ are produced at a total cost of $100 and that, in a competitive market, $P_y = \$6$. Further, we can imagine it is also possible to produce $31Y$ with $10X$ at a total cost of $101. Substantially, therefore, $MC_y = \$1$; the firm would apprehend the profitability of producing more Y, with X constant, whenever P_y exceeded $1. Fixing the output of X, profits could be increased whenever the additions to total cost made by a further unit of Y were less than the additional proceeds procured from its sale. In competitive equilibrium, therefore, ·we would have $MC_y = P_y$ (or MR_y under monopoly).

Precisely the same analysis would be relevant for X. If the Y output is fixed, with $MR_x > MC_x$, more X output would be in order. Equilibrium would require that the addition to total cost, with the associated output constant, equal the addition to total receipts. Ostensibly, when the proportions are variable a type of marginal cost can be deduced once the volume of the other output is stipulated. In equilibrium, on the special definitions of MC_x and MC_y,

$$P_x + P_y \geqq MR_x + MR_y = MC_x + MC_y, \tag{1}$$
$$P_x \geqq MR_x = MC_x, \tag{2}$$

and

$$P_y \geqq MR_y = MC_y. \tag{3}$$

Unless these equalities are established simultaneously, by fixing the output of one commodity and altering the output of the other, total profits can be enhanced.

Diagrammatic Solution of Variable Proportions

The problem can be illuminated by an adaptation of the indifference- and transformation-curve technique. In Figure 1, we measure the output quantities of commodities X and Y along OX and OY. Production is possible in any of the proportions indicated by the paths $1, 2, 3, 4$ $\cdots$. Ultimately, the only restriction for the case of joint production in variable proportions is that the paths cannot coincide with OX or OY—it is not possible to produce one good to the exclusion of the other. The more numerous the possibilities of variation, the greater the density of the paths; joint production in fixed proportions implies that production can expand along only one path, as that with index 1, and no other.

A total-cost curve, CC_1, can be mounted on Figure 1 to combine all those outputs that can be produced at a given total cost outlay; a constant total sales revenue curve as RR_1 can also be constructed to

connect all those output combinations that yield a given total revenue.*
The revenue curve will be linear when sales markets are competitive and
convex (or irregularly concave-convex) under monopoly; the constant
total-cost contour ought always be concave.

From earlier discussions it will be perceived that for each total cost
outlay a firm will produce the output combination that is indicated at
the tangency of a cost and revenue contour, for at the tangency position
the total revenue obtainable for the cost outlay will be at a maximum,

touching the highest-revenue
curve. Sketching in the cost and
revenue field, and then connecting
the points of tangency, we could
construct a type of output expansion path where each combined
output volume is contingent upon
a given total cost outlay. At each
point on the expansion path the
marginal rate of transformation of
product X for Y, for any cost
outlay, would equal the marginal
rate of substitution in the sales
markets of X for Y as revenue
producers of a fixed volume of
receipts. This is, of course, tan-

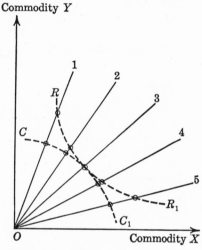

FIGURE 1

tamount to an implicit condition embodying conditions (2) and (3)
above, meaning that

$$\frac{MC_x}{MC_y} = \frac{MR_x}{MR_y}.$$

As this relation holds at each outlay level, for the full equilibrium the
increase in total cost outlays—the joint marginal cost—must equal the
increase in total revenue—the joint marginal revenue. Thus:

$$\Delta TR = \Delta TC,$$

where

$$\Delta TR = MR_x + MR_y$$

and

$$\Delta TC = MC_x + MC_y.$$

As an implication of this analysis, under monopoly conditions, where the

* The total cost curve CC' is to be distinguished from the earlier isocosts in that we now
measure combined output quantities rather than factors along OX and OY.

constant-revenue curves are no longer linear configurations, the combined output-expansion path may swerve from one production combination to another, because the rates of change in the marginal revenue of the separable commodities are different.

Conceivably, the number of technical production paths may be so few as to preclude the drawing of continuous total-cost or total-revenue curves. Nevertheless the principle is clear: for each total cost outlay the output combination that maximizes sales revenue will be chosen, while in the ultimate equilibrium configuration the joint MC will equal the joint MR. As before, the marginal revenue of each good must be positive. A shift in demand or a realignment in costs is likely to alter the expansion path and the equilibrium output combination. Inferentially, the more numerous are the possibilities of substitution the smaller is the likelihood that each increase in X, because of improved demand for X, will be accompanied by more Y output.

As a final remark, though the two goods are jointly produced, to prepare them for market may involve some separable expenses. The marginal revenue of each good must be computed net of the separable expenses, by deducting the latter from the independent market-demand schedules.

COST INTERDEPENDENCE

The analysis of joint products just elaborated assumed that the technical production complementarity was a resultant of natural causes, the physical impossibility of separate production. Among other causes of joint production there is the fact that the production of commodity B simultaneously with A may *lower* the variable cost of producing A. Let us consider the equilibrium relations under these circumstances.

Cost Complementarity

Let us postulate that 100 units of X can be produced by the application of a definite quantity of labor to a fixed volume of equipment. Suppose that to produce commodity Y the same equipment (essentially) can be utilized and that as labor is hired for the production of Y, MC_x is reduced, lowering AC_x and enhancing profits. As more Y is produced, each increment in its output may push MC_x lower down in the chart field. In Figure 2, D_y and D_x are the respective demand curves. As OM of Y is produced, the relevant MC_x is MC_1 in Figure 2B while as Y advances to ON, the curve MC_2 is generated for commodity X. As Y mounts to the OL output level, MC_3 emerges for X.

Pondering the causes of the volatility in MC_x, we may assume the answer to be that the productive factors hired for the Y output are complementary to those in X, lifting the marginal products of the latter and enabling any X output to be produced with fewer variable factors. As Y output expands, and more factors are hired for its production, the joint pressure on the fixed productive facilities ought to compress the ensuing rise in the marginal productivity of the factors engaged for producing X, so that the successive downward dislodgments of the MC_x curve should be smaller. Ultimately, the ΔY output should fail to depress the MC_x curve or it might even raise it, for otherwise it would appear that the special costs of producing the given quantity of X would be nil.

The output equilibrium conditions are now more involved, for on produc ing ΔY not only are there the additional sales pro-

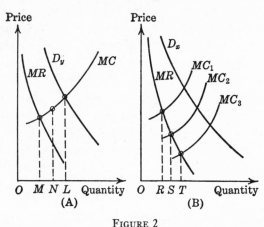

FIGURE 2

ceeds in Y, but also additional profits in the X commodity $(=\Delta R_x)$ due to the downward swing in the MC_x curve; hence the condition for output equilibrium is

$$MR_y + \Delta R_x = MC_y.$$

Patently, it will be profitable to push the production of Y beyond the simple equality of $MC_y = MR_y$. In Figure 2A, the ON output level for Y may prove more lucrative than that at OM. These relations should be symmetrical; if a greater application of factors hired to increase Y output raises the marginal productivity of the factors engaged to produce X, the reverse should also be true. Figure 2A can thus be conceived as belonging to X and Figure 2B to Y. Hence a similar equilibrium condition turns up for the production of X. But this also entails that if ΔR_x occurs through a greater output of X, then the total cost of producing the given Y amount will be reduced by the expansion of X, in sum say, ΔC_y. Thus the full equilibrium condition becomes

$$MR_y + \Delta R_x = MC_y - \Delta C_y.$$

If the X increment responsible for ΔR_x is small, its influence on the MC_y curve is negligible and ΔC_y approaches zero. A similar relation can be written for commodity X. If we assumed merely the expansion in Y output and then noted the change in profitability due to the changed X output, the complication of ΔC_y could be avoided, being subsumed in MC_y.

This is a curious pattern in that each separate equilibrium condition entails such mutual output adaptations that for one commodity, $MC > MR$ and for the other commodity, $MC = MR$, while when we look at the dual adjustment it is possible that each $MC > MR$. This reciprocal influence will be missing only when one output is held rigid. Otherwise the expansion in one sets up forces favorable for the other, which react on the first, thereby exerting a positive tremor back on the second, etc. It is probably not too unrealistic to regard these reciprocal effects as of decreasing magnitude compared to the direct rise in each MC and fall in MR. Still for the combined output to be of maximum profitability we need the supplementary condition that for a joint output movement the addition to total profits must be nil. Thus:

$$\Delta TC_{x+y} = \Delta TR_{x+y}.$$

As the MC_x (or MC_y) curve is functionally contingent upon the volume of Y (or X) output, for each Y amount, the MC_x curve is determinate and therefore the maximum P_x is also determinate. Hence for each Y and P_y, the maximum profit P_x can be calculated. The price reaction curve analysis of Fig. 3A, p. 194 would thus be appropriate to the problem, since a rise in P_y, with less Y output, would lift MC_x and raise P_x. Similarly, for each change in P_x the maximum profit P_y can be computed. The position of maximum profitability would have to be the one of mutual compatibility indicated at the intersection of the price reaction curves; thereafter it would be unprofitable to raise or lower P_x and P_y jointly, or lift one and depress the other. This approach by way of reaction curves is alternate to that running in terms of marginal costs and marginal revenue, leaving these aspects of the adaptation to inference and implication.

Cost Substitution

Even if the effect is to raise the MC curve of the alternate product or products, it may often be less expensive for a single firm to direct its equipment to the production of several alternate products rather than for new and independent firms to be organized for the separate tasks.

If the multiple products can be produced without raising the production cost of the main product too greatly it may prove more economical than constructing specialized machinery on which capital costs, besides the special variable costs, must be recovered. However elusive the definition of excess capacity, if a firm possesses unused machinery or unoccupied floor space, or if the entrepreneurial talents are not fully engaged on the main product, then it does have excess capacity in some sense. Unless specialization, with its capital charges, promises to lower average costs below the average variable costs when the commodity is but a by-product fashioned on existing equipment, then multiple-product firms will appear in even an entirely competitive world. In view of the lower output level of the firm under monopoly pricing, the opportunities for diverse side products are multiplied, although it would be mischievous to ascribe all such phenomena to monopoly. The chief advantage enjoyed by the firm in by-product output is that the additional product varieties need only contribute, at a minimum, the separable expenses incurred in their behalf, permitting the omission of any capital charges.

There are two reasons why a multiple-product firm may experience higher production costs than specialist firms: (1) because the equipment is not designed specifically for the conceived by-products, the amount of variable factors required, per unit of output, may be relatively excessive; (2) as more of any one product is produced it may hinder the production of other "main" products by drawing off entrepreneurial abilities, special labor skills, floor space, machinery, etc., and thereby raising the latter's cost of production.

The first point ought be clear without undue amplification; in our discussion of the planning curves it was declared that ordinarily several types of equipment were able to produce a particular commodity and that it was the entrepreneurial task to select the most remunerative conglomeration of facilities. It is highly unlikely that the equipment most suitable for one product will also be superior in the processing of another good. Specialization, despite additional capital charges, is likely to be more efficient.

This leads us to the second point. Some outputs, it was averred, are economically complementary; when more factors were engaged for one product the marginal product of factors hired for the other commodity rose. Contrariwise, it is possible that as commodity Y expands, with more factors hired for this purpose, they interfere with the production of X, demanding more floor space, more machine facilities, entrepreneurial

attention, etc., so that the MC_x curve rises rather than falls.   Resorting
to graphics, with OM output of Y in Figure 2A, the MC_3 is the relevant
one for X.   As Y advances to the ON level, MC_2 is the appropriate
curve, while with OL of Y, MC_1 is pertinent.   Hence, as an offset to the
additional profits occasioned by a further unit of Y, there must be
deducted the losses suffered through higher costs on the production of
X.   The equilibrium condition for commodity Y under these circumstances becomes

$$MR_y - \Delta R_x = MC_y.$$

Production of Y will cease below the level at which $MC_y = MR_y$, or at an
amount at which $MR_y > MC_y$.   If the factor relations are symmetrical a
similar equality is applicable to commodity X.   If the X output contracts, this will entail some reduction in the total costs of Y, in sum
ΔC_y.   Thus the condition will be

$$MR_y - \Delta R_x = MC_y - \Delta C_y.$$

The change ΔC_y tends to ameliorate the situation, to some degree,
though normally ΔR_x ought exceed ΔC_y.   As before, if merely the Y
output is permitted to expand and MC_y computed only after the new X
adaptation, the ΔC_y component could be neglected, as subsumed in
the net MC_y.   The position of maximum profitability for the mutual
adaptation between the two commodities can again be given by the
intersection of a pair of price-reaction curves.   This time, however,
since a fall in the price of one creates a rise in the price of another, they
resemble the pattern indicated in Fig. 3B, p. 194.   The supplementary
condition of nil marginal profits for a joint output variation must also
be attached.

Whereas in competitive adjustments of $P = MC$ each firm would use
its capacities more fully on any one output, these substitute interrelations indicative of diminishing physical returns are likely to obtrude
very early as a limitation upon the by-product outputs associated with
the main commodity.   Under monopoly, as less of the "main" commodity is produced, this force is likely to be less effective in restraining
the by-product output.

Induced By-Product Outputs

Suppose that a firm producing the $P > MC$ output decides to utilize
its facilities in producing a differentiated by-product that competes
with products of other firms, although affecting any one product

insignificantly (the monopoly hypothesis). As demand curves for the main products of other firms are contracted, the latter firms may be provoked to contrive their own by-product concoctions. The process can go on interminably, each firm adopting a by-product, contracting the market demands of other firms, and thereby pressing them to diversify their own product list. A product equilibrium will be reached only when each firm doubts the feasibility of extending its list of by-product outputs. By and large, the production of more varieties and the encroachment of each firm on the market preserves of all others will reduce monopoly profits all around.

Despite the disappearance of monopoly profits from this model, many of the ingredients of wasteful production would remain regardless of the display of intense competition between firms. With demand curves for each product pulled back, and with the greater elasticity of demand for each product at each price, the degree of monopoly power in any one output may be sharply reduced, and yet each particular commodity may be produced at higher average cost than for specialist firms. If some of the firms selling an imposing array of by-products were induced to price according to $P = MC$ criteria, the expansion in the one output would, because of the upward shift on the MC curve for by-products, render the latter less profitable and lead to their abandonment, and would lead other firms through the lower $P = MC$ price to forego the more closely substitutable by-products. Thus the by-product outputs engendered under monopoly may be costly to the economy, despite the superficial benefit of the unused facilities being diverted to alternate by-product outputs. Under competitive pricing and homogeneous entry, the degree of nonspecialization and multiple-product production, as well as product diversity, could never go so far as under monopoly pricing and heterogeneous entry.

VERTICAL INTEGRATION

In the multiple-product analysis the firm added new products to its sales offerings. In the theory of vertical integration the relevant topic is that of the number of productive phases requisite to a finished product performed under the firm's own aegis. In weighing the degree of integration, the firm must compare the cost of interdepartmental "purchases" as against market transactions or buying from another firm. Parenthetically, the degree of integration accomplished will affect the number of markets in which the firm appears as buyer or seller. With five stages A, B, C, D, and E before the output is finished for sale to consumers, if a firm at D integrates the C stage with its own D stage, it will henceforward appear as a buyer in the market for B rather than C. Integrating backwards, completely through stage A, the firm will ultimately have to operate certain natural resources, as mines and farms, and be a buyer solely in the factor markets. Integrating forward from D, rather than sell to E, the firm will appear as a competitor in the sales markets of the various E-stage firms. Integration thus reduces the number of market transactions between firms prior to the final sale to consumers.

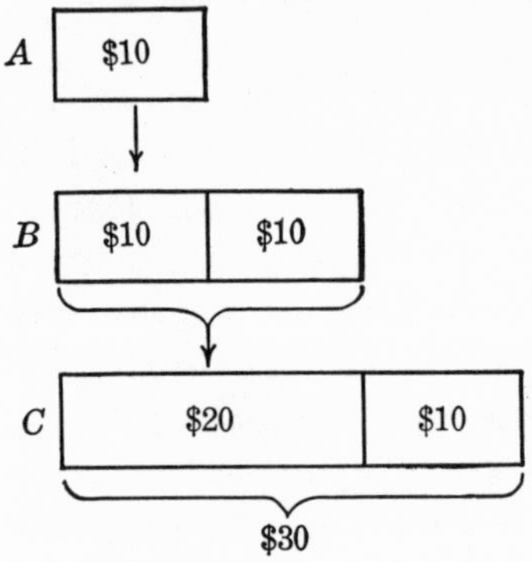

A Schematic Version

Figure 3 is a schematic version of a nonintegrated productive structure, and a pictorial view of the effects of integration. For simplicity, let us assume that bread making involves three distinct steps; namely, the growing of the wheat, the grinding of wheat into flour, and finally the baking operation. Let us say that the value of wheat is $10; these are then the sales receipts of each A firm as it sells its output to the millers (the B stage). In the milling process, by employing labor and equipment to mill the wheat, the millers transform wheat into flour and increase the value to $20: the B stage adds $10 of value to the output of the A stage. Flour is sold to C, the bakers, for $20; labor and equipment are applied in baking and the finished product, bread, is sold to consumers for $30. The total value of final output, in which the wheat growing and flour grinding are but ephemeral phases, is thus $30; in each stage $10 of value is added to the final product and $10 is the income of each productive phase. Although the total value of final output is $30, the total of transactions is $10 + $20 + $30 = $60. It is essential, then, to distinguish between the sum total of *transactions* and the net total *value of output*.

If the bakers decided not to purchase flour from the miller, but to integrate fully, they would be driven into growing their own wheat, grinding it into flour, and baking the latter into bread. Rather than three distinct market transactions there would now be but one transaction—the sale of the final product to consumers for $30. Rather than having factors of production hired by the A firms and the B firms, they would all be employed by the C firms, operating as a fully integrated

FIGURE 3

productive unit; there would be internal transfers of the raw material, (wheat) to the milling phase, and the semifinished material, flour, would flow along to bread making. The value of output and the sum of transactions would be one and the same; if operating costs were unchanged despite the integration they would be equal in our illustration to $30.

This simple diagram is useful in illuminating a wide array of problems; it is, for example, instructive in depicting why a sales tax is ordinarily imposed only at the final stage (the retail level), for otherwise those outputs that involve the most indirect transactions or are least integrated, with the cooperating firms connected only through the market nexus, would suffer most from the toll. A tax on all transactions would provide a strong incentive to firms to integrate their operations.

Nevertheless the diagram is deceptive unless carefully interpreted. For example, it is not imperative for the integration to be straightforward: firm C, for example, may be both baker and wheat grower yet may hire B for the milling. Or the baker may sell some of his output (old bread, say) to A for animal feed. All these variations and a multiplicity of others are possible when the diagram is expanded to include the fact that C purchases several ingredients rather than flour alone. It is these complications that render the concept of the structure of production immune to any simple diagrammatic statement.*

Economic Bases of Integration

In delving into the causes of integration, of why firms undertake the series of operations that they deem as falling within their province, realistically it must be confessed that the operations performed are attributable to a complex of historical, economic, and technical circumstances— the errors, the ignorance, and the caprice of the ancestral firms. And yet the degree of integration does change. Let us therefore examine some of the determining factors.

Economic and technical forces can be separated. Corresponding to the natural phenomena of fixed and variable proportions, one explanation for the full sequence of operations performed by the firm is the technical fact that certain processes must be executed (almost) simultaneously. In chemical mixtures the preparation must be viewed as a unit although the ingredients may come from other firms, but decisions for compounding them must generally be centralized within one firm, at least when the preparation must be consummated in one operation.

---

* F. Hayek once rested a full theory of the business cycle on diagrams of this sort. See the various figures in his *Prices and Production* (revised edition).

Besides the technical need for simultaneous processing, certain processes must be performed smoothly and successively, any disruption in the process chain being disastrous to the final result. Although it is not inconceivable for several firms to be charged with the different phases of the productive flow, there is always the chance of discord and nonfulfillment which, unless guaranteed by contract, might subject either the earlier or later participants in the process to burdensome loss. Hence integration is likely to be more successful than dividing responsibility at each stage among independent firms. As another aspect of continuity, a firm in possession of output contracts will have to assure itself that certain preliminary operations will be performed, that essential ingredients will be furnished to it on schedule, or that its particular specifications will be complied with. When these responsibilities are left to others, delays may occur and instructions may be slighted, making it advisable for the firm to extend its sphere of operations despite some diseconomies in so doing. In practice these factors bulk large and explain at least a minimum degree of integration within the economy.*

There will be an economic motive for integrating whenever the firm can lower its production costs. Intermediate factors that are purchased from other firms are, to the purchasing firm, a productive factor on a full parity with the labor, equipment, or natural resources it hires. When a firm can supply its own raw-material needs more economically than by purchasing materials in the markets, it can augment its profits by integration. Profitwise, it will be prudent for the firm to integrate backwards whenever the marginal cost of performing an additional process is below the market price for the same intermediate factor. If extra equipment is indispensable for the new task, the full condition is that $P = MC > AC$, where P is the market price for the material, MC is the additional cost of producing it within the firm, and AC is the full average cost of producing it within the firm. The inclusion of AC in the equilibrium condition is dictated by the fact that if MC lies below AC it would be foolhardy for the firm to incur the separable fixed costs to widen its productive sphere.

For integrating forward, the firm must be able to execute the further operations at an MC (and AC) not higher than the difference between the market price at the new stage and the market price at its former output place. In terms of Figure 3, if a firm at the B stage is to envelop C, the marginal and average costs of so doing must not exceed $10. Otherwise it will only suffer a diminution in profits for its integrating pains.

* Uncertainty is thus often a basic cause. See Chapter 15.

Forward integration may be countenanced because of sealed entry or institutional impediments, closing distributive facilities to the firm. Either it must build its own outlets or its entire productive endeavors will be abortive. Also, as a reminder of our discussion of joint products, integration is likely to occur if in performing phase B the cost of the A (or C) step is lowered. The equilibrium problem is the same problem as formerly, the difference being that the selection of the accompanying by-products entails integration. Besides MC curves being influenced, if successive output stages utilized similar equipment or other productive facilities that are otherwise not fully engaged, integration can reduce the joint AC, as compared to the growth of independent firms for the separate tasks.

MONOPOLY AND INTEGRATION

Let us consider the special influence of monopoly on integration. Specifically, two aspects of monopoly will be investigated: (1) the effects of monopoly pricing in intermediate output stages on backward integration; (2) backward integration as a device for strategic monopoly control of later stages.

Monopoly Pricing and Integration

A monopolist will often require materials which are themselves sold under monopoly conditions: hence we envisage a situation in which successive stages in a nonintegrated production structure are monopolized. To simplify the exposition we suppose that materials are bought by firm B from only one other firm (A) before being processed by B. Also, we assume that the B firm in buying materials from A is only one of many buyers of A's product and pays the market price, since its purchases are too small to influence A's monopoly sales price.

In Figure 4A, D is the market demand curve for B's finished output and MR is its marginal revenue curve. Cost of materials purchased from A is represented by mc, while MC is the curve of full marginal costs; the difference ($MC - mc$) thus represents the marginal cost of factors hired directly by the B firm to process the materials acquired from A into the finished goods of the B stage. The institution of a $P = MC$ pricing policy in the A stage would lower mc, thus lowering the full MC curve of our figure. Hence the new monopoly price adjustment for the B firm would be at a lower price than formerly. The extent of the price fall would depend on: (1) the price fall of the unfinished materials; (2) the importance of these materials in the cost curve of the B firm; and (3) the elasticity of the demand curve facing B. In the figure, the consequences of competitive pricing in the A stage are indicated by the dashed mc and MC curves.   The effect of A's monopoly price on B's output is to contract production from OS to OR.

When materials must be purchased from monopoly sellers it is conceivable, therefore, that backward integration, by B in our case, would lower B's MC curve and lead to a lower price to B's consumers despite the higher production costs involved in B's producing the materials compared to their costs to the A firm, inasmuch as A's monopoly price, and the excess of price over marginal costs, would afford an integrated non-

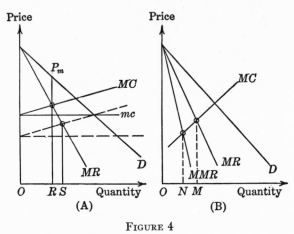

FIGURE 4

specialist firm an important means of absorbing minor diseconomies of production.

Although we have assumed that the B firm purchasing from A was itself a monopolist, this hypothesis is by no means crucial.   If B were one of a nucleus of competitive firms, the very same factors would motivate backward integration.   The analysis also indicates that we would underestimate the strength of monopoly pricing if we concluded that, because in any one firm the deviation between P and MC is small, monopoly pricing is unimportant.   Conceding this condition for the one firm, the conclusion is invalid when the final output contains materials processed by many monopoly firms.   The cumulative effects of monopoly pricing are thus more potent than can be detected merely by an examination of the price policy of an individual firm.   Let us develop this proposition further while proving that monopoly at an earlier stage with competition at later stages will elevate the final price just as effectively as competition in earlier stages with monopoly at the final stage.

Monopoly in Earlier and Later Stages

Let us assume that there are but two stages of production, with firms at the B stage providing the finished product and firms at the A stage providing the materials. Assume also, for simplicity that at B's stage production costs are zero; we shall remove this restriction in a moment but it is convenient to impose it in commencing this study.

In Figure 4B, the demand curve for the final product is D. Assuming numerous firms and competitive pricing, D is also the demand curve for the A-stage output, since each point on D reflects the maximum price that will be paid for each amount of the A wares. If at the A stage there is but one firm (so that A is a monopolist) to deduce its maximum price an MR curve, as in the figure, must be drawn and its intersection with MC (or A's marginal cost) observed. Output would then be OM. In contrast, suppose that the A product was sold under competitive conditions, so that MC now represents the supply curve of industry A, besides being the MC curve of firm B, which is now in a monopoly position. Firm B would purchase materials from the A firms in amount OM—the same quantity that would be sold if A priced monopolistically to B. Hence monopoly in either stage would affect the final purchaser identically; the difference is not to the consumers but to the distribution of the monopoly profits.

Lifting the hypothesis of zero costs at the B stage, suppose B's costs were constant and exactly those that would be experienced by A in integrating forward to the B stage; these constant amounts could be subtracted from each ordinate of the D curve. Palpably, on these hypotheses our conclusions would be unaffected. If A, on integration, was more efficient than the B firm which it supplants, the final MC curve of A ought to be lower than that of the B monopolist, with output enhanced and price reduced; the converse would be valid when B enjoys a productive superiority. Hence we have established that monopoly in the A stage, with competition in the B stage, will normally affect consumers in the same way as monopoly in later stages with competition in the earlier stages of the productive process. The proof of this proposition rests on the fact that the demand for A's output by the B firms is derived from the final demand curve for the finished product.

To conclude this analysis, both A and B firms may be monopolists, with B the sole seller to consumers and A the sole seller of essential materials to B. If there are no other buyers of A's product for other final sales uses, the problem is one of bilateral monopoly, with all of its indeterminacies.* In any event, B's demand curve for A's wares will be the MR curve to D. If we assume that because of the nature of the bargaining strength B must comply with A's price terms, A, in deciding on price policy, will in effect derive a curve marginal to B's MR curve, as MMR in Figure 4B. A's sales, and ultimately B's output, will thus be ON. Monopoly in the successive stages, therefore, will be more harmful to consumers than monopoly in but one stage. Hence fully integrated output will be superior from the consumer's standpoint even if there is some cost disadvantage attached to this development as compared to the economies of specialization.

Strategic Monopolies in Essential Materials

At this juncture it is superfluous to labor the importance of strategic monopolies exercised over an essential material that is used widely by all industry or by a particular industry. Possibly by patent right or by economic warfare, control can be acquired over some essential ingredient and dominance secured over an industrial structure which, in later processing stages, is highly competitive; the monopoly pricing will thus have widespread ramifications, exerting its influence in unsuspected quarters of the economic universe. A firm encircled by numerous competitors or caught in an oligopoly mesh can wend its way out and secure unitary power by acquiring control of a material vital to all firms at its own stage. Clearly, monopoly at the raw- and semifinished-material stages of the productive process can dissipate the price relief of competitive manifestations at later stages.

MONOPSONY AND INTEGRATION

Monopoly in earlier stages was shown to be a cogent influence in the backward integration of a firm. By similar reasoning it can be shown that monopsony in the later stages is conducive to forward integration. If the firm at the B stage is a monopsonist buyer, the firms at the A position will weigh the prospect of undertaking the B type of productive operation. The more unfavorable the monopsony price named by B the stronger the appeal that forward integration will carry to the A firms. Conceivably the monopsonist B firm may even sell in competitive markets. But this may be regarded as a highly unlikely concatenation, for if there were many competitors of the B firm its monopsony power over P_a would ultimately dissolve. It is most realistic to discuss

* Above, pp. 266–269.

the case in which B is a monopolist in its sales market and a monopsonist in its purchase of the intermediate A products—the monempory case discussed previously.* On these assumptions it can be shown that consumers would fare better by forward integration of the A firms, even while monopoly pricing persisted in the final market. Let us examine this situation.

In Figure 5, D is the market-demand curve for the end product of B's productive stage, and MR is the correspondent marginal revenue curve. Deducting from MR the cost to B of associated factors at each output level, the curve FMR emerges as B's demand curve for the intermediate product of the A firms. With MC as the supply curve of the A firms, and B the monopsonist, the A output would settle at ON. Conversely, if there was but one A firm whose costs were represented by the MC curve, and if it also controlled the B stage and enjoyed the same cost experience as the B firm, output would be OM. Hence the monempory at the B stage would be more adverse to final purchasers from the B stage than an integrated monopoly firm reaching back through both A and B operations.

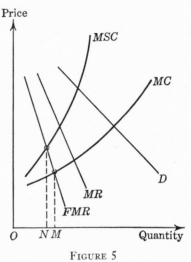

FIGURE 5

The Denial of Sales Outlets

Boycotts by dealers because of either contract commitments, or a reluctance to handle the products of a new firm, provide an obvious ground for forward integration. This can be construed as a manifestation of the monopsony power of dealer purchasers who abstain from buying in the thought of impeding the entry of the new producing firm. Owning and operating its distributing outlets may be the only straw that may be grasped by the producing firm, despite higher distributing costs. Forward integration is also likely when it offers the sole or best method of controlling selling policy at the retail stage, particularly when buyers associate price reductions with a deterioration of quality.

* Above, pp. 260–262.

BIBLIOGRAPHICAL NOTE

Recent contributions to the limited literature on multiple-product firms are: M. Reder, "Inter-Temporal Relations of Demand and Supply Within the Firm," *Canadian Journal of Economics* (1941), R. H. Coase, "Monopoly Pricing With Interrelated Costs and Demands," *Economica* (1946), and J. C. Weldon, "The Multiproduct Firm," *Canadian Journal of Economics* (1948). Also, on the theory of joint production, Marshall, pp. 388–390, and S. Carlson, *Theory of Production*, Chapter V. G. Stigler, *The Theory of Price* devotes Chapter 16 to the theory of multiple products. The equilibrium conditions for fixed proportions under monopoly are described in M. Colberg, "Monopoly Prices Under Joint Costs: Fixed Proportions," *Journal of Political Economy* (1941).

The article of D. Patinkin, "Multiple-Plant Firms, Cartels, and Imperfect Competition," *Quarterly Journal of Economics* (1947) is cited as one of the few treatments of multiple-plant firms. Also, the comment by W. Leontieff on this article in a later issue of the same journal, same year. The ingenious argument on induced by-product outputs consequent upon monopoly pricing is contained in N. Kaldor's "Market Imperfection and Excess Capacity," *Economica* (1935). The effects of monopoly in successive stages of a non-integrated output structure are analyzed in A. C. Hoffman, "Large-Scale Organization in the Food Industries," *Temporary National Economic Committee* (Monograph No. 35).

CHAPTER 14

Interrelated Demand

ALTHOUGH OUR FIRM HAS NOW BEEN endowed with control over multiple products, the reasons assigned for the phenomenon stem entirely from the cost side. In this chapter we examine several situations in which demand interrelations preponderate. The analysis generally entails a redefinition of the concept of marginal revenue.

DISCRIMINATORY PRICING

Consider first the problem of discriminatory pricing where the firm may be conceived as offering separate products for sale in the different markets. There are at least three degrees of price discrimination to be untangled. In discrimination of the first degree,* the monopolist may charge the same buyer a different price for each unit bought in order to extract the utmost in sales proceeds. Second-degree discrimination covers those situations in which different prices are charged, not for each unit but for each batch of goods bought. For example, the first 10 units might carry a price of $1, the next 30 a price of $.75, the next 50 a price of $.40, etc. Third-degree discrimination involves the ability of the firm to segregate customers according to income, individuality, or the use to which they will put the good or service and to charge different prices in each purchase category despite equivalent costs incurred in serving them. As long as the demand elasticities among different buyers are unequal, it will be profitable to post separate prices whenever possible.

The Condition for Discriminatory Pricing

Secondary markets must be eliminated for successful price discrimination. Middlemen must be prevented from buying in the cheaper market and reselling in the higher-priced market, a condition usually

* A. C. Pigou, *Economics of Welfare*, fourth edition, Pt. II, Chapter XVII.

satisfied for personal services.   Doctors can exact higher fees from rich patients than from the poor;* dentists and attorneys can act in the same way in the conviction that the lower-priced buyer cannot resell to those who pay the more exorbitant prices.   In the sale of electricity, discrimination is usually practiced between household, industrial, and other users.   International "dumping," wherein goods are sold for less in overseas markets than in home markets, is a recurring political grievance.

Discriminatory pricing is also occasioned, implicitly, in the practice of granting free delivery to all despite locational differences.   Discounts in excess of interest savings for prompt payment, or above the cost reductions for handling large shipments, are also forms of discrimination. Similarly the practice of granting uniform and liberal "trade-in" allowances regardless of the value of the unit surrendered discriminates against those who surrender superior units: when there is a conscious effort to evaluate the returned item the trade can be looked upon as a part-cash, part-barter operation.   Minimum bills submitted by public utilities also retain a flavor of discrimination against those who fail to utilize the permissible minimum service; a more baneful consequence is that it is likely to foster uneconomic use in order to utilize the minimum service.   Numerous other practices with a discriminatory aspect can undoubtedly be cited.

Discrimination of the First and Second Degree

In discrimination of the first degree we can assume either that each purchaser has an inelastic demand and will purchase at most but one unit, or that a continuous demand schedule can be written for each buyer.   The first hypothesis provides a good introduction, inasmuch as it can be treated succinctly; it can also be characterized as a special instance of third-degree discrimination.

If the individual demand curves are perfectly inelastic at one unit, with an uppermost price roof for the inelasticity, and if the roofs of the curves occur at different levels for each individual, by compounding the separate curves we can derive a fairly smooth and continuous aggregate market-demand curve.   If the seller was compelled to announce but one price to all buyers, the usual $MR = MC$ pricing rules would dictate the market price.   Since the seller is able to charge separate prices to each consumer, the total revenue for any volume of sales will equal the full

* Even here the policy is not uniformly successful, for in the larger cities individuals with higher incomes who can afford to pay for private treatment occasionally appear at clinics run mainly for the poor.

area under the demand curve rather than (as in the normal case) the
rectangular area formed by the demand price and perpendiculars to the
OX and OY axes. In this illustration of price discrimination the
demand curve itself emerges as the relevant MR curve for the discriminating monopolist. In Figure 1A, AR is the aggregate demand
curve formed from individual demands for but one unit, while MR is the
ordinary marginal revenue curve for the nondiscriminating monopolist.
Simple monopoly price would be OL ($= DP$) and output would be OD,
with total sales proceeds $OLPD$. In contrast, with inelastic unit
demands and price discrimination, each unit of output sells for the

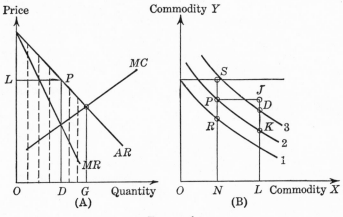

FIGURE 1

demand price above the unit in question. As further units are sold,
sales proceeds are increased by the additional area included under the
demand curve. The discriminating monopolist would push output to
OG, with each unit marketed at a different price. The total revenue
would equal the full area under the demand curve, or alternately, OG
multiplied by the average price per unit sold. This result is interesting
because it indicates that despite the objectionable features on the score
of price, sales are greater than under simple monopoly.

When the same consumer is charged a different price for each unit
purchased, the analysis is only slightly more formidable. An analysis
similar to our monopsony scheme is then pertinent. Strictly speaking,
if the discriminating monopolist extracted the maximum outlay from a
purchaser for each additional unit, the buyer would be confined to the
same satisfaction level that would be attained if the good were removed
completely from the economy. If we measure money on OY and
commodity X on OX, and recall that the relevant indifference curve at

the given income level would now originate on OY, the seller could collect the maximum purchase price for one unit at this indifference level. After the transaction for the first unit is completed, the seller could then extract the maximum demand price for a second unit, etc.; in this fashion a full demand curve consisting of marginal-demand prices could be traced for each consumer. Manifestly, the demand curve so constructed would be the pecuniary expression of the diminishing marginal rate of substitution between money and the monopolist's commodity, along the fixed indifference curve. The marginal-demand price curve of each consumer would also be the marginal-revenue curve to the seller. In selling to each individual the monopolist will push sales so far that the marginal revenues secured from each buyer will be equal, and each will be equal to the firm's marginal cost. The equilibrium marginal revenue will also be the price charged to each buyer for the final unit that the firm is prepared to sell to each. The average price paid by each buyer for the full stock purchased will, of course, exceed this marginal price.

In discrimination of the second degree, illustrated in Figure 1B, the consumer may be willing to pay a total sum of SR for ON units of X or a price per unit of SR/ON. If the market price is but SP/ON, well-being will be enhanced; thereupon the consumer would offer as much as JK/NL per unit for an additional quantity NL; any price below this, such as JD/NL, will elevate well-being. So long as the successive prices for each block of purchases are less than the maximum-demand price for the block, monopoly discrimination of the second degree is less injurious to consumer well-being than first-degree discriminatory pricing.

Price Discrimination of the Third Degree

Discrimination of the third degree, between classes of consumers, where each group buys freely at a separate price, is the most interesting and important of all the discrimination analyses. The monopolist is able to segregate two classes of consumers, conceiving independent D and MR curves for each grouping; the equilibrium condition is that the marginal revenue in each market must be the same and equal to the marginal cost of production. Unless the MR's are equal, output of the firm will be transferred from markets of low marginal revenue to markets in which it is higher. It follows that it is remunerative to expand output until MC is equal to the MR obtainable in each market.

Whereas under simple monopoly we summate the demand quantities in each market to derive the market-demand curve, and then extract the *MR* curve as a prelude to the derivation of price and output policy, in discriminatory-pricing problems we summate not the demand quantities at any given price but *the sales quantities for any given marginal revenue*. Equating the *MR* curve so derived to *MC*, we discover first the firm's output, and after allocating the total output among the several markets so as to secure the same *MR* in each we then learn the prices in each market corresponding to the equilibrium *MR*.

In Figure 2, MR_1 is the marginal-revenue curve in market 1; MR_2 is the marginal-revenue curve in market 2. Summating these curves laterally we establish the aggregate *MR* curve, MR_t. As the quantity demanded in market 1 is zero until price falls to OP_1, the MR_t curve coincides with MR_2 until this price height is reached. Drawing *MC* as the relevant marginal-cost curve, we observe that total output will settle at *OL*; the

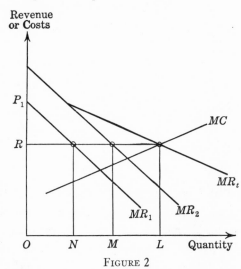

FIGURE 2

MR in each market will be OR_1 with an output amount *ON* absorbed by market 1 and *OM* (= NL) absorbed by market 2. The price in each market will be the demand price of the respective quantities.

As a special case of discriminatory pricing, the demand may be perfectly elastic in one market while in the other it may assume a normal downward trend. Conceivably, the former may be a foreign market where sales are subject to local competition, while the downward-sloping curve reflects the monopoly facts in the domestic market. In this case the aggregate marginal-revenue curve follows the *MR* curve of the domestic market so long as the domestic *MR* lies above the overseas price, after which MR_t merges with the perfectly elastic demand curve.*

Demand Elasticity and Price Discrimination

Discrepancies in the elasticity of demand are responsible for price discrimination; if at each price the demand points on the demand curves

*⸱Mrs. Robinson, p. 184.

for the several market classes were isoelastic, discriminatory pricing would be unprofitable and simple monopoly pricing would prevail. To prove this, and to deduce that price will be highest in markets in which demand is least elastic, we can invoke a variant of one of the earlier formulas, thus:

$$MR = P(1 - 1/E).*$$

Since MR is the same in each market, using the subscripts 1 and 2 to denote the different markets:

$$P_1(1 - 1/E_1) = P_2(1 - 1/E_2);$$

therefore

$$\frac{P_1}{P_2} = \frac{E_2E_1 - E_1}{E_2E_1 - E_2}.$$

Hence if

$$E_1 > E_2,$$

then

$$P_1 < P_2.$$

Simple and Discriminating Monopoly Output

Let us analyze the relations between simple and discriminatory monopoly output. One consideration alone almost suffices to establish the proposition that the discriminatory output will exceed simple monopoly output—namely, that discriminatory pricing may be effective profitwise even in circumstances where a singular price policy cannot promise profits because the AC curve lies everywhere above the simple D curve. For conclusive proof, however, it is necessary to compare the MR curves under simple and discriminating monopoly.

The demand and marginal-revenue curves under simple monopoly are clear and straightforward. Under discriminating monopoly of the third degree, at each MR the sales quantity and price in each market can be learned and hence the total sales proceeds for any given output volume can be computed. Dividing this last sum by the sales quantity, we can calculate the weighted average price for the volume of transactions; this would be the demand point on the relevant demand curve under discrimination. To supplement this average-revenue curve composed of weighted average prices we can append the discriminatory marginal revenue curve, as MR_t, in Figure 2. Except in the limiting case where they coincide, the AR per unit of sales for each sales quantity

* Above, p. 43.

under discrimination exceeds the simple monopoly AR. Consequently as total sales proceeds for any output are greater under price discrimination, and as the integral sum of the marginal revenues comprise the total revenue for any volume of sales, the discriminatory MR curve will ordinarily be above the simple MR curve, though over some ranges this may not be true. The crucial item is that of the relationship of the two MR curves at the output at which $MC = MR$ under simple monopoly. There is the strong presumption that the discriminatory MR curve will be to the right of the simple MR curve, and hence that output under discriminatory pricing exceeds output under a singular price policy.

It can be proven that with linear demand curves in the several markets the simple and discriminatory MR curves coincide, and total output is the same under price discrimination as under simple monopoly, although prices, profits, and the allocation of sales differ from the results achieved under a uniform price policy. In the event total output is *reduced* under discriminatory pricing, at the simple monopoly price the less elastic demand curve will have to be concave and the more elastic curve will have to be linear or convex. If the more elastic curve is concave, then output under discriminatory pricing will exceed simple monopoly output.*

***

* These results are due to Mrs. Robinson (*Economics of Imperfect Competition*, pp. 190–195). The fact that the simple MR and discriminatory MR curves are the same when market- and individual demand curves are linear can be proven as follows:

$$D_1 = x_1 = \frac{a - P}{k} \tag{1}$$

$$MR_1 = a - 2kx_1$$

$$x_1 = \frac{a - MR_1}{2k} \tag{2}$$

$$D_2 = x_2 = \frac{b - P}{r} \tag{3}$$

$$MR_2 = b - 2rx_2$$

$$x_2 = \frac{b - MR_2}{2r}. \tag{4}$$

To form the aggregate MR curve for discriminatory monopoly (MR_D), it is necessary to assume $MR_1 = MR_2$ and add (2) and (4):

$$x = x_1 + x_2 = \frac{a - MR}{2k} + \frac{b - MR}{2r},$$

$$MR_D = \frac{ar + bk - 2krx}{k + r}. \tag{5}$$

Similarly, to form the aggregate demand curve under simple monopoly, add (1) and (3)

$$x = x_1 + x_2 = \frac{a - P}{k} + \frac{b - P}{r}.$$

As price (P) is the same along each individual demand curve:

Price Discrimination and Universally Lower Prices

It is intriguing to ask whether discriminating monopoly can precipitate lower prices than can simple monopoly in all markets and benefit all consumers, even though the gains are shared unevenly.   If output is approximately the same despite discriminatory pricing, it is inevitable that in some markets price will be higher, and elsewhere lower, than with a uniform price policy.   Discriminatory pricing is likely to lower prices universally only when the MC curve is falling.   In the latter event (which also implies falling AC), the discriminatory AR at the $(MR_t = MC)$ output may be sufficiently below the simple monopoly price to confer upon all consumers a price lower than under a uniform price policy; with falling MC it may be that consumers can be profitably served whose demand prices are below the simple monopoly price.   If a firm abandons its maximum-profit objectives, perhaps being restrained by law as are public utilities, it is easy to conjure situations where, even without falling marginal costs, price under discrimination is universally below a single monopoly price.   For example, demand in a particular category of the market, as industrial demand for electric power, may be highly elastic, but at a price only *below* the simple monopoly price yet above the monopoly MR.   Some portion of this market, then, can be served profitably under price discrimination.   Hence the earnings amassed on the latter group will swell the total above the legal amount, fostering a price reduction in the more lucrative and inelastic market sectors in order to restore the aggregate profit balance to the permissible sum.   It is thus plausible to argue that discriminatory pricing between classes of consumers redounds beneficially even to those who pay the superficially exorbitant rates.

Price discrimination distorts both the relative economic position implicit in any income division and the real income obtainable from any given expenditure.   If a wealthy man has to pay more for the same medical services (say) than a poor man, the relative differences in money income fail to reflect the ratios of real purchasing power possessed by the two.   Substitute and complementary goods will also be affected by the

---

$$P = \frac{ar + bk - rkx}{k + r}.$$

Hence the simple monopoly MR curve (MRs) is:

$$MR_s = \frac{ar + bk - 2krx}{k + r}. \tag{6}$$

Thus equations (5) and (6) are identical.

bounties conferred and levies imposed through the multiple-price system. Although there are situations in which discriminatory pricing might work some positive benefits as compared to simple monopoly pricing, output under price discrimination will seldom equal the competitive output, for the simple market-demand curve will generally be to the right of the (third-degree) discriminating monopolist's MR curve. However, if the firm were compelled to equate MC to the AR curve evolved through discriminatory pricing—with each AR point being a weighted average price—output might well stretch beyond the competitive figure. This leads to the provocative query: does price discrimination merit a place in an optimal order, especially when cost proceeds can be recovered by discriminatory pricing tactics and market segregation, but not by a universal $(MC = P)$ policy? In those instances in which demand is too narrow to permit a $(P = MC)$ adjustment, or even a uniform $(P = AC)$ arrangement, discriminatory pricing might be advocated on the grounds that it can evoke outputs from which most consumers benefit, as revealed by their willingness to pay discriminatory prices. Nonetheless, there are elements of arbitrariness and favoritism in this procedure.

SUBSTITUTE GOODS

In the theory of pricing substitute goods, buyers of the firm's commodity A may also be potential purchasers of the $B, C, D \cdot \cdot \cdot$ varieties sponsored by the multiple-product firm; the demands for the several varieties are interrelated. Compared to discrimination where the costs of preparing goods for each market were identical, we can now suppose that costs are unrelated.* There is an implicit element of discrimination so long as the prices of the firm's several varieties are disproportionate to their marginal costs, but this is typical of all discrepancies in the degree of monopoly power among markets. As a simple illustration of the problem of pricing substitute goods, there is the practice of pricing theatre seats according to their location; this practice has a discriminatory element in that the cost of serving all patrons is almost indistinguishable. In a sense the propagation of substitute goods by a firm is reminiscent of discriminatory pricing in that the firm makes an effort to ferret out individuals and market sectors with different demand elasticities, and then produces goods designed to profit from the taste idiosyncracies.

---

* There may be some separable costs but, analytically, these can be deducted from the demand curves of the particular markets, after which the solution follows directly.

Diagrammatic Analysis

Diagrammatically, the equilibrium can be depicted by measuring the total revenue of commodity B (that is, TR_b) along the vertical axis and the price of B on the horizontal axis.   If we fix a price P_a for the substitute commodity A, the TR_b curve will be bell-shaped: as P_b rises TR_b will rise, reach a maximum, and then fall as the demand for P_b enters a stretch of inelasticity.   Similarly, when P_b is zero sales in A at the given P_a will be at a minimum; A's sales will expand, by and large, as P_b mounts.   Given the P_a, the total revenue in A for each P_b can thus be superimposed upon the TR_b curve, resulting in a combined TR_{a+b} curve, consisting of the total revenue obtained in both markets for the stipulated P_a linked to each possible P_b.   Presumably, as P_b rises the spread between TR_{a+b} and TR_b will widen.   At some P_b, however, the composite curve will attain a maximum and then decline.

Total costs (TC) of the implicit A and B outputs can also be included on the same diagram in order to compute the price combination of maximum profit.   As P_b ascends, the TC_b will decrease.   But as P_b rises the sales of A increase, so that TC_a will mount.   Weighing the opposing forces, we might assume provisionally that the total sum TC_{a+b} for the relevant quantities demanded at the respective prices is fairly constant. The most profitable P_b, given the P_a, can then be extracted.

A similar diagram would have to be drawn for each and every possible P_a and the true maximum P_a, P_b combination would have to be selected from among the various particular maxima computed in this way. With more than two substitute commodities sold by the firm, a similar technique could be improvised; P_a and P_b, for example, would have to comprise the data, the maximum P_c being derived in the light of them. As the number of substitutes widens, the diagrammatic technique becomes extremely cumbersome, since an interminable succession of diagrams must be drawn.   In practice the firm would have to form a rough estimate of the likely price arrangement for maximum profits, thereby reducing the pricing problem to manageable dimensions.

Alternately, the equilibrium price relations of a multiple-product firm can be depicted by means of a system of profit contours, where either outputs or prices are measured along the axes, and each point thus represents a definite total revenue and total cost outlay.   If all the profit contours are circular in shape there will be several P_a, P_b price combinations that promise maximum profits.   Any choice among them would be arbitrary.*

* It is not always easy to complete diagrammatically the total revenue and total cost

Equilibrium Conditions

The equilibrium position can also be expressed in marginal terms; for experimental maximum-price determination this is often more informative than operating with aggregates. Positing any P_a, B output will expand until the MC_b equals MR_b minus the diminution in profits on A at the constant P_a. Symbolically,

$$MC_b = MR_b - \Delta R_a,$$

where ΔR_a represents the loss in profits on A due to its constricted sales at the fixed P_a (as P_b falls), minus the reduction in the total costs of producing A. Thus:

$$\Delta R_a = \Delta TR_a - \Delta TC_a,$$

where ΔTR_a equals the fall in sales receipts on A at the given P_a as B expands by one unit, and ΔTC_a represents the fall in the total cost of producing the diminished A volume. If the marginal cost of A output rises with output, then the decline in sales proceeds will outweigh the decrement in total costs by an ever greater margin as P_b falls, restraining the B volume of output. Hence, given the P_a, as $MC_b < MR_b$, and as A's sales fall off, the production of B will be checked as a result of these roundabout market repercussions. Similar equations could be written for each P_a, enabling us to associate the maximum P_b to each P_a. From these various maximum price combinations the true maximum P_a,P_b price set could be selected. Equivalent equations can be written if P_b, instead of P_a, is regarded as the datum. Price-reaction curves can be employed that reveal at their intersection the maximum-price combination.

---

contours whose differences comprise the profit totals. For example, if we measure the A output vertically and the B output horizontally, it will be possible to ascertain the total costs and total sales proceeds for each output combination in the chart field. By the earlier principles, if both commodities conform to the rule of increasing marginal costs, the A and B combinations that can be produced for any given total cost are found along a transformation curve concave to the origin; a family of concave contours can be generated by varying the total cost outlay. But when we consider the sales revenue possibilities, simple indifference-curve diagrammatics appear futile. Consider the case where the aggregate total expenditure on the substitutes is always constant, whatever the price and output sets; all points in the chart field belong to the same isorevenue "curve" and the firm would maximize profits by desisting entirely from production! Or, conceivably, for each price or output combination the total purchase outlay may vary; each point then is an individual isorevenue. Even if several price sets release the same consumer expenditure, there is still little warrant for assuming that they form a smooth curve. However, if a continuous family of isorevenue curves can be drawn, the tangency points of isocosts and isorevenues indicate the possible equilibrium output sets for choosing the price combination for maximum profits.

The equilibrium condition discloses that the B output, with any given P_a (or vice versa), will be restrained whenever the two products are monopolized by one firm, as compared with each being offered for sale by independent firms.   From this it would be tempting to conclude that multiple-product monopoly harbors a greater threat to consumer well-being than a series of independent monopolists.   But this conclusion is unwarranted, for when markets are closely interrelated we are tied to a typical duopoly problem with all of its indeterminacies, rendering any positive conclusion tenuous.

Price Relations and the Cross Elasticity of Demand

If commodities A and B are but faint substitutes they may be treated as independent goods by the monopolist and their demand interrelations can be ignored.   Nevertheless at some price ratios the relationship, as measured by the cross elasticity of demand, will be closer than at others. As P_b declines and the cross-elasticity rises, this action will, by its signals of profit distress in A, check further decreases in P_b and output expansion of B.   Conceivably, the cross elasticity may be large only when P_b is high, diminishing as P_b falls—"conspicuous consumption" attitudes can cause a greater transference of demand from A to B at a higher rather than a lower P_b.   Thus a low cross elasticity of demand, even with substantial price discrepancies, will enable the firm to serve identical income groups with diverse functional substitutes which best suit them.   Possibly if the firm were compelled to price at least one commodity according to competitive principles, and if the cross elasticity were then high, the demand for the other good might so contract as to preclude its profitable production.   Rather than reflecting strong consumer preferences, multiple products would then appear as a creature of the monopoly pricing of one variety of the commodity type.   This is a familiar conclusion after our earlier monopoly studies, the novelty being merely that instead of a new firm being organized for the additional product, the product is contributed by a going firm.

COMPLEMENTARY GOODS

Goods were generally complementary, we recall, when a fall in the price of one led to an increased demand for the other.*   Let us examine the pricing problem when a complementary pair of goods are sold by the same firm.   With two separate firms in the field there would be a

* This is not strictly accurate, as a review of the earlier treatment will make plain.   But it will do for our purposes here.   See pp. 19–21 above.

tendency to keep the joint output low and the price of each item of the pair high, for each firm would perceive the futility of a price cut followed by a price rise of the complement.

Complementarity in Variable Proportions

Again we must posit the price P_a and assume that A and B are independent in production. Demand and the total-revenue curve for B, with P_b the variable, can then be derived. Superimposing on TR_b the total revenue amassed in the A market at the given P_a and the

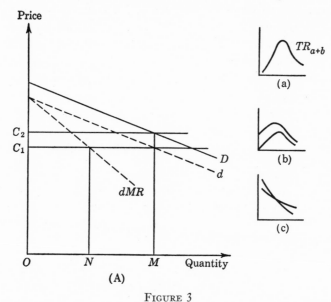

FIGURE 3

variable P_b, we can construct a TR_{a+b} curve. This aggregate-revenue curve will taper off to the right, as in Figure 3a, for (at some level) as P_b keeps rising, A's sales will be unaffected, since the complementary bond, gradually weakened by the ΔP_b, dissolves completely. Total revenue in A will be at its peak when P_b is zero; as P_b rises, TR_a diminishes, so that the widest gap between TR_{a+b} and TR_b occurs on the OY axis; the likely curve relations are indicated in Figure 3b. If A's only use was one complementary to B, as P_b rose sufficiently to drive demand for both A and B to zero, TR_{a+b} and TR_b would merge and fall to zero off to the right.

The combined output at the fixed P_a, clearly, will be greatest when P_b is zero. Total costs of A plus B will, therefore, reach their peak on OY and drop as P_b increases. Typically, profits will be at their highest where the spread between TR_{a+b} and TC_{a+b} is at a maximum. To find the maximal of the various maximum-price combinations, similar diagrams would have to be drawn for each P_a and the true maximum ferreted out from among all the particular maximum P_a, P_b price sets.

Equilibrium Conditions

The marginal conditions for profit maximization necessarily resemble those adduced for substitute goods, but whereas in pricing substitute goods the firm pondered the loss in revenue in the A market which accompanied the additional output of B, for complements the reverse holds true; an increase in the output of B will, with elastic demand for B, evoke additional revenue not only in B but also, (through the fall in P_b) in A. On this score we may infer that when complementary goods are controlled by a single firm, the output volume will surpass that of independent firms.

Symbolically, the equilibrium condition for the B output, holding P_a constant, is

$$MC_b = MR_b + \Delta R_a,$$

where ΔR_a represents the augmented profits in A at the constant P_a as P_b falls. The value ΔR_a is the compound resultant of an increase in sales revenue as more A units are sold at the fixed P_a through the fall in P_b minus the increase in TC_a in meeting the new A demand quantity.* Thus:

$$\Delta R_a = \Delta TR_a - \Delta TC_a,$$

where

$$\Delta TR_a = P_a \Delta A$$

and

$$\Delta TC_a = MC_a \Delta A,$$

where MC_a is the marginal cost of producing a further unit of A, while ΔA may exceed one unit.†

Since the A commodity becomes more remunerative as B production expands, the B output will be pushed beyond the simple $(MC_b = MR_b)$ equality to a level at which $MC_b > MR_b$. As this equality would be satisfied at each possible P_a, of all the partial maximum-price combina-

---

* Conceivably, the firm may be unwilling to furnish the full quantity of A demanded at the fixed P_a if this would involve $MC_a > P_a$. Rationing of sales may be considered although this will itself have repercussions on the sales of B. Ruling out rationing as inexpedient, the ensuing ΔP_a would, with the failure to produce more A, check the fall in P_b.

† This might be written more elegantly in formal mathematics; the expression, however, is accurate enough for our purposes.

tions, the price combination that promised the largest profit sum of all would be announced by the multiple-commodity monopolist. The same equilibrium equality could be written for P_a, when P_b is held constant. In the final equilibrium this condition would have to prevail for both A and B; otherwise a price movement in one direction or the other would augment the profit position of the firm. In terms of the price-reaction curves, these would have to intersect at the maximum price set. In view of the complementary price relations, measuring prices along the axes, the curve pair would take the path indicated in Figure 3c.

The equilibrium analysis for multiple-product firms producing complements or substitutes has been couched in terms of a postulated price of one product, while the output and price of the other product varied. The results would be much the same if instead of positing, say, P_a with A sales, P_b and B sales flexible, the A output was frozen and P_a allowed to fluctuate. In some ways this procedure is simpler, for with A output and sales rigid, A's total production costs are likewise constant, so that ΔR_a (the profit variation) reduces itself merely to a change in total sales proceeds on the stable A output. The implications for the B output are the same: a contractionist tendency appears for substitutes and an expansionist force appears for complements.

Complementarity in Fixed Proportions

As a partial proof of the proposition that the output of complementary goods under unified control will surpass the combined total output when they are separately produced, we may consider the extreme illustration of complements demanded in a fixed proportion—as, for example, a pair of shoes. The demand curve for the pair is represented by the linear demand curve D in Fig. 3A. The marginal-cost curve of the right shoe is constant and equal to OC_1 while the marginal cost curve of the left shoe, also constant, is C_1C_2. If both items are processed by one firm pricing competitively, output would be OM and the sales price for the pair, OC_2. Under monopolistic pricing the output would be ON or $\frac{1}{2}OM$, the "competitive" total.

Suppose that each of the shoes is supplied by several independent firms and that a price equal to marginal cost, C_1C_2, is exacted for the left shoe.* Subtracting this sum laterally from D, we can derive a new demand curve, d, for the right shoe. If the latter were priced monopolistically, OC_1 would be equated to the marginal-revenue cor-

---

* To obviate the prospect of duopoly complementarity we can assume that there are numerous suppliers of the shoes.

respondent of d; recalling that the MR curve would fall twice as fast as curve d, and as d cuts C_1 at OM output, production would settle at ON. Hence when the shoes are manufactured under separate ownership, and the specialists producing the left shoe seek to equate price and MC, the output volume for the fixed complementary pair equals only that of a single monopolist producing the complementary pair of items. At separate monopoly prices, or at a price for the left shoe in excess of C_1C_2, the total output would fall short of ON, the amount for a multiple-product firm producing the complementary pair.* Complementary demand is thus likely to confer a strong incentive to the creation of a multiple-product firm.

Loss Leaders and Tie-In Sales

"Loss leaders" provide an illustration of the pricing of complementary goods. The term refers to the practice of retail stores of selling certain goods sharply below the customary price and publicizing this fact through advertising, intending the loss leader to arouse consumer interest in the goods and, through purchase and sampling and the cultivation of a taste for it, to swing future demand permanently to the right. Here the complementarity is between present and future demand. Alternately, retail shops will underprice well-known brand commodities in order to attract shoppers and stimulate concomitant purchases of other merchandise. If commodity A is the leader, it is quite possible for $MC_a > MR_a$ and even MC_a to be greater than P_a: the direct losses are incidental so long as they are overshadowed by the indirect gains in the accompanying complementary lines. For a loss leader to be effective the cross elasticity of demand between A and $B, C, D \cdot \cdot \cdot$ will have to be strong. There is likely to be some asymmetry here; the cross elasticity resulting from a fall in P_a may well exceed the cross elasticity of a fall in P_b Besides involving a high cross elasticity, the direct elasticity of demand ought to be low, and that of supply high, for otherwise the direct losses are likely to outweigh the indirect complementary gains. A zero direct-demand elasticity and an infinite but negative cross elasticity would comprise the ideal loss-leader conditions. Frequently, purchasers of loss leaders will be rationed as to the quantity provided at the submerged price. This serves, implicitly,

---

* For the original diagram and the famous illustration of knife handles and blades, but in another context, see Marshall, p. 384*n*. A criticism of some of the more far-reaching conclusions drawn from this diagram in the theory of distribution is contained in G. Stigler, *Production and Distribution Theories*, pp. 84–87.

to cut the demand elasticity and limits the direct losses suffered by the seller while still evoking complementary buying of other commodities.

"Tie-in" sales provide another concrete example of complementarity; here the buyer is compelled to combine other purchases with the featured goods.* In effect, a joint good is offered the purchaser and the relevant valuations are those respecting the commodity pair. The result is to create an unnatural indivisibility. Largely, though not entirely, the practice will enable the firm to alleviate the rigors of competition in the tied-in product, extending its monopoly power over the commodity pair. Literally, there is an infinite array of tie-in arrangements: $1Y$ may be tied to $1X$, $2Y$ to $1X$, etc., with the firm choosing the combination that maximizes profits. Sometimes the tie-in proviso requires that an aggregate value sum of other goods must be bought with $1X$; this sum would, in principle, be chosen in such a way as to maximize profits. Normally, "tie-ins" will be effective when it is difficult to dispense with the main commodity and, of course, when the terms of the "tie-ins" are attractive. Where substitution for the presumed "lever" commodity can be readily accomplished the policy is a notorious failure. Packaged sales, with an offer to "buy one and get one free," is a form of tie-in practice that is often commended to the firm as a means of introducing a new commodity to a potentially receptive audience.†

The "Two-Part" Tariff

The "two-part" tariff may also be treated under the general heading of the pricing of complementary goods. Here the consumer is called upon to pay two different sums, a fixed charge independent of utilization and another charge varying with use. For example, public utilities usually exact a minimum bill and then levy a toll contingent upon extra services rendered. Or an amusement park will charge an entry fee and then charge a separate sum for each individual entertainment. Eco-

---

* The American Shoe Machinery Co. furnishes the classic example of a "tying" agreement in intermediate products. Possessing an exclusive and essential patent in shoe-making machinery, it compelled shoemakers to buy other materials and machinery as a condition of purchase of the former. See A. R. Burns, *The Decline of Competition*, pp. 452–453. For an interesting article on related practices in the consumer market, see W. A. Lewis, "Notes on the Economics of Loyalty," *Economica* (1942).

† Another type of tie-in sale, "full-line forcing," compels a dealer to store and sell all the multiple products of the parent firm as a condition of purchasing one of them. When the dealer is obliged to purchase the sundry list of items, the distributive facilities may be effectively closed to a vast array of competitive producers because of the limited physical and financial facilities of dealers. This tends to stifle competition at the distributive level and to narrow the list of alternatives open to consumers.

nomically, the two-part toll would seem to be merited if one payment referred, say, to installation costs of essential supplementary equipment, such as the telephone and wiring, or the transmission and distribution lines for gas and electric-power service, and if the other payment was levied to cover the costs involved in rendering the variable flow of services that are actually consumed.   In this event, the facilities and the services can be conceived as complementary items in variable proportions.   However, the dual toll appears to lend itself to abuse when we consider the relatively inelastic installation demand compared to the more elastic demand for the service flow.

INTERRELATED DEMAND AND COSTS

It remains to combine the analyses of the last chapter on cost interrelations with the demand interrelations developed in the present chapter.   Specifically, we have to deal with the following patterns: (1) substitutes in consumption produced by the identical production facilities;* (2) natural joint products which are related in consumption; and (3) production substitutes and complements associated with demand substitutes and complements.†

Demand Substitutes Produced by Identical Production Facilities

Under price discrimination, output was allotted to separate markets although the units were produced by identical technical processes; there was but one MC curve although there were several independent MR curves.   Separable costs of serving the unrelated markets could be handled by the simple expedient of deducting them from the demand price for each output quantity.   The analysis is only slightly more complex when the goods are produced by the same processes and yet have demands in the selling markets that are closely interwoven.   For example, the firm may use the identical ingredients but devise several brands to appeal to various segments of the market as an instrument of discrimination, yet at some price ratios the cross elasticity of demand for these several brands may be particularly strong.   Similarly, in geographical price discrimination buyers may at certain prices switch en masse from one buying center to another.   For the moment we can disregard any

* We ignore demand complementarity, although the theory would follow the same pattern.

† For a recent classification of cases of interdependence which relies largely on the value assumed by the coefficient of cross elasticity, see Y. R. Maroni, "Discrimination Under Market Interdependence," *Quarterly Journal of Economics* (1947).

separable costs in either branding and packing the items or in transporting them, or we can view these charges as equal for all markets.

The main principle of the solution is evident: the MR in each market must be the same, and equal to MC, for otherwise it will be profitable to deflect output from a market of lower to one of higher MR, or to curtail or expand production. The complication is that the demand curve for any one market (and hence the MR) cannot be known until the prices in other markets are fixed.

A solution can be approached in this way. It is easiest to begin with a volume of output to be allocated among the several markets in such wise that, at the ensuing prices, total receipts (and thus profits) are maximized. With this structure of prices the producer, in reaching a decision on whether to produce another unit, must assess not only the direct marginal revenue in the market to which the unit is destined but also the fall in price and revenues for the quantities hitherto disposed of in other markets. Thus if there are three substitute commodities A, B, C sold by the firm in amount X_a, X_b, X_c, and at prices P_a, P_b, P_c, the marginal revenue obtained from the sale of a further unit of A is

$$MR_a = (P_a - \Delta P_a)\Delta X_a - X_a\Delta P_a - X_b\Delta P_b - X_c\Delta P_c$$
$$= (P_a - \Delta P_a)\Delta X_a - (X_a\Delta P_a + X_b\Delta P_b + X_c\Delta P_c).$$

Since A, B, C are substitutes, however, the increased sales in A, and price fall there, will occasion the price drops ΔP_b and ΔP_c in B and C. Normally, when MR_a is positive, the first two terms on the right— the direct MR—will exceed the latter two terms (the indirect effects), for at the reduced P_a there will be a transfer of expenditure from other substitute commodities produced by other firms as well as from commodities B, C. In equilibrium, MR_a will equal MC and will also be equal to MR_b, MR_c $\cdot$ $\cdot$ $\cdot$ computed in the same way. As long as the firm can discern an MR in excess of MC it will be lucrative to devote further output to this segment of the market. It is quite possible that when total output is small the allocation of the output volume may be such that $P_a > P_b > P_c$, while at higher levels a complete price reversal may set in. If one of the varieties is sold in a perfectly competitive market the price ruling in that market will either govern the equilibrium MC and MR in the other substitute markets of the firm or set the minimum floor for these in the event the firm by-passes as less profitable the sales possibilities in the competitive market.

Conceivably, if the goods are identical technically but the different brands are viewed as complementary by deluded purchasers who, say, always buy more of the "better" grade simultaneously with more of the poorer grade, the indirect terms $X_b \Delta P_b$ and $X_c \Delta P_c$ are rendered positive, providing an uplift that works to advance total output. But this case of complementarity rests on some consumer ignorance.

Limited Geographical Price Discrimination

An analogous problem occurs when a firm sells the same technical commodity to consumers situated in cities separated economically by transport costs in amount equal to a sum denoted by the letter T. To obviate the problem of special transport costs involved in serving the separate markets we can assume that the plant, if not always equidistant from the markets, is located an equal amount of transport costs away from each. Denoting the markets as X and Y, the maximum price spread between them is thus $\pm T$. Given P_x, the demand curve in Y has a stretch of perfect elasticity at

$$P_y = P_x \pm T.$$

At the upper P_y of perfect elasticity all consumers located at Y switch their purchases to the X center, while at the lower P_y of perfect elasticity sales at Y are expanded by the transfer of custom from X. For each P_x, therefore, a distinct demand curve with a perfectly flat ceiling and floor emerges in Y. Manifestly, so long as the price differential does not exceed the transport costs a degree of price discrimination can be practiced between the markets. Rising transport costs will, of course, open the door wider to discrimination. Conversely, as transport costs approach zero the opportunities for discrimination tend to vanish.

Typically, the equilibrium price set P_x, P_y would be so chosen as to maximize profits. As long as D_x is elastic, further output and a lower P_x would always add revenue in X but, by the fall in P_x, the inelastic portion of D_y would be constricted, probably affecting price and sales proceeds in the Y market. This indirect influence renders this geographical problem one of pricing substitute goods—in our case, of pricing identical technical varieties produced under the same cost conditions. Marginal cost would have to equal marginal revenue, whether computed for an additional output unit to be allocated to the X or the Y market.

Fixed Proportions and Interrelated Demand

We deal now with natural by-products produced in fixed proportions, as $1X$ inexorably accompanied by $1Y$, with the demand for X and Y also interrelated.

Assume first that the goods are demand substitutes. If we postulate a given total output, the P_x, P_y combination must maximize total sales proceeds for this output. With a fused unit of (say) $1X$ and $1Y$ being produced, the direct marginal proceeds recovered in selling X would be reduced as the $1X$ was offered for sale, because of the indirect effect through the fall in P_y. Thus the net MR derived from ΔX would be

$$MR_x = (P_x - \Delta P_x)\Delta X - (X\Delta P_x + Y\Delta P_y),$$

where $Y\Delta P_y$ represents the lost-sales proceeds in Y due to the lower P_x. As the accompanying $1Y$ is also produced and offered for sale, there is a similar equation for the $1Y$. Thus the total MR obtained from a further unit of joint output is:

$$MR_{x+y} = [(P_x - \Delta P_x)\Delta X - (X\Delta P_x + Y\Delta P_y)] + \\ [(P_y - \Delta P_y)\Delta Y - (Y\Delta P_y + X\Delta P_x)].$$

If we are at liberty to assume that the price drop ΔP_y (or ΔP_x) due to an ΔX (or ΔY) is of the same size as that due to a ΔY (or ΔX), and suppressing $\Delta P_x \Delta X$ and $\Delta P_y \Delta Y$ by interpreting P_x and P_y as the *new* prices, the equation can be simplified to

$$MR_{x+y} = P_x\Delta X + P_y\Delta Y - 2(X\Delta P_x + Y\Delta P_y). \\ = P_x + P_y - 2(X\Delta P_x + Y\Delta P_y).$$

Whenever this total MR exceeds the combined MC, it will be lucrative to expand output. Neither MR may be negative: the seller would prefer to destroy the good rather than dispose of it at a negative MR.

The substitutionary demand relations thus operate to restrain the output of goods produced in fixed proportions, for both of the direct marginal revenues are reduced by the indirect effects. If the goods are complementary in consumption, and if the ΔP_x fall due to ΔX is offset by the ΔP_x rise due to ΔY (and similarly for ΔP_y), the terms $X\Delta P_x$ and $Y\Delta P_y$ tend to cancel out, leaving us with

$$MR_{x+y} = P_x\Delta X + P_y\Delta Y \\ = P_x + P_y$$

rendering a patently exhilarating effect on total output, for the combined MR now consists only of the sum of the new prices named in each market, devoid of the usual negative component in the MR expression.

Variable Proportions and Interrelated Demand

For commodities related in demand but produced in variable proportions the equilibrium conditions turn out to be more intricate. Fixing the total cost outlay, we can imagine the firm to experiment until it attains the output combination which maximizes total sales proceeds. In brief, as the firm expands the Y output, it will be compelled to withdraw some X output; the firm will find it fruitful to modify the output combination so long as the additional proceeds from the Y output exceed the revenue sacrifices on the X output. Thus with each ΔY, and holding X output constant temporarily, there is the gain in sales proceeds equal to

$$MR_y = (P_y - \Delta P_y)\Delta Y - (Y\Delta P_y + X\Delta P_x),$$

or, dropping $\Delta P_y \Delta Y$, then

$$MR_y = P_y\Delta Y - (Y\Delta P_y + X\Delta P_x),$$

where ΔP_x is the fall in P_x because of the substitutionary nature of demand.

Similarly, as there is a decrement in the X output (ΔX) in amount sufficient to keep the total cost outlay rigid while production expands in amount ΔY, there is a revenue *loss* equal to

$$MR_x = X\Delta P_x - P_x\Delta X - \Delta X\Delta P_x + Y\Delta P_y,$$

or, dropping $\Delta X\Delta P_x$, then

$$MR_x = X\Delta P_x + Y\Delta P_y - P_x\Delta X,$$

where ΔP_y is the rise in P_y due to the diminution in X output, and ΔP_x represents an increment rather than the customary decrement in P_x. Hence so long as the revenue gain MR_y exceeds the revenue loss MR_x, it will be profitable to expand Y at the expense of X. The equality condition must be satisfied for each total cost outlay. If we are entitled to assume that the decrement ΔP_x due to an expansion ΔY is of the same order as the increment ΔP_x due to the contraction ΔX, and similarly for ΔP_y, then the appropriate equilibrium condition reduces to the simple statement (where P_x and P_y are the *new* prices)

$$P_y\Delta Y = P_x\Delta X.$$

Only the direct gain in sales proceeds (by diverting most of the total cost to Y), and the loss in proceeds in X, need be appraised. Since the goods are substitutes in consumption, as the outlay level expands the substitutionary relations serve to check the final output level as compared to production under variable proportions and consumption independence.

Production Substitutes and Interrelated Demand

These analyses prepare us for those instances in which X and Y are substitutes in production (so that an increase ΔY will lift the entire MC_x curve) and substitutes in consumption (so that the ΔY output, and subsequent fall in P_y will dislodge the demand curve for X, pulling it to the left). At each volume of X output there will be one quantity of Y output which maximizes total profits. Fixing the X output, to deduce whether it is profitable to augment the Y volume, we must assess the direct MR_y minus the fall in profits on X resulting from both the rise in TC_x and the fall in TR_x. Thus for MR_y we can write

$$MR_y = P_y\Delta Y - Y\Delta P_y - (X\Delta P_x + X\Delta AC_x)$$
$$= P_y\Delta Y - (Y\Delta P_y + X\Delta P_x + X\Delta AC_x),$$

where ΔP_x is the decrease in the price of the fixed quantity of commodity X due to the lower P_y, and ΔAC_x is the increase in the average cost of producing the fixed amount of X when more Y is produced.

Manifestly, the dual substitutionary relations will serve to restrain output rather severely, inasmuch as each link between the markets indicates a profit decrease in X as the Y output expands. The stronger are the commodity ties, the smaller the likelihood of a marked enlargement of the production of the substitute. Analogously, where the goods are substitutes in production but complements in consumption, the rise in costs, ΔAC_x, will tend to be neutralized by the rise in price, ΔP_x, with results less adverse for output. If the demand complementarity outweighs the cost interdependence, Y output may actually be stimulated despite the rise in AC_x.

Production Complements and Interrelated Demand

Finally, the goods may be interrelated in demand and complementary in production. An increase in Y output will therefore lower MC_x and AC_x; this is favorable to an expansion in Y output. Insofar as X and Y are substitutes in consumption, however, the Y output will tend to be depressed on this score. Thus:

$$MR_y = P_y\Delta Y - Y\Delta P_y + X(\Delta AC_x - \Delta P_x).$$

The expansion in Y output will depend partly on the strength of the opposing forces poised against the fixed amount of X. Easily the most favorable conditions for the expansion of Y (and indirectly of X) occur when the goods are complementary in both consumption and production. Then ΔAC_x and ΔP_x are both treated as positive and added to

$P_y \Delta Y$, facilitating the growth in Y output.   Besides deducing the equilibrium condition on the assumption of constancy in X and an advance
in Y output, the identical relations would have to be fulfilled for ΔX as
well as for ΔY; the equilibrium conditions must obtain in both directions
(or in all directions, for the n-commodity case) rather than in one direction alone.

MONOPSONY DISCRIMINATION

After the protracted analyses of monopoly price discrimination the
exposition of monopsony price discrimination can be more modest.
Instances of monopsony discrimination can undoubtedly be found; purchasers may pay different prices to various sellers of identical products
or pay equally skilled workmen different wages.

It would be possible to distinguish various types of monopsony price
discrimination.   In discrimination of the first degree a different price
would be paid by the buyer to the seller for each *unit* purchased.   To
the buyer the effective supply curve (the *MSC*) would be the seller's
ordinary market-supply curve; purchases would cease at the transaction
volume at which this intersected the (marginal) demand curve.   But
before proclaiming that output and price will, therefore, rest at the competitive level we must remember that the demand curve under monopsony is drawn under different assumptions than the normal demand
curve.*   Moreover, the seller will recoup proceeds only equal to the
area *under* the supply curve rather than equal to the rectangular area
formed by the price and sales of the n units of output.   Economic rent,
in effect, would be obliterated; the monopsonist buyer would pay solely
the sums necessary for compensating the necessary versatile factors.

Monopsony of the second degree, of "step" prices for different quantities, is also possible; bonuses may be paid by the buyer as part of a plan
to stimulate production, just as price discounts may be given by the
seller to accelerate sales.

In monopsony discrimination of the third degree—monopsony discrimination proper—the principles of discrimination follow familiar
lines.   When the supply and marginal supply (*MSC*) curves are drawn
for each seller and the quantities offered by each seller at each *MSP*
summated, the monopsonist is pictured as equating the aggregate *MSC*
to his demand curve, thereafter paying each seller the price implicit at
the equality.   Hence the basic condition is the equality of demand price
and marginal-supply price in each segment of the market.   But prices
paid each supplier will be different.

* Above, pp. 254–255.

All this is consistent enough with our previous analyses, enabling us to dispense with the diagrammatics. It should be observed, however, that if the supply curve of but one selling firm is falling, the corresponding MSC will lie below the supply curve and the volume of purchases ought to surpass the competitive norm, with market price lower. Where the demand curve is one of factor hire, however, this would involve the monopsony firm in aggregate losses, for the monopsony-factor price would exceed the MVP of the factors. However, as the one selling firm with decreasing supply price will capture the entire sales market, to the exclusion of the other firms, ultimately the relationship should degenerate into one of bilateral monopoly, although the presence of potential alternate suppliers will strengthen the hands of the buyer—the discriminating monopsonist—against the seller.

Monopsony and Interrelated Supply

Paralleling the discussion of demand interrelations, we may state that a monopsonist will have to exercise a keener sense of price discretion, and occasional restraint, when supply curves are interrelated. For example, if X and Y are complements in production, buying fewer units and paying a lower price per unit for commodity X might lift the supply curve of commodity Y, which may also be bought by the monopsonist. Taking Y purchases as fixed in amount, the MSP_x must be reduced by $Y\Delta P_y$, for this decrease in expenditure on the fixed amount of Y occurs as more X is bought and a higher P_x paid. In view of these ramifications the monopsonist would be disposed to buy more and pay a higher price for X than indicated at the simple $D_x = MSC$ equality. Conversely, when X and Y are production substitutes, buying but a few units and paying a lower P_x might lower the supply curve for Y, forcing it to the right and lowering P_y. This would impel the monopsonist to buy fewer X and pay a lower P_x than in those situations in which these ramifications could be overlooked.

BIBLIOGRAPHICAL NOTE

Besides the writings listed at the close of the preceding chapter (some of which are pertinent to the problems of this chapter) the following additional references are particularly germane. Mrs. Robinson virtually charted new vistas in the theory of price discrimination, simplifying and extending old ideas enormously; see Chapters 15 and 16 of her book. Also, Professor Pigou, *Economics of Welfare*, Chapter XVII and his *Economics of Stationary States*, pp. 238–239. The intricacies in the rigorous proof that output under discriminating monopoly exceeds that of simple monopoly are indicated by P. Samuelson in his *Foundations of Economic Analysis*, pp. 42–45. The indifference apparatus for multiple-products, which is of limited use applied to cases of interrelated demand, is expounded by Stigler, *Theory of Price*, pp. 314–319. The equilibrium interrelations for multiple products with related demands are discussed briefly in Allen, *Mathematical Analysis*, pp. 359–362 and Hicks, "The Theory of Monopoly," *Econometrica* (1935). Also, an older discussion in F. Y. Edgeworth, *Papers Relating to Political Economy*, Vol. I, p. 174, and later comments by Harold Hotelling on "Edgeworth's Taxation Paradox," *Journal of Political Economy* (1932), pp. 602–603. C. Roos, in *Dynamic Economics*, elucidates the loss-leader problem. E. A. Robinson, *Monopoly*, pp. 72–73 has some comments on the practice of full-line forcing. The two-part tariff is reviewed at length in W. Arthur Lewis' article, "The Two Part Tariff," *Economica* (1941), with additional remarks by R. B. Rowson and Lewis in a later issue, same journal, same year. An interesting analysis on geographical discrimination, disclosing the curious result that a reduction of transport costs can raise price in *both* markets, is in W. Leontieff "The Theory of Limited and Unlimited Discrimination," *Quarterly Journal of Economics* (1940). Monopsony discrimination is covered by Mrs. Robinson in Chapters 17–19, and more thoroughly by W. Nicholls in Chapters 12–17 of his *Imperfect Competition Within Agricultural Industries*.

Part IV

DYNAMIC ANALYSES

Introduction

The task of the following chapters is to reorient the equilibrium analyses in recognition of dynamic phenomena. Largely the conversion requires the injection of the idea of the forward-looking nature of the economic process into the conceptual scheme. Production and consumption take time; decisions and actions in these spheres are guided by an estimate of the future. Heretofore we have been extremely vague on the time span to which our analytic models refer, although in stationary conditions this is not a serious shortcoming, for whatever the time length studied, each period is but a replica of every other interval; dissecting one is to diagnose all others. But in conditions of economic change this proposition is invalid and we are obliged to be explicit on the time span being investigated.

Chapter 15 deals with some broad aspects of uncertainty, introducing the concept into our framework and indicating its influence on economic behavior and social institutions.   Chapter 16 contains a statement of the conditions in which economic plans and actions will be compatible with the unfolding events; this study discloses the need for some revision of the equilibrium concept.   Chapter 17 allows for the effects of longer period anticipations of prices and costs on immediate market behavior. Completing this, in Chapter 18 we discuss the time lengths appropriate for economic study: thereafter all our analytic constructions can be locked to a definite time span.   This portion of the study is concluded in Chapter 19, where the response of the price mechanism to economic change is investigated; we examine also the manner and path through which prices move and the way in which equilibrium is restored under the impact of change in the forces of supply and demand.   Attention to these elements ought to give our study greater relevance and reality.

CHAPTER 15

Anticipations and Uncertainty

UNCERTAINTY COLORS ALL ECO-
nomic behavior.   Seldom does an economic subject have full and accurate information of all the data relevant for his purchase, production, or
sale decision.   Some idea of the dimensions of the new problems can be
detected when we ponder the fact that consumers make purchases in
advance of consumption; at the time of buying they must predict what
their tastes will be when they are actually using the goods.   Producers
must estimate not only consumer wants (and hence market prices—or,
under monopoly—demand) but also factor prices and productivity.
Capital goods must be erected years ahead of their actual use; their productivity and complementarity with other resources must be predicted.
Individuals must acquire special skills and prepare to enter definite
occupations well in advance of the application of their knowledge.
All of these decisions and preparations are made in an atmosphere
enshrouded in uncertainty, by individuals cognizant that the future is
but dimly foreseeable.   Any study pretending to relevance cannot
ignore these facts.

Uncertainty will thus affect the maximizing decisions of the two elemental units, consumers and firms.   For consumers the unsureness may
envelop either tastes, incomes or prices.   For firms, the vagueness may
touch either market product prices (or demand under monopoly), factor productivity, or factor prices.   It is also instructive to contemplate
the special effects of uncertainty on the choice of occupations by owners
of productive factors.

UNCERTAINTY ALLOWANCES

Let us examine the methods of coping with uncertainty when the
future in buying, selling, and producing is obscure and uncertain.

339

Under conditions of economic certainty, fixing the subjective and the external market data makes the equilibrium of the individual consumer determinate. Being cognizant of price (or demand) and cost data, producers can make adaptations that are likewise unequivocal. What is imperative now that uncertainty has been introduced, is to exhibit the *uncertainty allowances* of the economic units when the ultimate data for conduct are vague and indefinite, shorn of the certitude posited heretofore. Dealing with the concept of uncertainty allowances, the next step is a reconciliation of the actions sponsored by the subjective anticipatory data with the unfolding market facts.

The problem posed can be stated briefly. Decisions are made, despite uncertainty, and, in reaching decisions it is generally necessary to predict some facts whose exact dimensions belong to the future. When the predictions (and hence the bases for action) are accurate, the full equilibrium is assured. Correct forecasts, therefore, occasion no further obstacles. Erroneous judgments, however, rear further complications, involving subtleties in analysis and corrective fluctuations in the relevant markets. One way of resolving the dilemma and salvaging the neat solutions of equilibrium structures is to posit that anticipations *are* accurate. Although this assumption would have the merit of recognizing the futurity and forward-looking nature of the economic process, it would welcome in at the rear door the very uncertainty and subjective disquietude that led to the decision to lock the front gate. Hence this assumption will not do; when uncertainty is acknowledged, error-making and human fallibility must also be admitted as an inevitable concomitant, which can be mitigated but never fully eradicated so long as change and anticipations mark, mar, or enhance economic life.

The Effective Expected Price

The uncertainty allowances refer to the difference between the estimated value of a future event, held with less than complete confidence, and the value of a perfectly certain event that evokes the same conduct as the expected value, tinged as the latter is with uncertainty. For example, in competitive markets the producer must anticipate future price in calculating output policy. After the most probable price is estimated, there is still some uneasiness, for the forecast will not be held with 100% assurance. Nevertheless a decision on output must be made. Equivalent to this probability and the concomitant uneasiness there is one perfectly certain price which would have led to the same behavior; the latter may be termed the *effective* expected price (or the value of the expectation).* The difference between the most probable price and the effective price, or the mental provision for uncertainty and error, can be designated as an uncertainty allowance. Its magnitude will depend on both the confidence in the estimate and the particular individual's attitude towards action when he is less than fully confident; in short, it denotes his aversion to subjective uncertainty.

By means of this device of reducing vague probabilities to definite effective values we may be able to preserve intact much of the stationary analysis even after the intrusion of dynamic elements. For insofar as the effective value corresponds to the ultimate real value there is a coincidence between the anticipations and events so that, despite uncertainty, the actions fostered are precisely those that would be forthcoming in a perfectly sure world where future events were always foreseen. In this way we can partially "dynamicize"† the static theory and make it a more inclusive and representative model for depicting the real factors operative when less than perfect foresight pervades and for uncovering the chain of repercussions engendered by their movement.

CONSUMER ESTIMATES

In the theory of consumer behavior, prices and incomes were objective facts known with certainty. The taste schema, similarly, was a subjective fact and fully known to the consumer—that is, the consumer could foretell the relative significance of goods in consumption. The scope for correction is betrayed by the mere restatement of the data on which certainty was previously postulated.

Area of Consumer Estimation and Error

Consider first the possibility of divergence in the consumers' subjective estimates of prices and the objective price facts. For one thing, in buying commodity A in market A the buyer's prescience must extend to the ultimate prices in markets $B, C \cdots$, for otherwise errors in buying would occur. If in shopping in market A the prices $P_b, P_c \cdots$ are predicted as being, by and large, lower than they in fact come to be, they will buy too little of A. This error normally can be rectified without too much time lost in reshopping. Conversely, if they expect higher prices in other markets than those ultimately forthcoming, they will overstock on good A. With perfect markets they would be able to dispose of their excess purchases without loss: in actual markets excess

---

* The uncertainty allowance is termed the *risk premium* by Lange, *Price Flexibility*, p. 31.

† Compare J. Tinbergen's use of the term, *Statistical Testing of Business Cycle Theories* (League of Nations), p. 14. The word might well be corrupted to "dynamize."

purchases would entail both financial and psychic loss through the irksomeness of having to return the goods or behave as temporary sellers, or stock the goods as an inventory at home. Ultimately, the possible errors due to price uncertainty of this sort are attributable to the brute fact of the spatial separation of markets.

An even greater source of uncertainty and loss is inherent in the fact that the consumer, at the time of purchase, must foretell what his tastes and the tastes of those for whom the purchases are made, will be at the time when consumption actually takes place. Perforce, these anticipations will be imperfect. Knowledge of the physiological, environmental, psychological, and social circumstances—as we may term the tastes and proclivities of the dinner guest, for example—cannot be complete. Everything must be predicted. The plaint that preparations would have been different "if I had only known" is a familiar refrain.

A solution compatible with stationary equilibrium may be approached in this way. On the basis of imperfect knowledge of the circumstances surrounding consumption we can visualize the indifference system of the individual and, given the price line, the maximum-purchase position. Allowing for uncertainty and the fact that the consumer will forecast all the surrounding conditions of consumption as best he can, substituting in his taste schema items of more assured positiveness for the more "certain uncertainties," his indifference map will ordinarily differ from that constructed on the supposition of perfect knowledge. Conceivably, after discounting the subjective uncertainties the preference relations may unfold as a perfect image of the facts at the time of consumption, so that effective purchases and actual ex post preference quantities merge. Or possibly, the equilibrium along the estimated curve system may establish a fortuitous coincidence with the maximum-purchase combination on the real system; that is, a curve on the estimated indifference map would be tangent to the price line at the same combination of goods as the indifference curve drawn on the hypothesis of perfect foresight. Well-being would be just as fully maximized on this supposition, despite the uncertainty and erratic forecast, as it would be with full knowledge. Any other set of indifference relations, however, would presage some loss in well-being, assignable entirely to the inadequate knowledge on which behavior is predicated.

The chief way in which consumers can overcome the uncertainty of future tastes and climb closer to the maximum-consumption summit is through narrowing the time dates between purchase and consumption, or by increasing the frequency of purchases; if the cost of shopping is nil (and selling outlets were always open) purchases could be made almost simultaneously with use.   In the real world, there are of course definite elements of irksomeness involved in frequent trips to the store; moreover, retail outlets are not open for business at all hours so that purchase must, to some extent, antedate consumption.   If purchases had to precede consumption by a longer time length, the best way of limiting purchase losses would be to buy varieties of goods appealing to a diversity of palates and with manifold alternate uses.

Other than in prices and tastes, there is just the chance that income prognoses may go awry, particularly for those purchases, such as installment purchases, that are made in anticipation of a definite income stream in the (near) future.   Perhaps it is not too inaccurate to surmise that errors here are less likely than errors with respect to the other data. A monopsonist, rather than having to estimate merely the market price of a commodity, must extend his forecast to the full course of the supply curve; the greater possibilities for error need not be labored.

PRICE PREDICTIONS

If we visualize a competitive firm that regards price as external and uninfluenced by its own behavior, there appear to be three critical elements involved in predicting the market price over the time period during which output is to be sold.   The first of these consists of estimating the probability of each of the possible prices.   The second element is the need to determine the most probable figure.   Third, there is the matter of the degree of confidence with which one's own predictions are held.

Probability Distribution of Prices

In Figure 1A, the chances that each price will materialize are measured vertically.   Perfect certainty—a probability of 100 per cent for a particular price—would be the maximum value possible.   The possible prices are enumerated on the horizontal axis.   A frequency distribution of prices and probabilities can thereafter be described.   In Figure 1A this is drawn as of normal form.

After evaluating the frequency distribution, the entrepreneur will have to reduce his expectations to a single price value.   That is, he must decide whether it is the mean, mode, median, or some other value that he deems most likely.   In reaching this decision he will probably appraise the entire distribution, its skewness, or shape; the size of the standard deviation might also have some bearing on the matter.   It is vain to strive for more precision here; the estimate of the most probable value will depend upon the knowledge and individuality of the estimator.

The degree of confidence with which the estimates are held must also be injected as an additional element, because a change in certitude,

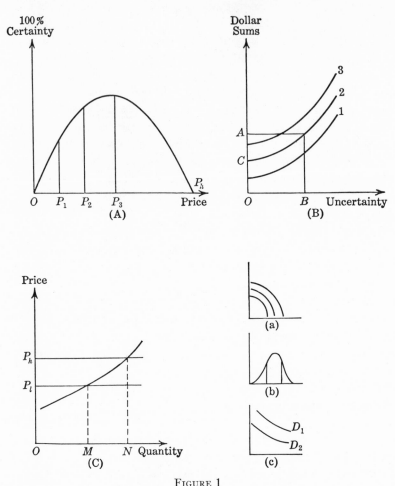

FIGURE 1

without any change in the estimated probability distribution or mean value, is likely to lead to new behavior. For example, with more assurance in his forecast and less hesitancy in acting upon it, the probability distribution which formerly gave rise to the same behavior as a positive and certain P_1 may now lead to the same action as a positive P_2, where $P_2 > P_1$. Alternately, after sketching the most likely probability distribution the entrepreneur can be expected to draw other probability distributions for comparative purposes, each held with a different degree of assurance, and then estimate the probabilities of the various "most probable" prices, finally arriving at a summary figure. We have termed the latter the *effective* value; it is this that becomes the basis for action. Because of the subjective uncertainty over the prediction, the *effective* estimated value will not coincide with the most *probable* estimated value, the difference between the two being the uncertainty allowance.*

Probable and Effective Price

Other aspects of the anticipatory procedure can be illuminated by the indifference system of Figure 1B. Most probable prices are measured vertically, beginning at a price of zero and rising indefinitely; the horizontal axis indicates the degree of uncertainty of each price eventuating. Rather than measuring cardinal values, the abscissae have only an ordinal meaning; at the origin on OX there is full certainty or zero uncertainty, and as we move rightward the degree of expectational assurance fades away. Hence a positive price of OC expected with full assurance provokes the same behavior as any of the higher prices along indifference curve 1 viewed subjectively as less than fully certain. Suppose OA were the most probable price, but held with assurance OB: measured by the action it evokes it is equivalent to a price OC forecast with certainty. The difference $(OA - OC)$ has already been described as the *uncertainty allowance* (or risk premium), while OC stands for the *effective* (subjective) price.†

Figure 1C demonstrates that despite subjective uncertainty over the future market price, so long as an entrepreneur feels there are some fairly rigid bounds to the price potentialities, output will be determinate, at least within limits. Suppose a price higher than P_h or lower than P_l is so unlikely as to be excluded from calculations. With the MC curve known, the firm's output must at a minimum be OM, and at most ON: output indeterminateness is limited to this range until an effective

---

* The widely quoted passage from Keynes' *General Theory of Employment, Interest and Money* (p. 24n.) will bear repetition here: "An entrepreneur, who has to reach a practical decision as to his scale of production, does not, of course, entertain a single undoubting expectation of what the sales proceeds of a given output will be, but several hypothetical expectations held with varying degrees of probability and definiteness. By his expectation of proceeds I mean, therefore, that expectations of proceeds which, if it were held with certainty, would lead to the same behavior as does the bundle of vague and more various possibilities which actually makes up his state of expectations when he reaches his decision."

† For buyers' price anticipations, the curve family of Figure 1B would be concave to the origin, as in Figure 1a, because greater uncertainty would have to be compensated by a *lower* most probable price.

price estimate is formed. The P_h and P_l limits may be regarded as either the high and low price points at which the probability distribution of Figure 1A cuts the OX axis, or it may be that although the entrepreneur believes that prices outside this range are possible they are so unlikely as to be disregarded in policy; the high-low range in Figure 1A can thereby be narrowed—all price chances of less than, say, 10 in 100 are dismissed as unlikely. Vertical lines from OX can be erected to cut off this range of the frequency distribution, as in Figure 1b. In terms of Figure 1B, if some prices are estimated as being wholly improbable and devoid of significance for conduct, the lowest effective curve on the indifference system will begin at the P_l height on OY and the highest indifference curve at P_h.

As the probability distribution of prices is but an individual estimate, it will be shaped by the state of mind of the prognosticator, his factual preparation, his assurance in making forecasts, and the timidity or tenacity which guides his judgment. However much he strives for objectivity in forecasts, the subjective element can never be completely allayed. After the probable facts are appraised, precisely the same mental attitudes govern the degree of assurance with which the most probable view is maintained. Different individuals, therefore, appraising the same future event are likely to hold diverse views; the high-low values, probable values, degree of assurance, and the attitude towards uncertainty (and hence the effective actions) are unlikely to be identical.

Other than referring to it as the *effective* price, the price that evokes the entrepreneurial conduct in competitive markets may also be called either the subjective market price, the imagined market price, the prospective price, or the ex ante price. All of these terms will be used interchangeably.

ANTICIPATED DEMAND AND COST CURVES

While the competitive firm must prejudge merely the future market price, the prognostic problem of the monopolist is more complex: rigorously, he must estimate the alignment of prices and output that comprise the market-demand curve. Whereas heretofore we assumed that the monopolist knew the market-demand curve, which was something objective and real, the market-demand curve which now obtrudes to disconcert us, is of the *ex ante*, *imagined*, or *subjective* variety. Let us see how the subjective demand curve can be formed; after the analysis of the elements involved in price predictions the ex ante demand curve is immediately comprehensible.

Even in competitive markets, where the individual firm had merely to forecast future price, if the estimate was thorough, endeavoring to include and decompose all the future price determining facts, the firm would have to assay both market demand and supply factors, including in the latter the outputs of all fellow producers. Normally, in competitive markets there will not be the need for such a detailed survey: extrapolating prices in the past, modified in the light of current and expected circumstances, may function sufficiently well as a basis for estimating the most probable price and then estimating an effective price, from which output decisions can be prepared. Under monopoly, the situation is at once different; projecting the past experience will be suitable only if the perception of change did not prey upon the monopolist's mind —that is, in stationary conditions. In conditions of expected change the firm must estimate the most probable price and, after allowing for uncertainty, the *effective* price at which it presumes it can dispose of *each* quantity of output, although it might dispense with estimates for output quantities differing substantially from its output in the recent past —the extremities of the new as well as the old demand curve.

For each output, therefore, a probability distribution of prices can be formed and the most probable price selected, reduced because of uncertainty to an effective value; it will be the latter price (the probable price minus the precautionary allowance) that will be associated with the output. Connecting the series of effective prices for each output, we can trace the locus of the subjective demand curve. Just as with competitive price, it would also be possible to predicate minima-maxima output determinacy by drawing demand curves containing the most optimistic price estimates for each output and then drawing the most pessimistic tones; the MR correspondents can be appended to each curve; the latter, with the MC curve, would depict the high-low output range. Rather than working with the single-valued subjective-demand curve we can substitute this solid demand *band* or zone of most probable high-low values; an upper and lower MR curve can then be drawn and output will be determinate within these limits. The more cautious business man would be likely to hold production towards the lower-output intersection, while the more optimistic and venturesome soul, with less of an aversion to risk and loss, or more confidence in his forecasts, will press towards the upper portion of the range. Thus the demand band will be the area between the curves D_1 and D_2 in Figure 1c. If market conditions appear to be more uncertain and unsettled, or if the entrepreneur's attitude towards the forecasts is more hesitant than before, the spread in the potential demand-zone can be widened to reflect these new facts.

The Subjective Cost Curves

After the alarming plasticity exhibited by what seemed to be a rigid, objective demand structure, it would be reassuring to learn that the cost concept remained firm and unwavering despite our excursion into the realm of subjectivism. Unfortunately this hope is also doomed. Perhaps not entirely commensurate with the demand phenomena, the cost curves nevertheless are also subjective projections and appraisals of ultimate facts which may diverge from the real manifestations. Cost experience over the full range of output will rarely be established by past operations; firms will not have at their command all the factual data relating costs and output. Hence there is ample justification for distinguishing the *expected*, *ex ante*, or *subjective* cost curve from the *actual* cost curve.

In cost analysis the probability dispersion of cost potentialities for a given output is likely to be more compressed than sales-price estimates for the same output. Usually there is some cost experience to serve as a yardstick, abstracting from the disruptions caused by radical technological innovations or important dislocations in relative factor prices which require a large reshuffle in factor use; demand forecasts, on the other hand, must encompass all the external vagaries of market purchasers and the price policies of competitors. As a rule, however, after the probable cost is estimated the forecast will be deemed to be a practically certain figure.

The Monopsonist's Cost-Curve Estimate

Normally, buyers will not have any reason to estimate the cost curve of the seller; a monopsonist, however, would have to do so. Hence, not only will the individual sellers frame their estimates of their cost curves, but the monopsonist buyer will also hold some ideas on this element of the adaptation. Under monopsony we have to distinguish between: (1) the "real" supply curve; (2) the sellers' individual estimates of it; and (3) the buyers' estimate of its course. Likewise, in some duopoly problems sellers will strive to estimate their rival's cost structure.

UNCERTAINTY AND ECONOMIC DEVELOPMENT

Digressing from the investigation of the effects of uncertainty on the demand- and cost-curve apparatus, and refraining from the use of our new information in equilibrium analyses, let us consider some of the more general influences of uncertainty on the nature and content of economic life. Uncertainty allowances will, in all real situations, undoubtedly distort the structure of production and consumption as compared to a perfectly sure world. But there are even deeper implications; to combat the uncertainty, operations, and institutions that would not exist in an economy where the future was perfectly foreseeable become commonplace when the unfolding events are obscure and unforeseeable. To enumerate, there is the use of money, the parallel existence of numerous independent firms, the place for entrepreneurial talent, speculators, Stock Exchanges, forward markets, and the like. With complete awareness of the future by all participants in the economic process, neither the functions implied, nor the institutions intimated, could subsist. Let us consider a few of them. It is superfluous to add that the list is but a partial one.*

If the future expenditure plans were known with certainty, no one would want to hold money, for it is an unprofitable cash balance; interest-yielding investments would always be sought. Money to use for discontinuous purchases out of income could also be dispensed with; goods could be shipped directly to consumers in sum exactly equivalent to their projected expenditure plan and claims could be recognized for their temporary or permanent savings. The circulation of money would be unnecessary under this idyllic scheme.

The entrepreneur has traditionally been associated with the function of risk bearing. But risk arises only in a world of uncertainty. Likewise, the separate and independent existence of firms can be explained only by reference to the world of change whose future dimensions are vague and conjectural; giant amalgamations would be more pervasive and would probably be unobjectionable because of their susceptibility to regulatory control under full foresight of the future. Speculative markets are indubitably linked with the reality of change and risk, the by-product of uncertainty; speculation would disappear, for it would be without purpose if the future were known—speculation and certainty being mutually contradictory terms. Contracts that transfer future claims could be entered into at the full future price, discounted only at

---

* It is fascinating to contemplate political or social institutions in a perfectly certain world. Policemen would be needed only at the moment of crime, firemen only at the time of fire; laws could be more pointed to cover precisely the specific objectionable future occurrence, etc. The mere knowledge of future developments would not always be sufficient to prevent antisocial outbreaks, for some of them may not be amenable to advance control.

the going interest rate in a known environment; there would be no uncertainty as to the probability of fulfillment of the contract, and no need for hedging or shifting the risk to others. Interest rates would depend solely upon the rate of time preference in the world of perfect certainty; liquidity preference phenomena, representing the demand to hold money for precautionary and speculative motives, would likewise dissolve under stationary circumstances.*

Certainty Seeking and Disproportionate Development

Turning from institutions to individuals, the proposition that uncertainty will color choice is irrefutable. Well-being might be permanently constrained by the reluctance of consumers to experiment and purchase new-fangled substitutes that, if tried, might improve their real-income position. Like consequences ensue when individuals decide to postpone consumption on the grounds of an uncertain future and yet the future continues uncertain. Limitation in the span of human life may make consumption and enjoyment ultimately impossible, while, by a subsequent fortuitous twist, future events may make a mockery of all the years of denial; hindsight would have told us that these events were inevitable. Production plans must be flexible in the face of unforseeable contingencies. Economy in a certain world, or on an ex post view, would require that they be rigid and precise, directed to definite events. Whereas capital equipment would probably be more widely adopted under known conditions, labor will be substituted for machinery when uncertainty preponderates, when price and output fluctuations are expected downward as well as upward. Exceptions would be found among those individuals who, blinded by optimism and heedless of cost, go on building monuments to themselves in the way of capital projects; some overexpansion thus supplies a compensating tendency despite the pessimism that uncertainty usually breeds. The fact of uncertainty thus affects the exact content of consumption, prices, and production in the unfolding equilibria.

Unproductive Labor

An incidental effect of uncertainty, as remarked, is the creation of a professional body of speculators and a retinue of clerks and legal aids, whose functions would dissolve in the certain economy; on these grounds, they can be labeled unproductive in a way that agents contributing to form, time, and place utility cannot be. Their services are

* See Keynes, Chapter VIII.

wanted and they perform a valuable function only in the uncertain (the real) world; so long as uncertainty is the fact it is idle to deny their usefulness or to talk of dispensing with their services.*

Incomes will, as a rule, be lower to the extent that certainty prevails in particular trades. Choosing occupations, learning trades, considering shifts, all involve future estimates. The greater the uncertainties of the future in one line, with a wide dispersion of the earning probabilities, the more attractive will be the acceptance of lower incomes in other more certain fields, all in the pursuit of security. Removal of uncertainty—to indulge for the moment in a pipe dream—would thus modify rather substantially the allocation of economic resources and the distribution of incomes. Everyday institutions and a good portion of the normal run of occupations would display a sharply altered status if knowledge of the future were increased or predictions were rendered more accurate.

Economic Insurance

Insurance plans are the usual response of our society to risk. Consequently we may well ask why insurance against uncertainty and losses cannot succeed in the economic world. There is copious evidence that it cannot, and that economic uncertainties are uninsurable risks; there is the brute fact that insurance companies have disdained to underwrite such policies.

Ostensibly, we are devoid of any actuarial basis on which to write premiums and reduce the risks to insurable certainties; the movements in the data are too irregular and incalculable. Under properly executed insurance plans the amounts collected would have to be just large enough to absorb the losses sustained. In the economic process the actuarial imponderables are too numerous and the movements too haphazard to be intelligently charted or foreshadowed.† Laws governing changes of taste or changes of inventive, legislative, and productive resources have yet to be discovered and reduced to precise mathematical formulas. Furthermore, an insurance scheme would be utterly impracticable in a world of recurring boom and depression. During the boom, profits are general and premiums ought exceed any insurance payments.

---

* Davenport, *Economics of Enterprise*, Chapter IX is recommended reading for some unusually pithy remarks on productivity in our economic world.

† This is not to be construed as a rejection of health, old-age, or unemployment insurance. In great part no thorough actuarial base is ascribed to these plans and their problems are not comparable to those that would be encountered in insuring entrepreneurs against losses.

Depression, however, cannot be accurately predicted in amplitude and duration. It is fantastic to expect that a balanced collection of premiums to cover the general losses could be made; if accurate forecasts of aggregate depression losses were possible, we could take more intelligent action to avert these social catastrophes, obviating the very need for the insurance.

It is fortunate that such insurance is impossible. Compensating firms for losses would lead to uneconomical output; entrepreneurs would have less incentive to keep costs down and to predict the future accurately; the entrepreneur would have scant reason to prepare output in the quantities and types wanted by consumers for the insurance would (largely) protect him from losses, while larger profits would tend to be partly dissipated in paying premiums. A system of resource organization that succeeded in freezing output or relieving the pressure on entrepreneurs to make correct decisions on output types and quantities would be almost indefensible; the very backbone of the private-enterprise economy is the element of risk and the social advantages when risk is borne by the more venturesome spirits in the community who are willing and able to assume it.

BIBLIOGRAPHICAL NOTE

The following literature on uncertainty, as distinct from anticipations, may be consulted: A. C. Pigou, *Economics of Welfare*, Appendix A, 4th edition; J. R. Hicks, "The Theory of Uncertainty and Profit," *Economica* (1931); H. Makower and J. Marschak, "Assets, Prices and Monetary Theory," *Economica* (1938); J. Marschak, "Money and the Theory of Assets," *Econometrica* (1938); P. Rosenstein-Rodan, "On The Role of Time in Economic Theory," *Economica* (1934); O. Lange, *Price Flexibility and Employment*, Chapter VI; A. G. Hart, *Anticipations, Uncertainty, and Dynamic Planning*, Chapter IV; and "Risk, Uncertainty, and the Unprofitability of Compounding Probabilities," in *Studies in Mathematical Economics and Econometrics* (In Memory of Henry Schultz); G. Tintner, "The Theory of Production Under Non-Static Conditions," *Journal of Political Economy* (1942), and "A Contribution to the Non-Static Theory of Choice," *Quarterly Journal of Economics* (1942).

The indifference technique of reducing uncertain values to equivalent certain sums is elaborated in Lange, *Price Flexibility*, p. 31. A. G. Hart is critical of endeavors to substitute certain values for the vague and hazy expectations of the businessman, contending that, with uncertainty, behavior does not have any simple, *certain* counterpart. See his *Anticipa-*

tions, Chapter IV. Chapter IX of his *Money, Debt, and Economic Activity* iş also informative.

Mr. Kaldor appears to have been the first one to distinguish, at least in an emphatic way, the subjective demand curve in a review article in *Economica* (1934), pp. 340–341. There is a careful discussion of the subjective curves, as well as remarks germane to uncertainty theory proper, in A. J. Nichol, "Probability Analysis in the Theory of Demand, Net Revenue, and Price," *Journal of Political Economy* (1941), and "Production and Probabilities of Cost," *Quarterly Journal of Economics* (1942). Further references on this literature, as well as the equilibrium implications, are contained in my article on "Demand Anticipations and Monopoly Equilibrium," *Journal of Political Economy* (1942).

Adam Smith is still fresh reading on the effect of uncertainty on the choice of an occupation. (*The Wealth of Nations* [Cannan ed.], Vol. I, Bk I, Chapter X.) A modern expression of the social conflict between uncertainty and security is A. G. B. Fisher's *The Clash of Progress and Security*. Lastly, on all these topics, and offering stimulating if hard reading, there is F. H. Knight's exemplary dissertation on *Risk, Uncertainty, and Profit*.

CHAPTER 16

Imperfect Equilibrium Adaptations

THE EQUILIBRIUM ANALYSES OF
the firm were predicated on the supposition that the firm knew the pertinent facts on price, or demand, and costs.   The disclosures of the preceding chapter, however, threaten to undermine the whole system of thought along with the conclusions reached via the conventional fiction of full knowledge.   When it is anticipations that provide the urge to output, the maximum position of a firm viewed prospectively may diverge seriously from the maximum position viewed retrospectively, either with full or improved knowledge.   It becomes important, therefore, to investigate the possible equilibrium configurations when output plans are prepared in advance and are guided by anticipations even in fundamentally stationary conditions, where the knowledge of constancy is denied to the planning subjects so that their policies are open to error. Besides the departures from the objective ex post maximum position caused by uncertainty, the same factor, we can surmise, attends the selection and installation of the plant layout of the firm.   It will thus be convenient to include in this chapter an analysis of the consequences of imperfect knowledge on the long-run profit position and on the size of the firm.

COMPATIBLE ANTICIPATIONS

We consider first some possible deviations from the real maximum position because of imperfect estimations by the firm of price, demand, or costs.   For the consumer the preceding chapter demonstrated that the maximum *real* position, as discovered by a retrospective glance at the relevant facts, could be achieved either by: (1) full knowledge of the data; (2) by a fortuitous coincidence of the estimated indifference system and prices (both reduced by uncertainty allowances) and the actual indifference and price state at the maximum satisfaction position of the latter; (3) errors in prognosticating both tastes and prices that induce, nevertheless, the same purchase intake as with full knowledge. Whatever the data conditioning the purchase decision, and however many the errors betrayed by the unfolding market facts, as the purchase intake in all these circumstances corresponds to the maximum-purchase plan with full knowledge, it can persist without revision, even as knowledge progresses, so long as the determining conditions are expected to remain unchanged.

Similarly, let us diagnose the conditions of compatibility between the entrepreneurial sales program calculated to maximize profits and the market facts that would permit an equilibrium adaptation, devoid of tendencies to change, despite erroneous ideas on demand and cost facts. Monoply markets are dealt with first.

Demand Anticipations Compatible with Equilibrium

Ignoring for the moment the cost curves, and postulating that a subjective demand curve is fixed in the entrepreneurial mind, let us consider the equilibrium possibilities between expected sales and the actual sales at the intended price. The point to emphasize is that unless expectations are realized the production rate will not be maintained even without further changes in the supply or demand schedules. The congruence of estimates and unfolding facts is indispensable to an unvarying equilibrium continuum through time.

Firstly, if the subjective demand curve is an accurate projection of the real market curve, the problem dissolves: this possibility deserves mention solely for expositional completeness. The equilibrium is fully determinate and will continue through time, excluding only the usual dynamic changes in data. All the ordinary propositions of monopoly theory apply without modification.

Secondly, we can envisage the real market-demand curve as tangential to the subjective demand curve at the point of prospective maximum monopoly revenue. Here, to the undiscerning eye of the monopolist seller, the actual sales at the planned equilibrium price will coincide with the expected sales; this equilibrium position can also be maintained through time despite the erroneous image of the full course of the market-demand curve. Propositions derived from an uncorrected comparison of monopoly and competitive output, where both are presumed to rest on the real objective manifestations, would however have to be amended.

Next, suppose the subjective demand curve *intersects* the real market demand curve at the output which, ex ante, has been deemed most profitable. That is to say, both demand curves cross at the output at which the anticipated net revenue was calculated to be a maximum.* Although the resulting equilibrium is unlikely to be the one that would prevail with full foresight, it is perfectly determinate because the planned adaptations are compatible with the real conditions. The adaptation can endure unless entrepreneurial views waver or the market-demand curve alters.

Cost Compatibility

Provision must now be made for the influence of the estimated and the actual costs on the equilibrium adaptation; the prices announced, outputs prepared, and sales planned will result from the subjective views of demand and cost: the output level will be pushed to the point where the expected *MR* equals the expected *MC*. Stipulating either (1) the coincidence of the real and expected demand curves, or (2) the tangency of the two demand curves at the demand price envisaged by the ex ante views, or (3) intersection of the two demand curves at the same critical point, then market demand will be fully consistent with the price and production plan, and on appraising his own market conduct the entrepreneur will congratulate himself in the thought that his predictions were correct.

Now let us examine the situations in which the expected cost situation will be compatible with the actual cost results; for when the real cost facts are divulged they may diverge from the advance estimates. To begin with, in the fairly trivial cases of identity and tangency of subjective and actual *total-* (and *average-*) cost curves, the real and imagined *MC* points are also identical. Briefly, for the equilibrium the subjective *MC* curve must cut the subjective *MR* curve at an output where not only the actual and imagined demand (or total revenue) curves intersect, but also where the estimated *average-* (or total-) cost curve cuts the actual *average-* (or total-) cost curve. This is the full condition of subjective and objective compatibility and continuing equilibrium in stationary real conditions; unless it is fulfilled a revision in price and output will be in order. Examining his total cost outlay for the completed output, the entrepreneur would observe that it differed from what he expected, indicating that marginal costs were wrongly

---

* For costless output the intersection would have to occur at the output at which the anticipated marginal revenue is zero.

computed ex ante. The belief that plans were correct could be confirmed only when the subjective and actual average-cost curves coincided at the planned output, simultaneously with the equality of estimated and actual demand points; the facts would then corroborate the entrepreneur's advance calculations and delude him into thinking that it would be unnecessary to reconsider costs or to rearrange price and output policy.

If the estimated and actual AC equality is satisfied through time at the planned output, the cost-curve pair could diverge only through the rest of their length by virtue of miscalculations of input-output relations, for cost curves are a resultant of the dual forces of factor prices and factor productivity. A disparity between the estimated and the actual factor prices would soon be detected and inspire its own corrective; an inaccurate assessment of factor productivity could be concealed for a long time. Hence any discrepancy between the cost curves must originate in this source.

Although erroneous demand anticipations may be compatible with equilibrium in monopoly markets, under competition the anticipated price must be the ultimate market price; for in shaping his output decision the individual producer will equate estimates of MC and P and, if the actual events disclose the falsity of the original forecast, a review of output policy is inevitable. As the competitive firm, just as the monopoly firm, must prejudge the full course of its cost curve, opportunities for miscalculation abound here: if the actual AC is equal to the expected AC at the output at which expected MC equals both actual *and* expected P, then any suspicion of error in the forecast will be dispelled. Confused ideas on the full course of the TC or AC curves may persist for a long time and yet be consistent with equilibrium in competitive markets, so long as actual and expected AC coincide at the output chosen for the ex ante maximum adaptation.

Monopsony Markets

The analysis can be extended to encompass monopsony markets. The monopsonist's offer price will be contingent upon the subjective demand curve image which, in consumer markets, is itself a function of the estimated supply curve.* If at the output at which the subjective $D_x = MSP_x$, the actual and estimated S curves either merge, are tangent, or intersect, then the monopsonist's offer price will be fully compatible with equilibrium, in the sense that the amount of the product

* See above, pp. 254–255.

or factor forthcoming for sale at the monopsony price will be exactly the quantity anticipated. This situation can endure until either the actual supply phenomena change or estimates, income, or tastes of the monopsonist change.

Stable Equilibria

Apparently a determinate equilibrium may evolve despite erroneous ideas on the full course of the demand or cost curves. Pushing this inquiry a step further it is instructive to outline the conditions under which this balance will be stable. Stability, it will be remembered, refers to the question of whether or not a slight departure from the equilibrium adjustment evokes forces to restore the original balance.*

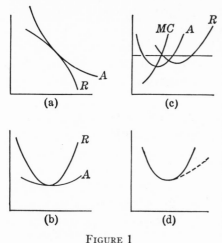

FIGURE 1

The problem may be envisaged in the following way. Suppose the monopolist produces, by accident or design, a little more or a little less than the ex ante amount which, by virtue of the subjective and objective curve relations, and as revealed by experience, are known to be compatible with equilibrium. In order that the seller revert back to the compatible adjustment, and to discourage further experiments with price and output, the anticipated revenue for the greater (or smaller) quantity must exceed the actual receipts; the disappointment will presumably hasten a retreat to the safety of the known equilibrium position. The compatible adjustment could then be described as a truly stable one. From the standpoint of costs, the contrary must be true for stability; realized costs must exceed those contemplated prospectively. In terms of the full curves, whether output accidentally falls below or progresses beyond the adjustment compatible with equilibrium, for complete stability the realized demand curve must lie underneath the anticipated one; similarly, the realized cost curve must stand above the estimated curve. Consequently for real linear curves and subjective demand curves that intersect one another at the output where the imaginary MR and MC are equal, stability on the demand side is to be

* Chapter 5.

found only on one side, *but not on both sides*, of the demand-curve intersection. Full stability, apart from irregularly shaped demand curves, would devolve only from the juxtaposition of a convex anticipated, and concave realized, demand-curve combination tangent at the ex ante equilibrium demand price, as in Figure 1a, where A refers to the anticipated demand curve and R, to the realized or market curve.

Normally, if the real and imaginary cost curves intersect at the subjective equilibrium output, one average-cost curve will lie above the other at one side of the initial equilibrium position, but not at the other. For U-shaped curves, however, if the realized curve is more tightly constricted than the anticipated cost curve, as in Figure 1b, with the two curves tangent at the ex ante equilibrium adjustment, then the equilibrium will be fully stable for output movements in both directions.

Incomplete stability will predominate when only cost curves or demand curves, but not both, satisfy the stability criteria. If the anticipated demand curve lies above the actual one for an output beyond the equilibrium, while the actual cost curve is lower than the expected cost curve, it is the cost-curve relationship that exercises a destabilizing influence. Whether the monopolist would prefer the new position or revert to the old would turn upon whether a comparison of the wholesome cost facts outweighed the ominous demand tidings. Over a longer period, however, even though the initial price-output position may be temporarily stable because of the losses occasioned by the accidental expansory adaptation, once the monopolist apprehends that his original views on either cost or revenue are erroneous, then demand and cost recalculation and price experimentation at a later date are an extremely likely development.

A Symbolic Statement

The argument of this chapter can be recapitulated and restated more concisely in symbolic form; a few equalities and inequalities are all that is necessary. The abbreviations MC and MR, AC and D, TR and TC, retain their usual meanings; the appended subscript a always refers to an anticipated value and r to a realized value. The main propositions follow.

(1) The firm's production volume and price policy are based upon the equality $MC_a = MR_a$. The maximization problem of the firm is resolved subjectively. It is anticipations that activate the output and price decisions.

(2) For the planned price and output adjustment to be compatible

with the actual data and continuing stationary equilibrium, when the data are constant, the relations that must be satisfied are

$$D_a = D_r \quad \text{and} \quad P_a = P_r \tag{a}$$
$$\text{(under monopoly)} \qquad \text{(under competition)}$$

and

$$AC_a = AC_r. \tag{b}$$

Or, alternately,

$$TR_a = TR_r, \tag{a}$$

and

$$TC_a = TC_r. \tag{b}$$

(3) For the equilibrium to be not only determinate but also stable in monopoly, the following relations must hold for a slight increase (or decrease) in output:

$$D_a > D_r, \tag{a}$$

and

$$AC_a < AC_r, \tag{b}$$

or

$$\frac{D_a}{D_r} > 1$$

and

$$\frac{AC_a}{AC_r} < 1.$$

If but one of the latter stability conditions is satisfied, the test of whether the equilibrium is temporarily stable will depend on whether

$$D_a - D_r \gtreqless AC_a - AC_r,$$

with the understanding that $D_a - D_r > 0$ implies unexpected losses and $AC_a - AC_r > 0$ indicates unexpected profits.

Hence, although it will be anticipations that guide the firm in its maximization endeavors, its program must be reconciled (in the way stipulated) with external events if a continuing equilibrium devoid of tendencies for change in either prices or outputs is to evolve, when both anticipated views and the real price-determining data are inflexible.

INCOMPATIBILITY OF PLANS AND EVENTS

The analysis demonstrates that an equilibrium may be achieved in immanently stationary real conditions despite imperfect knowledge of the full course of the actual demand and cost curves; the conditions of compatibility of plans and events for the individual firm are less stringent than a complete coincidence of subjective and objective schedules. The firm may go on uncritically in the conviction that its prognostications are accurate so long as the actual average-revenue and average-cost curves synchronize with their subjective counterparts at the planned output, which also becomes the actual output. It is interesting to ponder upon the outcome in those contingencies in which the planned sales and output prove to be inconsistent with the quantity wanted at the announced price.

Outputs Incompatible with Equilibrium

When the entrepreneur perceives that his views are in error, he will of course be pressed to revise his ideas on his future market plan. Recalling the earlier discussion of stable equilibria under competition, perhaps we can write that as the ratios D_r/D_a and AC_r/AC_a deviate from a value of unity, then in each period of time $\Delta P/\Delta t > 0$, with ΔP itself depending upon the magnitude of the error, and whether the error is an unpleasant shock or pleasant surprise. Often, however, if the seller is pleasantly surprised by sales exceeding estimates at the price named, what may happen is that, instead of a price rise occurring, inventory (if available) will function as the shock absorber, being worked off in the interim pending the correction of the original sales ideas through a combined price rise and expanded output. Temporarily, in any event, there is an income loss to the seller because of the mistaken judgment; earnings will fall short of the maximum potential and buyers will reap the income benefits of the lower price. Ultimately, only when the prospective views are fused with the real demand facts, either by identity, tangency, or intersection, will the planned output have any chance of enduring. The conclusion is essentially the same when anticipations turn out to be erroneous because expected sales at the announced price were on the optimistic side; inventory will accumulate until the original price policy is corrected and a landing somehow made onto the actual demand curve.

When flaws are detected in the original cost calculations, a similar train of events will be set in motion. When costs have been overestimated, actions to expand output will provide the corrective; when cost estimates are shown to have been understated, the output level will contract. In general when estimates are contradicted by events the planned output and price policy will have to be revised; changes in plans will occur until a reconciliation of estimates and facts is established. It is futile to attempt to portray the process and path of adjustment because the problem is overly determinate in the sense that there are all sorts of possibilities.   Moreover, it is impossible to foretell the length of time and the number of successive trials before an equilibrium balance is attained.   With stationary real conditions, each market price and output trial of the monopolist conveys information on the real demand and actual cost situation; as knowledge of the data thus improves, in the (relatively) stationary world an incompatible original position will illuminate some of the real facts and contribute to a correct reconstruction of ideas on the cost and demand curves.

It was declared that with erroneous and incompatible plans, inventory would function as the shock absorber, either accumulating or being depleted too rapidly.   But this is only one view of the contingencies; to illustrate, suppose a price was named for the planned (and actual) output which, in the light of the demand facts, was too low.   Among the possibilities, consider a situation in which inventory carry-over from the past is nil.   If the announced price is rigid, or if the cost of altering it in the short period is prohibitive,* then the error will redound to the benefit of consumers whose real income on the current output is enhanced— although really they wanted more of the good.   If the seller apprehends his folly very early in the time interval and if the costs of a price change are not excessive, price will be raised to a more lucrative figure and the initial error will become partially repaired—although profits could have been greater with larger production and better foresight.

With inventory present and price understated, where the announced price cannot be altered because of the administrative costs attached, the next question is whether to allow the inventory to run down or to ration sales out of current output among consumers.   In making this decision, expected future demand and cost will dominate policy.   Optimistic sellers will generally be reluctant to sell out of inventory; rationing of current output is the more likely policy.   When future views lean towards pessimism, the opportunity for inventory clearance will be seized.   Conversely, when unfolding events reveal that the announced price is too high, so that sales lag behind the intended rate, the output flow will be reduced if sales are roughly synchronized with production— unless future prospects warrant the inventory expansion.   If the output has been prepared in advance of sales, the problem is to decide whether to lower current price and accelerate the rate of sales, or to maintain the higher price in the light of the future demand potential.   Anticipations

* See pp. 430–432.

of the still longer future thus enter into the determination of policy; some of the relevant elements are analyzed in the following chapter.

Multivalued Expectations

Although the analysis has made provision for the subjective and anticipatory nature of the maximum adjustment of the firm, one defect of the argument is its reduction of the price and sales estimates of the entrepreneur to a single figure. It can be contended that if the firm is vague on the future then it will not make precise estimates but instead will regard demand and costs as consisting not of unique values but comprising a high-low band. It is true that output must still be single-valued, determinate at least within this range. Yet there is another possible role that may be assigned to inventories. Suppose that the entrepreneur is inclined toward pessimism but is still conscious of his fallibility. Although the price that will be named and sales that are expected fall in the lower range of the demand band, where the lowest possible MR cuts the highest possible MC curve, in the uneasy thought that he may be proven unduly depressed in his forecasts, the entrepreneur may direct that some additional production be undertaken, with the proviso that it be destined for inventory if his views on the most probable events are upheld, but that it be sold if his views should prove mistaken. Here too the inventory serves as a buffer, yet it consists of new production rather than a past carryover. However, after price is once named and sales run as fast, or faster than estimated, the firm will probably want to reconsider its announced price in view of the overt falsity of its forecasts. If the entrepreneur fears a false sense of overoptimism, provision will be made for the higher output level, with the possibility of a price reduction or inventory accumulation foreseen if the plans should prove to be wrong. Critical elements in this analysis are thus the length of the time period of sales for which the output is prepared, the ability to alter an announced price and the costs of carrying inventory. Unless market conditions are subject to wide and rapid fluctuations, however, each market effort of the firm ought to yield new and better information, tending toward single-valued demand and cost projections.

ACTUAL AND OPTIMAL OUTPUT

There are some important price and output implications in this analysis. First, consider errors in anticipations, with all firms overoptimistic and producing in excess of the output flow that would prevail under better foresight.   As disappointment will be the common lot, the output and employment position will not be maintained through time.   If all views have been unduly pessimistic, a later expansion will be the upshot despite the immanently stationary real conditions.   Normally, the views of individual producers will not lean preponderantly in the one direction or the other, but if there is an "average" tendency that can be isolated, these conclusions will be substantially correct.   If equilibrium is to exist in the stationary economy, the expected and actual facts on prices, sales, and costs must synchronize.   The harmony should in time be accomplished as clearer ideas on the market are uncovered, unless in the very process of equilibrating the shift of income to or from producers because of price miscalculations, and the demands of entrepreneurs for capital equipment engendered by the errors, push the equilibrium inherent in the initial data beyond recall; by modifying the income and equipment data a new and different equilibrium becomes implicit.

Coincidence of Estimates and Facts

That a stationary equilibrium may perpetuate itself even without fully correct ideas on demand or costs implies that the actual price and output adjustment, though compatible with the real facts, may diverge from the maximum position that would obtain under perfect foresight. Let us consider the implications of this proposition.

To begin with competitive firms, while price anticipations had to be correct to prevent output revision, the adjustment could continue through time so long as $AC_a = AC_r$ despite muddled ideas on the full course of the AC_r curve.   Suppose the two curves resemble those in Figure 1c, with the actual output confined to their intersection.   Assuming that the AC_a curve is the one to the left, indicating some innate caution and conservatism at the bottom of the mistaken cost calculations, more enlightened views would promote an output expansion.   If the same phenomena affect all the firms in the competitive field, output would be repressed much below the real maximum, while price would be higher than necessary.   Contrariwise, if it is the AC_r curve that lies closer to OY, then the overoptimism and the misinformation on cost data would foster greater output and lower prices than with fuller knowledge.

Under monopoly the equalities $D_a = D_r$ and $AC_a = AC_r$ may be on either side of the real monopoly maximum position so that the actual output is indeterminate relative to the real maximum $MC_r = MR_r$ position: a priori there is no reason why the errors should lean one way or the other.   Wherever the actual output falls, the effects of monopoly on the economic system will depend upon a comparison of the actual output and the real competitive output, and not on a comparison of the real monopoly maximum under perfect foresight and the real competitive output.

Part of the answer on the likely direction of error will be contingent upon the monopolist's attitude toward production. If despite the monopoly power he is disposed to be a large producer, with an urge to lead a "big" producing firm, the actual output is likely to advance toward the competitive optimal. Where the monopolist prefers to live a small and peaceful business life, the output level ought to be relatively compressed. If both types of monopoly personalities enjoy decision-making authority in the real world, so that some surpass the real monopoly maximum output and others fail to approach it, then the level of employment, if not the composition of output, ought to correspond approximately to the monopoly level so that employment propositions that derive their support from monopoly and full-knowledge hypotheses for the full system may be largely unimpaired. With the mistakes falling in one direction or the other, then the usual conclusions on the actual effects of monopoly have to be corrected upon the recognition of imperfect foresight.

Ex Ante Plans and Economic Well-Being

The conclusion that miscalculations compatible with equilibrium may push monopoly output closer to the competitive $MC_r = P_r$ output than heretofore suspected is hardly to be construed as a defense of monopoly. Nor should it foster complacency on the ground that little damage is wrought upon the structure by monopoly domination: such a conclusion does not follow. So long as man is committed to ex ante judgments and decisions, and fallibility and imperfect foresight mark the human lot, the crucial issue is one of *intent*—the output planned and executed as compared to the policy that an optimal adaptation would condone. Measured by this standard, the monopoly-price practice does restrain outputs in which it prevails as compared to a competitive motivation in the sense of a conscious effort to equate P_a and MC_a. If the firm sought to equate $P_a = MC_a$, then, with the same anticipatory bases, particular outputs would undoubtedly be greater. In the light of the respective ex ante urges and objectives the usual criticisms of monopoly behavior retain their force even though fortuitously, rather than for any reason that reflects credit on the monopolist, the monopoly decision may actually correspond more closely with the real competitive facts. But just as this may happen, the reverse may also be true: the actual monopoly output curtailment may drive the adaptation further from the real competitive level. It would be irrational to advocate actions that on a forward-looking view are deprecated just because occasionally and accidentally they may achieve the desired ends.

UNCERTAINTY AND PLANT LAYOUT

It would be possible to deduce similar relations of compatibility between estimates of the planning curve and demand facts and the real planning curve and the real demand curve. But this analysis is of limited scope, for after the equipment is once chosen and installed, if an error in anticipatory calculations is disclosed it is the analysis surrounding that of a definite layout that is applicable rather than one running in terms of the planning curve. Let us, therefore, deflect the analysis slightly and consider the influence of uncertainty on the scale of plant chosen. In an earlier passage it was argued that if economic changes were expected in either market price or demand, then the entrepreneur would erect a plant that, while not least costly at any one output level, was flexible enough to involve lowest average costs over a wider output range than more specialized layouts. But this analysis presumed that the entrepreneur merely anticipated the change and then acted with full certitude, as if the very fact of expectations of market change did not create some uneasiness and disquietude over the question of the right plant to erect. Contemplating that the new firm will require financing, normally neither entrepreneurial borrowers nor lenders will display such calmness and confidence in an uncertain future; the uncertainty will color the choice of layout in devious ways.

Lenders' Risk

Whatever the prospects of a business, the very fact of uncertainty will compel lenders to exact a higher rate of interest on loans for the *same* expectation than they would require if the future were an open book, transparent to all, with the expectation elevated to the status of a certainty. In itself this interest-rate factor will elevate the full ACP curve. If all AC curves subsumed in the ACP curve were lifted proportionately, it probably would not affect the choice of the particular layout installed. However the vagaries of the capital markets are such that for relatively small sums interest charges are severe, declining somewhat as borrowings grow, and then rising as sums requested exceed conventional levels and the variety of securities offered lenders multiplies. If this is the typical capital market situation, it should work to pinch the *ACP* curve somewhat, to push both extremities closer together while lifting the course of the entire curve. Because of lenders' risk, therefore, the plant layout is likely to assume dimensions different from those it would take in a more certain world.

Moreover, some firms may learn that the sums open to them are "rationed"; although we could draw the usual array of U-curves corresponding to the diverse technical installations, the maximum sum at the firm's command will limit the layouts that might be chosen, leaving the extreme right-hand portion of the planning-curve chart field blank. In Figure 1d, the heavy line is the actual *ACP* curve to the firm in view of the capital rationing, while the potential *ACP* is the broken-line extension which, because of the reluctance of lenders, is blocked to the firm.

The aversion of lenders to unlimited commitments is a less extreme illustration of the consequences when firms and individuals are unable to borrow even when they envisage an investment opportunity. Even though lenders' profit prognostications may be more accurate than borrowers', nevertheless the significant and perhaps unwholesome fact is that entry can be throttled as successfully by the refusal of finance funds to production aspirants as it can by the bleak entrepreneurial estimates of potential *ACP* and *P* relationships.*

Borrowers' Risk

Besides lenders' risk we have to allow for the borrowers' restraint and unwillingness to borrow because of the fear of default and the stigma of bankruptcy, unless it is expected that the borrowed sums can be recovered through sales revenues with some margin to spare. The entrepreneurial group may refrain from implementing their entry plans unless a "risk allowance," over and above average costs, can be earned at each output level. Hence entry may be retarded through entrepreneurial abstention from the capital markets until there is the mental assurance that the venture will cover potential costs with a surplus to spare. Although the equation of *MCP* and *MR* and the relation of *P* and *ACP* may warrant the installation, the equilibrium unit excess $(P - ACP)$ may be too narrow to overcome the entrepreneurial misgivings of a minimum "safety margin." The effect of including these sums in the *ACP* curve is to lift the full envelope upward; if the borrowers' risk allowance varies with the output, the *MCP* curve will also be affected, tending to modify the ultimate layout chosen.

As another aspect of the same class of phenomena, entrepreneurs may

---

* These very real elements have been virtually ignored despite their importance even in the most rarified accounts of the theory of entry.

forecast an excessive annual rate of depreciation as part of their capital charges that are included in the *ACP* curve. This too will have the effect of elevating the entire *ACP* curve, perhaps relatively more so in the rightward portions of the curve where a greater amount of capital equipment lies implicit. All allowances of this nature, attributable ultimately to uncertainty, will dislodge the stationary *ACP* curves elucidated earlier. The *ACP* curve is thus a highly subjective phenomenon, in large measure a creature of the mentality of the entrepreneur.

Conventional Practices, Flexibility, and Uncertainty

There are still other channels through which uncertainty will condition the choice of equipment. In practice there are all sorts of conventional criteria that have to be observed, most of which must work to raise costs, at least when they are superfluous to the operations of the business. Often, for example, it is deemed prudent to observe certain corporate-balance-sheet relations, such as the ratio of common stocks to bonds, as a matter of form. Similarly, there is the practice of placing eminent citizens on the directorate of the firm despite their ignorance of its particular affairs; also, firms often concur in common marketing arrangements or credit terms, or maintain inventory at a customary magnitude, or keep a substantial demand deposit as evidence of liquidity, etc. The cost of following these common practices will have to be appraised by the firm in advance; in contrast to the lenders' fright, if there is a departure from the conventions and rules of thumb, observing these conventions may lower the interest charges and the *ACP* curve to the firm, though not to the economy. If deviation from the conventions were possible, cost calculations might be reduced.

There are numerous other ways in which uncertainty may exert its influence even at the planning stage. To overcome lenders' risk, collateral security is often required in borrowing operations; a wealthy entrepreneur may have a substantially lowered *ACP* than a less affluent adventurer; one with more entrepreneurial talents may be without access to funds because of the paucity of his personal property rights. Elements of this sort are usually of decisive importance in deciding entry and the exact dimensions of the new layout.

THE SIZE OF FIRMS

Once we acknowledge the fact of uncertainty and the borrower's and lender's risk which it engenders, we can understand some of the forces limiting the size of the firm. Hitherto the possible divergence between the maximum size of operating plant and the size of the firm has not been labored.   A little reflection will reveal that the two phenomena are distinct; in stationary conditions the plant and firm coincide only under very special assumptions on the nature of the ACP curve.   This subject deserves to be pursued further.

The U-Shaped and Discontinuous ACP Curves

Positing a continuous U-shaped ACP curve, there are some ostensible limits to the growth of the firm: beyond the $P \geq MR = MCP$ equality, profits would fall short of maximization.   The technical diseconomies of larger scale, plus the limited demand under monopoly, would constitute valid explanations of the size of firms—at least, of firms producing a single definite commodity.   It would scarcely matter whether all equipment implicit in the ACP curve was physically located within the four walls of a plant or whether separate small plants were removed by greater or lesser geographical distances, or whether the plant contained several discrete wings.   All that would be important is that there would be a unique organization and layout created.   Hence monopoly, or technical diseconomies of scale under competition, could account for the numerous firms of the economy even under inherently stationary conditions.

In contrast, suppose the ACP curve continues to fall as the size of the productive unit grows, or (as a more tenable hypothesis) that it contains several discontinuous segments each with a minimal dip at (approximately) the same AC level.   An instance has already been furnished (Fig. 4A, p. 90) where the firm has been described as able to erect several replicas of the operating plant and where management is assumed to be able to cope efficaciously with the successive volumes of output.   Under stationary conditions this is not an unreasonable supposition; as product and factor prices are constant, and as productivity is unchanged, there are few fundamental tasks of entrepreneurship; the organizing, the exercise of judgment, the implementation of decisions, belong to a changing economy.   Of course, for monopoly the force of market demand in restricting the size of the firm is an indisputable fact. But barring technical diseconomies, we are, under competition, devoid of an explanation of the size of firms: any one firm might grow without limit and absorb all the others.

Even acknowledging the rule of monopoly as universal and as the solution to the impasse in the question of size, this argument breaks down when we recognize multiproduct firms, for then the task becomes one of explaining why firms cease adding to their product scope or commodity varieties.   Just as with the competitive case, unless some limiting factor can be stipulated the firm should steadily grow until all production comes under its wing.   Unless we concede the reality of technical diseconomies, in a stationary state the size of firms (as distinct from operating plants) is indeterminate: rather than a multitude of firms existing, any one firm could expand without limit, swallowing all others without evincing any digestive pains by way of higher costs.   Here is another disconcerting reminder of the sterility of stationary theory in explaining certain very patent facts: in this case the stationary model either admits monopoly or it is unable to explain the size of firms.

Uncertainty and the Size of the Firm

Once we transcend the rigid stationary confines, a whole host of factors can be cited as retarding the growth of firms.   One suggestion is that "personality and historical accident rather than intelligible general principles"* account for the size of firms.   Unfortunately, "personality" is as suitable a rationalization for one-firm industries as for industries with multiplicity of firms.   Moreover, if the firm is a result of historical accident and chance, it is a creature of imperfect foresight, otherwise the "accident" would not have occurred.   Emphasizing accidental factors is but a circumlocution for stressing uncertainty.

Another view, unequivocally premised upon uncertainty, contends that with the limited personal capitals of entrepreneurs they will be increasingly reluctant to borrow the sums required for expansion and personal domination of the particular industry.   For they will not wish, through selling stock, to let new equity stockholders share their current rate of profits; funded debt, on the other hand, is regarded as unsatisfactory because additional borrowing reduces the margin of safety between earnings and fixed charges, and hence any miscalculation invites bankruptcy and financial loss to present owners.†   This explanation, predicated upon uncertainty, provides scant relief to the theorist intent upon fitting the firm into the competitive stationary framework of perfect foresight; ultimately this explanation can be reduced to the inability to borrow unlimited funds at a fixed rate of interest and the uncertainties that create the fears of default.

* Knight, *Risk, Uncertainty, and Profit,* preface to the reissue edition, London School of Economics series of reprints, Scarce Tracts in Economic and Political Science (1933), p. XXI.

† M. Kalecki, "The Principle of Increasing Risk," in his *Theory of Economic Fluctuations,* pp. 95–106.

Another suggestion holds that capital rationing is the factor limiting the size of firms.* Either lenders will proffer to the firm certain definite sums and no more, or will offer larger sums only at graduated rates. Competing firms could thus enter the field, for they could procure at least a limited quantity of capital funds at lower costs than those charged to expanding firms borrowing additional capital amounts. If interest rates for greater amounts of money capital are graduated upward, the deterrent to the firm must be the lack of further technical economies to scale, for further economies could neutralize the higher capital charges. But once again the firm comes to be the product of an uncertain world: capital rationing would vanish in a world of certainty and assurance.

Either of the last two reasons, the increasing cost of funds because of borrowers' risk and the increasing cost of funds because of lenders' risk, should in most instances explain the size of firms. To these can be added actual technical diseconomies when scope is allowed for the exercise of the entrepreneurial functions of judgment and decision-taking. To illustrate: in small enterprises a frequent limitation is distrust in the ability of the available administrative personnel; there can thus be diseconomies of scale long before the firm has exhausted its borrowing facilities. In large-scale duopoly and oligopoly enterprise the stress on an alleged financial limitation is likely to miss the mark entirely; more likely is the aversion to the economic warfare and the struggle for power that would accompany further growth. The inevitable conflict after expansion will be cause for sober reflection and will temper any rash act of growth that will provoke a costly internecine struggle. Lastly, in a regime' of private property, public policy on size cannot be ignored: statutory laws may obstruct growth or the public hostility to combination may foster new legislation, impelling firms to forego the profits of combination and to abstain from tempting the legislative fates.

CHANGE AND PROFIT CALCULATIONS

It is time now to exhibit some of the implicit assumptions that all but demolish the planning-curve apparatus in handling all but stationary problems; it offers a precise version of the process of equipment selection only in highly rarified stationary circumstances where the following conditions are met: (1) the sales price or demand curve is expected to be

* A. G. Hart, *Anticipations, Uncertainty and Dynamic Planning*, Chapter III, p. 39, especially. If the firm, under perfect foresight and certainty, can borrow more, but only at higher rates, it is the imperfect lending market that limits the firm's size. In determining its borrowing volume the firm is in the position of a monopsonist.

constant through time; (2) the service life of all the equipment implicit in the planning curve is of the same duration; (3) prices of the complementary variable factors engaged for each layout remain constant through time or their alterations leave the relative position of the individual cost-curve components unaffected. Let us see the consequences of a breach in any of these stipulations.

Defects in the Planning Curve

When the market price or demand curve is expected to fluctuate from period to period, in each period there will be a different output (and implicit equipment) at which the planned MR equals MCP. For each equation apparently a different equipment will maximize earnings. Hence the ACP and MCP curves are practically useless in detailing which layout will be chosen. It will be recalled that when changing output levels was acknowledged, we resorted to the subterfuge of describing the maximum-profit U-shaped curve as being attributable to a flexible plant that is economical for both high- and low-output levels.

Similarly, if the various equipments subsumed in the planning curve have a service life of different duration, the planning curve would be misleading; it could be a satisfactory cost portrait only when the layouts maintained their relative position in the chart field through equal lengths of future time. If the planning curve is presumed to represent, say, average costs for each output level conceived as an annual rate, then if some equipments last 10 years and others 15, etc., as soon as the least durable equipment wears out, the planning curve disintegrates, because some of the individual AC curves comprising the envelope ACP vanish. Hence, the ACP curve cannot serve as a vehicle for exhibiting the layout that conforms to maximum-profit calculations—the objective for which it was designed—when some equipments last longer than others.

Finally, each layout implicit in the planning curve combines variable and fixed factors in different proportions. Consequently, a relative change in factor prices in any future period will disrupt completely the statement of cost relations implicit in the planning curve. If in the second year wage rates are expected to fall, then those equipments that hire relatively most labor promise a more severe cost reduction than other layouts that use more capital. A planning curve drawn to mirror unit costs over a per annum time interval will fail to depict the relative cost positions in year 2 even if it successfully exhibited these relations for year 1. Not uncommonly the layout most profitable when the facts of year 1 prevail is seldom the maximum plant in the cost circumstances of year 2.

Arithmetical Calculations

As the planning curve offers an outline of some basic relations only with stationary phenomena, we are driven inexorably to perform laborious arithmetic profit calculations for each layout and, thereafter, to compare the ultimate profit prospects of each.

Drawing our time periods to encompass periods of constant demand, factor costs, and productivity phenomena, and including in each period's cost calculations both variable and fixed costs, it is possible to compute the current value of each period's surplus (S) of receipts over the current value of its costs and summate these differences. Thus for layout 1, the current value of these surpluses will be

$$S_c = S_1 + S_2 \cdots + S_n.^*$$

Performing these calculations for layout 2 and for each layout, and in each time interval planning to equate $MC = MR$, we find that there will generally be one plant that promises most profits. With complete subjective certainty, and with ready access to the requisite funds for its installation, the entrepreneur would order that this layout be constructed—provided the person of the entrepreneur could be located and imbued with a profit-maximization conviction. With uncertainty present, especially when the "entrepreneur" consists of a promotional group sponsoring the firm and anxious to demonstrate the profitability of the business prior to the sale of their investment holdings, if the most profitable layout amasses most of its earnings toward the close of the period (instead of the plant being extremely profitable in the early years) this is likely to be a force militating against the layout's adoption. The shape of the prospective profit stream may thus be highly important, whereas with complete certitude and access to loan markets one time-stream of income can always be converted into another by appropriate borrowing and lending operations.† Recognizing all these contingencies, we find that one plant will appear best—perhaps because of its flexibility in being diverted to an alternative use if planning errors are disclosed; perhaps because of the greater certitude of its cost elements; perhaps because of limitations of finance; or perhaps because financing groups entertain views on the correct scale of layout through their abil-

---

* The final surplus S_n, rather than representing a sales-receipt-production-outlay difference, may represent the ultimate scrap value of the equipment.

† I. Fisher, *The Theory of Interest*, Chapter V.

ity to sell one volume of securities more readily than another. The plant that satisfies these many requirements will ultimately be ordered.

BIBLIOGRAPHICAL NOTE

Although the subjective demand and cost curves are widely recognized today as instrumental in the firm's maximization decision, there is almost no material dealing with the conditions of compatibility between subjective elements and external events that can culminate in stationary equilibrium. As one contribution on the subject, there is R. H. Coase's "Some Notes on Monopoly Price," *Review of Economic Studies* (1937). My article on "Demand Anticipations and Monopoly Equilibrium," *Journal of Political Economy* (1942) is an attempt to deal with this problem on the lines of the first portion of this chapter.

The influence of both borrowers' *and* lenders' risk on capital growth was stressed by Keynes, *General Theory*, pp. 144–145. On the size of firms, besides the articles alluded to in the chapter, there is the closely reasoned article of N. Kaldor, "The Equilibrium of the Firm," *Economic Journal* (1934). The refusal to study the rules of thumb and arbitrary criteria often erected by capital markets, which have implications for the size of firms, constitutes an evident shortcoming of economic theory. A. G. Hart has done a great deal to close the gap in his *Anticipations, Uncertainty, and Dynamic Planning*. Another admirable attempt to synthesize the facts of capital markets and the hypotheses of economic theory is N. Buchanan, *Economics of Corporate Enterprise*. The relationship between income streams, and a frank and explicit statement of the assumption of a firm able to borrow unlimited amounts of funds, is found in the lucid and brilliant volume of Irving Fisher, *The Theory of Interest*.

CHAPTER 17

Multiple-Period Anticipations

ALTHOUGH THE COMPELLING FORCE of anticipations has been acknowledged, we have assumed that the purview of the economic participants extends only to the time interval in which transactions are consummated. That is, if the firm launched its production program in January (time period t_0, say) with the aim of selling in February (t_1), its forecasts extended solely to t_1, forsaking a longer outlook. The mere recital of the hypothesis conveys its defects; it is imperative to remedy the omission and proffer some account of how views on the longer future affect present events. For just as the immediate market events are anticipated, there will be some notions, obscure and hazy though they be, on the longer trend of events.

Inscribing the period in which the firm's (or buyer's) plans are made as t_0—where t_0 lies in advance of market events—and t_1 as the period towards which the plans are directed, we want to examine the influence on markets in t_1 of expectations held in t_0 of events of periods t_2, t_3, t_4 $\cdots$. Until the following chapter, however, we continue to be vague and evasive as to the length of a time interval.

Our economic subjects will be described as "discounting future values"; the concept has already been employed several times. In the discussion of uncertainty the vague uncertain values were *discounted;* because of the uncertainty the economic subjects were willing to accept in its stead a lower certain value. In temporal analyses the term recurs even more frequently; it refers to the fact that a dollar obtainable in the future is not the equivalent of a dollar currently on hand, because a current dollar, due to the operation of the rate of interest, automatically grows into a larger sum in the future. If the rate of interest is five per cent, $1 today is the equivalent of $1.05 a year from date. Hence, if the expectation is of the receipt of $1.05 a year hence, its present value or the *discounted future value*—the indifference relation between present

375

and future sums—will be $1. If we write S as the future sum, r as the rate of interest (assuming interest compounded but once annually), and n as the number of years in the future that must elapse before S is received, then V, the current value of the accruing sum, is given by the equation

$$V = \frac{S}{(1 + r)^n}$$

The higher the rate of interest, and the more distant the receipt of S, the greater the absolute amount of discount. At a low rate of interest, and with n approaching zero, V and S become equal.

CONSUMER PLANS AND EXPECTED PRICE CHANGES

A full treatment of the time aspects of consumer expenditure is not intended, for it would plunge us too deeply into the theory of savings—a recondite and conjectural subject in which the strength of the rate of interest and the purely rational motives in accumulation and decumulation are obscure. Our remarks cover only some temporal price influences affecting the current purchase scheme and, perforce, the immediate volume of savings.

Expected Price Changes

Let us postulate that price changes are expected between t_1 and t_2, with the income stream constant. Writing P_1 and P_2 for the expected prices of commodity X, in t_1 and t_2 respectively, where P_1 is also the price that materializes, let us suppose first that $P_1 > P_2$. If the individual is completely indifferent about the date of consumption, all purchases of X will be deferred until t_2. When the goods are regarded as imperfect substitutes by virtue of the discrepancy in their time availability, we can mark off the indifference relations by plotting X_2 on the horizontal axis and X_1 on the vertical axis. Disregarding all thoughts of the future (t_2), with P_1 known the allocation of expenditure to X_1 is determinate. A price line can then be drawn, emanating from the fixed money sum on OY, signifying its availability for expenditure in t_1 or t_2: the tangency of this price line and the indifference system will disclose the relevant purchase intake in t_1 together with the rational saving in t_1 for expenditure in t_2. The equilibrium condition is (as always) between relative prices and the MRS between the substitute, though physically identical, goods available at the different dates. If the curves are convex and flat, almost horizontal, then X_2 is a limited substitute for X_1 and a lower P_2

hardly dents current consumption; with a convex but vertical curve system, there would be a more marked purchase postponement.

Conversely, when the opinion is that $P_1 < P_2$, the individual will endeavor to hasten all purchases, to buy in t_1 all the quantities that will normally be consumed in $t_2, t_3 \cdot \cdot \cdot$, etc., even borrowing money for the purpose. If the price was expected to rise in t_2 the consumer might even emerge as a speculator in the good, not only buying for personal inventory but for eventual resale. Crucial in this decision are (1) the degree of perishability of the product, which is generally equivalent to the cost of storage; (2) the uncertainty of the expectation; (3) the amount of finance; and (4) the rate of interest. If the latter is high enough it could offset any saving incurred by current purchase compared to future purchase at the expected higher price: it would render the lending of money more profitable than the holding of goods.

This is probably as far as we need go. The conclusion, amenable to common sense, is that an expected price rise in t_2 will hasten purchases while an expected price fall will presage some deferment of demand. The substitutionary effect will be especially strong when consumers are indifferent to the time dimensions of consumption. Insofar as a consensus of views one way or the other prevails in the market, prices in t_1 will reflect the expectations of $t_2, t_3 \cdot \cdot \cdot$, etc. After the decision to speed or postpone purchases are framed and executed in t_1, behavior and prices in t_2 will inevitably be influenced by these earlier decisions—especially as deferment originally begun in t_1, say, becomes an ordeal so that purchases can no longer be delayed; if purchases were already postponed from t_1 to t_2 and later to t_3, the t_3 demand may become largely independent of, say, $t_4, t_5 \cdot \cdot \cdot$, etc. expectations, despite a belief in even a precipitate price drop. As the postponement interval lengthens the potency of future expectations wanes.

Income Streams

Just as prices may be expected to vary in time, estimates made by individuals of their flow of income will contract or grow. Suppose it is surmised that $I_2 > I_1$ and, for the individual's optimum consumption plan, it is desired roughly to equalize consumption through time. Here, if possible, the individual will borrow so long as the anticipated increase in current well-being exceeds the future deduction. The purchase plan then hinges on the expected income stream, the optimum-consumption scheme, the relative price movements between periods, and the rate of interest. When the optimum-consumption plan tends toward equal purchases through time, while income is expected to grow, with prices constant and interest rates fairly unimportant, borrowing will be the typical response.   When high income is expected in the near future but later regarded as likely to taper off, current savings and lending at interest will appear as a rational twist to give to the time dimension of the income flow.   If views were so unanimous that all consumers expected a future in which *real* income steadily rose, purchases in t_1 would be swollen by the optimistic wave.   If a drying up of the income stream is generally foreseen, expenditure in t_1 is almost sure to be restrained.

Rather than viewing it as a method of balancing expected income and consumption streams, installment purchases can be regarded as a form of "pay-as-you-use" purchase, with incremental amounts of the good used and paid for in each time period.   Thus the scheme is inherently sensible, although the price paid for the rigid purchase plan may be excessive.   The major considerations are the satisfaction afforded by the good relative to other goods in each time interval and the periodic price paid.   As tastes, income, and relative prices per time interval must all be anticipated, the purchase plan can come to grief for the customary reasons—namely, imperfections of foresight.   As most time-purchase schemes are heavily weighted to favor the seller, the burden of error will generally devolve upon the purchaser.   When anticipations of future income are optimistic and prices are expected to rise, installment buying will grow; in itself this is likely to perpetuate the aggregate income and employment level.

INTERTEMPORAL DEMAND AND COST RELATIONS

Transferring the emphasis from the consumer to the firm, let us examine some problems wherein the firm's activities in t_1 affect the profitability of operations in $t_2, t_3 \cdot \cdot \cdot$.   Generally, the significant patterns are those in which production in t_1 affects costs in t_2, t_3, etc., and price in t_1 influences demand and profits in t_2, t_3, etc.   Inherently, the temporal interrelations are entirely analogous to those discussed in the study of the multiple-product firm.   The difference is one of asymmetry; the activities of t_1 influence t_2 profits but t_2 events, which unfold after t_1 is already part of past history, are unable to exert an influence on t_1 operations.

User Costs

Normally, the typical cost interrelation will be that in which production in t_1 affects the ability of the firm to produce in t_2: mainly it will be the capacity of the equipment to render services that will be impaired. The uplift inflicted upon the marginal-cost curve of t_2 (or later time periods) and the consequent loss of profits can be designated as the *user* cost of t_1. Recalling the multiple-product analysis in which the cost curves of the respective outputs were related, and using subscripts $_1$ and $_2$ to refer to t_1 and t_2 values, we can state the condition for t_1 profit maximization as:

$$P_1 \geqq MR_1 = MC_1 + \Delta R_2,$$

where ΔR_2 is the current value of the decrement in profits in t_2 due to t_1 activity, and is the user cost of current output, which must be added to MC_1, operating to limit output in t_1. Alternately, t_2 profits may be enhanced because t_1 production and maintenance of equipment in good order reduces t_2 costs; ΔR_2 would then have to be deducted from MC_1, providing a stimulus to t_1 production to surpass the simple $MR_1 = MC_1$ volume. When costs are temporally interdependent whether ΔR_2 is positive or negative, production will fail to correspond to the $P = MC$ rule, even in competitive market conditions and perfect foresight. If costs in several future intervals are influenced by t_1 operations, the ΔR concept would have to be extended to encompass these ties.

To portray these relations, assume for the moment that the firm's productive facilities were idle in period t_1. For period t_2, supposing the firm sells in a competitive market and the expected price is (say) OP, the MC_1 curve in Figure 1A would describe the appropriate cost path; total output in t_2 would thus be OM and total profits would be PKR. But when one unit of output is produced in t_1, production costs, because of the wear and tear on equipment, will be higher in t_2: more labor, for example, might be necessary for each level of output so that the relevant t_2 marginal cost curve would rise from MC_1 to MC_2. The estimated maximum output in period t_2 would consequently recede to OS and profits to PTJ, a reduction of $JKRT$.

Writing MC_v in Figure 1B for the curve of actual t_1 marginal cost outlays, as one unit of current output reduces future profits by $JKRT$, this last sum, discounted to its present value, must be added to the MC_v of one unit of t_1 output to calculate the full marginal cost: the full t_1 cost consists of both immediate cash outlays and curtailed future profit opportunities. Ordinarily, small amounts of current outputs will not diminish future production potentialities, and might even improve them, so that the user costs for small amounts of current output will be zero or negative. As current production expands, however, the *mar-*

ginal user cost—the MC increment at each output representing future profit displacements—will become positive and more substantial. This is shown in Figure 1B by the widening gap between MC_u and MC_v. Concentrating on MC_u, which includes both marginal user and marginal cash outlays, we observe that MC_u cuts the market price line PP' to the left of the MC_v and PP' intersection. Total t_1 sales proceeds would then be $OP \cdot OG$, of which total variable cash cost outlays would be $OBEG$, with the difference $PCEB$ consisting of profits. But in obtaining this volume of current profits there would be the sacrifice of future profits, discounted to date and equal to BCE. Besides depressing future earn-

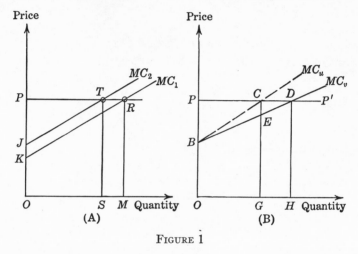

FIGURE 1

ings by this amount through the advance harvest, there is the net current income of PCB. Output, however, would not surpass OG because to do so would mean relinquishing future profits in excess of the added current earnings.

Although it should be apparent, it is best to make explicit that the user cost refers solely to the *avoidable* depreciation, that due to use; it must not be confused with the total of depreciation allowances which, if rightly calculated, is a composite sum consisting of the losses in the value of equipment attributable to both time and use.

Introducing user costs imparts a serious indeterminateness to mental models of equilibrium relationships even under competitive conditions, for if all the numerous firms foresee different future prices, even if they possess identical equipments there will not be any simple, uniform relation of P and MC_v. When the economic horizon extends beyond the two periods of our model, the user cost chargeable to a unit of output can be derived as follows: First, we can find the effect of a unit of current t_1 output on t_2 profits. Next we can suppose t_2 output to be zero and then appraise the movement in t_3 profits due to t_1 output; continuing, we can suppose zero output in t_2 and t_3 and discover the effect of t_1 output on t_4 profits; etc. The user cost attributable to a unit of output in t_1 will be the *value of the greatest of the potential profit reductions* discounted to date. In the event that producing a unit of output "today" lowers costs "tomorrow" but raises them the "next day," then we must strike a balance among the positive and negative items in computing the net user cost, positive or negative. The factors that predominate in determining the magnitude of marginal user cost are (1) the age of the equipment —new equipment will seldom involve a (serious) positive user cost; (2) the rate of interest, which influences the rate of discounting of future profit expectations—with a high rate of interest only substantial future profit opportunities will persuade an entrepreneur to repress current output for an uncertain future gain with a low current value; and (3) expected future prices, or demand under monopoly conditions, and expected factor costs, both of which shape the magnitude of the expected future profits—with optimistic entrepreneurial profit views, user-cost phenomena will bulk larger in the economy and hence in the emergence from depression they are likely to be extremely important.

Price Policy and Future Demand

Just as current output will influence future production costs and profits, a monopolist will also perceive a relationship between the t_1 price and the $t_2, t_3, t_4 \cdot \cdot \cdot t_n$ demand. There are at least three discrete cases to be distinguished: (1) firms frequently conclude that consumers can be encouraged by a low current price to purchase their product and thereby become permanent purchase adherents; this might be termed the "introductory offer" case, essentially an evidence of complementary demand; (2) firms will predict the extent to which consumers will accelerate their purchases and advance them to t_1 from $t_2, t_3 \cdot \cdot \cdot$ dates by lower current prices below the expected (perhaps publicized) future levels; this can be called a case of "accelerated selling" wherein current and future purchases are substitutes; and (3) firms will weigh the consequences of low current prices on future demand fearing the possibility of "spoiling the market." That is to say, a low current price may engender a reluctance of the buyers to pay more in the future in the belief that the commodity "is not worth more," or because of the revulsion towards the ethics of a seller whose price is unduly raised. Although there are elements common to each, to delineate their distinctive features each case is accorded a brief and independent exposition.

In introducing new goods or to enlarge the market for known goods a monopolist will often reason that a lower current price will encourage some consumers to experiment and purchase the good in lieu of substitute commodities, with the result that he builds some lasting attachments and future demand is permanently shifted to the right. Alternately, just as low prices stimulate experimentation, relatively high prices will deter even customary demand and encourage the trial of substitute commodities. Hence monopolists will be willing to charge prices below the immediate maximization figures, foregoing present profits in the expectation that these will be recouped in the future. The action pattern, however, can pertain only to monopoly markets, for the thoroughly competitive firm would be unable to exert more than an imperceptible influence over future demand and price.

In terms of the cross elasticities of demand, where the relative current price change constitutes the denominator and future purchases the numerator, the cross elasticity would be negative—the usual complementarity relation. The principle determining the extent to which it will pay to forego current profits (or accept current losses) may be stated tersely: it will be worthwhile to lower the current price and suffer a diminution in current profits so long as the immediate sacrifice is outweighed by a future gain in profits, with the latter discounted to date. In the continuous case where the future gains in profit stemming from a current fall of price successively diminish, equilibrium will emerge at the equality of the two. Equationally, we have:

$$MR_1 + \Delta R_2 = MC_1,$$

where ΔR_2 is the increment in profits in t_2 caused by the rightward movement in the t_2 demand curve emanating from the decrement ΔP_1 in P_1. Hence when account is taken of the temporal relationships, output and sales will be greater and price lower than if the firm were blind to this interdependence. Diagrammatically, a construction similar to the user-cost construction of Figure 1B could show the equilibrium position; rather than add on "user costs" to MC_v, we could deduct sums in amount equal to the discounted value of the greater future profits occasioned by each t_1 price fall and output advance. If there are user costs of equipment, however, these could neutralize the future demand and profit rise. If a lower t_1 price favored profits through a longer future extending beyond t_2, the full current value of these sums would constitute the ΔR component.

In contrast to the preceding analysis where a lower t_1 price increased demand and profit opportunities in t_2, a firm will often conclude that as price falls in t_1 demand in t_2 will be depressed, with the t_2 demand curve shifting to the left, as with all substitute goods. The cross elasticity of demand between the goods is thus positive; from each current MR there must now be deducted (or to each current MC there must now be added) this additional cost of the expected loss in future revenue: ΔR_2 in the preceding equation is a negative quantity. User costs become unduly repressive, with future-cost curves raised and future-demand curves contracted. Needless to say, this bodes ill for output and price in t_1: production will be restrained and price will be higher than with an uncorrected $MR = MC$ policy in t_1. Any suggestion of reducing t_1 prices will arouse misgivings; firms will shy away from advancing customer purchase dates and destroying future profit opportunities. As a possible exception, however, if the firm plans to go out of business or convert its facilities to another commodity variety, this negative future effect will be disregarded, for the firm will literally want to advance consumer purchase dates.

The notion of a price policy "spoiling the market," historically associated with the name of Alfred Marshall, is, unfortunately, unduly vague in many respects. To Marshall it appeared to mean an unwillingness to sell at lower prices because of the depressing influences on future demand; consumers in the future would be unwilling to pay higher prices.* In a period of low current demand and costs, as in the midst of a business depression, a firm in contemplating current price below "normal" past levels will apprehend that in a future business upsweep consumers may rebel at higher prices, forestalling their purchases from t_2 to t_3, t_4 · · · , etc., in the belief that the t_2 price rise is but temporary. This effect must be weighed before proclaiming a low current price; it has its analogue, in principle, in the version of accelerated selling.

But more than this the firm will reason that the subsequent "necessary" price rise in t_2, because of changed cost circumstances say, will incur the wrath of consumers and dissipate their "good will," transferring their custom to more "ethical" competitors. The suspicion that the firm is "unfair" will grow, that it charges low prices until an advan-

---

* This appears to be the usual impression although Marshall was not very specific. (*Principles*, pp. 377, 849.) Professor Pigou in one place interpreted it as "selling a thing in bad times at such a price, and, therefore, in such quantities, that in subsequent good times the market is already stocked." We have already included this relationship under the heading of temporal substitutability and accelerated selling. (*Industrial Fluctuations*, 2nd edition, p. 186.)

tage can be gained. Rather than inflame some very human sentiments a firm might hold prices in t_1 *above* the immediate minimum that would be counseled by a more rigid application of the current maximum-profit rule.

As an alternative interpretation of "market spoiling" through a current price fall, in the partly irrational real world a lowering of price may cast an aura of cheapness about the commodity so that not only is the demand quantity at lower prices immediately reduced in t_1—rather than enlarged—but forever after there will lurk in the minds of uninformed consumers an aversion to the commodity and a belief that it is essentially an inferior variety. Future demand may never recover from this hapless price move—a phenomenon that has its roots in the consumer ignorance of quality and the "conspicuous consumption" attitudes of buyers of some goods. Hence a firm will be wary of temporary "low-price" innovations: the higher current income may augur substantial losses through time.

PRICE POLICY AND POTENTIAL COMPETITION

There are a few more cases akin to the intertemporal demand relations that deserve some scrutiny; they can be joined in this section for expository convenience. Briefly, the subjects are (1) the influence of potential competition on current price policy; (2) the effect on monopsony price policy of the interdependence of current price and future supply; and (3) advertising outlays and future demand.

Potential competition is often declared to be a potent force checking maximum monopoly pricing on the grounds that the resulting swell of profits will hasten the entry of producers of substitutes; this will, it is averred, enforce a less avaricious price policy in order to forestall future competition and enable the firm to enjoy a lower but more permanent level of profits. In a similar vein it is alleged that a nonmaximum monopoly price policy will be instituted to banish the spectre of government regulation. But there is a subtle difference in the two cases: to block entry of new sellers, price will have to be depressed to levels *below* the monopoly level; however, to still the clamor for regulation it is only essential that profits do not appear exorbitant. The latter result can be achieved, and the issue obscured just as effectively, by an inordinately high price as by a low one; for net income is reduced on both sides of the monopoly price.

The main principle covering these cases is scarcely novel. It will be prudent, where new entry is threatened, to lower current prices, and maintain them low, so long as the expected discounted future additions to revenue in forestalling entry exceed the current revenue sacrifices through lowering price. Each further lowering of current price that succeeds in deterring entry will work to sustain the future demand curves for the firm. A higher t_1 price, say, which invites entry in t_2, would reduce the t_2 and later demand curves of the firm. Price policy is thus transformed into a persuasive instrument that enables the firm to live a quieter, more secure, but less spectacular profit life. As the lower current price is correlated with greater future demand, so that the cross elasticity of demand is negative, we witness another case of complementarity.

Despite frequent protestations and professions of its validity, the weight to be assigned to such phenomena in the real world is rather dubious. When entry is easy because fixed and specialized equipment is unimportant to a new firm, it is hardly likely that a firm would forego the bird in hand for the hypothetical and very uncertain future bird in the bush. If entry is difficult, requiring expensive equipment, only if the existing firm scents plans for encroachments by a new and huge transgressor need it commence a low-price policy. In brief, it is most likely that the bludgeon of price reductions will be exhibited only when the rumblings of entry are audible, for until they crystallize the firm will perceive the advantage in a maximum current price policy designed to enrich it immediately and gird it for a lasting conflict.* In the same way, the view that the fear of government regulation invariably restrains monopoly-price exactions seems altogether too sanguine. Everything will depend on the political climate and the shrewdness, deliberateness, and callousness of the monopolist. If the atmosphere is ominous and charged with the threat of government regulation, the monopolist will have to assess the degree to which this can be deflected or mitigated by judicious price manipulations. In times when regulatory control is unlikely, caution and price restraint can be discarded.

Temporal Aspects of Monopsony and Sales-Outlay Policies

Under monopoly it was demonstrated that the firm might well maneuver its price policy to sway future demand or supply. A monopsonist may likewise ponder the influence of its current price policy on future profits. For example, a low wage may dissuade labor from moving to the area, may prejudice the acquisition and development of skills, etc.

---

* Rightly this aspect of the case falls in the realm of strategy and tactics of economic warfare. See Chapter 7.

A calculating monopsonist, therefore, will weigh the future perturbations evoked by the present market-price policy. As future profits will be affected, the discounted value of these sums, positive or negative, must be set off against t_1 profits at each t_1 price. Thus at each point on the MSC curve of Figure 1a, Chapter 11, we must add or deduct the discounted incremental future profits or losses through paying the associated supply-curve price. Injecting "user" costs in this way the effect ordinarily will be to drive current monopsony price closer to the $(P = S)$ alignment. Writing ΔR_2 for the future gains attributable to a *higher* current price, the maximum condition becomes

$$MDP + \Delta R_2 = MSP.$$

In a similar vein, it was presumed in the earlier analysis of sales outlays that the augmented demand that was attracted accrued in precisely the same time period as that in which the promotional disbursements were incurred. Although this assumption is of course false, for the demand rise is maintained through successive time intervals, the corrections to be made are quite minor. Whatever the sales outlays, the firm must be conceived as weighing its effect on demand in t_1, t_2, t_3 $\cdots$ t_n. The estimated surge in profits through the future must be discounted to date, and balanced against sales outlays, prior to embarking upon the selling program. Insisting on the time dimensions of the problem it seems unlikely that a firm will, in t_1, recoup the full amount of t_1 sales outlay, especially if the product is a new one, struggling for a place on the consumer's purchase scale and requiring heavy educational expenditures. Immediate losses, rather than profits, may be the conspicuous element.

INVENTORY AND PROFIT EXPECTATIONS

More so than most phenomena, inventory accumulations cannot be poured into the stationary mould, however ingenious the effort: they belong only to the dynamic and uncertain world. Holding stocks of goods is costly; businessmen must expect to reap some gain from the idle stock pile. If prices never changed, and if future demand and cost were invariant, inventories would be practically nil, arising mainly from physical discontinuities in production and consumption, such as seasonal harvests and recurring daily consumption. Briefly, the following motives might be distilled to explain the vast majority of inventory accumulations, where these include the saleable goods that the firm, at its discretion, chooses to carry over to a future period:

(1) The prospect of financial gain through a price rise or, under monopoly, a future lift of demand and/or cost—it is a notorious fact that when price optimism pervades, stock piles increase sharply.

(2) The firm's desire to guarantee its ability to accommodate an abnormally high volume of sales so that unforeseen custom is not refused; here inventory is a buffer—an uncertainty allowance whose additional cost may be small and whose potential lucrativeness may be large.

(3) The desire to save on transportation charges by making "block" purchases rather than piecemeal purchases—dealers are likely to hold abnormal stocks that fluctuate discontinuously between the high point at moment of delivery to the low point just prior to replenishment.

(4) The desire to insure stability of operations when dislocations are foreseen, such as strikes, physical factors, etc.

(5) The observance of customary business practices that call for window displays and well-stocked shelves as sales-promotion measures (in this instance the inventories are a form of selling cost).

(6) A final reason (though not a motive) for inventory accumulations is found in the unexpected and unplanned accumulations due to a rate of sales below that expected; this last case will be analyzed in the concluding chapter in discussing the reaction of the system to change; for these stocks, which are utterly unplanned, are not the result of conscious entrepreneurial calculations.

On a general plane these are probably the major reasons for holding goods that are already complete and ready for resale. For goods in process, in various states of completion, there would have to be added the rate of input and the t me length of production. In the list enumerated above, we can ignore the third, fifth, and sixth reasons as irrelevant at this stage, while the fourth reason itself involves an expectation of future demand and costs, for dislocations are ultimately costs. Hence the prospect of price rises and a rate of sales greater than estimated (the first and second reasons above) command our attention; the buffer motive, however, may be disposed of rather summarily.

If a firm holds on hand quantities in excess of those required for current sales or expected future price rises, the cause will mainly be the lack of complete confidence in its sales forecasts.* The cost of holding inventory may be small, whereas the prospects may be good that prices or sales will currently or in the near future vastly exceed estimates. On the balance of considerations, the firm will be led to hold stocks. The firm may rule out as highly improbable those prices and sales that are

* See page 363.

lower than estimated, with better prospects possible even if not likely; inventory holdings will impart to the firm the flexibility to profit by a favorable turn in fortunes.   Virtually we are led to argue that after the firm's forecasts are completed it engages in another series of estimates to allow for undue pessimism in its projected estimates.*   The maximum inventory total will then be selected after an appraisal of inventory-holding costs compared with the possible augmentation of price proceeds over and above the most probable levels.

Before elaborating the effects that potential price movements under competition, or demand and supply changes under monopoly have upon decisions to produce for inventory, we might enumerate the costs associated with inventory carry-over.   They are: (1) interest costs on the current money value of the inventory; (2) storage and maintenance cost on the stockpile; (3) physical depreciation and possible obsolescence of the inventory components; (4) insurance charges, to guard against fire, theft, malfeasance, etc.; and (5) a risk allowance for loss through erroneous predictions.   These elements will appear as instrumental in the ensuing analysis.

Production for Inventory: Competitive Markets

Figure 2 facilitates the analysis of the degree of production for inventory by competitive firms when their forecast for prices for t_2 differs from the opinion held for t_1.   The horizontal P_2P_2 line represents the expected t_2 price and P_1P_1, the current price; MC is the current marginal cost curve.   Drawing $P_2P_1'P_2'$, the ordinate amounts $P_2 - P_1$ at each output summarize the additional carrying costs for the corresponding unit of output when held over in reserve for sales in t_2.   Consequently, the curve $P_2P_1'P_2'$ embodies the *net* t_2 price expectation on each unit of current output.

Considering these relations, until an output OM is reached it will be profitable to assign t_1 output to inventory rather than to sell it currently, for this will enlarge aggregate income in amount $P_2P'P_1$.   But beyond OM, current sales will be more lucrative than withholding for future disposal.   Clearly, if the current price P_1 rose relative to P_2, the inventory carryover would be cut; in the limit if $P_1 \geqq P_2$, inventory holdings will be nil.   In the event that the horizontal P_1P_1 line cuts MC at or below the intersection of MC and $P_2P_1'P_2'$, all of t_1 output would be destined

---

* Calculations of this nature lend credence to A. G. Hart's insistence that in an uncertain world the uncertainty allowances cannot be discounted and equated to a simple indifference equivalent.

for inventory and t_2 sale.   If we posit the t_2 price expectations of each competitive firm, so long as the general view is that $P_2 > P_1$, there will be production for inventory.   If the spread in expected prices is at all large then current output may vastly exceed the current rate of sales. Even if there are discrepant views on the future, with a scatter of individual ideas involving $P_1 \gtrless P_2$, some inventory production will appear. By a like analysis we can determine whether it will be remunerative for the firm to consign to future sale inventory that has been built up in the past, or to unload it immediately; if the carry-over amounted to OM or less, all of it will be reserved for t_2; if it exceeds OM, the excess will be disposed of currently.

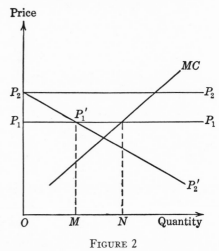

FIGURE 2

When the time horizon is enlarged to include $t_3, t_4 \cdots$, etc., although the diagrammatic analysis is cumbersome, the principle governing the time dimensions of sales is obvious enough: the firm will plan to sell quantities of current output until the marginal net revenue expected in each period is equal to current market price and marginal cost.   This plan will entail that the future price expectations exceed the t_1 price, by some positive balance even after deducting carrying costs.   Inventory will not be consciously accumulated if $P_1 > P_2 \geqq P_3 \cdots$, etc.

Production for Inventory: Monopoly

The usual monopoly $P > MC = MR$ output principle may also be suspended when provision is made for production for inventory; the current output may surpass the simple, single-period output foreshadowed at the $MR = MC$ adjustment.

In general terms the equilibrium condition of monopoly production for inventory can be concisely stated.   Glossing over the complication due to the discounting of future MR's and the carrying costs on holding current output till the future, in the final equilibrium there must be the full equality of

$$MR_1 = MR_2 = MC_1 = MC_2,$$

where the subscripts $_1$ and $_2$ refer to t_1 and t_2 respectively.   Otherwise, if

$MR_2 > MR_1$ it would be profitable to carry over some units of stock while, if $MC_2 > MC_1$, current production would be a profitable substitute for future output.

There is, however, a supplementary note that must be appended, for these relations apply only when inventory is actually accumulated. If in t_1 the equation $MR_1 = MC_1$ exceeds the direct equation $MR_2 = MC_2$, then inventory carry-overs will vanish, for in this case the firm would (if it were physically possible) transfer t_2 output to t_1 in order to enhance its profits. Thus, production for inventory is dependent on an antecedent condition, namely, that

$$MR_1 = MC_1 < MR_2 = MC_2.$$

If this relation holds, then inventory opportunities are open and the full condition will hold. Equilibrium in a multiperiod scheme will require the equalities

$$MR_1 = MR_2 = MR_3 \cdots = MR_n = MC_1 = MC_2$$
$$= MC_3 \cdots = MC_n.$$

The theory lends itself to exposition by means of the diagrammatic apparatus of Figure 3. Initially, as a simplification it is supposed that the later MR's are not discounted so that \$1 forthcoming in t_2 is regarded as equivalent to \$1 in t_1; likewise, carry-over costs are nil so that an MC of \$1 incurred for t_1 output to be held until t_2 imposes the same expense as an MC outlay of \$1 in t_2.

Curves MR_1 and MC_1 in each diagram of Figure 3 are the curves belonging to t_1, prior to any appraisal of the profitability of inventory accumulations for t_2. MR_t represents merely a lateral summation of the MR curves for the two periods, computed by adding to MR_1 the quantity that can be sold in t_2 at equivalent MR's. Similarly, MC_t requires the lateral addition to MC_1 of the quantities that can be produced in t_2 at equivalent marginal costs.

According to Figure 3A, simple single-period analysis would evoke the production of OM in t_1 and sold to yield an MR of R_1. In these circumstances production for inventory would be distinctly unprofitable, for to equalize

$$MR_1 = MR_2 = MC_1 = MC_2,$$

or

$$MR_t = MC_t,$$

it would be necessary to produce and sell the quantity ON over the two periods at an MR of R_2, requiring that OL be produced and sold in t_1, a quantity at which $MR_1 < MC_1$.   In doing so, the firm will sustain some avoidable losses in period 1; hence the aggregate profit realized over both periods cannot be a true maximum.   Thus with

$$MR_1 = MC_1 > MR_2 = MC_2,$$

the monopolist will secure maximum profits by producing in each period the normal single-period quantities for immediate sale.

Figure 3B offers a marked contrast, for now the equation of MC_t $= MR_t$ occurs at a higher MR level than does $MR_1 = MC_1$.   Simple single-period analysis would lead the monopolist to equate $MR_1 = MC_1$

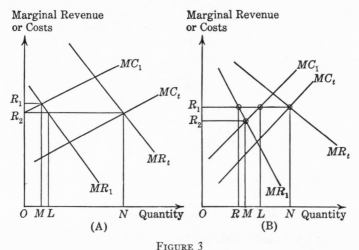

FIGURE 3

and produce OM for immediate sale.   But because future events are propitious, a deeper vision would order a t_1 production of OL, corresponding to the MC at which $MR_t = MC_t$, of which OR would be disgorged in t_1 while RL would be withheld for inventory, comprising part of the RN sales of t_2.   Thus an MR in each period equal to R_1 would ensure maximum profits over the full time interval.

A perusal of the MR_2 and MC_2 curves of Figure 3 will show that under monopoly it is a rise in either the future MR or MC curve, or a concerted movement, which is responsible for inventory.   Under competition it was solely the movement in future prices, not costs, that favored production, for inventory, although palpably an expected cost movement, might be taken as an omen of a higher t_2 price.   A monopolist who expected the MC_2 curve to rise relative to MC_1, even if the MR_1 and MR_2 curves were identical replicas of one another, would still profit from inventory carryover and t_2 sale.

We need to erase the assumption that a future MR is viewed as equally valuable with a current MR. The correction is evident: MR_2 must be discounted, in the light of the effective interest rate and subjective uncertainty, to a current value. Thereafter, the sales that yield a present MR, and the sales in t_2 that yield an equally valued current MR, need be summated laterally to comprise the MR_t curve of our diagram. The equilibrium equality, when inventory is profitable, is thus

$$MR_1 = DMR_2,$$

with DMR_2 signifying the discounted MR_2 value. Likewise, when the carrying costs per unit of t_1 output are acknowledged, each MC_2 is equivalent to a smaller MC_1, so that our lateral addition of MC curves consists of the output at each MC_1 level plus that MC_2 level minus carrying costs which equals MC_1; the equality is then

$$MC_1 = AMC_2,$$

where AMC_2 is the MC_2 equivalent of MC_1 after subtracting carrying charges from MC_2. Reflection will disclose that the reduction of future MR values to a current value, and the intrusion of carryover charges on t_1 output, will operate to reduce the volume of production for inventory. In the final equilibrium the pertinent inventory equality for maximum profit will be

$$MR_1 = DMR_2 = MC_1 = AMC_2.$$

Some Complex Combinations

Curiously enough, when we consider simultaneous combinations of expected events, as user costs along with inventory, the problem is not rendered the more complex: current output raises the future cost curve and hence the current MC must contain user cost as an element. In the final equilibrium, neglecting the time discounting and carrying costs, if

$$MR_1 = MC_1 < MR_2 = MC_2,$$

where MC_1 includes user cost, then in the final equilibrium, for maximum profit,

$$MR_1 = MR_2 = MC_1 = MC_2.$$

For those cases in which a firm can influence future demand through present price policy, if at the t_1 price and output of maximum profit $MC_1 < MC_2$, where the latter is the t_2 maximum, then producing for inventory is a likely result. In the final equilibrium,

$$MR_1 \gtrless MC_1 = MR_2 = MC_2,$$

where MR_1 is indeterminate depending on whether the temporal demand relations are those of substitution or complementarity. In the independent t_1 and t_2 demand case, then $MR_1 = MR_2$. Marginal costs would ultimately have to be equal for, barring $MC_1 > MC_2$, the opportunities for profitable inventory accumulation insure this equality and the larger equality of both t_1 and t_2 MC's with MR_2.

A NOTE ON SINGLE-PERIOD VERSUS STREAM ANALYSIS

This is perhaps as far as we need go in demonstrating the influence of expectations of the longer future on the immediate behavior of the firm. Because of the manifest temporal deficiencies of single-period analysis of the economic process, there is a growing absorption with models of equilibrium processes through time, recognizing that the horizon of the economic participants, both consumers and firms, extends beyond the immediately unfolding time period. The consumer is conceived to anticipate his stream of tastes, incomes, and prices in periods t_1, t_2, t_3 $\cdots t_n$, and to adjust his consumption intake accordingly. The firm is portrayed as estimating a stream of revenues and costs over a multiple-period time span and is described as selecting that behavior plan which, out of all the alternatives, maximizes its income. Ultimately, an equilibrium in time, covering successive dates, is analyzed and described.

But this approach can be charged with an even higher degree of sterility than traditional methods. Although the proponents of "stream analysis" are to be commended for the explicit introduction of time into the analysis, yet with only a wavering faith in the reality of the equilibrium concept in single periods, it requires a stronger faith to entertain thoughts premised upon an equilibrium *through* time. For unless in each unfolding period of time the successive facts dovetail with the preceding plans, the plans will have to be altered: once they do alter, the original planning relationships are immediately disrupted. Hence, while it is not too great a strain on our credibility to suppose that plans for the short future will be compatible with events, over the longer multiple-period analysis, this is well-nigh impossible. There seems to be few occasions, therefore, to erect elaborate models of equilibrium through time in the thought that they may have some empirical counterpart in the world we know.

It would be more in conformity with traditional analysis, and more nearly approximating the facts, to work with models of the world that depict and analyze events in only one time period, the forthcoming t_1 period, say, with due cognizance that events in t_1 will be influenced by expectations of t_2, t_3 $\cdots$, etc. The effects of the longer planning views on t_1 activity will thereby be included, and the analysis can then be directed to the consequences of longer plans, whatever their time length, on prices, incomes, and outputs in t_1, describing the conditions under which the plans will be realized, along with effects of errors in planning. Although the time dimensions of the equilibrium flow are too seldom made explicit, this is an approximate description of the method of most of economic literature when given a time context. There are some occasions, such as in the construction of capital equipment, when we shall want to lay out the longer-period plans more carefully; but concentration on them to the exclusion of their effects on economic affairs in t_1 is likely to be fruitless.

On this view, if in the original formulation of plans for the longer future, there is compatibility in period t_1 between plans and events, then the original plan can continue on to t_2 unless new events are foreseen on the horizon. If the foresight is also proven justified by the unfolding events in t_2, the t_1 plan for t_3 can be implemented. In this way, with correct foresight, the advancing single-period analysis would coincide exactly with the stream analysis. But it is artificial and unrealistic in the extreme to stake out the full future time dimensions of planning and then argue as if the subjective model had a firm prospect of enduring. Realistically, even with the best-planned actions, these models simply will not fit in a world of change.

Of course, if our t_1 period has exactly the same time duration as the full t_1, t_2 $\cdots$ t_n period in the stream analysis, then this criticism is misdirected. Whereas in the stream analysis the time periods might refer to days, our t_1 might extend to a decade. As everything depends on the length of t_1, we consider in Chapter 18 the matter of defining the length of the economic period.

BIBLIOGRAPHICAL NOTE

More elaborate formulas for ascertaining the present value of future sums, when there are discontinuities in the receipt of the future sums and in the compounding of interest, are described in Allen, *Mathematical Analysis*, pp. 232–237. Speculative activity, its conditions and consequences, are dissected minutely in the recondite and abstruse but important series of papers beginning with N. Kaldor, "Speculation and Economic Stability," *Review of Economic Studies* (1939), and the ensuing "Symposium on the Theory of the Forward Market," same journal, 1940, to which Kaldor, J. C. R. Dow, and R. G. Hawtrey contributed. A résumé of these discussions is contained in

G. Blau, "Some Aspects of the Theory of Futures Trading," *Review of Economic Studies* (1944–1945).

The classic description of the process of changing the time dimensions of an income stream by appropriate borrowing and lending activities is found in Chapters V–VI of Irving Fisher's *The Theory of Interest*. See also the more recent treatment of this topic in Hicks' volume, pp. 184–188. The need for some scheme of rental hire or installment purchase to overcome the indivisibility of goods, such as pianos, which otherwise reduces well-being, was argued by Wicksteed in his *Commonsense*, Vol. I, Chapter III.

Although the concept can also be termed one of intertemporal cost complementarity, this phenomenon was resuscitated by Keynes in the short-run analysis of the business cycle and designated as *user* cost, a concept badly neglected outside his own volume. See the *General Theory*, Appendix to Chapter VI. Its value for the theory of the firm was demonstrated in Alfred C. Neal's, "Marginal Cost and Dynamic Equilibrium of the Firm," *Journal of Political Economy* (1942), reprinted as Chapter III in his *Industrial Concentration and Price Inflexibility*. G. Tintner has drawn diagrams of cases in which user cost is negative, though he sedulously refrains from describing the phenomena in these terms. See his graphic article on "The Theory of Production Under Nonstatic Conditions," *Journal of Political Economy* (1942). A recent discussion of the influence of potential entry on price policy is J. S. Bain's article, "Pricing in Monopoly and Oligopoly," *American Economic Review* (1949).

The diagrammatic presentation of the theory of production for inventory is derived from the excellent article of E. Shaw, "Elements of the Theory of Inventory," *Journal of Political Economy* (1940). Samples of the stream analysis which have intrigued contemporary theorists are provided in Hicks, *Value and Capital*, Part V, and Hart, *Anticipations, Uncertainty and Dynamic Planning*, Chapter II especially. The late Irving Fisher was perhaps the precursor in this mode of thinking.

CHAPTER 18

Clock-Time Sequences

CONSIDER NOW THE DURATION OF the clock-time interval to which our constructions are appropriate. Time, it was alleged earlier, can be ignored in the stationary-flow equilibrium. In the repetitive stationary processes of production and consumption it matters little how long a time interval is dissected for study: the economic phenomena of a week represent a seven-fold projection of the events of a day, and a month represents a supply-demand multiple of 30 days, etc. Lengthening the time period compels us, however, to introduce the rate of interest in an explicit and conscious way.

But the study of temporal processes is urgent in a world of dynamic development where changing real phenomena, and changing ideas about the real phenomena, disturb the stationary flow, dislodging the economy from any undulating norm to new levels of adaptation that may not always be equilibrating. On this view the traditional conception of the economic pattern in time must be reformulated. Besides the dynamic disruptions there are some interesting discontinuous processes containing important time lags which invite study, even in immanently stationary conditions.

OPERATIONAL AND CLOCK TIME

The time dimensions that pervade Marshall's famous Book V have been aptly described as *operational* time. Although it conveys an air of clock-time, the impression is deceiving: periods are immediate, long, or short, not according to the revolving hands of the clock, but according to the adaptations of producers and consumers to changing circumstances, whether these are but temporary, partial, or complete.* The actual length of time involved—a day, week, month or year, etc.—can be

* See page 101.

arbitrarily stipulated, for this is a matter of indifference when only functional differences in the demand and supply curves are stressed. Conceivably, when time is envisaged operationally, given a change in demand or cost the long-run forces might *precede* the short-run; output from existing facilities may utilize so much clock time because of natural causes that new equipment can be installed prior to any output flow emanating from existing "facilities." Here the long-run analysis supplants the short-run. Extreme care, then, is required in translating Marshallian time into clock-time lengths. A shortcoming of Marshallian analysis is that the actual time interval to which the curve constructions apply is undefined, being independent of the problem under analysis. There is need for a theory to fill the analytical void—the discrepancy between operational and clock-time lengths.

Among the alternatives to Marshallian time, with its functional rather than hourglass flavor, it has occasionally been proposed that an arbitrary "slice of time," long or short, be isolated and abstracted from the historical sequence and dissected for study.* Although the technique has largely been expounded in business-cycle literature it is likely to win adherents in price theory when once the problem of the length of the time period is broached. Unfortunately, the admonition to study a period of time is merely to raise the issue, not to resolve it; the unsettled question still remains as to the appropriate time span to subject to study. If the time span is too short, there will be many processes either missing or uncompleted in the period. If it is too long, there will be too great a mass of material to digest, so that we must discriminate and reserve our energies for what we regard as essentials, abstracting from other details. Eventually we shall study "time slices"; their length, however, is still vague.

The Week as the Appropriate Time Interval

Recently, the "week" has been prescribed as the proper time span for study. But this is an elusive and functional "week"; for rather than stipulating a rigid clock length, Professor Hicks, its leading proponent, explains that it can be compressed or elongated, since it is viewed simply as that period during which variations in prices can be ignored.† Lit-

---

* Professor D. H. Robertson is responsible for the phrase "slice of time," one of the many colorful creations in his word armory. For his views on the time length of economic analysis, see his *Essays in Monetary Theory*, page 137. It is to be remarked that Professor Robertson's "day," in his customary usage, is not congruent with the chronological 24-hour day; instead, it too is a functional day wherein a "piece of money" circulates once.

† Hicks, p. 122.

erally, it is assumed that production, sales, and deliveries occur continuously within the week, although prices are settled on "Monday." It is on this one day of the week that all prospective buyers and sellers gather in the "market place" and, as a result of the mutual interactions, settle the price for the subsequent week. Conceding the artificiality of the construction, it is defended as a simple approximation to reality compared to the greater web of complexity in working with market models in which price making is visualized as a continuous phenomenon. In stationary markets, pricing on each successive Monday would coincide with prices on the first Monday. In the dynamic world, unless we are intent on detailing each change, however trivial, it can be argued that this procedure provides an accurate glimpse of reality by extracting frequent sample readings of the unfolding economic process. Time is thus explicitly introduced into the analysis although the analytical barriers occasioned by continuous and frequent change are subdued but not wholly suppressed.

An obvious criticism of this procedure is that it assumes the continuity of economic processes which, paradoxically, are studied discontinuously: a good part of normal economic activity fails to conform to this continuity postulate. Moreover, as the "weekly" readings omit many of the changes, we cannot refrain from asking questions on these matters. If we can shorten our time interval without inviting a prodigious amount of detail, then the analysis would commend itself as a substitute or supplement to the discontinuous weekly-level study. Finally, the assumption of all price making confined to the same day (Monday) does too much violence to the facts to secure universal assent. We are still not absolved from probing continuous (that is to say, realistic) market structures.

Continuous and Point Time

When we regard time abstractly, it needs only be mentioned that clock time is fully continuous, just like the number system of mathematics. Thus between any two fleeting time movements we can write as many time dates as we wish. Seizing upon output-sales sequences as decisive for economic study, we can define a continuous economic sequence as involving production and sales at each momentary interval of passing time. Less than this, the process contains a discontinuity.

Actually this concept is too fastidious for purposes of economic analysis. Let us suppose that our economic subjects think only in terms of

days or that our time meter measures only days and not hours or minutes
That is to say, on a horizontal line each point represents one day, while
"in-between" points are excluded.   Conceiving time as always advancing by one day, with Δt always consisting of twenty-four hours, we will
find this to be a continuous enough development for our purposes; sales
markets are continuous if sales occur in each day; production will be
continuous if there is a forward flow of output each day.   Within the
day itself, however, there will be discontinuities that we disregard;
transactions are consummated and production processes are confined
almost wholly to the normal business hours.   Even when these discontinuities are overlooked, it is also true that on some days of the week—
Sundays and holidays—there may be neither production nor sales.
Despite these temporal transgressions it will be harmless to describe output and sales as continuous if they occur within each *business* day.

Many operations, on the other hand, are confined to a point in time,
happening on one day and thereafter, never again to be duplicated or
repeating themselves only after the lapse of a number of ordinary business days.   These activities are designated as *point-time* phenomena.
For example, a concert artist's performance can be denoted as point-
time production even though, rightly, it is compressed not within a point
but a small interval of chronological time.   Sales, too, might be poured
into a point-time mould—witness sales solely for festive occasions; for
example, turkeys for Thanksgiving.   (Here, strictly speaking, it is a
minor time range, a few days, rather than a fleeting 24-hour period that
is involved).

Point-time activities that repeat themselves irregularly are special
types of discontinuities.   For example, certain outputs may be assigned
to several discrete dates during the year so that it is a discontinuous
production sequence rather than a "once-and-for-all" point activity.
Nevertheless, when events are unpredictably discontinuous, then point
analysis will establish substantially correct results.   Discontinuous
sequences are those in which business days elapse before a recurrence of
either sales or output processes, but in which provision must be made for
the effects of the activities of one date on the economic phenomena of
other dates: certain dates are blank in the stream of history although
occasionally, regularly or not, our business calendar will register repeti-
tious sales or output activity.   We can thus direct our major concentration to point and continuous sequences, restricting our study to the
following temporal combinations: (1) continuous output, continuous
sales; (2) continuous output, point sales; (3) point output, sales; (4)

point output, continuous sales.* These sequences will be elucidated in the pages to follow, although some discontinuous point patterns will also be examined.

DAILY PRICE FORMATION

As our clock lengths are days, in the continuous sequence both demand and supply curves have a daily periodicity. With discontinuous point demand or point output sequences we might decide to relate the time dimensions of demand or output to the full interval that has been closed. For example, if in agriculture the output belongs to but one "day" in the year, we might declare it to be the "annual" output. Likewise, when output is continuous and demand occupies only a point, enabling us to take demand to cover the full past interval, it will generally be convenient to refer the supply curve to exactly the same time dimensions as those of the demand curve.

But there are some stumbling blocks in endeavoring to give the conceptions even a 24-hour life. For if we sought empirical counterparts for these categories, it would appear that the supply-demand curves enjoy but a fleeting, instantaneous existence: at each moment of the day another set of constructions would, realistically, have to be drawn. But if the curve apparatus has but a transitory life it will literally be shorn of its vitality. As a practical matter it is not accurate to argue that decisions to buy or to sell are rigid only within and when directed towards moments of time: a day probably is the minimum period of time for which action patterns are planned. On this basis it seems to be in concurrence with the preponderance of facts to attribute to our conceptions a 24-hour interval, freeing our analysis from the mountain of detail which would be amassed against us if we acknowledged the passage of continuous fractional days.

Let us elaborate our mental model. Suppose that the supply and demand curves have a 24-hour time length and that at the close of the previous business day, t_0, individuals plan their purchase and sales behavior for the following day, t_1. Further, on the ensuing t_1 day we can visualize *all* purchases and sales compressed into but one instant of that day, permitting us to omit those complications and modifications that are associated with the passage of time within the daily period. On this hypothesis only one price would rule each day in the various markets, although under discriminatory monopoly, of course, a different

---

* For a somewhat different application of point and continuous concepts see F. Hayek, *The Pure Theory of Capital*, p. 66. The terminological originality is accredited to R. Frisch.

price can rule in each transaction: in the latter event the discriminatory prices even when spread out through the day are the same as would materialize if all sales were consummated simultaneously. In most cases this assumption of a single price prevailing through the day, being generally a projection of the historical price ruling on the previous day, synchronizes pretty well with the facts, even if the description of the concentration of sales within the one instant is artificial; however, it can be argued that these differences in the exact moment of transactions within the day can be disregarded as extremely insignificant. Still, we must make the necessary emendations for those circumstances in which this price hypothesis is violated, as well as the important question of whether the price named to rule for the day is an equilibrium price—a hypothesis difficult to justify because its empirical proof is elusive in the extreme.

In dealing with this last item, the prices named in the several markets can be equilibrium prices arrived at by simple maximum-profit criteria; they can evolve out of more complex maximum calculations in which, say, present price is named by a monopolist with thoughts of the future; they may represent duopoly configurations, etc., or they may be nonequilibrium prices, transitional phases on the equilibrium path or nonequilibrium responses that may not even culminate in any ultimate equilibrium. The various equilibrium cases have been analyzed previously; the last two analyses will be deferred until the following chapter. Temporarily, we can postulate that our daily prices are equilibrium prices.

Once this is done for those markets in which the price is constant throughout the day, it remains to make the necessary qualifications and contrasts for those markets in which this assumption of daily price constancy is likely and for those markets in which the assumption fails to reflect the facts. Immediately the theoretical structures can be extended to some cases in which price, to a superficial observer, evidences changes during the day. For example, many prices are settled through the day by individual bargains between buyer and seller, in which other sellers of perfect substitutes are not present or in which buyers are unable to purchase the seller's product for resale. These instances in which the individual market participants haggle over the price terms in each transaction fit the conventional picture of bilateral monopoly. Whether each transaction occurs separately in time, spread out over the 24-hour day, or whether all transactions of this nature are compressed into a brief moment, would be a matter of indifference: the results are likely to be the same and therefore our theoretical constructions would not have to be modified.

Markets of Continuous Price Formation

The image of 24-hour price constancy is likely to be shattered occasionally even in markets where this model is a serviceable representation; sometimes price will be altered during the course of the day because of a reappraisal by sellers of the current market phenomena.   Normally this phenomenon can be envisaged as one of market readjustment, a movement towards a new equilibrium.   Its study can be postponed until the following chapter.

Our model performs badly mainly in those markets in which prices are in continuous flux as a result of momentary purchase and sales decisions of buyers and sellers—largely in the great security and commodity exchanges of the world in which incessant price oscillations are commonplace.   Several procedures are open to us.   First we could declare that our tools are inadequate for the analysis; but this would be a counsel of unnecessary abstention and unbecoming flight from an important problem without a test and struggle.   Alternately, we can assign an instantaneous life to our constructions to cover those market sequences in which price displays ceaseless fluctuations.   Undoubtedly this solution would, in essential respects, reflect the facts.   But this solution suffers from the defect of the inclusion of imponderable detail, for if we concur in the premises of general equilibrium analysis and stress the interrelations of prices, the ramifications of each price aberration in these markets on other markets would have to be pursued, even though the links are frequently small and inconsequential.   It would be worth some effort to preserve the more discontinuous techniques of infusing the supply-demand conceptions with a full 24-hour life.   Let us consider how this might be done, allowing at the same time for the effects of frequent price changes during the entire day upon the number of transactions, and upon the market price, and taking into consideration the nature of the reverberations on phenomena in other markets arising from the movements in the particular markets.

One artifice worth trying is to assume that in the particular markets the total daily expenditure is of a constant magnitude whether all transactions are executed simultaneously within a momentary time interval, or whether sales are strung out through the day at innumerable prices: repercussions on other markets can then be neglected.   But those sellers fortunate enough to dispose of their holdings at a price above the daily average will gain an income benefit at the expense of buyers; the same would apply for buyers who purchase at a price below the average. This income redistribution may affect the number of transactions within the particular market unless we inject the additional proviso that the marginal utility of money (income) is constant, after which the last set of effects can be neglected.

If the hypothesis of a constant aggregate outlay within the market, despite innumerable prices, and a constant marginal utility of income cannot be granted, then the volume of transactions and prices will deviate from the total eventuating when but one price rules for the full day. But there is, however, a further complication: buyers' and sellers' attitudes on future prices, and hence their decisions to trade immediately, will frequently be colored by events just passed. Only if a unique price prevailed through the entire day would the opening demand-and-supply schedules of the ensuing day be unaltered. Thus if there are interminable price fluctuations throughout the day the concept of a given demand-and-supply structure can be overworked: although these situations must be admitted, if we can argue that the day's price swings are rather limited it is perhaps not as demolishing to the structure as may be feared. In any event it applies only when uncertainty is rife and anticipations are highly volatile.

To conclude, the assumption that our constructions have a 24-hour life is likely to fit most market analyses. Further qualifications are necessary for those markets in which prices are always wavering in perpetual flux. The main criticism still to be faced is the supposition that where price constancy prevails the price actually rests at an equilibrium level.

TIME SEQUENCES AND COSTLESS OUTPUT

Assuming the price is fixed daily, generally by the seller to rule for the day, let us examine temporal sales sequences, beginning first with markets in which goods are at hand and priced independently of cost considerations. Actually, under the heading of costless output, we can simultaneously investigate markets in which (1) the goods are really costless, in the sense that their present form is independent of any human exertions but ascribed to natural causes; (2) the present stock and variety of goods cannot be reproduced; (3) the goods have already been produced and can be reproduced and replenished, but perhaps at cost levels substantially different from the historically incurred costs. We begin first with the point-time sales interval, where the stock of goods is to be disposed of instantly or, more generally, in a short interval of time.   Both monopoly and competitive hypotheses are in order; as we are well acquainted with the solution of this type of problem our analysis can be brief and peremptory.

Point-Time Markets

With point-time markets and numerous buyers and sellers, all of whom are informed of prices at the alternate sales outlets so as to guarantee competitive pricing, one price will emerge in these markets— namely, that price at which demand and supply quantities are equated. There is no need to dwell further on this case; it has become the imperishable material of the elementary textbooks.   When the goods are owned by but one seller the simple monopoly problem appears.   The seller must detect the correct shape of the demand schedule or else name, fortuitously, an equilibrium price; otherwise the results will be at variance with stationary equilibrium analysis.

Continuous Sequences

For the competitive case of fixed stocks and continuous markets running daily, the analysis does not raise any untoward difficulties.   Each buyer and seller is concerned in estimating prices over some future intervals and executing their market decision in a propitious time interval. Postponing sales when the goods are on hand entails an inventory decision: sellers, in estimating the expected future price, will have to discount for time, storage, and uncertainty.   Insofar as expectations are justified by the unfolding events the initial sales and purchase plans are likely to be implemented.   If the daily price is a true equilibrium price, decisions to buy at the market price will be exactly commensurate with decisions to sell, otherwise the daily price will engender either unsated demands or unwanted inventory accumulations.   When either sellers or buyers apprehend that their forecasts have gone awry, revisions for future dates in the time continuum are inevitable.   For the moment, however, we abstract from this possibility; the theory of errors will be developed later.

Discontinuous sequences can be treated even more concisely.   Supposing a continuous market pattern to consist of days t_1, t_2, $t_3 \cdot \cdot \cdot t_n$, sales markets may develop on only certain dates, as t_3, t_7, t_{20}, with a time hiatus intervening between the market dates.   Each potential buyer and seller must weigh the importance of purchases and sales at one date rather than another.   If the dates are far enough apart, so that purchases cannot be deferred and withholding is too costly, the case becomes even more definitely one of point-time analysis.

Just as continuous temporal competition requires the daily presence of numerous buyers and sellers and knowledge of one another's actions, monopoly entails numerous purchasers striving to buy from just one seller at several possible prices on each day. With fixed stocks of goods the task for the monopolist is to allocate them to different sales periods so that the MR obtainable in each period is the same; thus

$$MR_1 = MR_2 = MR_3 \cdots \geqq 0.$$

When holding costs and time discounting are important, each MR must be reduced to a net current sum. When current price influences future demand, the sales quantities allotted to each period must be such as to maximize profits over the full time span envisaged: the MR's of the respective dates would still be equal but they are now interdependent values, with the equalities being a resultant of the inclusion of future revenue events; one restriction for costless output, however, is that in the last planned sales interval the expected $MR_n \geqq 0$. Discontinuous monopoly sales intervals can also be tackled by the same technique: whatever the discontinuity in market dates, deducting waiting and carrying costs, prospective MR's must be equated to one another and must equal or exceed zero, at least when the temporal demand curves are independent of one another.

Hence for constant prices through time with costless output, under competition it is essential that the demand and supply curves intersect at the same price height in each daily time interval. If unanimous views on the future are held, they must be such as to forecast price constancy, otherwise price will immediately change. Where the goods cannot be stored or purchase decisions deferred, the unfolding D and S curves for the same price and sales through time, must, if they are not replicas of the previous curves, at least intersect at the same price. For constant prices—under monopoly when demand curves are independent over time—the MR and MC equality must occur at the same elasticity of demand in all time periods, for according to the formula

$$P = MR(E_d/E_d - 1),$$

the mere constancy in the level of the MR-MC intersection is not enough to assure the constancy of prices.

OUTPUT-SALES SEQUENCES

Whenever goods have already been produced, the fixed stock hypothesis just elaborated is the valid one, because (past) production costs are then powerless to affect price, except as they influence the expectations of future costs and prices (and thus current buying and selling decisions). Advancing to the more realistic situations in which current prices are aligned with current output, the adjustment of rates of output to rates of sale is typically the key problem of the firm and the one that our theoretical superstructure ought to illuminate.

Point-Output and Point-Sales Phenomena

Point-output-point-sales phenomena may be illustrated by the example of the concert artist who has a recital only once a year (or at irregular intervals). The illustration also has an additional attribute, a point-input-point-output conjunction. The analysis of this phenomenon fits the single-period textbook discussions in which costs are assigned a part in price determination. If the producer maintains a monopoly foothold, the price that maximizes the total revenue for the output actually produced can be announced. When production is still in the planning stages the endeavor is to balance MC against the expected MR; excluding errors the expected and actual MR will coincide. In competitive markets the output is sold at the ruling price and if errors are not committed the market price will have evoked that output at which $P = MC$.

Point Output, Continuous Sales

Agriculture furnishes some rough approximations of point-output-continuous-sales phenomena. Once output is produced the farmer has the option of selecting the most advantageous selling dates. But after the crop is harvested the analysis parallels that of costless output and continuous sales. If expectations are fulfilled then, for the competitive seller disposing of output in each period, $P_1 = DP_2 = DP_3 \cdots$ etc., where the DP's are the future unit price receipts reduced to a current value because of holding costs—this is the competitive inventory problem expounded earlier. For a monopolist, assuming the demand curves between the different dates are independent, $MR_1 = DMR_2 = DMR_3 \cdots$ etc. Inventory depends not only on demand and cost-curve movements between the several dates but also on carrying costs.

Continuous Output, Point Sales: Competitive Selling

Let us consider now what appears to be a quixotical case, that of continuous output and point sales. Essentially the analysis devolves into the theory of inventory; on reflection, we can detect many applications of this conjunction. For example it encompasses, with certain qualifications, most of the seasonal selling problems. Products turned out continuously during the year might realize a selling outlet, say, only during the Christmas holidays.*

The competitive case can be quickly handled. If we restrict the concept of the *MC* curve to a "day," the expected future price must first be reduced to a current value, and from this reduced price there must be deducted the marginal storage costs attached to each unit currently produced that must be consigned to inventory. It will be to the latter—the daily price residue—that the daily *MC* curve will be equated. Hence production furthest in time from the date of sale will tend to be depressed for two reasons: (1) the current value of the expected future price will be at its lowest daily ebb; and (2) storage costs, because of the time and risks involved, will be high. Therefore, for commodities sold only at the Christmas season say, production should literally collapse the week after Christmas. On each successive day, as the weight of the factors enumerated lightens, the daily outputs are likely to expand with the approach of the sales date.

Some interdependence between the amount produced on t_1 and consigned to inventory, and the cost of storing output of t_2, t_3 $\cdots$ to the date t_n (the sales date) is a likely contingency. When this interrelation is significant the solution can be sought on these lines: to each *MC* point of t_1 there can be added the highest *addition* to storage costs engendered in either t_2, t_3 $\cdots$, etc., by the utilization of storage space in t_1. It will be the latter *MC* curve, inclusive of "user" storage cost, that is equated to the daily "reduced" price expectation.

During the production interval prior to the selling date, as the day of ultimate sales approaches price expectations may change. If they are revised upward this will give a lift to all future output: the firm would even regret its failure to produce in greater volume in the past. But if views suddenly take a more pessimistic tone, then production will thereafter be contracted. Although past output may now appear excessive in the light of the newly forecast market facts, only if the future price is not expected to cover the storage costs over the remaining time length

* Generally sales will recur through the year; but their volume may be so small as to be dismissed from the calculations of the business man.

will the present holdings be abandoned, being either destroyed or allowed to deteriorate. So far as output over the full interval is concerned, if unduly pessimistic expectations loom larger only as the final output date approaches, they are likely to be far less serious for the total output volume than similar views entertained in the beginning of the continuous output sequence and persisting until the end, unless storage costs are so high as to require that the greater part of production be reserved until near the final sales date.

Autonomous changes in factor prices, like revisions in price forecasts, may arise during the production sequence. Rises in costs, while future price or demand expectations are unchanged, work in the usual way, to contract output; cost declines will augment the production volume. There seems to be much scope for some curious types of production anomalies not visualized in the conventional price analysis. As one example, firms with point-sales dates, perhaps because of seasonal unemployment in neighboring industries, can reap the benefit of this temporary phenomenon, hiring more labor in their "off" period and accelerating the production tempo on these dates. The portion of the labor force ordinarily subject to seasonal unemployment could, in theory, secure continuous employment if the production programs of different seasonal trades were effectively synchronized.

Continuous Output, Point Sales: Monopoly Markets

Continuous-output-point-sales analysis under monopoly is more complex than the competitive juxtaposition: under competition, in each day the MC curve was equated to expected price. Under monopoly a daily D and MR curve to suspend against the daily MC curve is lacking. Instead, to solve the problem of production over the full time interval until the point-sales date, the lateral sum of each day's MC curves must be combined in a composite "annual" MC curve, which is then balanced against the "annual" D and MR curves, to decide each day's contribution to the annual output. The subtlety lies in defining equal MC's, for the ultimate equilibrium principle is clear: the MC on the composite of the daily cost curves must equal the MR of the point-demand curve. Manifestly, to the daily MC curves we must add the carrying costs associated with each unit of output until the final sales date. As these costs diminish when output is produced later on, assuming factor prices as constant, the later MC curves will lie further to the right than the earlier ones, so that production will be enlarged toward the end of the time cycle. In equilibrium the "annual" MR will equal the composite "annual" MC and both will equal $MC_1 = MC_2 = MC_3 \cdots$, etc., where the latter are the daily cost phenomena inclusive of carrying costs. For it would always be remunerative to produce later on if current MC exceeded future MC, or produce earlier if the relations were reversed.

Introducing a revision in anticipations as the sales date approaches, the major point lies in the recognition that once production has been completed nothing very much can be done but plan to dispose of the output at the best price obtainable and adjust subsequent output in the light of the new estimates. If by chance the volume of output already completed exceeds the quantity at which MR is zero, further production will cease. As an interesting conjecture, with perhaps some occasional applications in agriculture, if both demand and production costs fall while storage costs increase it may prove profitable to destroy existing stocks and produce fresh output for the approaching sales date.

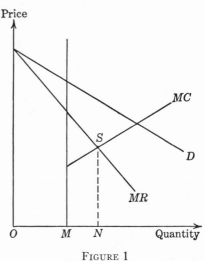

FIGURE 1

Figure 1 contains a diagrammatic analysis of the problem. Suppose that at the date when the former anticipations of the still future point demand are revised, OM quantity has already been produced. D is the newly estimated demand curve and MR is its correspondent, while MC is compounded out of the daily MC curves remaining until the sales date. Over the remaining period then, MN output will be produced, being distributed among each remaining day in such wise that the sum of the daily output levels is MN and the daily MC level is NS, equal to the composite MC. If OM were so large that the appended composite MC lies everywhere above MR, further output would cease. Under competition, however, whatever the dimensions of inventory, as long as even the downward estimates of future price enabled current production to promise profits, output would continue: inventory would be sold ultimately for whatever price it could fetch, being destroyed only if the remaining carrying charges were expected to be excessive relative to the future price.

As another interesting ramification of these ideas, it is quite within the realm of possibility that discontinuous demand—either point or intermittent demand through the year—may be conducive to the growth of multiple products.   For example, where the cost of storing goods for inventory is too excessive, or where all the output that can be most profitably produced can be most economically concentrated into a time sequence shortly preceding sales, then for the rest of the annual period the firm will seek out by-products, being anxious to devote its facilities to any profitable pursuit.   A simple illustration of this principle can be drawn from the ice wagon that is converted into a coal delivery cart in winter.   Seasonal demand and highly perishable (and therefore costly) storage products, or products that are subject to the vicissitudes of taste, can foster a series of supplementary commodity types to occupy the firm in the interim periods.

Continuous-Output–Continuous-Sales Sequences

The continuous-output–continuous-sales sequence is undoubtedly the most important of the temporal categories and is the model most commonly envisaged when temporal processes are described.   Approximating this continuous-output and continuous-demand sequence are many items in which output is continuous but in which the regularly recurring demand is confined mainly to one or two days a week.   These are hybrid cases susceptible to attack by the methods to be outlined.   Bread, newspapers, milk, are prize illustrations of output-sales continuity.   With each of them, too, the analysis of inventory accumulation, of the finished product at least, can generally be discarded.

Impounding any temporal interrelations, the result appears as the traditional price theory, with conscious stress on the multiple-period equilibrium continuum and with firms in each daily interval foreseeing their market correctly and equating MC and MR.*   A revision in estimates will have its effect on output almost immediately—the "next day"—unless this is technically impossible.   Each day in fact, or the preceding "day" (t_0), firms must be conceived to plan their program for the ensuing t_1 day.   Normally, as in stationary conditions, the programming will consist of nothing more than a passive adherence to the previous day's schedule, which is likely to have been laid out some time in the past, and projected for the "quarter-year" without further reconsideration, unless there are violent eruptions in the business scene: normally it will have to be a severe business storm that shakes a firm from its

---

* Realistically we might often take a time lag between production and sales of one "day."

plotted and lethargic ways. When a monopoly firm revises its production schedule downward because of the pervading business gloom, it may deem it prudent to eliminate even inventory holdings prior to undertaking new production. Competitive firms, however, may dispose of inventory as best they can while sustaining profitable *new* production.

Discontinuous Production and Multiple Products

As another multiple-product implication of this analysis, a firm with continuous sales may perceive the greater profitability of discontinuous production over continuous production. For example, say that the AC curve is U-shaped, and that the demand curve intersects AC at the minimum point on the latter. Also suppose that in view of the shape of the demand and cost curves, the monopoly output is exactly one half the competitive total. It may well be profitable in these circumstances for the firm to produce the minimum AC quantity, the volume indicated at the $P = MC$ position, and sell one half currently while storing the remainder until the next sales date, when it can be disgorged. The procedure might prove more profitable than equating MC and MR in each period and producing continuously. The critical elements are the carrying costs and the minimum AC, compared to the AC at the daily $MC = MR$ output. By and large, the analysis applies to those nonperishables that are subject to decreasing AC and can be stored without excessive cost. When the firm is producing the large quantity, its equipment will be idle in every alternate time period. This fact should exert a strong incentive for the propagation of suitable by-products.

The important point is that firms will not, when the continuous time dimensions of the equilibrium adaptations are discerned, produce the output that is disclosed at the point at which the single-period $MR = MC$. Future time intervals of sale and production are an integral part of the problem. Not infrequently the AC at the single-period $MR = MC$ output volume is drawn as about double the level at the minimal AC. Unless inventory costs are prohibitive this solution indubitably conveys a wrong impression; temporal sequences are far more appropriate for the problem.

INPUT-OUTPUT INTERVALS

The assumption of the simultaneity of input and output (where inputs consist of the application of productive factors in order to obtain output results) must also be relaxed, if not generally dropped.   The alternate hypotheses are: (1) input, applied continuously or not, ripens into output on one date; in farming this approximates the facts; (2) input, however applied, yields output over a series of dates; (3) input can create output on several possible *alternate* dates; if the input is directed to output on one date the output that might be secured on other days is foregone.   As a fourth hypothesis there is a simultaneity, or negligible time lag, between input and output, ultimately a special case of (1) above.

Input-Output Lags and Output-Sales Sequences

When there is simultaneity, or an inappreciable time lag between input and output, as in bread baking or newspaper publishing, the earlier analyses can stand firm.   Likewise, when output emerges at but one date, even when the time lag is not negligible, the earlier analyses are unaffected.   Part of the productive costs, however, are interest charges associated with the application of variable factors; sales sequences may, however, be of the continuous or point variety.   A homely illustration of a continuous input that culminates in a continuous output sequence, with each unit of output related to a definite input, is the sausage machine, where after an initial time lag the rate of output is synchronized to the rate of input.   If the latter ceases, output may not be immediately affected although, after a time lag, it soon dries up.*   This technical production lag can accompany either continuous or point sales phenomena.

When output from current input accrues on not one but several ultimate dates, the factor's marginal-revenue product (PMR) is the current value of its full series of future outputs.   If we denote its marginal-revenue products by PMR, with the numeral subscripts indicative of their dates, and with D signifying the appropriate discount factor applied to each price separately, then

$$PMR = D(PMR_1 + PMR_2 + PMR_3 \cdots).$$

So long as the PMR sum, so computed, exceeds the price of the factor,

---

* From D. H. Robertson, *Money*, p. 112.   Although the "production period" is measurable in simple cases of this sort, attempts to measure it almost invariable conclude that it is infinite, stretching back to the beginning of time.   On this point there is of course the endless controversy surrounding the work of Böhm-Bawerk.   For a recent article reviewing the enormous literature, see N. Kaldor, "The Recent Controversy on the Theory of Capital," *Econometrica* (1937), and the reply and rejoinder by Professor Knight and Mr. Kaldor, same journal (1938).

the factor will be hired: the equilibrium condition is the equality of the two, as observed earlier.*

If sales markets are continuous, even though the marginal product is really a joint product in time, it hardly disrupts (though it somewhat complicates) the analysis. For point sales, however, all outputs that accrue *after* the selling date must be written off as valueless. If the selling is discontinuous, costs of storage until the sales dates must be included in computing the marginal-revenue products. Either way, these considerations combine to reduce the effective PMR of the factor.

If input can be made to sprout output on several alternate dates, it is likewise true that only output obtainable before the marketing date is valuable. For the continuous sales pattern, with this input-output relation the firm would direct the input to that output date on which the PMR was highest: the largest of the alternate PMR's would be the aim of policy. By and large, the largest physical output attributable to the given input would be selected unless this occurred at a very late date, rendering its current value low, or if it ensued at an early date when either price or MR was extremely low.

Hence the relaxation of the simultaneous input-output hypothesis does not greatly damage our output-sales sequence analyses. Realistically, the theory must acknowledge the temporal disparity between input and output. For the study of market phenomena, however, apart from the theory of the equilibrium of the firm, it is the output-sales patterns that form the main objective of our intellectual labors.

Isoquants and Input-Output Lags

It is pertinent to examine the validity of the isoquant apparatus when input and output belong to different dates. When the two are simultaneous, then of course the isoquant field is an enlightening tool, of geometrical elegance and eloquence. Even if output is not strictly coterminous with input, so long as the services of the two factors are addressed to the same output date, even if applied at different times, then here too the structure is not demolished: part of the factor costs, however, is an associated interest charge because of payment in advance of production. But when the output attributable to the different factors ripens at different dates the isoquant approach is futile, for the product curves are deprived of any single and straightforward interpretation. The analysis of factor hire can then best proceed in terms of the ratio of the factor's PMR to the factor's price.

* Above, p. 139.

Finally, it was argued earlier that an entrepreneur might be badly informed in his estimates of the actual shape of the cost curve by an incomplete appraisal of input-output relations. When there is an important time discrepancy between the two, and especially when outputs recur on several dates from a given input dose, the chances of obscure and muddled ideas are multiplied.

BIBLIOGRAPHICAL NOTE

A more valuable account of Marshall's method and conception of time is R. Opie, "Marshall's Time Analysis," *Economic Journal* (1931). Erik Lindahl, *Studies in the Theory of Money and Capital*, in describing a temporal equilibrium uses the artifice (p. 60) of confining price changes to the interstices of time between market dates—price being named actually before the market opens—and thereafter directs his attention to sales and production phenomena. This is not different in essentials from the ideas set forth in this chapter on daily price formation. The classic, if artificial, descriptions of the means by which knowledge of market phenomena is transmitted to the market participants are stated in L. Walras, *Elements d'Économie Politique*, p. 44 (1927 edition) and F. Y. Edgeworth, *Mathematical Psychics*, pp. 18–19. A concise survey of these methodological tactics is provided in Hicks, *Value and Capital*, pp. 127–129.

CHAPTER 19

Path Analysis

IT REMAINS TO ANALYZE THE MAN-
ner in which markets react to dynamic change, conducting the investigation in a clock-time setting. Constancy in the data, we can surmise,
will culminate in equilibrium; it is change and the dynamic shifts in the
data that arouse our misgivings over the equilibrium postulates. In
the timeless comparative statics, rather than trace the processes of
adjustment and the path traversed before the equilibrium is realized
after a change in the data, the transitional study is omitted in the haste
to picture the essential features of the final equilibrium configuration.
The analytic boldness of this procedure can be excused only if we
are convinced that new obstacles would not obtrude along the path to
impede the equilibrium development; the theory is suspect until this
proof is forthcoming.

THE COBWEB THEOREM

Let us envisage a model in which the market is in competitive balance
with $D_x = S_x$. If we superimpose an increase in demand onto our
mental scheme, equilibrium analysis will immediately conclude that if
supply is a rising function of price, price will be higher and output
greater.

Pondering the process by which this equilibrium is reached, we conclude that either of two hypotheses are available: (1) All producers
estimate the new equilibrium price implicit in the demand shift correctly, and implement their estimates by correct production schedule
variations; the old equilibrium is thereby transformed into a new equilibrium immediately and mechanistically, in one smooth stage. This
hypothesis might provide the sustenance for the method of comparative
statics. (2) Producers may be individually ignorant of the spontaneous

change in demand. One assumption—one of many—is that they continue to produce the former equilibrium output despite the demand rise. Price may immediately be elevated to the new demand price for the former equilibrium output quantity, and an equilibrating process may be touched off whose content, duration, and amplitude is contingent upon the anticipations of producers on the price course over the subsequent "days."

Incremental Adaptations

In Figure 1A, D_1 and S_1 are the demand and supply curves for date t_1 in a competitive market, with the equilibrium price P_1, and output, OM. Demand, on t_2 say, rises to D_2. Assuming that producers had expected P_1 to persist to t_2, an output of only OM would be forthcoming. The impact effect of the demand shift would be to elevate price to P_2, the ordinate height on D_2 above the abscissa OM.

Suppose that entrepreneurs expect P_2 to prevail on t_3 and strive to equate MC to P_2. If this could be accomplished immediately, output would advance to OR, well beyond the equilibrium quantity ON. However, it may be impossible in the short daily period to advance output by more than finite incremental amounts, equal to the horizontal lengths of the small steps engrafted upon S_1 and D_2 in Figure 1A. Thus if the ultimate equilibrium output ON exceeds OM by 1,000 units and the daily output can be increased by but 100 units, it will be ten days before the new equilibrium is achieved. With each "day," despite the daily price fall, output will expand until a total daily production rate of ON is reached and the equilibrium price P_3 is established. But the transition to equilibrium is in orderly stages rather than in one heroic plunge. Hence, when only incremental output variations are possible, and sellers' actions are predicated on the ruling price, the equilibrium is determinate: the theory of the path in this case buttresses conventional analysis. Symbolically, if ΔP denotes the daily price decrement, Δt the passage of 24-hour unit time, and ΔX the daily production increment, then after the final equilibrium stage

$$\frac{\Delta P}{\Delta t} = 0$$

and

$$\frac{\Delta X}{\Delta t} = 0.$$

The movements in price and output can be assigned to the excess demand price in each day. Perhaps it can be posited in all these problems that as excess demand price decreases, then the daily rate of price decrease $\Delta P/\Delta t$ will be smaller. Hence as the equilibrium is approached the daily rate of price change will slow down.

Even waiving the hypothesis that sellers expect the t_2 price to be a

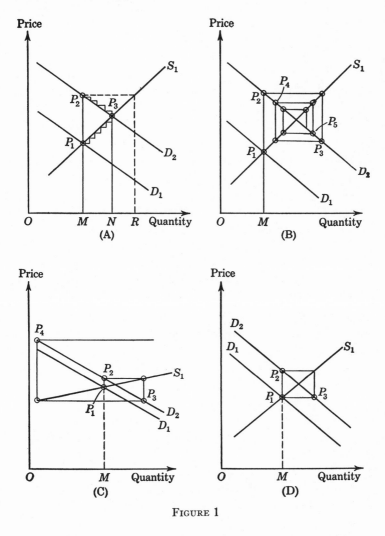

FIGURE 1

perpetuation of the t_1 price, equilibrium is still determinate so long as the expected t_2 price exceeds the MC of the maximum daily augmentable output rate. Equilibrium, in the competitive case of incremental adaptations, would be indeterminate only if the *expected* price fell below the MC of the current output rate. Then the t_1 output rate might not be maintained even if on the objective market facts an output increase would be justified. So long as producers act on misguided beliefs of the direction of price change, until the erroneous price expectations are corrected market determinateness cannot be posited: the theory of the path would then become a proper vehicle for study while equilibrium analysis would distort market events.

Output Fluidity

We now examine the possible consequences of more fluid output adaptations in which substantial daily variations in the productive flow are possible: here rather than $\Delta X/X$ approaching zero, it is possible for it to be greater than unity. The argument probably fits discontinuous temporal sequences better than continuous daily output sequences; for example, in agriculture substantial additions to the output volume (exclusive of the influence of weather) are possible from one harvest season to another.

In Figures 1B, 1C and 1D we presume that OM is initially produced, for this is the equilibrium volume prior to the upward tilt in demand. Price, after the demand rise, immediately rises to P_2, after which all firms are able to and do expand output to a total indicated by the relevant S_1 point at the price P_2. But this output can be sold only at the demand price shown on D_2. Output will subsequently contract, to the supply point at price P_3; price will thereupon rise to P_4, etc.

Working through the adaptative process in Figure 1B, each successive $\Delta P/\Delta t$ movement ensures a closer approximation to the $D_2 = S_1$ equilibrium price. Equilibrium will be the ultimate outcome whenever, for linear curves, the gradient of the supply curve exceeds that of the demand curve (neglecting its negative sign). Figure 1C depicts a thoroughly unstable configuration, with each successive adaptation bringing a more serious departure from the $D_2 = S_1$ equilibrium intersection. This explosive development accompanies a linear supply curve of lesser slope than that of a linear demand curve. Equilibrium will be indeterminate unless expectations or adjustments are recast; otherwise, even with fundamentally constant supply-and-demand phenomena, markets will display a series of sustained fluctuations rather than culminate in equilibrium.

Figure 1D illustrates a range of neutral oscillations, with the price and output amplitude fluctuating regularly about equilibrium at the same level. Here the slopes of the linear S and D curves are equal, though their directions differ. Price alternates between P_1 $(= P_3)$ and

P_2. Surveying the skein sketched in Figure 1 makes the etymology of the "cobweb" term apparent.

Other than the assumption that firms expect market price to continue constant, a major presupposition of the cobweb theorem is that during the full course of the adaptative process it is assumed that the D and S curves are rigidly fixed despite the passage of time, independent of the course of adaptation and income redistribution among buyers and sellers occasioned by the price flurries. Once this assumption is relaxed the diagrammatic presentation of the cobweb skein becomes hopelessly intricate, for there are too many alternate types of propagation to unravel. In all but special circumstances, entrepreneurs must for equilibrium predict one way or another in the adaptative process the $D_x = S_x$ equilibrium price. Then, after planning their output on this hypothesis, they must cling to it tenaciously for future output decisions.

Repercussions in Other Markets

Substitutes and complements will, of course, experience some shocks and tremors as the price in market A oscillates along the adaptative path. With each new P_a the demand curve in the varying B markets will be dislodged. Along the course of the cobweb, therefore, other markets will be upset, echoing the perturbations in P_a, with the degree and amplitude of the reverberations determined by the degree of commodity interdependence. This very interdependence constitutes a new threat to stability and equilibrium in the market for A. It was observed earlier that when P_b remains constant while P_a fluctuates, the demand curve for A is rendered flatter and more elastic than when P_b follows P_a upward and downward. This very steepness of D_a might, given the supply curve, provoke an explosive cobweb. Hence markets that promise equilibrium when other prices are presumed constant during the equilibrium course may be rendered unstable by roundabout price interrelations. It need not, however, be part of our present task to trace these ramifications; regardless of how other prices react, we can consider their movements as already subsumed in the demand curve for A. So long as they are posited as being of a given order, this part of the problem can be neglected.

CHANGE AND EQUILIBRIUM PROCESSES

The next step is an analysis of a shift in either or both of the D and S functions while the market is in the throes of adaptation to a previous D or S displacement; here new data erupt along the equilibrium path.

Several common types of market phenomena can be clarified only by according incessant change a place in our mental model.

Continuous Demand Changes

Recalling the incremental adaptation process, suppose that the supply curve is rigid while the market-demand curve grows continuously. Writing ΔD as the lateral daily demand shift at each price (assuming this to be uniform at each price), and ΔS, as the daily output increment, then if

$$\frac{\Delta D}{\Delta t} > \frac{\Delta S}{\Delta t},$$

obviously, with the lateral shift in demand exceeding the daily increment in output, equilibrium in the sense of $D_x = S_x$ is impossible. Hence, everything rests upon the degree and frequency of demand shifts, the price forecasts, and the degree of output fluidity. If output is fluid, as in the cobweb analysis, and price expectations are accurate, equilibrium may evolve. Likewise, when demand advances in the course of the cobweb adaptation, an otherwise unwarranted expansion in output may be absorbed by the demand rise. Situations could be concocted in which price swings are wide and explosive, and other situations in which, in alternate periods, price is close to and farther from the equilibrium levels. But it is unavailing to dwell on these points unless we care to outline precise, but probably uncommon, sequences. In sum, incessant demand changes, like all continual changes, are inimical to equilibrium concepts unless the changes are foreseen and output is fluid.

"Supply Catching Up with Demand"

In part, the popular phrase "supply catching up with demand," so commonly employed in describing postwar market phenomena, can be construed as signifying sustained changes in demand. Unfortunately the phrase is ambiguous, with at least two reasonably distinct ideas that can be distilled: (1) that the demand curve is rigid while the rate of output is well below equilibrium levels, and (2) that current demand is unduly high and, as output is produced and sold, the demand curve will recede. The former might describe commodities of daily recurrent demand, such as bread, milk, newspapers, etc. The latter might fit items of nonrecurring demand, such as automobiles and refrigerators, where current purchasers, procuring a unit of the commodity today, drop out of the market for several "tomorrows."

For goods of recurring demand the analysis is simple. In Figure 1A, perhaps OM is produced while ON is consistent with equilibrium. If output can be expanded only incrementally, equilibrium is eventually determinate, although it may be several time periods before it is realized. If output is volatile, immediately expansible, and equilibrium price forecasts accurate, the time-lag characteristic of supply "catching up with demand" vanishes. The cobweb theorem comes into its own, however, if prevision is wrong and the output expansion fluid.

With nonrecurrent (daily) demand phenomena, as with automobiles, the "current" demand level is conceived as abnormally high while output is abnormally low. There are two dynamic demand properties here that should be distinguished: (1) the Δt growth in demand from new sources superimposed upon the unfilled demands of those waiting to purchase from the past; (2) the daily Δt diminution

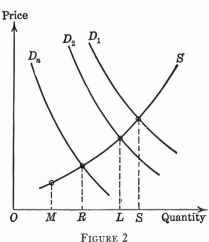

FIGURE 2

of demand as new output is produced and sold and former purchasers removed from the market. Let us disregard (1) and concentrate on the second element.

In Figure 2, for t_1 we commence with D_1 and S; output in t_1 is OM while the t_1 equilibrium output is OS. As OM is marketed, the demand curve for t_2 will recede, reduced say by OM in the upper reaches; although, since the t_1 buyers may desire additional units at very low prices, the t_2 demand curve (D_2) approaches the D_1 of t_1 in the lower regions. Each week, as the rate of output advances, the demand curve recoils at a faster rate; perhaps a temporary equilibrium is secured at output OL; thereafter with demand continuing to fade, there must also be a retrenchment in output. The demand fall ultimately subsides and the curve settles, say, at D_n, which becomes the "daily" level of *recurring* demand (even though the daily purchasers are different individuals). The ultimate equilibrium output is at OR, although supply can be described as having "caught up with demand" in the range between OR and OS.

Simultaneous Demand and Supply Changes

Simultaneous movements in both D and S need to be briefly covered. Conceivably, at the same time that demand has swung to the right, longer-run forces might dislodge the supply curve and push it to the right. The equilibrium solution is obvious: the market mechanism by which the equilibrium is attained is far more obscure.

As a first principle, the new supply curve is the one relevant for the market analysis. Complexities that troubled us in the cobweb theorem also disconcert us now, for whatever the stage from which the equilibrium adaptation commences, the ultimate equilibrium is given by the demand curve that prevails on the market date and the supply curve that is real at the date output is prepared. If sellers delude themselves into thinking that the last price will persist, and if they have faith in its permanence, equilibrium demonstrations are futile when both D and S are subject to simultaneous variation and intersection at other than the preceding period's price. Most damaging to the equilibrium concept would be the combination of continuous demand increases and supply decreases or, conversely, demand decreases and supply increases. Equilibrium models that proclaim external determinateness in such an atmosphere are undoubtedly misleading.

Oscillating movements in demand and supply are entitled to some mention; undoubtedly interesting specimens can be envisaged, but without knowledge of market facts it becomes but a mental pastime to proceed to unravel them. It is, of course, the unforeseen oscillations that matter; merely seasonal switches in demand can ordinarily be prognosticated with a fair degree of certitude without gravely upsetting markets.

Speculation and Change

A notable omission in the discussion of change has been the failure to advert to the role of speculation. In its simplest form speculation obtrudes whenever buyers or sellers predict future prices as a guide to their current actions: any belief that these will diverge from current prices will foster "speculative" operations. Added to this, whenever prices are expected to change there will be scope for the proclivities of a professional and specialist group interested in buying and selling solely to profit from the price movement.

Manifestly, whenever important price swings are expected, the field is rife for speculation, at least where commodities are standardized without legal and institutional obstructions to the practice. A priori we cannot argue that the price swings will be tempered by the practice unless we have in mind some particular types of expectations, recognizing that in each period the activities of speculators must be added to either or both the demand and supply side. Their activities may sometimes accentuate, rather than dampen, the price swings. For example, given underlying future data as but a replica of the present, and assuming the market already in equilibrium, prices will fluctuate so long as speculators *expect* them to change; in this chain of events speculators can hardly be described as restraining price movements. In other sequences, however, when their views on the future are more nearly accurate than those of producers, they can render a signal, stabilizing influence.

MONOPOLY PRICE MOVEMENTS

The discussion of dynamic phenomena so far has been conducted wholly within a competitive framework. This assumption needs to be lifted and some attention devoted to the response of monopoly markets to economic change. We shall find that although the theory of the path is simpler, the effects of change are more indeterminate than in competitive analysis. In the latter, when the theory of the path was disregarded and the method of comparative statics applied, we could be sure that when the demand curve moved to the right that price and output would rise so long as the supply curve sloped upward. But even this elementary proposition cannot be vouchsafed when monopoly prevails.

Equilibrium Theory and an Increase in Demand

Since it is not the demand curve but the MR curve that is instrumental in monopoly equilibrium analysis, it requires but a modicum of perspicacity to apprehend that even if the full demand curve moves rightward, its slope may change so that price or output may be *lower* after the demand lift than before. Let us prove this statement, for it offers a strange contrast to competitive theory where a demand rise always evoked a price-output increase.

In monopoly equilibrium, $MC = MR$ and $P/MR = E_d/E_d - 1$.* Invoking the assumption that MC is constant, thereby fixing MR in the new equilibrium despite the demand shift, if we can show that price may *fall* it can be inferred that even if MC is (slowly) rising, price may still be lower. Examining the formula, we see that all that is required for price to be reduced despite a growth in demand is that the elasticity

* Above, p. 43.

of demand should be so increased as to overshadow even an MC rise. Considering that the demand shift need not be a uniform lateral movement, we are divested of any analytical warrant for concluding that price will rise.   In competitive analysis, where MC curves had to be rising, so long as the demand quantity at the former price increased, price had to go higher.   In monopoly, when we ponder the fact that falling MC phenomena are not precluded, there is further reason for suspecting a possible price fall.

To make matters worse, there is the possibility that after the demand curve shifts, the new MR curve may be steeper than the old.   Conceivably, it may intersect the MC curve to the *left* of the old intersection so that price will be higher than prior to the demand change, but—and this is curious—output will be lower.   If price is higher, and MC ($= MR$) lower than before, the elasticity of demand in the new equilibrium will be reduced.

Fortunately, movements in the cost curve under monopoly do not imply the same indeterminateness: a rise or fall in the MC curve operates in the usual way.   Still, we are left with the uncomfortable thought that with monopoly we are without a simple theory of comparative statics as a guide to the final effects of a change in demand on price and output; not even the directional tendencies of change are assured to us.

An Increase in Demand and the Adjustment Path

Under competition, after an increase in demand the cobweb theorem assumed that each firm sold all of its current output which, it was first supposed, was less than the equilibrium amount.   Even if firms disgorged some of their inventory holdings, so long as the amount unloaded plus current output was exceeded by the ultimate equilibrium quantities, and so long as constant price hypotheses dominated the entrepreneurial outlook, the cobweb skein would develop.

To cover the same terrain in monopoly markets, in Figure 1A, we can suppose that the D_1 curve is the initial MR_1 curve, while D_2 represents the MR_2 after the lift in demand and S_1 is an MC curve.   The original equilibrium amount is OM and the new equilibrium volume, ON.   If OM quantity was produced because of faulty prevision of the demand upsurge, and if the firm persisted in naming the previous "day's" price, it would discover sales proceeding at a faster pace than before and sooner or later it would revise its demand views.   If we suppose that on the day the output is ready for sale the firm learns of the new demand situation, it will announce the new demand price for the OM volume.

Retaining the hypothesis of incremental daily output adaptations, equilibrium is perfectly determinate but some time must elapse before it evolves.

If output is more fluid the firm would have to calculate the prospective $MC = MR$ price and output. Assuming an error is made in the direction of undue output optimism, the firm would have to compute whether the MR of its actual output volume is negative, besides weighing inventory costs and the effects of a nonequilibrium current price on future demand. If it does decide to dispose of the full production turned out for that day, price will be below the final equilibrium level. This would precipitate a reappraisal of views and the calculation of a new $MC = MR$ position. By this experimental process of producing and selling, if the new demand curve is durable the firm should acquire sufficient information on it to attain an equilibrium position of *estimated* $MC = MR$, which need not always coincide with the *real* $MC = MR$ position.*

This analysis seems mild and unexciting compared to the cobweb spectacle of competitive analysis. The reason is not hard to see: the cobweb oscillations were attributable to the faulty price expectations of entrepreneurs; the equilibrium required not only that price be foreseen by each seller but also that the sum of the outputs of the individual firms be exactly equal to the amount that the market wanted to purchase at that price. Under monopoly, however, these wild aberrations need not follow; with each output the monopolist will glean some new information on the market demand curve; in fairly short order the firm should be able to form some accurate ideas on the market-demand curve. This in itself ought preclude explosive or neutral cobweb phenomena.

Just as under competition, the demand points on the monopolist's demand curve are contingent on the outputs and prices in other markets; unless the latter prices follow a given configuration the monopolist's demand curve is not unique, contributing a new element of indeterminacy. Hence these interrelations must be specified; for if they alter, the equilibrium development will be affected.

Incomplete Equilibrium and Economic Change

If further changes in the data occur while the monopolist is adjusting to previous developments, the determinacy of the results centers upon the direction of the new change and the accuracy of the prognostications of the seller: if the new changes are small, a wide departure from equilib-

---

* Above, pp. 359–360.

rium should not be imminent.   In general, we are left with the conclusion reached in competitive analysis, namely that stationary equilibrium
requires that the demand and cost curves possess sufficient durability to
enable producers to know them.   Otherwise the stationary strictures
are devoid of descriptive significance and are indicative only of the
equilibrium relations compared with actual market results.

Situations similar to those discussed under the heading of "supply
catching up with demand" also have a place in monopoly theory, with
the same distinction as before between rigid demand curves of recurring
demand and the "backward-moving" curve system of nonrecurring
demand.   As no new subtleties are involved, it is superfluous to repeat
the analysis.

Duopoly, Change, and Equilibrium Analysis

Nothing has been said of the response of duopoly and oligopoly markets to change.   Little need be done here for we already know that even
when demand and cost phenomena are stationary, these markets might
display some strange aberrations.   Analytically, not very much can be
said as to the transition process or the final equilibrium in the event of
change; we can surmise that a general "market" rise in demand or costs
should raise prices and a fall should lower them.   But when we reflect
on the diverse reaction patterns and the importance of the psychology
of the participants, the security of even this trite conclusion is denied us.

RIGID PRICES

Price inflexibility may be the response to change.   Rigid prices, for
our purposes, can be defined analytically as prices that are constant in
the historical time-sweep, even when market forces are conducive to
price change: the price mechanism can be conceived as suspended
although output and sales quantities may disclose some substantial
fluctuations.   Rigid prices are characteristic of many markets; some
writers have gone so far as to ascribe most, if not all, of the economic ills
of the system to the "stickiness" of prices in many sectors of the
economy.

Price rigidity, patently, is wholly a matter of degree.   A price that
fluctuated daily could be labeled "rigid" in the sense of being inflexible
over the one day in which it prevailed.   On this interpretation, unless
all prices manifested the hypersensitivity of prices on the commodity
and stock exchanges, they could be characterized as rigid.   Palpably,
it would be grotesque to construe price rigidity so severely: an economic

system in which prices fluctuated continually would contain irrationalities of its own, rendering, for one thing, the use of the price system a chore rather than a help, and reducing the economic process to a huge price-guessing contest. What is largely intended by price rigidity is fixity despite strong upheavals in demand or supply conditions.

Rigid Equilibrium Prices through Time

Let us eliminate some causes of rigidity that are unworthy of inquiry. In competitive markets, as one example, if marginal costs are constant, however exaggerated the swings in demand, price will be stable. Or if demand was always perfectly elastic at the same level—implying usually rigid prices of perfect substitutes—then price will not yield despite the passage of time. Analogously, demand and supply may move simultaneously and in such wise as to maintain price constant even though the changes may evoke some wide output gyrations. Finally, unchanging supply-and-demand data would be the simplest cause of price rigidity. In all these circumstances price rigidity through time would be perfectly compatible with the equilibrium postulates, while price flexibility would itself denote a market imbalance. Disregarding these relationships, prices in smoothly working competitive markets will oscillate with the ebb and flow of supply and demand.

Under monopoly a price variation is unnecessary if supply and demand forces are rigid. Similarly, movements in D, MR, and MC may so neutralize one another that for profit maximization remedial price action is unnecessary although output will fluctuate. Hence monopoly price rigidity is sometimes explicable by the course of the demand curve in the neighborhood of equilibrium after the shift in MR and MC. All too frequently these perfectly comprehensible causes óı price rigidity are disregarded in observations on real markets.

Let us cite some of the causes of rigid prices when the underlying D and S facts appear to warrant a price change. In competitive markets speculative activity can be listed as a cause of price rigidity, if somehow we can divorce speculative purchase and sale activity from the "real" forces. As a pseudo-competitive case, the government may stabilize particular prices either by purchase-sale operations or price-fixing injunction. In monopoly markets we have a more imposing array of causes of price rigidity. As a trivial case, the monopolist in examining the daily demand curve may invariably misjudge the situation and name the same price as formerly. Eliminating such flagrant errors, the more substantial reasons for price rigidity that can be detected are (1) the practice of market planning of price and output for a definite length of time; (2) costs of administering price changes; (3) estimates of the effects of price changes on future demand; (4) duopoly and oligopoly price interdependence; (5) full-cost pricing ideas. The list could undoubtedly be extended.

Constant Price Expectations and Price Rigidity

Even in competitive markets prices will be constant and rigid if buyers and sellers have grown accustomed to a particular price as normal, so that they guide their market decisions by it. For buyers it would involve demand quantities falling off precipitately to zero, and expanding to "infinite" levels above and below the normal price. For sellers, it would involve an unwillingness to sell below the "normal" level and a readiness to unload their full stocks above this figure. In this environment price is almost certain to be constant through time. Of course the problem would still be to explain why (all) views should converge and center on the same price expectation.

Nonetheless, more than mere concurrence on *future* price is required to bring current price to this level: buyers and sellers must be willing to accelerate current purchases or dispose of all supplies (which must be ample for the purpose) if current price is to be held equal to the expected future price. Otherwise, merely a widespread conviction on the likely *future* price will not suffice to equate D and S at this price in the present.

Monopoly Price Policy for a Rigid Clock Length

Monopoly control provides more scope for price inflexibility.* There is as a trivial case a monopolist naming the previous day's price because of mistaken ideas on *today's* demand. Likewise, we need not bother with a monopolist who forecasts so badly each day that he produces an output (all of which is sold) that does not maximize profits but succeeds in holding the price constant. Both of these cases are based upon error, ignorance, or irrationality. Let us concern ourselves with the more purely rational motives for price inflexibility.

Empirically, in monopoly markets the prime cause of price rigidity, in the short period at least, seems to be that firms plan their price and output policy for a finite time length—say a quarter year or full year—and, in general, refuse to reconsider their judgment until this time has elapsed. One reason for this adamancy may be the cost of administer-

---

* See the remarks of J. K. Galbraith, "Reflections on Price Control," *Quarterly Journal of Economics* (1946).

ing price change; nonetheless, whatever the precise explanation is we must accept the constant-price policy over the time length as a datum. Let us see how a rational decision on a maximum price would be formed if it is stipulated that this price is to be effective for the full time interval.

Immediately, we might inquire into the factors determining the length of the pricing period. Frequently this will be fixed by custom, by directorate interest, by ideas and persuasions of what is "sound management practice"—a set of rule-of-thumb precepts. Logically, a firm would plan output and price only for that period forward for which it felt it could gauge demand and costs. If errors are made, and if these were disclosed by unfolding incidents and events, production plans would be recast whenever the new information justified the change. Sometimes, as in agriculture, technical factors may prevent alterations in output plans; when they cannot be revised there is of course nothing to be gained by pondering the future anew. In clock time, in all but periods of rapid change, perhaps a quarter-year is not too long a time horizon for planning.

In forming its price decision to cover a quarter-year, say, the sum of daily sales at each possible price would have to be estimated in order to mould the daily demands into the period composite. Likewise, the daily MC curves can be summated into a quarterly aggregate. Thereupon the price that maximizes profits, at which $MR = MC$, would be learned. Although this by now appears elementary, there are some complications: if sales do not proceed at an even daily rate, but are higher in the later stages, there will be need for some early production for inventory, which will entail some added costs. Or, the other way, output may initially have to be pushed beyond the ultimate ($MC = MR$) equality, or sales will have to be rationed, either consciously or haphazardly.

So far it is presumed that the firm's estimates on the sales volume at the stipulated price are correct. But this may not be so. If the firm had been too optimistic, inventories would accumulate towards the end of the period, perhaps uncomfortably; the firm could, of course, reconsider and retrench in its output scale. If sales are outrunning the production rate a decision will have to be made on whether or not output is to be accelerated. Perhaps the management is so obdurate as to refrain from any alteration in its plans until the next quarter-year. Generally, however, even if the fixed price pronouncement is maintained, there will be some latitude granted management to adjust the output flow to sales rates. Still, unless rates of sale and output are uniform the maximum profit implicit in the daily equality of MC and MR will not be attained. Hence a rigid price policy imposed for a length of time will not maximize profits; a truly maximum price policy would oscillate with daily flurries in demand and costs. Even if total sales at the period price equal the sum of sales at each *daily* maximum price, profits from the latter would be greater—unless each day's D and MC curves were identical replicas—because of the time distribution of output and price differences, the total sales receipts would be different.

That periodic price announcements fail to secure maximum monopoly profits is a significant proposition. And yet firms persist in the practice. When a proposition flagrantly violates actual operating principles there is need to inquire whether there are some ameliorating forces at work tending to soften the theoretical strictures.

Cost of Administering Price Changes

Daily fluctuations in D and MC may be so small that the profit discrepancy accruing from a daily maximum compared to a periodic rigid price may be minute. In items of daily recurring demand, it may be surmised that a price fixed for a fairly short period ahead is likely to be tantamount to a daily maximum-price announcement. For items of nonrecurring demand, however, where sales are bunched rather than flowing at a uniform daily rate, a more flexible price policy would probably repay itself. Yet this is just the paradox: it is in these fields— the "durable goods" outputs—that price rigidity is most rampant. Holding in abeyance the matter of the cost of administering a price change, we must seek one explanation of the anomaly in the opportunities for speculation when prices of durable goods are subject to frequent fluctuation. Dealers, likewise, would largely become speculators in inventory. Rather than incur their wrath and rancor through a fluctuating price policy, and perhaps lose custom to rigidly priced substitute wares because of dealers who refused to be partners to a speculative venture, a measure of rigidity is inevitable if other firms adhere to rigid price policy. Thus in items of recurring demand there is usually little to be gained by daily price fluctuation; in items of nonrecurring demand both speculative buying and the reluctance of dealers to participate in the speculative scheme would militate against the practice. We are committed then to a substantial degree of price rigidity in the economy over at least short periods of time. Departures from the practice would invariably entail a waste of resources: (1) a greater number of individuals would be engaged in purely "speculative" endeavors; (2) when we recognize the frictions in the hire of factors it is clear that "daily" variations in production would in most cases require that a substantial number of productive factors alternate each day between employment and unemployment.*

Other than the reasons intimated in the last paragraph is this fact: to surmount the objections of middlemen who intervene between the early stages of production and final consumers, the practice of compensating them for their losses introduces a new cause of price rigidity, namely the *cost* of administering price changes. Retailers, for example, must carry an inventory as part of the cost of doing business because of the vagaries of sales and conventional modes of shop-keeping, that is, of stocking goods for display purposes. Constant price fluctuation will make merchandising a highly speculative pastime; custom is likely to be diverted to primary sellers who do maintain prices. To overcome their aversion to price changes, the retailers are frequently reimbursed for losses in inventory holdings when the sales price is reduced. Even when the atmosphere is favorable for a price change, the sums that will have to be expended for their price protection will be a persuasive deterrent to frequent price reductions. For price rises, on the other hand, especially in duopoly or oligopoly circumstances, unless rivals are ready to follow suit, an upward price adjustment may not be feasible.

But there are other expenses involved in varying the price by the firm. Large merchandising outlets will incur at least nuisance expenses in varying price placards, in changing the nature of the sales appeal, and in disseminating information on price movements, besides reaping the bad harvest of greater price consciousness on the part of shoppers. For the manufacturer, there will be the need to recompute and arrange for credits on purchases on which price reduction allowances are granted, to reconsider price, sales and production schedules on their product (in practice, many products), to notify salesmen by printed matter or otherwise of the impending price change, and in general to publicize the price trend. All this will involve cost and will militate against minor price fluctuations that do not vastly enhance the net revenues of the firm. Hence we can conclude that for a monopoly firm, after a change in D or MC, if the calculated new monopoly price differs from the old price, the price change will be announced only if the profits at the new price exceed the profits at the old known and effective price by an amount large enough to offset the cost of making the price change.

---

* See the argument of E. F. M. Durbin on the consequences of excessive resource fluidity, in *The Problem of Credit Policy*, p. 49.

Writing R_1 as the total profits ensuing from perpetuating the historical P_1 price, R_2 as the profits from a new price P_2 that would maximize the firm's profits, and C as the cost of changing the historical price, then for a price change we must have, for whatever time length the price change is planned,

$$R_2 - C > R_1.$$

This is the condition of price change in a dynamic world where prices are named by individuals in response to changing circumstances. The point has been sorely neglected in the peremptory application of the methods of comparative statics. Thus if the existing price was $1 and the new market forces indicated a price higher or lower—$1.10 or $.90—the new price would of course be named if (barring nonpecuniary motives) markets operated mechanistically, and the price alteration could be accomplished without costs. The cost of administering the price modification, however, might well exceed the additional profits captured by the price change.

Oligopoly, "Kinked" Demand Curves, and Price Rigidity

Although the analysis has dealt chiefly with competitive and monopoly price rigidity, frequently it was declared that rigid prices could be attributed to the loss in custom to a constant price rival. However pernicious it is to economic analysis, consumers *do* gauge quality by price: very frequently, quality can be appraised only by qualified technicians. Consumers are thus likely to be wary of the quality of commodities whose prices fall relative to those of other firms. Likewise, in the field of durable consumer goods they are prone to rebel against the speculative flavor of purchasing items subject to chronic price fluctuations, preferring to direct their expenditure to the presumed safety of a constant price rival. We need not dwell on any of the several reasons why rivals maintain their price; we need merely note that when the tendency exists it will limit the upward price freedom of firms competing in an oligopoly market of close substitutes. Oligopoly relations must be viewed as a major factor in price rigidity.

If price rises are largely stifled, and if price falls are unattractive because of competitors following suit in a "market" of demand inelasticity, changes in the demand for the product of any one firm will spend itself largely in narrowing or expanding sales at the fixed price. Depending on the initial relationship of P and MC, if $P > MC$, a rise in demand will establish a closer rapprochement of the two, perhaps lifting MC

above P unless the firm chooses to ration sales. A fall in demand, if $P > MC$, would widen the gap and raise the index of monopoly power even further. Full cost pricing, with constant MC, should also be mentioned as another possible reason for price rigidity. If firms are motivated by thoughts of a fair profit per unit of sales, this is likely to result in constant prices despite big swings in demand. Cost movements alone, but not demand changes, will drive prices up or down.

BIBLIOGRAPHICAL NOTE

Most of the dynamic price analyses have, unfortunately, devoted a disproportionate amount of space and attention to a competitive setting; hence it is difficult to decide on what ought to go into a study more specifically concerned with the problems of a firm. Among the writings on the theory of the path and market price dynamics are: P. A. Samuelson, "The Stability of Equilibrium: Comparative Statics and Dynamics," *Econometrica* (1941); L. A. Metzler, "Stability of Multiple Markets: The Hicks Conditions," *Econometrica* (1944). Also, O. Lange, *Price Flexibility*, Appendix, pp. 94–99, as well as the fine résumé in M. Reder, *Welfare Economics*, Chapter IX.

There are several interesting studies on the "cobweb theorem": N. Kaldor, "A Classificatory Note on the Determinateness of Equilibrium," *Review of Economic Studies* (1933–1934); N. S. Buchanan, "A Reconsideration of the Cobweb Theorem," *Journal of Political Economy* (1939); M. Abramovitz, *Price Theory for a Changing Economy*, Chapter II; W. H. Nicholls, *Imperfect Competition*, Chapter XVIII, and M. Ezekial, "The Cobweb Theorem," *Quarterly Journal of Economics* (1938).

The price and output indeterminateness of a demand change under monopoly has been investigated by Mrs. Robinson in her *Imperfect Competition*, pp. 65–66; Hicks, "Theory of Monopoly," *Econometrica* (1935), and A. J. Duncan, "Monopoly Adjustments to Shifts in Demand," *Econometrica* (1942).

A survey of the literature on rigid prices is in Alfred C. Neal's *Industrial Concentration and Price Inflexibility*. For an analytical statement of motives for price rigidity, see T. de Scitovsky, "Prices Under Monopoly and Competition," *Journal of Political Economy* (1941).

APPENDIX

Welfare Aspects of Pricing

W‌ITH FEW EXCEPTIONS WE HAVE refrained from drawing the welfare implications of the different modes of price determination. And yet we cannot help but raise questions on their significance for well-being. We want to know whether we ought prohibit monopoly pricing, whether competitive pricing is socially superior, whether there is not another alternative better entitled to be designated as optimal. We want answers on whether nonprice competition is a wholesome development, whether multiple-product firms born of profit motivation rather than natural causes are in the public interest. Similarly, we reflect on whether commodity diversification has gone too far or, alternately, whether greater commodity standardization would confer greater benefits. Should prohibitions on entry be removed or, in some cases, should barriers be erected? Should pricing, in industries where demand is too small to permit profitable operations with a $P = MC$ adjustment, be subject to $P = MC$ precepts, with a government subsidy redressing the balance, or should the price be based on average costs? Is discriminatory pricing preferable to a uniform price policy? Should monopsony price practices be corrected? Should the volume and nature of sales outlays be circumscribed? Should firms, through current price policy, be free to influence future demand? These, and a host of other questions, immediately suggest themselves.

These questions must be answered. They cannot be evaded by the economist, especially when recognition of the phenomena emanates from his investigations. Ultimately, if economics (or any science) has any social pretensions it is because it aims to improve the lot of mankind. Nonetheless, the positive portion of the study—the diagnosis of the precise causes and nature of the practice—must be mastered as an essential preliminary to prescription and policy making. This volume has been devoted to this first phase of the matter.

Acknowledging that price theory can provide us with some answers to these queries, it is by itself incomplete and inadequate to the task. For any change in prices, through altered modes of price conduct, involves not only a reapportionment of relative outputs and a reallocation of productive factors, but may also have implications for the normal *level* of productive activity—the level of aggregate income and the aggregate employment in the economy.* Even if it is postulated that full employment is always maintained, either through the natural recuperative forces of the private enterprise economy or by interventionist measures on the part of government, there is the further complication that any change in the modes of price making will alter the incomes of owners of productive factors. Usually, when examining the implications of a change in the mode of pricing, it is assumed that tastes, income and productivity conditions remain constant. Plainly this will not do when, as a result of the price change, incomes *are* modified. Hence the study of optimal modes of price conduct should come after, and not before, a comprehensive study embracing not only the theory of price determination but also the theory of aggregate income and the theory of income division.

There are other difficulties connected with current welfare theory. The one proposition around which its constructions have revolved is that, as economists, we can sanction only those changes that confer

---

* I have, in another place, attempted to trace the effects of monopoly, rather than competitive price making, on income and employment. See my article, "Monopoly Pricing and Unemployment," *Quarterly Journal of Economics* (1946).

benefit on some (or all) without simultaneously working injury upon others. Normally, any new policy will affect some individuals adversely. In most cases, therefore, it is suggested that a system of bounties be arranged whereby those hurt by the change are compensated out of the gains obtained by others. But here is the rub: there is the need to prescribe techniques and, usually, administrative agencies of government, by which this can be accomplished. Hence, the study of economic analysis alone falls short; political mechanisms must also be provided, requiring that we invade the normal preserves of the political theorist. There has been an unbecoming reticence about these matters. The bare statement of the principle of economic sanction, the justification for compensation without details on the means of doing so and its *cost*, and other economic implications of its implementation, impart an air of vagueness and unreality to most of these discussions.

Much of the comment on the superiority of competitive modes of price making is barren for similar reasons. Often it is taken for granted that these competitive modes are optimal, without inquiring whether there are other adjustments that approach the ideal even more closely, satisfying it in more respects: the optimal may have more than one facet. From the scanty remarks the student is led to believe that we ought precipitately, and universally, institute $P = MC$ pricing modes. This must leave the economist open to the charge of reasoning in a vacuum. If we are to be frank about the matter we must confess that we do not possess any simple device for restoring competitive price making, even if we are convinced of its manifest superiority. Exhortation to businessmen to change their pricing tactics would surely not suffice, so long as stronger reasons, profitwise, counsel their current behavior. Every plan of government supervision contains its share of disadvantages: these ought be made explicit, so long as we are meddling in policy, so that the best of the alternatives is secured. Even when these disadvantages are held to a minimum, we are not entitled to assume, once we recognize that price making must be an ex ante phenomenon, that it will, ex post, surpass the results obtained under an unregulated, partially monopolized, mechanism. Further, it is a spurious, and perhaps dangerous, pastime to suggest price changes as a means of improving the resource-allocating efficiency of the price mechanism without first probing the effects of price changes on such dynamic phenomena as commodity innovation and commodity progress, and the impact of controls upon the spirit of business enterprise. So much of the analysis presumes that we have an original choice of instituting one mode of price making rather than another, while realistically we must always remember that the economy is a "going" one; any change will work hardships and will be resisted by those adversely affected. Policy cannot assume this problem away by presupposing that the damages are unimportant, that the hostility is misguided, or that the ill effects fall only upon powerful "vested interests" whose welfare can be disregarded. Animated by a bitter political philosophy, the policy will be self-defeating, inimical as it is to our institutions, ethics, and concepts of freedom. Perhaps this accounts for the signal failure of modern price theory to influence legislative patterns. Undoubtedly, the greater explicitness of aggregate income theory on the instruments necessary to implement its welfare implications accounts in good measure for the success of thinking in this sphere on economic policy, in contrast to the practical impotence of price theory.*

Despite this view that the Economics of Welfare, or more appropriately, the Economics of Control, largely represent a virgin field, there are some excellent writings that must be consulted for genuine progress in these directions. A bibliographical list of titles is attached.

BIBLIOGRAPHICAL NOTE ON THE ECONOMICS OF WELFARE

The monumental volume of A. C. Pigou, *Economics of Welfare* (4th ed.), the work of A. P. Lerner, *Economics of Control*, and the recent publication of M. W. Reder, *Studies in the Theory of Welfare Economics*, are the most important of the works on analytic economics devoted exclusively to what has become the theory of welfare economics. A short and excellent compendium of some of the ideas of Professor Pigou is contained in J. E. Meade and C. J. Hitch, *Economic Analysis and Policy*, Pt. II, Chapter III. Largely in the same vein, with more modifications because of monopoly, is R. F. Kahn's "Some Notes on Ideal Output," *Economic Journal* (1937). A résumé of some aspects of the ideas of Professor Pigou and the surrounding literature is presented in the article by Howard S. Ellis and William Fellner, "External Economies and Diseconomies," *American Economic Review* (1943).

Some of the more important recent articles can be listed as follows: J. R. Hicks, "Foundations of Welfare Economics," *Economic Journal* (1939); N. Kaldor, "Welfare Propositions in Economics," *Economic Journal* (1939); O. Lange, "The Foundations of Welfare Economics," *Econometrica* (1942); T. de Scitovsky, "A Note on Welfare Propositions in Economics," *Review of*

* See A. Radomysler, review article, "Welfare Economics and Economic Policy," *Economica* (1946).

Economic Studies (1941); A. Bergson, "A Reformulation of Certain Aspects of Welfare Economics," *Quarterly Journal of Economics* (1938). Also, the discussion between William J. Baumol and N. Kaldor on "Community Indifference," *Review of Economic Studies* (1946–47). Paul A. Samuelson, in *Foundations of Economic Analysis*, devotes Chapter VIII to this topic, presenting an excellent evaluation of the literature and subject matter. See also the discussion between G. Stigler and Samuelson, "The New Welfare Economics," *American Economic Review* (1943). An important article advocating pricing according to marginal-cost criteria is H. Hotelling, "The General Welfare in Relation to Problems of Taxation and of Railway and Utility Rates," *Econometrica* (1938), and the discussion between Hotelling and Ragnar Frisch, same journal (1938). A critical voice sounding an alternate view in at least some applications is R. H. Coase, "The Marginal Cost Controversy," *Economica* (1946). Also, on the same subject, see the remarks of J. A. Nordin and Coase, same journal (1947). Some objections to marginal cost pricing are appraised by William Vickrey, in an article so titled, *Journal of Political Economy* (1948).

Index